Analytical Methods and Qualitative Analysis for Differential Equations

Analytical Methods and Qualitative Analysis for Differential Equations

Guest Editor

Fengping Yao

MDPI

Basel • Beijing • Wuhan • Barcelona • Belgrade • Novi Sad • Cluj • Manchester

Guest Editor
Fengping Yao
Department of Mathematics
Shanghai University
Shanghai
China

Editorial Office
MDPI AG
Grosspeteranlage 5
4052 Basel, Switzerland

This is a reprint of the Special Issue, published open access by the journal *Mathematics* (ISSN 2227-7390), freely accessible at: https://www.mdpi.com/journal/mathematics/special_issues/K4FSIEWU56.

For citation purposes, cite each article independently as indicated on the article page online and as indicated below:

Lastname, A.A.; Lastname, B.B. Article Title. *Journal Name* **Year**, *Volume Number*, Page Range.

ISBN 978-3-7258-7845-1 (Hbk)
ISBN 978-3-7258-7846-8 (PDF)
https://doi.org/10.3390/books978-3-7258-7846-8

Contents

About the Editor

Fengping Yao

Fengping Yao is a Professor in the Department of Mathematics at Shanghai University. He received his Ph.D. in 2008 from Peking University and joined the faculty of Shanghai University the same year. From 2010 to 2011, he was a visiting scholar at the University of Iowa, USA. His current research interests include regularity theory and the applications of elliptic and parabolic partial differential equations.

Preface

As a fundamental mathematical tool for describing natural phenomena and dynamic evolutionary laws, differential equations are widely applied in physics, engineering, biology, electronics, fluid mechanics, mathematical physics, and other related fields, serving as a crucial bridge between abstract theory and practical applications. Within this broad framework, ordinary and partial differential equations represent the fundamental language for characterizing evolutionary laws, whereas analytical methods and qualitative analysis serve as the two core pillars in uncovering the structure, stability, bifurcation, chaos, and dynamical properties of solutions. Over recent decades, the rise in fractional calculus, stochastic differential systems, and nonlinear wave models has further expanded the depth and breadth of this field, enabling more accurate descriptions of the memory effects, hereditary properties, randomness, and complex nonlinear interactions.

This Special Issue collects cutting-edge contributions centered on analytical methods and qualitative analysis for differential equations, covering theoretical innovations, methodological breakthroughs, and engineering applications. The collected works address a rich spectrum of topics: bifurcation and chaotic dynamics of time-fractional nonlinear Schrödinger equations; integrability and bifurcation analysis of the KPP equation; soliton dynamics and stability in fractional Biswas–Arshed equations; exact solutions and modulation instability of the Lonngren wave model in semiconductor electronics; nonlinear wave structures and multistability in quantum dusty plasmas; numerical methods for linear fractional differential equations using fractional B-poly bases; large-angle analytical solutions for physical pendulums; fractional soliton theory for generalized water wave equations; stochastic wave solutions for the Wu-Zhang system in quantum mechanics; and Melnikov-type perturbation analysis for classical dynamical models. Together, these studies reflect the diversity, depth, and vitality of modern differential equation research. This Reprint compiles these high-quality papers published in the journal *Mathematics*, presenting systematic developments in exact solutions, Hamiltonian structures, phase portraits, bifurcation mechanisms, stability theory, chaotic dynamics, and numerical–analytical hybrid methods. It highlights the interplay between fractional operators, nonlinear wave equations, dynamical systems, and applied physics, while showcasing original techniques.

We sincerely hope that this collection serves as a valuable reference for researchers, instructors, and students in pure and applied mathematics, nonlinear analysis, mathematical physics, and computational engineering. It is also our wish that these studies inspire further exploration into nonlinear dynamics, fractional models, stochastic systems, and wave phenomena, fostering new discoveries and cross-disciplinary collaborations.

As the Guest Editor of the Special Issue, I express my deepest gratitude to all authors for their outstanding contributions, to the anonymous reviewers for their rigorous and constructive feedback, and to the editorial team at MDPI *Mathematics* for their professional support and efficient collaboration. Special thanks are due to the managing editorial team for their meticulous coordination and professional support, which have guaranteed the successful completion and publication of this Special Issue and its Reprint edition.

I would also like to express my sincere gratitude to Ms. Hannah Lu, Managing Editor of this Special Issue, for her outstanding collaboration, consistent guidance, and invaluable assistance throughout the entire process.

Fengping Yao
Guest Editor

mathematics MDPI

Editorial

Preface for "Analytical Methods and Qualitative Analysis for Differential Equations"

Fengping Yao

Department of Mathematics, Newtouch Center for Mathematics, Shanghai University, Shanghai 200444, China; yfp@shu.edu.cn

As a fundamental mathematical tool for describing natural phenomena and dynamic evolutionary laws, differential equations are widely applied in various fields, serving as a crucial link between abstract theory and practical applications. Ordinary and partial differential equations constitute core branches of differential equations and share fundamental theoretical frameworks including calculus, functional analysis, stability theory, perturbation techniques and numerical methodologies. Qualitative theories of ordinary differential equations (covering stability, bifurcation and chaos) as well as analytical construction strategies lay an essential theoretical foundation for analyzing the local behaviors of partial differential equations. Conversely, research on boundary-value and initial-boundary-value problems of partial differential equations further complements and refines the boundary constraint theory for ordinary differential equations. Over recent decades, the rise in fractional calculus, stochastic differential systems, and nonlinear wave models has further expanded the depth and breadth of this field, enabling more accurate descriptions of memory effects, hereditary properties, randomness, and complex nonlinear interactions.

This Special Issue "Analytical Methods and Qualitative Analysis for Differential Equations" aims to bring the newest results of the study on analytical methods and qualitative analysis for ordinary and partial differential equations. Ordinary differential equations (ODEs) and partial differential equations (PDEs) are important tools to describe dynamic systems and physical phenomena. They are widely used in many fields such as engineering, physics, chemistry, biology, control theory, astronomy, quantum mechanics, general relativity, elasticity, electromagnetism, finance, economics, and so on. Analytical methods provide tools for accurately solving ODEs and PDEs, while qualitative analysis methods help us understand the global behavior and properties of solutions, both of which are indispensable in mathematical analysis. We launch this Special Issue with the intention of collecting the newest research progress and trends in the study of analytical methods and qualitative analysis for differential equations of one variable and several variables, which thus push forward the development of both branches and, at the same time, inspire parallels between them.

Featuring theoretical innovations, methodological breakthroughs and engineering applications, this Special Issue collects cutting-edge contributions that focus on analytical methods and qualitative analysis for differential equations. The collected works address a rich spectrum of topics: Melnikov-type perturbation analysis for classical dynamical models (Contribution 1); stochastic wave solutions for the Wu–Zhang system in quantum mechanics (Contribution 2); fractional soliton theory for generalized water wave equations (Contribution 3); large-angle analytical solutions for physical pendulums (Contribution 4); numerical methods for linear fractional differential equations using fractional B-poly bases (Contribution 5); nonlinear wave structures and multistability in quantum dusty plasmas

(Contribution 6); exact solutions and modulation instability of the Lonngren wave model in semiconductor electronics (Contribution 7); soliton dynamics and stability in fractional Biswas–Arshed equations (Contribution 8); integrability and bifurcation analysis of the KPP equation (Contribution 9); and bifurcation and chaotic dynamics of time-fractional nonlinear Schrödinger equations (Contribution 10). Together, these studies reflect the diversity, depth, and vitality of modern differential equation research. This Reprint compiles these high-quality papers published in the journal *Mathematics*, presenting systematic developments in exact solutions, Hamiltonian structures, phase portraits, bifurcation mechanisms, stability theory, chaotic dynamics, and numerical-analytical hybrid methods. It highlights the interplay between fractional operators, nonlinear wave equations, dynamical systems, and applied physics while showcasing original techniques.

We sincerely hope this collection serves as a valuable reference for researchers, instructors, and students in pure and applied mathematics, nonlinear analysis, mathematical physics, and computational engineering. It is also our wish that these studies inspire further exploration into nonlinear dynamics, fractional models, stochastic systems, and wave phenomena, fostering new discoveries and cross-disciplinary collaborations.

As the Guest Editor of the Special Issue, I express my deepest gratitude to all authors for their outstanding contributions, to the anonymous reviewers for their rigorous and constructive feedback, and to the editorial team at MDPI *Mathematics* for their professional support and efficient collaboration. Special thanks are due to the managing editorial team for their meticulous coordination and professional support, which have guaranteed the successful completion and publication of this Special Issue and its Reprint edition. I would also like to express my sincere gratitude to Ms. Hannah Lu, Managing Editor of this Special Issue, for her outstanding collaboration, consistent guidance, and invaluable assistance throughout the entire process.

Funding: This research received no external funding.

Conflicts of Interest: The author declares that there are no conflicts of interest.

List of Contributions

1. Kyurkchiev, N.; Zaevski, T.; Iliev, A.; Kyurkchiev, V.; Rahnev, A. Investigations of Modified Classical Dynamical Models: Melnikov's Approach, Simulations and Applications, and Probabilistic Control of Perturbations. *Mathematics* **2025**, *13*, 231. https://doi.org/10.3390/math13020231.
2. Mohammed, W.W.; Ali, E.E.; Ahmed, A.I.; Ennaceur, M. Abundant Elliptic, Trigonometric, and Hyperbolic Stochastic Solutions for the Stochastic Wu–Zhang System in Quantum Mechanics. *Mathematics* **2025**, *13*, 714. https://doi.org/10.3390/math13050714.
3. Qawaqneh, H.; Al Naim, A.S.; Alomair, A. Novel Analytical Methods for and Qualitative Analysis of the Generalized Water Wave Equation. *Mathematics* **2025**, *13*, 2280. https://doi.org/10.3390/math13142280.
4. Fernandes, J.C. Very Large Angular Oscillations (Up to $3\pi/4$) of the Physical Pendulum—A Simple Trigonometric Analytical Solution. *Mathematics* **2025**, *13*, 2836. https://doi.org/10.3390/math13172836.
5. Rahman, M.H.; Bhatti, M.I.; Dimakis, N. Solutions for Linear Fractional Differential Equations with Multiple Constraints Using Fractional B-Poly Bases. *Mathematics* **2025**, *13*, 3084. https://doi.org/10.3390/math13193084.
6. Xue, H.; Zhang, L. Nonlinear Wave Structures, Multistability, and Chaotic Behavior of Quantum Dust-Acoustic Shocks in Dusty Plasma with Size Distribution Effects. *Mathematics* **2025**, *13*, 3101. https://doi.org/10.3390/math13193101.
7. Qawaqneh, H.; Alsharidi, A.K. Truncated M-Fractional Exact Solutions, Stability Analysis, and Modulation Instability of the Classical Lonngren Wave Model. *Mathematics* **2025**, *13*, 3107. https://doi.org/10.3390/math13193107.

https://doi.org/10.3390/math14122065

8. Zafar, A.; Razzaq, W.; Nazir, A.; Alomair, M.A.; Al Naim, A.S.; Alomair, A. Bifurcation Analysis and Solitons Dynamics of the Fractional Biswas–Arshed Equation via Analytical Method. *Mathematics* **2025**, *13*, 3147. https://doi.org/10.3390/math13193147.
9. Elmandouh, A. Nonlinear Dynamica Analysis of a Diffusion-Driven Bacterial Density Model: Integrability and Bifurcation Analysis. *Mathematics* **2025**, *13*, 3623. https://doi.org/10.3390/math13223623.
10. El-Dessoky, M.M.; Elmandouh, A.A.; Algharni, A.A. Qualitative Analysis for Modifying an Unstable Time-Fractional Nonlinear Schrödinger Equation: Bifurcation, Quasi-Periodic, Chaotic Behavior, and Exact Solutions. *Mathematics* **2026**, *14*, 354. https://doi.org/10.3390/math14020354.

mathematics

MDPI

Article

Investigations of Modified Classical Dynamical Models: Melnikov's Approach, Simulations and Applications, and Probabilistic Control of Perturbations

Nikolay Kyurkchiev [1,2], Tsvetelin Zaevski [2,3], Anton Iliev [1,*], Vesselin Kyurkchiev [1] and Asen Rahnev [1]

1 Faculty of Mathematics and Informatics, University of Plovdiv Paisii Hilendarski, 24, Tzar Asen Str., 4000 Plovdiv, Bulgaria; nkyurk@uni-plovdiv.bg (N.K.); vkyurkchiev@uni-plovdiv.bg (V.K.); assen@uni-plovdiv.bg (A.R.)
2 Institute of Mathematics and Informatics, Bulgarian Academy of Sciences, Acad. G. Bonchev Str., Bl. 8, 1113 Sofia, Bulgaria; t_s_zaevski@math.bas.bg
3 Faculty of Mathematics and Informatics, Sofia University "St. Kliment Ohridski", 5, James Bourchier Blvd., 1164 Sofia, Bulgaria
* Correspondence: aii@uni-plovdiv.bg

Abstract: We suggest a few kinds of extended classical oscillators in this study. We present a few specific modules for examining these oscillators' behavior. This will be an essential component of a broader web-based scientific computing platform that is in the works. The modeling and synthesis of radiating antenna designs is also taken into consideration as a potential use case for Melnikov functions. Additionally, we discuss strategies for achieving probabilistic control over system perturbations.

Keywords: extended classical oscillators; Melnikov's approach; antenna factor

MSC: 34C37

1. Introduction

A number of authors have researched the classical differential model:

$$\begin{cases} \dfrac{dx}{dt} &= y \\ \dfrac{dy}{dt} &= -\sin x + \epsilon F(x,y)y, \end{cases} \tag{1}$$

where $0 \le \epsilon < 1$. The literature on this subject is extensive and diverse. The outstanding studies of Tricomi [1], Stoker [2], Levi, Hoppensteadt and Miranker [3], Perko [4], and Guckenheimer and Holmes [5] provide the reader with comprehensive information. A universal escape nonlinear oscillator model describes a variety of oscillatory physical phenomena that occur in various fields, including mechanics, quantum optics, acoustics, hydrodynamics, electronics, and engineering. The equation of motion for the sinusoidally driven escape oscillator, which includes nonlinear damping terms as a power series on the velocity, has been examined by Sanjuan [6]. See [7–14] for additional results. We examine the following model in [15].

$$\begin{cases} \dfrac{dx}{dt} &= y \\ \dfrac{dy}{dt} &= -\sin x + \epsilon\left(a_1 + \sum_{i=0}^{\frac{n}{2}-1} a_{n-2i}x^{n-2i} + \sum_{i=0}^{\frac{n}{2}-2} b_{n-2-2i}y^{n-2-2i}\right)y, \end{cases} \tag{2}$$

where $0 \le \epsilon < 1$ and n is even. The classical differential model—the damped mathematical pendulum excited by horizontal harmonics—is the focus of several authors' studies [16–21]:

$$\ddot{x} + \epsilon\delta\dot{x} + \sin\, x + \epsilon\gamma\cos{(\omega t)}\cos\, x = 0 \tag{3}$$

or

$$\begin{cases} \dfrac{dx}{dt} &= y \\ \dfrac{dy}{dt} &= -\sin x - \epsilon(\delta y + \gamma\cos{(\omega t)}\cos\, x), \end{cases} \tag{4}$$

where $0 \le \epsilon < 1$. In this paper, we suggest some classes of extended classical oscillators. Studies are examined in the context of Melnikov's methodology [22]. We offer several simulations. Additionally, we present a few specialized modules for examining the dynamics of these fictitious oscillators. The obtained results can be included into a much broader scientific computing application—see [23–28] for additional information. The following is the paper's plan. In Sections 2.1 and 2.2, we provide our models. Sections 2.1.1 and 2.2.1 examine investigations in the context of Melnikov's methodology. Sections 2.1.2 and 2.2.2 contain a few simulations. Sections 2.1.3 and 2.2.3 address one potential use of Melnikov functions, which is in the modeling of radiating antenna designs. Section 3 brings us to a close. Appendices A and B provide probabilistic control over the perturbations.

2. The Models

2.1. The Model A

The following novel class of extended oscillators is examined.

$$\begin{cases} \dfrac{dx}{dt} &= y \\ \dfrac{dy}{dt} &= -\sin\, x - \epsilon\left(A\sum_{p=1}^{n} y|y|^{p-1} - \sum_{j=1}^{N} g_j\sin(j\omega t)\right), \end{cases} \tag{5}$$

where A is the damping level, $p \ge 1$ is the damping exponent, N is an integer, and $0 \le \epsilon < 1$. Specifically, we take into account the following model:

$$\begin{cases} \dfrac{dx}{dt} &= y \\ \dfrac{dy}{dt} &= -\sin\, x - \epsilon\left(Ay|y|^{p-1} - \sum_{j=1}^{N} g_j\sin(j\omega t)\right). \end{cases} \tag{6}$$

The equation $H(x,y) = \frac{1}{2}y^2 + 1 - \cos x$ represents the system's total energy ($\epsilon = 0$). Some details can be found in monograph [5]. The orbit is provided by (refer to Figure 1):

$$(x_0(t) = \pm 2\mathrm{arctan}(\sinh t);\ y_0(t) = \pm 2\mathrm{sech}\, t). \tag{7}$$

2.1.1. Observations in View of Melnikov's Methodology

The Melnikov function can be used to determine the transverse intersection of the stable and unstable manifolds and provides a measure of the leading order distance between them when $\epsilon \neq 0$. By definition, the Melnikov integral is provided by

$$M(t_0) = \int_{-\infty}^{\infty} y_0(t) \left(A y_0(t) |y_0(t)|^{p-1} - \sum_{j=1}^{N} g_i \sin(j\omega(t + t_0)) \right) \mathrm{d}t, \tag{8}$$

where Equation (7) defines the functions $x_0(t)$ and $y_0(t)$. The task of determining the root of $M(t_0)$ is more intriguing from a numerical perspective as the parameters that appear in the suggested differential model are subject to certain practical and physical constraints.

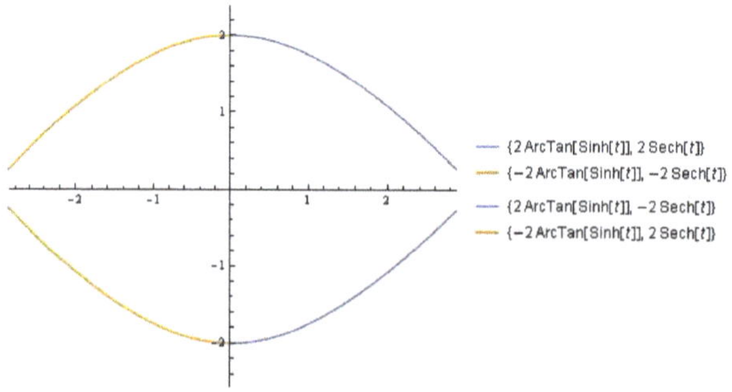

Figure 1. The orbits $(x_0(t), y_0(t))$.

Proposition 1. *The roots of the Melnikov function $M(t_0)$ are provided as equation solutions if $p = 2$ and $N = 1$*

$$M(t_0) = 2\pi\left(2A - g_1 \mathrm{sech}\left(\frac{\pi\omega}{2}\right) \sin(t_0\omega)\right) = 0. \tag{9}$$

$M(t_0) = 0$ (for $p = 2$; $N = 1$; $A = 0.015$; $\omega = 0.2$; $g_1 = 0.09$), for instance, is shown on Figure 2. In the interval $(0, 16)$, the roots are: 1.78742; 13.9205. Melnikov's condition for chaotic behavior of the dynamical model can be formulated by the reader from Proposition 1 (also see Figure 2).

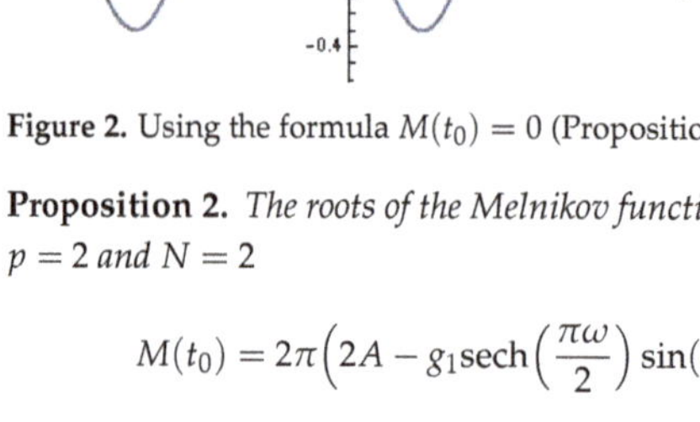

Figure 2. Using the formula $M(t_0) = 0$ (Proposition 1).

Proposition 2. *The roots of the Melnikov function $M(t_0)$ are provided as equation solutions for $p = 2$ and $N = 2$*

$$M(t_0) = 2\pi\left(2A - g_1 \mathrm{sech}\left(\frac{\pi\omega}{2}\right) \sin(t_0\omega) - g_2 \mathrm{sech}(\pi\omega) \sin(2t_0\omega)\right) = 0. \tag{10}$$

For instance, the formula $M(t_0) = 0$ is shown in Figure 3 (for $p = 2$; $N = 2$; $A = 0.015$; $\omega = 0.6$; $g_1 = 0.07$; $g_2 = 0.3$). The following are the roots in the interval of $(0, 10)$:

0.224036; 2.7794; 5.63804; 7.0665. We can demonstrate the following claim when $p = 4$ and $N = 1$.

Proposition 3. *The roots of the Melnikov function $M(t_0)$ are provided as equation solutions for $p = 4$ and $N = 1$*

$$M(t_0) = 2\pi\left(6A - g_1 \text{sech}\left(\frac{\pi\omega}{2}\right)\sin(t_0\omega)\right) = 0. \tag{11}$$

For instance, Figure 4 shows the equation $M(t_0) = 0$ (for $p = 4$; $N = 1$; $A = 0.015$; $\omega = 0.1$; $g_1 = 0.091$). The root in interval $(0, 16)$ is: 15.708 with a multiplicity of two.

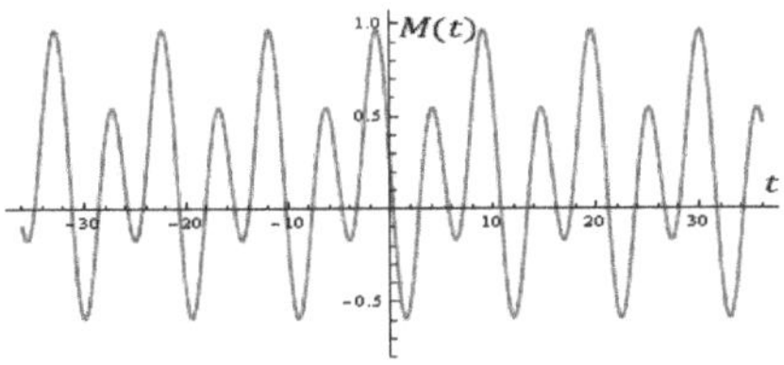

Figure 3. Using the formula $M(t_0) = 0$ (Proposition 2).

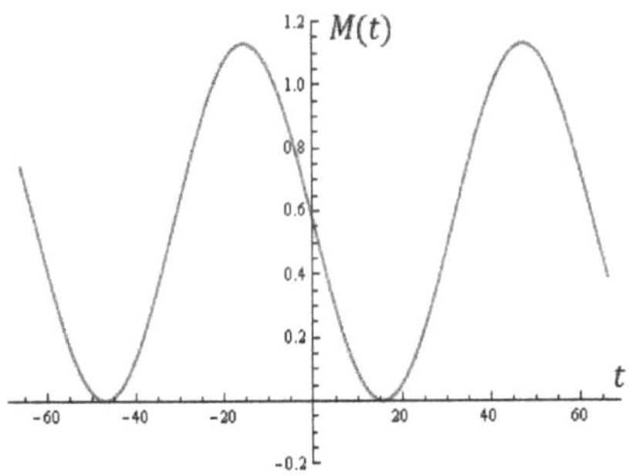

Figure 4. Using the formula $M(t_0) = 0$ (Proposition 3).

Proposition 4. *The roots of the Melnikov function $M(t_0)$ are provided as equation solutions for $p = 4$ and $N = 2$*

$$M(t_0) = 2\pi\left(6A - g_1 \text{sech}\left(\frac{\pi\omega}{2}\right)\sin(t_0\omega) - g_2 \text{sech}(\pi\omega)\sin(2t_0\omega)\right) = 0. \tag{12}$$

As an illustration, Figure 5 shows the equation $M(t_0) = 0$ (for $p = 4$; $N = 2$; $A = 0.011$; $\omega = 0.92$; $g_1 = 0.091$; $g_2 = 0.32$). The roots (with a multiplicity of two) at an interval of $(0, 10)$ are: 0.97718; 7.92402. $M(t_0) = 0$ is the equation (for $p = 4$; $N = 2$; $A = 0.02$; $\omega = 0.7$; $g_1 = 0.005$; $g_2 = 0.2$) and has no roots (see Figure 6).

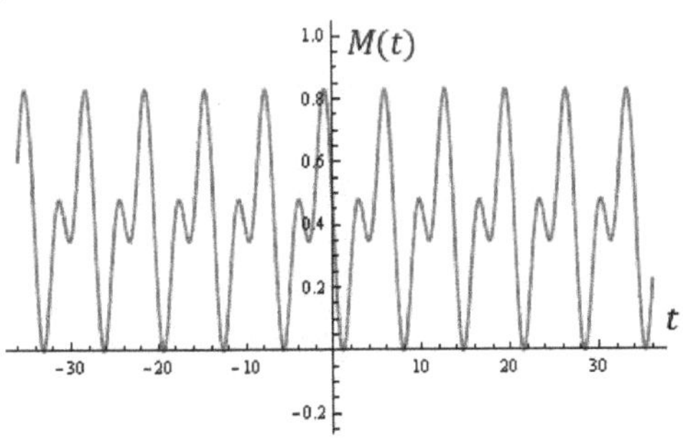

Figure 5. Using the formula $M(t_0) = 0$ (Proposition 4).

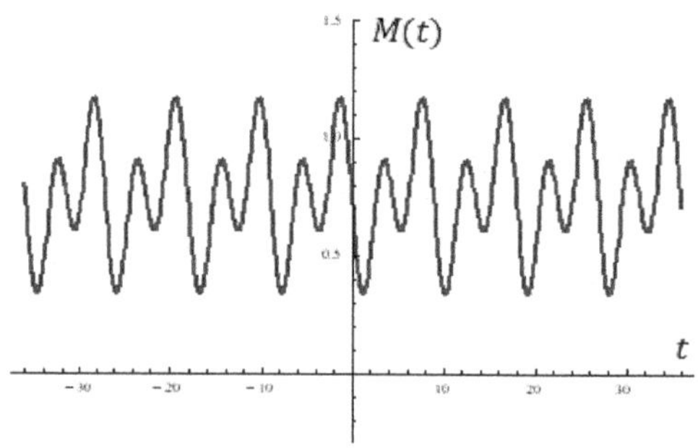

Figure 6. Using the formula $M(t_0) = 0$ (Proposition 4).

Proposition 5. *The roots of the Melnikov function $M(t_0)$ are provided as equation solutions if $p = 4$ and $N = 3$*

$$\begin{aligned} M(t_0) = & \frac{1}{-1+2\cosh(\pi\omega)} e^{-2it_0\omega}\pi\left(-ie^{2it_0\omega}g_1 + ie^{4it_0\omega}g_1 + 6Ae^{2it_0\omega}\cosh\left(\frac{\pi\omega}{2}\right)\right. \\ & +ie^{2it_0\omega}g_1\cosh(\pi\omega) - ie^{4it_0\omega}g_1\cosh(\pi\omega) - ig_3\cosh(\pi\omega) \\ & +ie^{6it_0\omega}g_3\cosh(\pi\omega) - ie^{it_0\omega}g_2\cosh\left(\frac{3\pi\omega}{2}\right) + ie^{5it_0\omega}g_2\cosh\left(\frac{3\pi\omega}{2}\right) \\ & -ie^{2it_0\omega}g_1\cosh(2\pi\omega) + ie^{4it_0\omega}g_1\cosh(2\pi\omega) \\ & \left.+6Ae^{3it_0\omega}\cosh\left(\frac{5\pi\omega}{2}\right)\right)\operatorname{sech}\left(\frac{\pi\omega}{2}\right)\operatorname{sech}(\pi\omega) = 0. \end{aligned} \tag{13}$$

For instance, the equation $M(t_0) = 0$ (for $p = 4$; $N = 3$; $A = 0.05$; $\omega = 0.09$; $g_1 = 0.6$; $g_2 = 0.3$; $g_3 = 0.1$) is depicted on Figure 7.

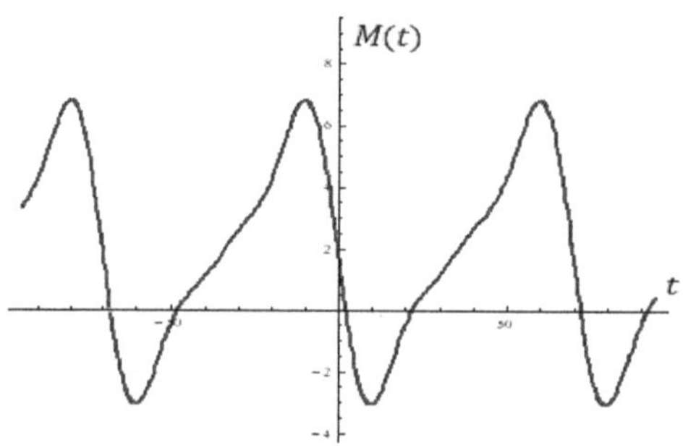

Figure 7. Using the formula $M(t_0) = 0$ (Proposition 5).

Proposition 6. *The roots of the Melnikov function $M(t_0)$ are provided as equation solutions if $p = 6$ and $N = 2$*

$$M(t_0) = 2\pi\left(20A - g_1\operatorname{sech}\left(\frac{\pi\omega}{2}\right)\sin(t_0\omega) - g_2\operatorname{sech}(\pi\omega)\sin(2t_0\omega)\right) = 0. \tag{14}$$

Melnikov's criterion for the occurrence of the intersection between the perturbed and unperturbed separatrixes can be formulated by the reader using Propositions 1 through 6. The analogous approximation issue for randomly selected p and N can be examined by the reader.

2.1.2. Some Simulations

We will concentrate on a few interesting simulations here:

1. For the given $p = 2$; $N = 2$; $A = 0.015$; $\epsilon = 0.1$; $\omega = 0.6$; $g_1 = 0.07$; $g_2 = 0.3$, the simulations on the system (6) for $x_0 = 0.6$; $y_0 = 0.2$ are depicted in Figure 8.

2. For the given $p = 4$; $N = 2$; $A = 0.011$; $\epsilon = 0.1$; $\omega = 0.92$; $g_1 = 0.9$; $g_2 = 0.2$, the simulations on the system (6) for $x_0 = 0.7$; $y_0 = 0.3$ are depicted in Figure 9.

3. For the given $p = 6$; $N = 3$; $A = 0.011$; $\epsilon = 0.1$; $\omega = 0.98$; $g_1 = 0.96$; $g_2 = 0.1$; $g_3 = 0.6$, the simulations on the system (6) for $x_0 = 0.8$; $y_0 = 0.4$ are depicted in Figure 10.

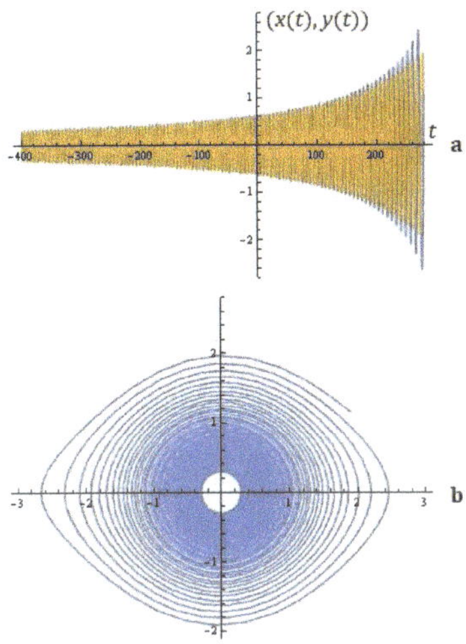

Figure 8. The system's solutions (**a**); phase space (**b**) (example 1).

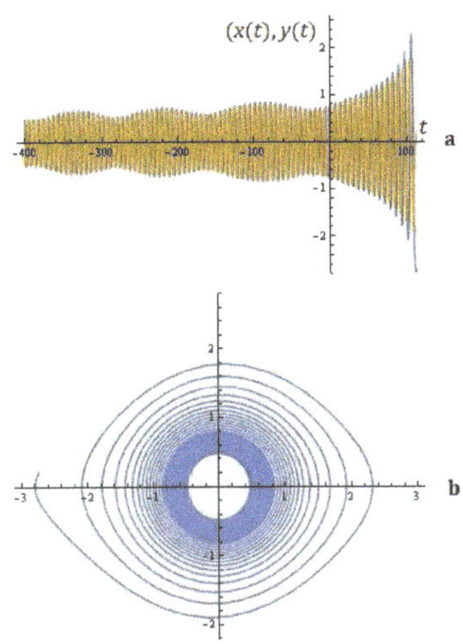

Figure 9. The system's solutions (**a**); phase space (**b**) (example 2).

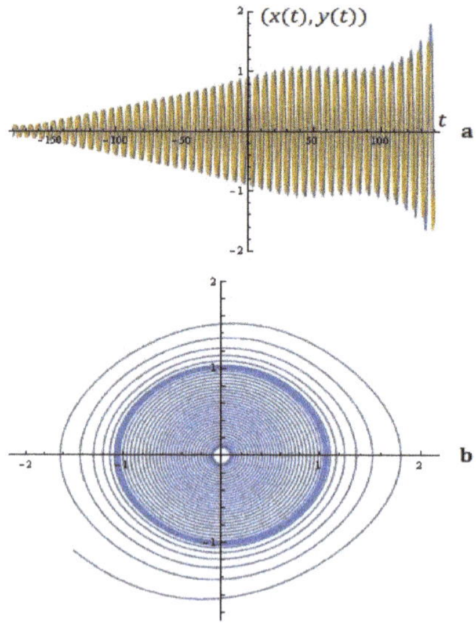

Figure 10. The system's solutions (**a**); phase space (**b**) (example 3).

2.1.3. The Modeling and Synthesis of Radiating Antenna Patterns Is One Potential Use for Melnikov Functions

This brings us to $M(t)$. The hypothetical normalized antenna factor is defined as follows: The formula is $M^*(\theta) = \frac{1}{D}|M(K\cos\theta + k_1)|$, where θ is the azimuth angle, $K = kd$; $k = \frac{2\pi}{\lambda}$; λ is the wave length, d is the distance between emitters, and k_1 is the phase difference.

For fixed $A = 0.0001$; $\omega = 0.27$; $g_1 = 0.6$; $g_2 = 0.001$; $K = 19.91$; $k_1 = 0.001$ (from Proposition 4), see Figure 11.

For fixed $A = 0.002$; $\omega = 0.27$; $g_1 = 0.07$; $g_2 = 0.001$; $K = 20.91$; $k_1 = 0$ (from Proposition 6), see Figure 12.

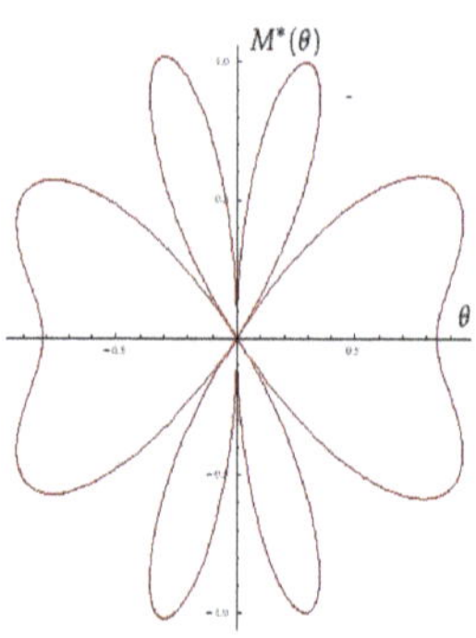

Figure 11. A typical Melnikov antenna array (from Proposition 4).

Naturally, the hypothetical Melnikov array that we provided can be viewed as an addition to the Array Antenna Theory, following careful evaluation by experts in this field of study.

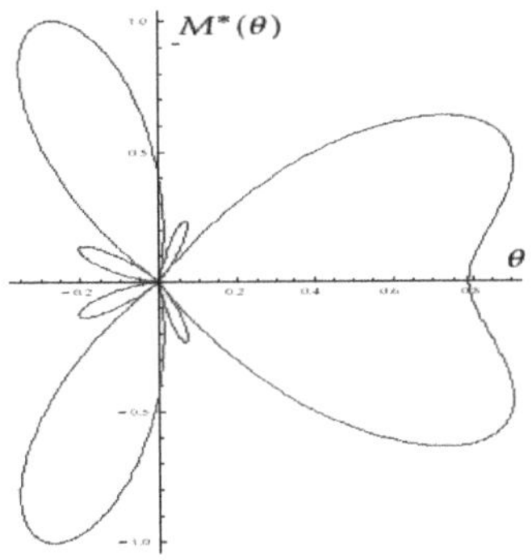

Figure 12. A typical Melnikov antenna array (from Proposition 6).

2.2. The Model B

The following novel class of extended oscillators is examined

$$\begin{cases} \dfrac{dx}{dt} &= y \\ \dfrac{dy}{dt} &= -\sin x - \epsilon\left(A\sum_{p=1}^{n} y|y|^{p-1} + \cos x \sum_{j=1}^{N} g_j \cos(j\omega t)\right), \end{cases} \quad (15)$$

where A is the damping level, $p \geq 1$ is the damping exponent, N is an integer, and $0 \leq \epsilon < 1$. Specifically, we take into account the following model

$$\begin{cases} \dfrac{dx}{dt} &= y \\ \dfrac{dy}{dt} &= -\sin x - \epsilon\left(Ay|y|^{p-1} + \cos x \sum_{j=1}^{N} g_j \cos(j\omega t)\right). \end{cases} \quad (16)$$

2.2.1. Taking into Account Melnikov's Methodology

The integral of Melnikov is defined as follows

$$M(t_0) = \int_{-\infty}^{\infty} y_0(t)\left(Ay_0(t)|y_0(t)|^{p-1} + \cos(x_0(t))\sum_{j=1}^{N} g_i \cos(j\omega(t+t_0))\right) dt, \quad (17)$$

where Equation (7) defines the functions $x_0(t)$ and $y_0(t)$.

Proposition 7. *The roots of the Melnikov function $M(t_0)$ are provided as equation solutions if $p = 2$ and $N = 1$*

$$M(t_0) = 2\pi\left(2A + g_1\omega^2 \cos(t_0\omega)\text{sech}\left(\frac{\pi\omega}{2}\right)\right) = 0. \quad (18)$$

As an illustration, the equation $M(t_0) = 0$ (for $p = 2$; $N = 1$; $A = 0.0025$; $\omega = 0.3$; $g_1 = 0.17$) is depicted in Figure 13. The roots in at an interval of $(0, 20)$ are: 6.47699; 14.467.

The reader can derive Melnikov's condition for the dynamical model's chaotic behavior from Proposition 7 (also see Figure 13).

Proposition 8. *The roots of the Melnikov function $M(t_0)$ are provided as equation solutions for $p = 4$ and $N = 2$*

$$M(t_0) = 2\pi\left(6A + g_1\omega^2 \cos(t_0\omega)\text{sech}\left(\frac{\pi\omega}{2}\right) + 4g_2\omega^2 \cos(2t_0\omega)\text{sech}(\pi\omega)\right) = 0. \quad (19)$$

As an illustration, the equation $M(t_0) = 0$ (for $p = 4;\ N = 2;\ A = 0.0025;\ \omega = 0.4;\ g_1 = 0.17;\ g_2 = 0.05$) is depicted in Figure 14. The root in interval $(0, 5)$ is: 3.74239.

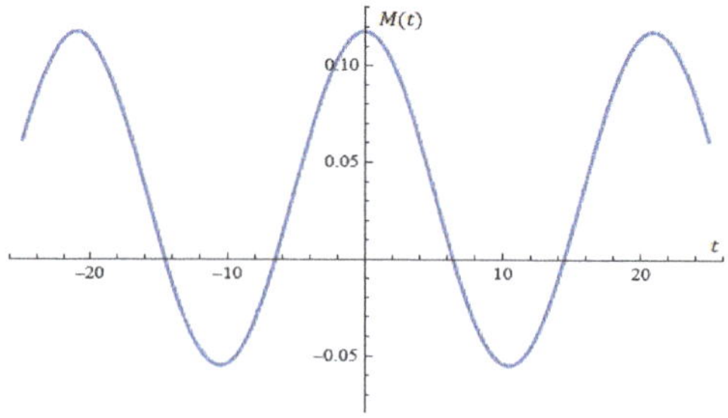

Figure 13. Using the formula $M(t_0) = 0$ (Proposition 7).

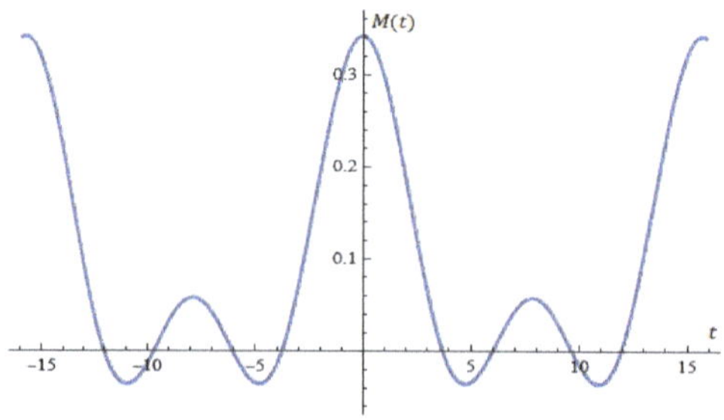

Figure 14. Using the formula $M(t_0) = 0$ (Proposition 8).

Proposition 9. *The roots of the Melnikov function $M(t_0)$ are provided as equation solutions if $p = 6$ and $N = 3$*

$$\begin{aligned} M(t_0) \quad &= \quad 2\pi\big(20A + g_1\omega^2\cos(t_0\omega)\operatorname{sech}\big(\tfrac{\pi\omega}{2}\big) \\ &\quad +4g_2\omega^2\cos(2t_0\omega)\operatorname{sech}(\pi\omega) \\ &\quad +9g_3\omega^2\cos(3t_0\omega)\operatorname{sech}\big(\tfrac{3\pi\omega}{2}\big)\big) = 0. \end{aligned} \tag{20}$$

As an illustration, the equation $M(t_0) = 0$ (for $p = 6;\ N = 3;\ A = 0.001;\ \omega = 0.7;\ g_1 = 0.1;\ g_2 = 0.05;\ g_3 = 0.01$) has a root of 2.15038 (in interval $(0, 3)$ (see Figure 15).

For $p = 6;\ N = 3;\ A = 0.001;\ \omega = 0.35;\ g_1 = 0.08;\ g_2 = 0.06;\ g_3 = 0.01$, the equation $M(t_0) = 0$ has no roots (see Figure 16).

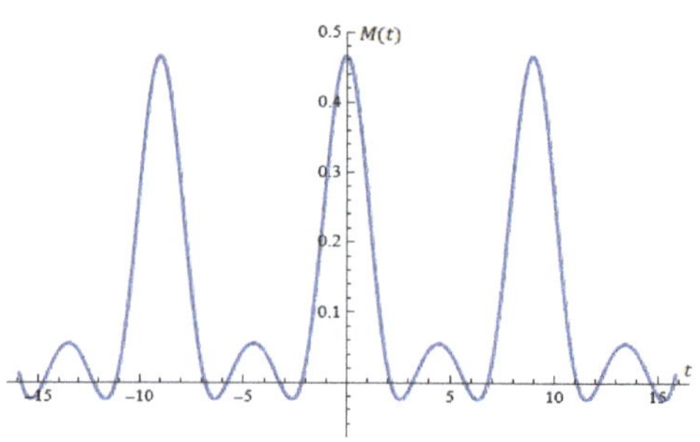

Figure 15. Using the formula $M(t_0) = 0$ (Proposition 9).

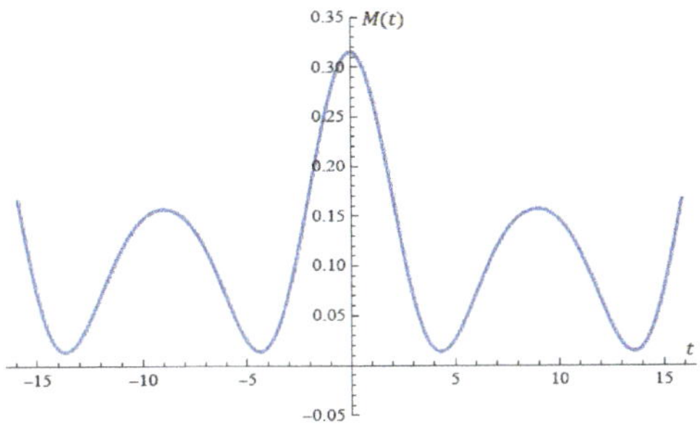

Figure 16. Using the formula $M(t_0) = 0$ (Proposition 9).

2.2.2. Some Simulations

We will concentrate on a few interesting simulations here:

1. For the given $p = 4$; $N = 2$; $A = 0.015$; $\epsilon = 0.01$; $\omega = 0.6$; $g_1 = 0.07$; $g_2 = 0.3$, the simulations on the system (5.16) for $x_0 = 0.6$; $y_0 = 0.3$ are depicted in Figure 17.

2. For the given $p = 6$; $N = 3$; $A = 0.005$; $\epsilon = 0.01$; $\omega = 0.3$; $g_1 = 0.07$; $g_2 = 0.3$; $g_3 = 0.5$, the simulations on the system (5.16) for $x_0 = 0.7$; $y_0 = 0.4$ are depicted in Figure 18.

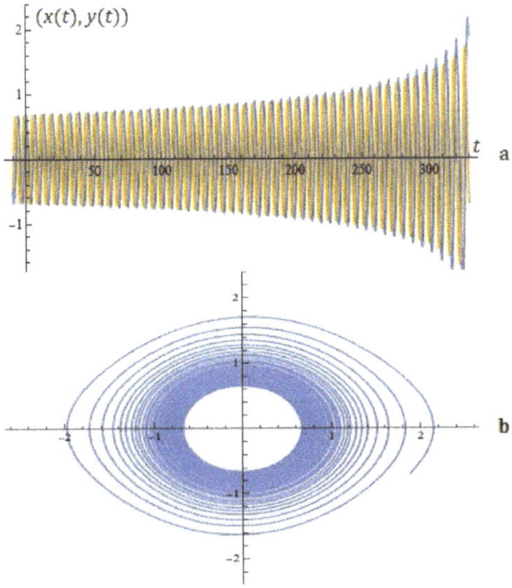

Figure 17. The system's solutions (**a**); phase space (**b**) (example 1).

2.2.3. The Modeling and Synthesis of Radiating Antenna Patterns Is One Potential Use for Melnikov Functions (See Section 2.1.3 for Additional Information)

For fixed $A = 0.0025$; $\omega = 0.4$; $g_1 = 0.17$; $g_2 = 0.05$; $K = 6$; $k_1 = 0.1$ (from Proposition 8), see Figure 19.

For fixed $A = 0.001$; $\omega = 0.6$; $g_1 = 0.16$; $g_2 = 0.1$; $g_3 = 0.01$; $K = 3.44$; $k_1 = 0.01$ (from Proposition 9), see Figure 20.

For arbitrarily selected p and N, the reader can examine the corresponding approximation problem.

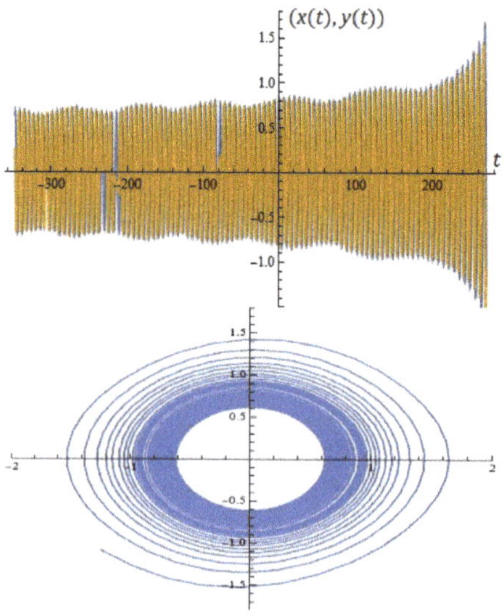

a

b

Figure 18. The system's solutions (**a**); phase space (**b**) (example 2).

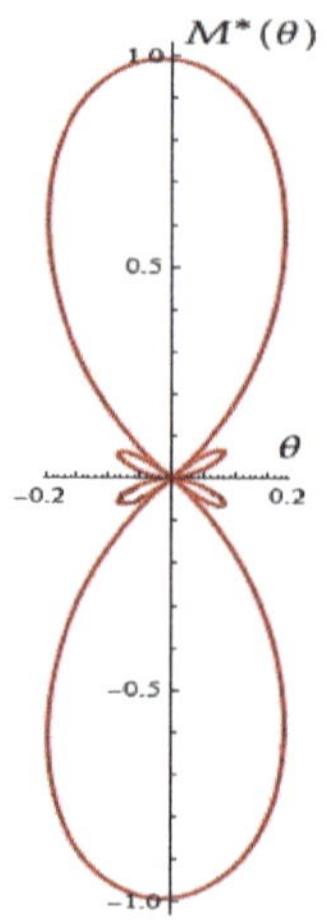

Figure 19. A typical Melnikov antenna array (from Proposition 8).

Proposition 10. *The roots of the Melnikov function $M(t_0)$ are provided as solutions to the following equation if $p = 8$ and $N = 4$*

$$\begin{aligned} M(t_0) \quad = \quad & 2\pi(70A + g_1\omega^2 \cos(t_0\omega)\mathrm{sech}(\tfrac{\pi\omega}{2}) \\ & +4g_2\omega^2 \cos(2t_0\omega)\mathrm{sech}(\pi\omega) \\ & +9g_3\omega^2 \cos(3t_0\omega)\mathrm{sech}(\tfrac{3\pi\omega}{2}) \\ & +16g_4\omega^2 \cos(4t_0\omega)\mathrm{sech}(2\pi\omega)) = 0. \end{aligned} \tag{21}$$

As an illustration, equation $M(t_0) = 0$ (for $p = 8$; $N = 4$; $A = 0.0001$; $\omega = 0.95$; $g_1 = 0.1$; $g_2 = 0.03$; $g_3 = 0.2$; $g_4 = 0.05$) is depicted in Figure 21).

For $p = 8$; $N = 4$; $A = 0.001$; $\omega = 0.4$; $g_1 = 0.1$; $g_2 = 0.03$; $g_3 = 0.1$; $g_4 = 0.05$), equation $M(t_0) = 0$ has no roots (see Figure 22).

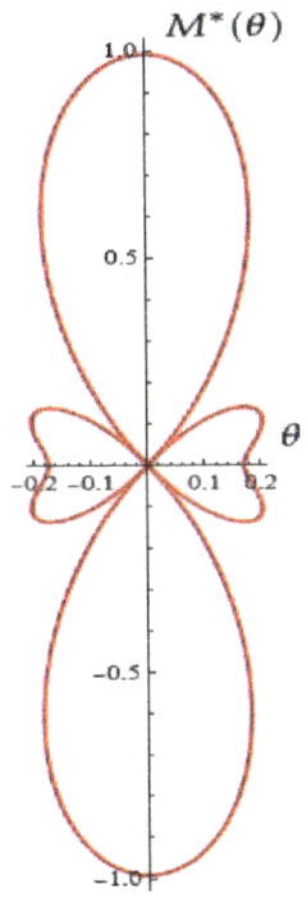

Figure 20. A typical Melnikov antenna array (from Proposition 9).

The potential normalized antenna factor $M^*(\theta)$ in the case $p = 8$; $N = 4$ and fixed $A = 0.0001$; $\omega = 0.95$; $g_1 = 0.1$; $g_2 = 0.03$; $g_3 = 0.2$; $g_4 = 0.05$; $K = 3.44$; $k_1 = 0.1$ (from Proposition 10), see Figure 23.

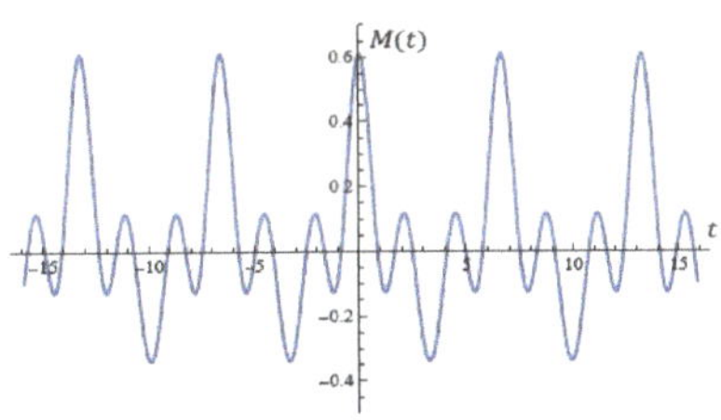

Figure 21. Using the formula $M(t_0) = 0$ (Proposition 10).

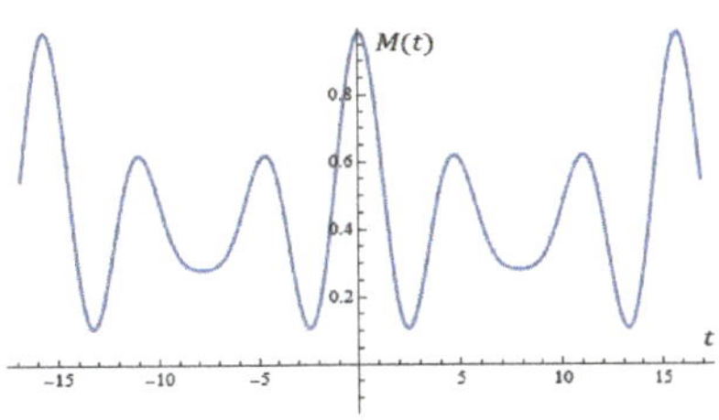

Figure 22. Using the formula $M(t_0) = 0$ (Proposition 10).

Proposition 11. *The roots of the Melnikov function* $M(t_0)$ *are provided as equation solutions if* $p = 10$ *and* $N = 6$

$$\begin{aligned} M(t_0) \quad = \quad & 2\pi\big(252A + g_1\omega^2\cos(t_0\omega)\mathrm{sech}\big(\tfrac{\pi\omega}{2}\big) \\ & +4g_2\omega^2\cos(2t_0\omega)\mathrm{sech}(\pi\omega) \\ & +9g_3\omega^2\cos(3t_0\omega)\mathrm{sech}\big(\tfrac{3\pi\omega}{2}\big) \\ & +16g_4\omega^2\cos(4t_0\omega)\mathrm{sech}(2\pi\omega) \\ & +25g_5\omega^2\cos(5t_0\omega)\mathrm{sech}\big(\tfrac{5\pi\omega}{2}\big) \\ & +36g_6\omega^2\cos(6t_0\omega)\mathrm{sech}(3\pi\omega)\big) = 0. \end{aligned} \tag{22}$$

The equation $M(t_0) = 0$ (for $p = 10$; $N = 6$; $A = 0.00001$; $\omega = 0.8$; $g_1 = 0.07$; $g_2 = 0.03$; $g_3 = 0.17$; $g_4 = 0.05$; $g_5 = 0.77$; $g_6 = 0.02$) and normalized antenna factor $M^*(\theta)$ for $K = 4.44$; $k_1 = 0$ are depicted in Figure 24.

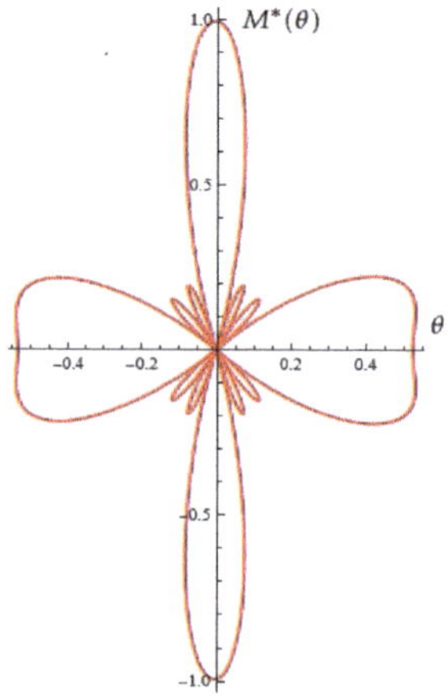

Figure 23. A typical Melnikov antenna array (from Proposition 10).

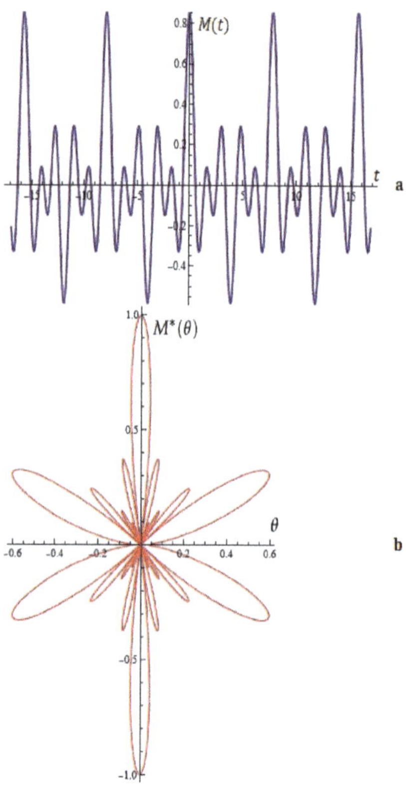

Figure 24. (**a**) The equation $M(t_0) = 0$ (Proposition 11); (**b**) A typical array of Melnikov antennas (from Proposition 11).

3. Concluding Remarks

In this study, we have examined a few kinds of extended classical oscillators. We present a few specific modules for examining these oscillators' behavior. For some of them, a cloud version is available that just needs a browser and an internet connection. This will be an essential component of a much broader web-based program for scientific computing that is in the works. In [29,30], numerical techniques for solving nonlinear algebraic equations are contained. The reader can formulate Melnikov's criterion for the appearance of the intersection between the disturbed and unperturbed separatrixes using Propositions 1 through 6. For arbitrarily selected p and N, the reader can examine the corresponding approximation problem. We observe that arbitrary point sets in the plane about uniform metric can be approximated using Melnikov polynomials. These kinds of activities are pertinent to the general theory of radiation diagrams and digital filter fabrication and analysis. To determine A_k coefficients, the standard N-element linear phased array factor is

$$AF(\theta) = \sum_{k=1}^{\frac{N}{2}} A_k \cos((2k-1)u) = M(x),$$

where $x = x_0 \cos u$ and x_0 is a design parameter, d is element separation, θ is the polar angle, and $u = \frac{\pi d}{\lambda} \cos \theta$. Soltis [31] used this concept in his creation of novel Gegenbauer-like and Jacobi-like antenna arrays. Naturally, this relatively new concept is a topic for defense, and experts in this field of science will conduct substantial research to support its legitimacy. The issue related to noise minimization (in decibels) also remains open.

Remark 1. *The monograph [32] is concerned with the control of chaos in dissipative non-autonomous system described by the differential equation*

$$\ddot{x} + \frac{\mathrm{d}U(x)}{\mathrm{d}x} = -\mathrm{d}(x\dot{x}) + F(t),$$

where $U(x)$ is a nonlinear potential, $-\mathrm{d}(x\dot{x})$ is a general dissipative force, and $F(t)$ is a general periodic function of period T. The planar system, corresponding to the damped pendulum, is

$$\begin{cases} \frac{\mathrm{d}x}{\mathrm{d}t} &= y \\ \frac{\mathrm{d}y}{\mathrm{d}t} &= -\sin x - \epsilon(Ay - g\, cn(\omega t; 0)), \end{cases}$$

where $A, g > 0$, and $cn(\omega t; m)$ is the Jacoby elliptic function of parameter m. In the book cited above, one can find a relatively precise bibliographic reference on the mentioned topic, as well as some modified but not sufficiently studied differential models. Following the considerations in this article, the reader can successfully formulate and investigate the dynamics of the following extended oscillators:

$$\begin{cases} \frac{\mathrm{d}x}{\mathrm{d}t} &= y \\ \frac{\mathrm{d}y}{\mathrm{d}t} &= -\sin x - \epsilon\left(Ay|y|^{p-1} - \sum_{j=1}^{N} g_j\, cn(j\omega t; 0)\right), \end{cases}$$

$$\begin{cases} \frac{\mathrm{d}x}{\mathrm{d}t} &= y \\ \frac{\mathrm{d}y}{\mathrm{d}t} &= -\sin x - \epsilon\left(Ay|y|^{p-1} - \cos x \sum_{j=1}^{N} g_j\, cn(j\omega t; 0)\right), \end{cases}$$

where $0 \le \epsilon < 1$, A is the damping level, $p \ge 1$ is the damping exponent, and N is an integer.

Proposition 12. *If $p = 8$, $N = 4$, and $|\mathrm{Im}(\omega)| < \frac{1}{4}$, then the roots of the corresponding Melnikov function $M(t_0)$ are given as solutions of the equation:*

$$M(t_0) = 70A - g_1 \cos(t_0\omega)\mathrm{sech}\frac{\pi\omega}{2} - g_2 \cos(2t_0\omega)\mathrm{sech}(\pi\omega) - g_3 \cos(3t_0\omega)\mathrm{sech}\frac{3\pi\omega}{2} - g_4 \cos(4t_0\omega)\mathrm{sech}(2\pi\omega) = 0.$$

For example, the equation $M(t_0) = 0$ (for $p = 8$; $N = 4$; $A = 0.00$; $\omega = 0.2$; $g_1 = 0.2$; $g_2 = 0.62$; $g_3 = 0.1$; $g_4 = 0.425$) is depicted in Figure 25.

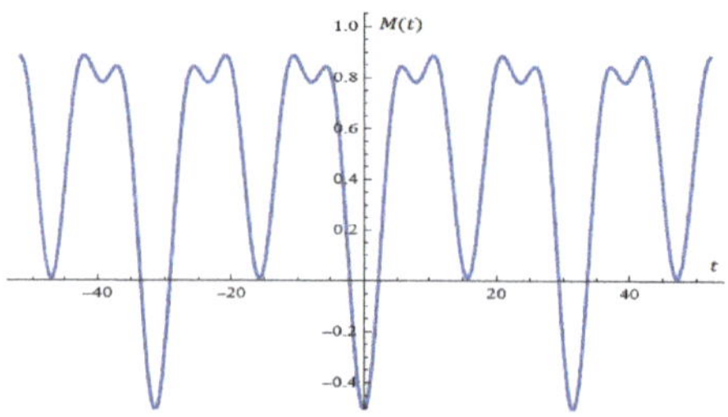

Figure 25. Melnikov function $M(t_0)$ (Proposition 12).

Remark 2. *The analytical study of controlling chaotic dynamics in spur gear systems is the subject of reflections by many authors working in the field of Mechanisms and Machine Theory (see [33–38]). Gear systems have been widely used in many industrial applications due to their advantages of having accurate transmission ratios, compact dimensions, and high efficiency. A nonlinear dynamic model of a spur gear pair with backlash and static transmission error is formulated in [33] as*

$$\begin{cases} \frac{dx}{dt} = y \\ \frac{dy}{dt} = -f_h(x) - \epsilon(Ay + g_1\cos(\omega t)), \end{cases}$$

where the backlash function $f_h(x)$ is a nonlinear displacement function and can be expressed as follows:

$$f_h(x) = \begin{cases} x - (1-\alpha); \ 1 < x \\ \alpha x; \ -1 \le x \le 1 \\ x + (1-\alpha); \ 1 < x, \end{cases}$$

where α is a mechanical parameter. The authors in [33] consider the following polynomial approximation (for $\alpha = 0$): $f_h(x) \approx -0.1667x + 0.1667x^3$ and study the dynamics of model using Melnikov analysis. The reader can formulate and explore the dynamics of the modified model of the type

$$\begin{cases} \frac{dx}{dt} = y \\ \frac{dy}{dt} = -f_h(x) - \epsilon\left(Ay - \sum_{i=1}^{N} g_i\cos(i\omega t)\right) \end{cases}$$

in which a trigonometric approximation for backlash function $f_h(x)$ of type $\sin x$ or $\sin x + cx$ is used, and then use the apparatus proposed in this article.

Remark 3. *A number of authors have devoted their research to the RF superconducting quantum interference device (SQUID) driven by an oscillating external flux (see, for example, [39–48]). In this regard, we would like to note that the detailed study of modified dynamic models of type*

$$\begin{cases} \frac{\mathrm{d}x}{\mathrm{d}t} &= y \\ \frac{\mathrm{d}y}{\mathrm{d}t} &= -\sin x - cx - \epsilon\left(by - \sum_{i=1}^{N} g_i \cos(i\omega t)\right) \end{cases}$$

will be the subject of our future research.

Remark 4. *For the purposes of our research (thankfully), the user does not need to have an explicit representation of the Melnikov polynomials corresponding to our differential model (for large values of the parameters), because the output of the first module used becomes the input for the second and most important module (implemented in the CAS Mathematica) used, designed to generate and visualize the corresponding diagrams of the radiating antenna array.*

Author Contributions: Conceptualization, N.K. and T.Z.; methodology, N.K. and T.Z.; software, T.Z., V.K. and A.I.; validation, A.R., T.Z., A.I. and N.K.; formal analysis, N.K. and T.Z.; investigation, T.Z., N.K., V.K., A.R. and A.I.; resources, A.R., T.Z., V.K. and N.K.; data curation, A.R., A.I. and V.K.; writing—original draft preparation, V.K., N.K. and T.Z.; writing—review and editing, A.R., V.K. and A.I.; visualization, V.K., N.K. and T.Z.; supervision, T.Z. and N.K.; project administration, T.Z.; funding acquisition, A.R., T.Z., N.K. and A.I. All authors have read and agreed to the published version of the manuscript.

Funding: The first, third, and fifth authors are supported by the European Union-NextGenerationEU, through the National Plan for Recovery and Resilience of the Republic of Bulgaria, project No BG-RRP-2.004-0001-C01. The research of the second author was carried out under project BG-RRP-2.011-0049, "Integrated Framework for Health Service Improvement via Analysis of Patient Reported Outcomes Data", funded by the Recovery and Resilience Mechanism as part of investment C2.I2, "Enhancing the Innovation Capacity of the Bulgarian Academy of Sciences in the Field of Green and Digital Technologies".

Data Availability Statement: Data are contained within the article.

Conflicts of Interest: The authors declare no conflicts of interest.

Appendix A. Stochastic Control on the Perturbations in Model A

Next, we discuss a stochastic control on the introduced perturbations. We first rewrite model (5) as follows

$$\begin{cases} \frac{\mathrm{d}x}{\mathrm{d}t} &= y \\ \frac{\mathrm{d}y}{\mathrm{d}t} &= -\sin x - \epsilon\left(Ay\frac{1-|y|^n}{1-|y|} - \sum_{j=1}^{N} g_j \sin(j\omega t)\right). \end{cases} \tag{A1}$$

We can assume without any restrictions that $\sum_{j=1}^{N} g_j = 1$ and, consequently, we can consider these coefficients to be the probabilities of a particular distribution. We shall follow the approach of [26–28]—we will briefly describe it. Using the complex presentation of the sin-function

$$\sin(x) = \frac{e^{ix} - e^{-ix}}{2i}, \tag{A2}$$

we can rewrite the y-dynamics (A1) as

$$\begin{aligned} \frac{\mathrm{d}y}{\mathrm{d}t} &= -\sin x - \epsilon\left(Ay\frac{1-|y|^n}{1-|y|} - \sum_{j=1}^{N} g_j \frac{e^{ij\omega t} - e^{-ij\omega t}}{2i}\right) \\ &= -\sin x - \epsilon\left(Ay\frac{1-|y|^n}{1-|y|} - \frac{1}{2i}(\psi(\omega t) - \psi(-\omega t))\right). \end{aligned} \tag{A3}$$

Above, by $\psi(\cdot)$ is denoted the characteristic function of a distribution taking values $\{1,2,\ldots,N\}$ with probabilities g_j, $j = 1,2,\ldots,N$. Note that we can generalize dynamics (A3) on the infinite support $\{1,2,\ldots\}$ as well as on some continuous domain. Thus, if we denote the domain of the probability distribution by D and its density by $g(\cdot)$, then the original dynamics (A1) turns into

$$\begin{cases} \dfrac{dx}{dt} &= y \\ \dfrac{dy}{dt} &= -\sin x - \epsilon\left(Ay\frac{1-|y|^n}{1-|y|} - \int\limits_D g(u)\sin(u\omega t)du\right). \end{cases} \tag{A4}$$

In contrast to the approach used in [26–28], we shift the time dependence from the sin-function to the function $g(\cdot,t)$, imposing the condition $\int_D g(u,t)du = 1$ for every fixed t. Thus, we view $g(\cdot,t)$ as the density function of a stochastic process. Thus, dynamics (A3) turn into

$$\frac{dy}{dt} = -\sin x - \epsilon\left(Ay\frac{1-|y|^n}{1-|y|} - \frac{1}{2i}(\psi(t,\omega) - \psi(t,-\omega))\right). \tag{A5}$$

Our suggestion is to use the characteristic function of a Brownian motion with drift μ and multiplied by a diffusion coefficient σ—its domain is $D \equiv \mathbb{R}$. Its characteristic function is

$$\psi(t,x) = e^{t\left(i\mu x - \frac{\sigma^2 x^2}{2}\right)}. \tag{A6}$$

Hence, dynamics (A5) can be written as

$$\begin{aligned} \frac{dy}{dt} &= -\sin x - \epsilon\left(Ay\frac{1-|y|^n}{1-|y|} - \frac{1}{2i}\left(e^{t\left(i\mu\omega - \frac{\sigma^2\omega^2}{2}\right)} - e^{t\left(-i\mu\omega - \frac{\sigma^2\omega^2}{2}\right)}\right)\right) \\ &= -\sin x - \epsilon\left(Ay\frac{1-|y|^n}{1-|y|} - \frac{e^{-\frac{\sigma^2\omega^2 t}{2}}}{2i}\left(e^{i\mu\omega t} - e^{-i\mu\omega t}\right)\right) \\ &= -\sin x - \epsilon\left(Ay\frac{1-|y|^n}{1-|y|} - e^{-\frac{\sigma^2\omega^2 t}{2}}\sin(\mu\omega t)\right). \end{aligned} \tag{A7}$$

We present in Figure A1a,c,e the x- and y-dynamics as well as the phase portrait for the following values: $p = 10$, $A = 0.0012$, $\epsilon = 1$, $\omega = 0.1$, $\mu = 0.1$, and $\sigma = 0.3$. The initial point is assumed to be $(0.1, 0.1)$.

Suppose now that the perturbations are driven by the characteristic function of a Poisson point process with intensity λ, i.e.,

$$\psi(t,x) = e^{\lambda t(e^{ix}-1)}. \tag{A8}$$

Using formula (A2), we rewrite

$$\begin{aligned} &\frac{1}{2i}(\psi(t,\omega) - \psi(t,-\omega)) = \frac{1}{2i}\left[e^{\lambda t(e^{i\omega}-1)} - e^{\lambda t(e^{-i\omega}-1)}\right] \\ &= \frac{e^{-\lambda t}}{2i}\left[e^{\lambda t(\cos\omega + i\sin\omega)} - e^{\lambda t(\cos\omega - i\sin\omega)}\right] \\ &= \frac{e^{-\lambda t}}{2i}e^{\lambda t\cos\omega}\left[e^{i\lambda t\sin\omega} - e^{-i\lambda t\sin\omega}\right] \\ &= e^{\lambda t(\cos\omega - 1)}\sin(\lambda t\sin\omega). \end{aligned} \tag{A9}$$

Hence, y-dynamics (A7) turns into

$$\frac{\mathrm{d}y}{\mathrm{d}t} = -\sin x - \epsilon\left(Ay\frac{1-|y|^n}{1-|y|} - e^{\lambda t(\cos\omega - 1)}\sin(\lambda t \sin\omega)\right). \tag{A10}$$

Some simulations based on this construction can be seen in Figure A1b,d,f. We use the values $p = 10$, $A = 0.03$, $\epsilon = 0.04$ and $\lambda = 0.1$.

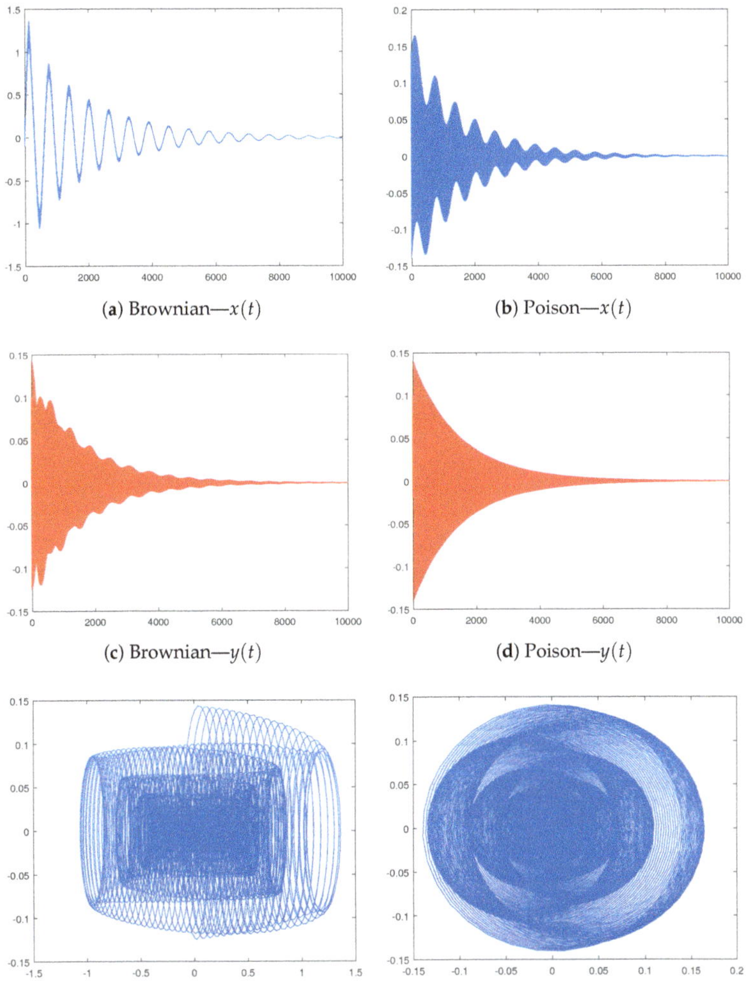

(**a**) Brownian—$x(t)$ (**b**) Poison—$x(t)$

(**c**) Brownian—$y(t)$ (**d**) Poison—$y(t)$

(**e**) Brownian, phase space (**f**) Poison, phase space

Figure A1. Oscillators based on the Brownian motion and the Poisson process.

Appendix B. Stochastic Control on the Perturbations in Model B

We discuss briefly Model B in light of the approach presented in the previous section. Using the cos-presentation

$$\cos(x) = \frac{e^{ix} + e^{-ix}}{2}, \tag{A11}$$

we transform dynamics (15) into

$$\begin{cases} \frac{\mathrm{d}x}{\mathrm{d}t} &= y \\ \frac{\mathrm{d}y}{\mathrm{d}t} &= -\sin x - \epsilon\Big(Ay\frac{1-|y|^n}{1-|y|} + \frac{\cos x}{2}(\psi(t,\omega)+\psi(t,-\omega))\Big). \end{cases} \tag{A12}$$

If we use the Brownian characteristic function (A6), we reach

$$\frac{\mathrm{d}y}{\mathrm{d}t} = -\sin x - \epsilon\left(Ay\frac{1-|y|^n}{1-|y|} + \cos x e^{-\frac{\sigma^2\omega^2 t}{2}}\cos(\mu\omega t)\right). \tag{A13}$$

If we apply the Poisson characteristic function (A8), then dynamics (A13) turns into

$$\frac{\mathrm{d}y}{\mathrm{d}t} = -\sin x - \epsilon\left(Ay\frac{1-|y|^n}{1-|y|} + \cos x e^{\lambda t(\cos\omega - 1)}\cos(\lambda t\sin\omega)\right). \tag{A14}$$

Some simulations based on the parameters reported in Appendix A are presented in Figure A2.

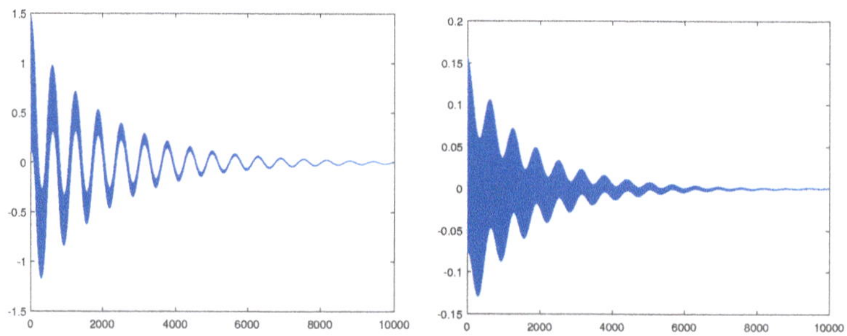

(**a**) Brownian—$x(t)$ (**b**) Poison—$x(t)$

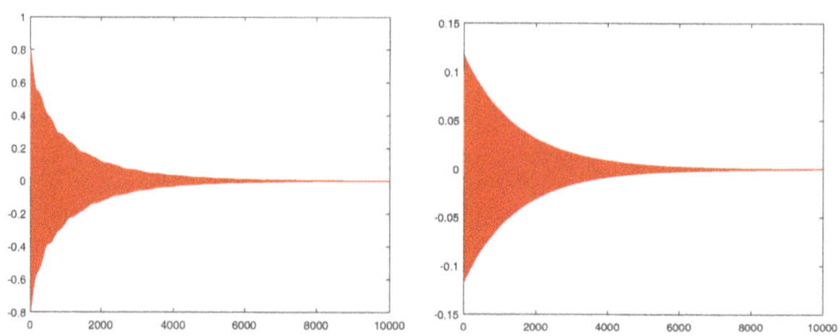

(**c**) Brownian—$y(t)$ (**d**) Poison—$y(t)$

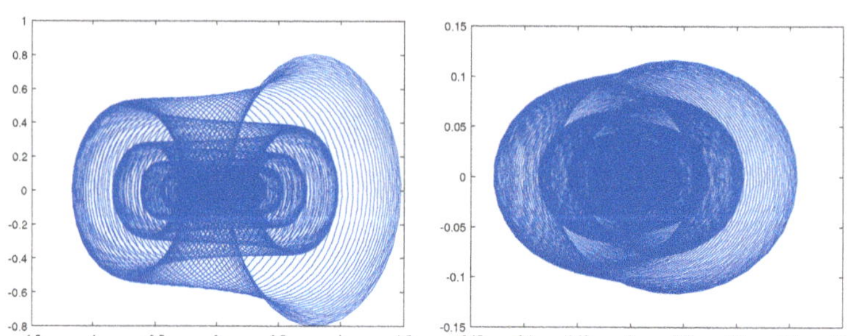

(**e**) Brownian, phase space (**f**) Poison, phase space

Figure A2. Oscillators based on the Brownian motion and the Poisson process.

References

1. Tricomi, F. Integratione di un' equazione differenziale presentatasi in elettrotecnica. *Ann. Della Sc. Norm. Super. Pisa* **1933**, *2*, 1–20.
2. Stoker, J. *Nonlinear Vibration in Mechanical and Electrical Systems*; Interscience: New York, NY, USA, 1950.
3. Levi, M.; Hoppensteadt, F.; Miranker, W. Dynamics of the Josephson junction. *Q. Appl. Math.* **1978**, *35*, 167–198. [CrossRef]
4. Perko, L. *Differential Equations and Dynamical Systems*; Springer: New York, NY, USA, 1991.
5. Guckenheimer, J.; Holmes, P. *Nonlinear Oscillations, Dynamical Systems, and Bifurcations of Vector Fields*; Springer: New York, NY, USA, 1983.
6. Sanjuan, M. The effect of nonlinear damping on the universal oscillator. *Int. J. Bifurc. Chaos* **1999**, *9*, 735–744. [CrossRef]
7. Soliman, M.; Thompson, J. The effect of nonlinear damping on the steady state and basin bifurcation patterns of a nonlinear mechanical oscillator. *Int. J. Bifurc. Chaos* **1992**, *2*, 81–91. [CrossRef]
8. Fangnon, R.; Ainamon, C.; Monwanou, A.; Mowadinou, C.; Orpu, J. Nonlinear dynamics of the quadratic damping Helmholtz oscillator. *Complexity* **2020**, *2020*, 8822534. [CrossRef]
9. Bikdash, M.; Balachandran, B.; Nayfeh, A. Melnikov analysis for a ship with a general roll-damping model. *Nonlinear Dyn.* **1994**, *6*, 101–124. [CrossRef]
10. Ravindra, B.; Mallik, A. Stability analysis of a non–linearly clamped Duffing oscillator. *J. Sound Vib.* **1999**, *171*, 708–716. [CrossRef]
11. Ravindra, B.; Mallik, A. Role of nonlinear dissipation in soft Duffing oscillators. *Phys. Rev. E* **1984**, *49*, 4950–4954. [CrossRef] [PubMed]
12. Sanjuan, M. Monoclinic bifurcation sets of driven nonlinear oscillators. *Int. J. Theor. Phys.* **1996**, *35*, 1745–1752. [CrossRef]
13. Holmes, P.; Marsden, J. Horseshoes in perturbation of Hamiltonian systems with two degrees of freedom. *Commun. Math. Phys.* **1982**, *82*, 523–544. [CrossRef]
14. Holmes, P.; Marsden, J. A partial differential equation with infinitely many periodic orbits: Chaotic oscillations. *Arch. Ration. Mech. Anal.* **1981**, *76*, 135–166. [CrossRef]
15. Golev, A.; Terzieva, T.; Iliev, A.; Rahnev, A.; Kyurkchiev, N. Simulation on a Generalized Oscillator Model: Web-Based Application. *Proc. Bulg. Acad. Sci.* **2024**, *77*, 230–237. [CrossRef]
16. Lenci, S.; Lupini, R. Homoclinic and heteroclinic solutions for a class of two-dimensional Hamiltonian systems. *Z. Angew. Math. Phys.* **1996**, *47*, 97–111. [CrossRef]
17. Lenci, S.; Rega, G. Controlling nonlinear dynamics in a two-well impact system. I. Attractors and bifurcation scenario under symmetric excitations. *Int. J. Bifur. Chaos Appl. Sci. Eng.* **1998**, *8*, 2387–2407. [CrossRef]
18. Lenci, S.; Rega, G. Controlling nonlinear dynamics in a two-well impact system. II. Attractors and bifurcation scenario under unsymmetric optimal excitation. *Int. J. Bifur. Chaos Appl. Sci. Eng.* **1998**, *8*, 2409–2424. [CrossRef]
19. Lenci, S.; Rega, G. Higher-order Melnikov analysis of homo/heteroclinic bifurcations in mechanical oscillators. In Proceedings of the 16th AIMETA Congress of Theoretical and Applied Mechanics, Ferrara, Italy, 9–12 September 2003; CD-Rom.
20. Lenci, S.; Rega, G. Optimal control of homoclinic bifurcation: Theoretical treatment and practical reduction of safe basin erosion in the Helmholtz oscillator. *J. Vib. Control* **2003**, *9*, 281–315. [CrossRef]
21. Rega, G.; Lenci, S. Bifurcations and chaos in single-d.o.f. mechanical systems: Exploiting nonlinear dynamics properties for their control. In *Recent Research Developments in Structural Dynamics*; Luongo, A., Ed.; Research Signpost: Kerala, India, 2003; pp. 331–369.
22. Melnikov, V. On the stability of a center for time–periodic perturbation. *Trans. Mosc. Math. Soc.* **1963**, *12*, 3–52.
23. Kyurkchiev, N.; Zaevski, T.; Iliev, A.; Kyurkchiev, V.; Rahnev, A. Nonlinear dynamics of a new class of micro-electromechanical oscillators–open problems. *Symmetry* **2024**, *16*, 253. [CrossRef]
24. Kyurkchiev, N.; Zaevski, T.; Iliev, A.; Kyurkchiev, V.; Rahnev, A. Dynamics of a new class of oscillators: Melnikov's approach, possible application to antenna array theory. *Math. Inform.* **2024**, *67*, 367.
25. Kyurkchiev, N.; Zaevski, T.; Iliev, A.; Kyurkchiev, V.; Rahnev, A. Modeling of Some Classes of Extended Oscillators: Simulations, Algorithms, Generating Chaos, Open Problems. *Algorithms* **2024**, *17*, 121. [CrossRef]
26. Kyurkchiev, N.; Zaevski, T.; Iliev, A.; Branzov, T.; Kyurkchiev, V.; Rahnev, A. Dynamics of Some Perturbed Morse-Type Oscillators: Simulations and Applications. *Mathematics* **2024**, *12*, 3368. [CrossRef]
27. Kyurkchiev, N.; Zaevski, T.; Iliev, A.; Kyurkchiev, V.; Rahnev, A. Notes on Modified Planar Kelvin–Stuart Models: Simulations, Applications, Probabilistic Control on the Perturbations. *Axioms* **2024**, *13*, 720. [CrossRef]
28. Kyurkchiev, N.; Zaevski, T.; Iliev, A.; Kyurkchiev, V.; Rahnev, A. Generating Chaos in Dynamical Systems: Applications, Symmetry Results, and Stimulating Examples. *Symmetry* **2024**, *16*, 938. [CrossRef]
29. Proinov, P.; Vasileva, M. On the convergence of high-order Gargantini-Farmer-Loizou type iterative methods for simultaneous approximation of polynomial zeros. *Appl. Math. Comput.* **2019**, *361*, 202–214. [CrossRef]
30. Ivanov, S. Families of high-order simultaneous methods with several corrections. *Numer. Algorithms* **2024**, *97*, 945–958. [CrossRef]
31. Soltis, J. New Gegenbauer-like and Jacobi-like polynomials with applications. *J. Frankl. Inst.* **1993**, *33*, 635–639. [CrossRef]

32. Chacon, R. Control of homoclinic chaos by weak periodic perturbations. In *World Scientific Series on Nonlinear Science*; Chua, L., Ed.; Series A; World Scientific Publisher: Singapore, 2005; Volume 55.
33. Saghafi, A.; Furshidianfer, A. The analytical study of controlling chaotic dynamics in spur gear systems. *Mech. Mach. Theory* **2016**, *96*, 179–191. [CrossRef]
34. Guerine, A. Dynamic response of a spur gear system with uncertain parameters. *J. Theor. Appl. Mech.* **2016**, *54*, 1039–1049. [CrossRef]
35. Dalpiaz, G.; Rivola, A.; Rubini, R. Dynamic modeling of gear systems for condition monitoring and diagnostics. *Congr. Tech. Diagn.* **1996**, 185–192.
36. Guerine, A.; El Hami, A.; Fakhfakh, T.; Haddar, M. A polynomial chaos method to the analysis of the dynamic behavior of spur gear system. *Struct. Eng. Mech.* **2015**, *53*, 819–831. [CrossRef]
37. Guerine, A.; El Hami, A.; Walha, L.; Fakhfakh, T.; Haddar, M. A perturbation approach for the dynamic analysis of one stage gear system with uncertain parameters. *Mech. Mach. Theory* **2015**, *92*, 113–126. [CrossRef]
38. Jin, B.; Bian, Y.; Liu, X.; Gao, Z. Dynamic Modeling and Nonlinear Analysis of a Spur Gear System Considering a Nonuniformly Distributed Meshing Force. *Appl. Sci.* **2022**, *12*, 12270. [CrossRef]
39. Ritala, R.; Salomaa, M. Odd and even subharmonics and chaos in RF SQUIDS. *J. Phys. C Solid State Phys.* **1983**, *16*, 477–484. [CrossRef]
40. Ritala. R.; Salomaa, M. Chaotic dynamics of periodically driven rf superconducting quantum interference devices. *Phys. Rev. B* **1984**, *29*, 6143. [CrossRef]
41. Fesser, K.; Bishop, A.; Kumar, P. Chaos in rf SQUID's. *Appl. Phys. Lett.* **1983**, *43*, 123–124. [CrossRef]
42. Schieve, W.; Bulsara, A.; Jacobs, E. Homoclinic chaos in the rf superconducting quantum-interference device. *Phys. Rev. A* **1988**, *37*, 3541. [CrossRef] [PubMed]
43. Ling, F.; Bao, G. A numerical implementations of Melnikov's method. *Phys. Lett. A* **1987**, *122*, 413. [CrossRef]
44. Salam, F. The Mel'nikov Technique for Highly Dissipative Systems. *SIAM J. Appl. Math.* **1987**, *47*, 232–243. [CrossRef]
45. Schecter, S. Melnikov's method at a saddle–node and the dynamics of the forced Josephson junction. *SIAM J. Math. Anal.* **1987**, *18*, 1699–1715. [CrossRef]
46. Grebogi, C.; Ott, E.; Yorke, J. Basin boundary metamorphoses: Changes in accessible boundary orbits. *Physica* **1987**, *24*, 243–262.
47. Bruhn, B.; Koch, B. Homoclinic and Heteroclinic Bifurcations in rf SQUIDs. *Z. Naturforschung* **1988**, *43*, 930–938. [CrossRef]
48. Ostrovskii, V.; Karimov, A.; Rybin, V.; Kopets, E.; Butusov, D. Comparing the Finite-Difference Schemes in the Simulation of Shunted Josephson Junctions. In Proceedings of the 23rd Conference of Open Innovations Association (FRUCT), Bologna, Italy, 13–16 November 2018; pp. 300–305.

mathematics

MDPI

Article

Abundant Elliptic, Trigonometric, and Hyperbolic Stochastic Solutions for the Stochastic Wu–Zhang System in Quantum Mechanics

Wael W. Mohammed *, Ekram E. Ali, Athar I. Ahmed and Marwa Ennaceur

Department of Mathematics, College of Science, University of Ha'il, Ha'il P.O. Box 2440, Saudi Arabia; ek.ali@uoh.edu.sa (E.E.A.); ath.ahmed@uoh.edu.sa (A.I.A.); mar.ennaceur@uoh.edu.sa (M.E.)
* Correspondence: w.mohammed@uoh.edu.sa

Abstract: In this article, we look at the stochastic Wu–Zhang system (SWZS) forced by multiplicative Brownian motion in the Itô sense. The mapping method, which is an effective analytical method, is employed to investigate the exact wave solutions of the aforementioned equation. The proposed scheme provides new types of exact solutions including periodic solitons, kink solitons, singular solitons and so on, to describe the wave propagation in quantum mechanics and analyze a wide range of essential physical phenomena. In the absence of noise, we obtain some previously found solutions of SWZS. Additionally, using the MATLAB program, the impacts of the noise term on the analytical solution of the SWZS were demonstrated.

Keywords: multiplicative white noise; stochastic exact solutions; stabilize by noise; mapping method

MSC: 35A20; 60H10; 60H15; 35Q51; 83C15

1. Introduction

Nonlinear evolution equations (NLEEs) are commonly employed to describe complicated phenomena in a variety of engineering and scientific areas, including fluid dynamics, acoustics, optical fibers, solid state physics, hydrodynamics and plasma physics. Consequently, it is crucial to solve these NLEEs. Recently, numerous powerful approaches for discovering exact solutions to NLEEs have been introduced, such as $exp(-\phi(\varsigma))$-expansion method [1], Jacobi elliptic function expansion [2], modified extended tanh-function method [3], F-expansion method [4], Riccati equation method [5], (G'/G)-expansion [6,7], exp-function method [8], sine–cosine method [9], etc.

One of these equations is the Wu–Zhang system [10]. The Wu–Zhang system is a well-known model in quantum mechanics that describes the dynamics of two coupled qubits, or quantum bits. The system exhibits a variety of interesting phenomena, including entanglement generation and quantum phase transitions. One essential consideration in the study of the Wu–Zhang system is the role of noise, or random fluctuations in the system's parameters, which can have significant effects on its behavior.

Noise in the Wu–Zhang system can come from a variety of sources, such as external electromagnetic fields or fluctuations in the system's energy levels. These random fluctuations can lead to decoherence, or the loss of quantum coherence, which is important for quantum computing and other quantum technologies. Understanding the effects of noise in the Wu–Zhang system is crucial for developing strategies to mitigate its impact and improve the system's performance.

In this article, we look at the stochastic Wu–Zhang system (SWZS) as follows:

$$\begin{aligned} &\Psi_t + (\Phi\Psi)_x + \tfrac{1}{3}\Phi_{xxx} = \varpi\Psi\mathcal{B}_t, \\ &\Phi_t + \Phi\Phi_x + \Psi_x = \varpi\Phi\mathcal{B}_t, \end{aligned} \tag{1}$$

where $\Psi = \Psi(x,t)$ presents the surface velocity of water and $\Phi = \Phi(x,t)$ indicates the elevation of the water; ϖ is the amplitude of noise; $\mathcal{B} = \mathcal{B}(t)$ is a Brownian motion and $\mathcal{B}_t = \frac{\partial \mathcal{B}}{\partial t}$. Due to their Lax pairs [11], the Wu–Zhang system (1) is integrable.

Due to the importance of the Wu–Zhang system in quantum mechanics, some authors obtained its solutions by using various methods including the dynamic analysis method [12], generalized extended tanh-function method [13], csch method, tan–cot method, extended tanh–coth method, modified simple equation method [14], extended tanh and Hirota methods [15], and extended trial equation method [16]. Moreover, the solutions of the fractal Wu–Zhang system with different fractional operators were obtained by using various methods including the modified auxiliary equation method [17], first integral method [18], and semi-inverse method [19], exponential rational function method [20], and iterative method [21]. However, the stochastic Wu–Zhang system with a noise term has not yet been addressed.

Our aim for this study is to obtain the exact stochastic solutions for the SWZS (1). To the best of our knowledge, the exact stochastic solutions for the SWZS (1) has never been obtained before. Several kinds of solutions may be found by using the mapping approach including periodic solitons, kink solitons, singular solitons and so on. In the absence of noise, we obtain some previous solutions of SWZS (1) such as the solutions stated in [13]. Furthermore, to study the effect of white noise on the discovered solutions, we present a number of two-dimensional and three-dimensional graphs.

The paper's outline is as follows: Section 2 provides the wave equation of the SWZS (1), and Section 3 explains the mapping method. In Section 4, we obtain the solutions of the (1). In Section 5, we may investigate the impact of the stochastic term on the solutions of the SWZS (1). Finally, the obtained results of this paper are stated.

2. Traveling Wave Equation for SWZS

The wave equation for SWZS (1) is obtained by applying

$$\Phi(x,t) = \varphi(\zeta)e^{\varpi\mathcal{B}-\frac{1}{2}\varpi^2 t} \text{ and } \Psi(x,t) = \psi(\zeta)e^{\varpi\mathcal{B}-\frac{1}{2}\varpi^2 t},\ \zeta = kx + \lambda t, \tag{2}$$

where the deterministic functions φ and ψ are real, and λ and k are non-zero constants. We note that

$$\begin{aligned} \Phi_t &= [\lambda\varphi' + \varpi\varphi\mathcal{B}_t - \frac{1}{2}\varpi^2\varphi + \frac{1}{2}\varpi^2\varphi]e^{\varpi\mathcal{B}-\frac{1}{2}\varpi^2 t} \\ &= [\lambda\varphi' + \varpi\varphi\mathcal{B}_t]e^{\varpi\mathcal{B}-\frac{1}{2}\varpi^2 t}, \\ \Phi_x &= k\varphi' e^{\varpi\mathcal{B}-\frac{1}{2}\varpi^2 t},\ \Phi_{xxx} = k^3\varphi''' e^{\varpi\mathcal{B}-\frac{1}{2}\varpi^2 t} \end{aligned} \tag{3}$$

where $\frac{1}{2}\varpi^2\varphi$ is the Itô correction term. Similarly,

$$\Psi_t = [\lambda\psi' + \varpi\psi\mathcal{B}_t]e^{\varpi\mathcal{B}-\frac{1}{2}\varpi^2 t},\ \Psi_x = k\psi' e^{\varpi\mathcal{B}-\frac{1}{2}\varpi^2 t}. \tag{4}$$

Substituting Equations (3) and (4) into Equation (1), we obtain the following system:

$$\begin{aligned} &\lambda\psi' + k(\psi\varphi)' e^{\varpi\mathcal{B}-\frac{1}{2}\varpi^2 t} + \tfrac{k^3}{3}\psi''' = 0. \\ &\lambda\varphi' + k\varphi\varphi' e^{\varpi\mathcal{B}-\frac{1}{2}\varpi^2 t} + k\psi' = 0, \end{aligned} \tag{5}$$

Considering the expectation on both sides of Equation (5), we arrive at

$$\begin{aligned} &\lambda\psi' + \tfrac{k^3}{3}\varphi''' + k(\psi\varphi)' e^{-\frac{1}{2}\varpi^2 t}\mathbb{E}(e^{\varpi\mathcal{B}}) = 0, \\ &\lambda\varphi' + k\psi' + k\varphi\varphi' e^{-\frac{1}{2}\varpi^2 t}\mathbb{E}(e^{\varpi\mathcal{B}}) = 0. \end{aligned} \tag{6}$$

Since $\mathcal{B}(t)$ is a Gaussian process, $\mathbb{E}(e^{\varpi\mathcal{B}(t)}) = e^{\frac{1}{2}\varpi^2 t}$ for any real number ϖ. Hence, Equation (6) becomes

$$\begin{aligned} &\lambda\psi' + \tfrac{k^3}{3}\varphi''' + k(\psi\varphi)' = 0, \\ &\lambda\varphi' + k\psi' + k\varphi\varphi' = 0. \end{aligned} \tag{7}$$

Integrating Equation (7) once and setting integration constant equal to zero, we obtain

$$\lambda\psi + \frac{k^3}{3}\varphi'' + k(\psi\varphi) = 0, \tag{8}$$

$$\lambda\varphi + k\psi + \frac{1}{2}k\varphi^2 = 0. \tag{9}$$

From Equation (9), we have

$$\psi = \frac{-\lambda}{k}\varphi - \frac{1}{2}\varphi^2. \tag{10}$$

Plugging Equation (10) into Equation (8) leads to

$$\varphi'' - \frac{3\lambda^2}{k^4}\varphi - \frac{9\lambda}{2k^3}\varphi^2 - \frac{3}{2k^2}\varphi^3 = 0. \tag{11}$$

3. The Clarification of Mapping Method

Let us explain the method that we utilize here (for more information, see [22–24]). We assume the solution of Equation (11) has the form

$$\varphi(\zeta) = \sum_{i=0}^{N} q_i \mathcal{P}^i(\zeta),\ q_M \neq 0, \tag{12}$$

where $q_0,\ q_1,\ q_2, \dots,\ q_{N-1}$ and q_N are undefined constants to be determined and $\mathcal{P}$ solves the following nonlinear elliptic function equation that is an ordinary equation:

$$(\mathcal{P}')^2 = \alpha_1\mathcal{P}^4 + \alpha_2\mathcal{P}^2 + \alpha_3, \tag{13}$$

where $\alpha_1,\ \alpha_2$, and α_3 are real numbers. Equation (13) has several solutions for $\alpha_1,\ \alpha_2$ and α_3 as follows (Table 1).

Table 1. The solutions of Equation (13) for distinct values $\alpha_1,\ \alpha_2$ and α_3.

Case	α_1	α_2	α_3	$\mathcal{P}(\zeta)$
1	ß^2	$-(1+$ß$^2)$	1	$sn(\zeta)$
2	ß^2	$-(1+$ß$^2)$	1	$cd(\zeta)$
3	1	$-($ß$^2+1)$	ß^2	$ns(\zeta)$
4	1	$-($ß$^2+1)$	ß^2	$dc(\zeta)$
5	$(1-$ß$^2)$	2ß$^2-1$	$-$ß^2	$nc(\zeta)$
6	$(1-$ß$^2)$	$2-$ß^2	1	$sc(\zeta)$
7	1	$2-$ß^2	$(1-$ß$^2)$	$cs(\zeta)$
8	1	2ß$^2-1$	$-$ß$^2(1-$ß$^2)$	$ds(\zeta)$
9	$\frac{1}{4}$	$\frac{(1-2ß^2)}{2}$	$\frac{1}{4}$	$ns(\zeta)\pm cs(\zeta)$
10	$\frac{1}{4}$	$\frac{(ß^2-2)}{2}$	$\frac{ß^2}{4}$	$ns(\zeta)\pm ds(\zeta)$
11	$\frac{1-ß^2}{4}$	$\frac{(1+ß^2)}{2}$	$\frac{(1-ß^2)}{4}$	$nc(\zeta)\pm sc(\zeta)$
12	$\frac{ß^2}{4}$	$\frac{(ß^2-2)}{2}$	$\frac{ß^2}{4}$	$\sqrt{1-ß^2}(sd(\zeta)\pm cd(\zeta))$
13	$\frac{ß^2}{4}$	$\frac{(ß^2-2)}{2}$	$\frac{1}{4}$	$\frac{sn(\zeta)}{1\pm dn(\zeta)}$
14	$\frac{(1-ß^2)^2}{4}$	$\frac{ß^2+1}{2}$	$\frac{1}{4}$	$ds(\zeta)\pm cs(\zeta)$
15	1	$2-4$ß^2	1	$\frac{sn(\zeta)dn(\zeta)}{cn(\zeta)}$
16	ß^4	2	1	$\frac{sn(\zeta)cn(\zeta)}{dn(\zeta)}$
17	1	ß$^2+2$	$(1-2$ß$^2+$ß$^4)$	$\frac{dn(\zeta)cn(\zeta)}{sn(\zeta)}$
18	$\frac{(1-ß^2)}{4}$	$\frac{(1+ß^2)}{2}$	$\frac{(1-ß^2)}{4}$	$\frac{cn(\zeta)}{1\pm sn(\zeta)}$
19	$\frac{1}{4}$	$\frac{(1-2ß^2)}{2}$	$\frac{1}{4}$	$\frac{sn(\zeta)}{1\pm cn(\zeta)}$

Where $cn(\zeta)=cn(\zeta,ß)$, $ds(\zeta)=ds(\zeta,ß)$, $sn(\zeta)=sn(\zeta,ß)$, $sc(\zeta)=sc(\zeta,ß)$, $dn(\zeta)=dn(\zeta,ß)$, are the Jacobi elliptic functions (JEFs) for $0<ß<1$.

JEFs generate the following hyperbolic functions when ß$\to 1$:

$$\begin{aligned} dn(\zeta) &\to \operatorname{sech}(\zeta),\ ns(\zeta)\to\coth(\zeta),\\ cs(\zeta) &\to \operatorname{csch}(\zeta),\ cn(\zeta)\to\operatorname{sech}(\zeta),\\ sn(\zeta) &\to \tanh(\zeta),\ ds\to\operatorname{csch}(\zeta). \end{aligned}$$

JEFs generate the following trigonometric functions when ß$\to 0$:

$$\begin{aligned} sc(\zeta) &\to \tan(\zeta),\ cs(\zeta)\to\cot(\zeta),\\ ds(\zeta) &\to \csc(\zeta),\ ds\to\csc(\zeta),\\ dn(\zeta) &\to 1,\ sn(\zeta)\to\sin(\zeta),\\ ns(\zeta) &\to \csc(\zeta),\ cn(\zeta)\to\cos(\zeta). \end{aligned}$$

4. Exact Solutions of the SWZS

First, let us equate φ'' with φ^3 in Equation (11) to calculate the parameters N as

$$N+2=3N\ \Rightarrow N=1.$$

With $N=1$, Equation (12) takes the form

$$\varphi(\zeta)=q_0+q_1\mathcal{P}(\zeta), \tag{14}$$

Putting Equation (14) into Equation (11), we obtain

$$\begin{aligned}&+[2\alpha_1q_1-\frac{3}{2k^2}q_1^3]\mathcal{P}^3+[\frac{-9\lambda}{2k^3}q_1^2-\frac{9}{2k^2}q_0q_1^2]\mathcal{P}^2\\&+[\alpha_2q_1-\frac{3\lambda^2}{k^4}q_1-\frac{9\lambda}{k^3}q_0q_1-\frac{9}{2k^2}q_0^2q_1]\mathcal{P}\\&+[\frac{-3\lambda^2}{k^4}q_0-\frac{9\lambda}{2k^3}q_0^2-\frac{3}{2k^2}q_0^3]=0.\end{aligned}$$

Inserting each coefficient of the various powers of $\mathcal{P}^j$, we have

$$2\alpha_1q_1-\frac{3}{2k^2}q_1^3=0,$$

$$\frac{-9\lambda}{2k^3}q_1^2-\frac{9}{2k^2}q_0q_1^2=0,$$

$$\alpha_2q_1-\frac{3\lambda^2}{k^4}q_1-\frac{9\lambda}{k^3}q_0q_1-\frac{9}{2k^2}q_0^2q_1=0,$$

and

$$\frac{-3\lambda^2}{k^4}q_0-\frac{9\lambda}{2k^3}q_0^2-\frac{3}{2k^2}q_0^3=0.$$

By solving the above equations, we have

$$q_0=\frac{-\lambda}{k},\ q_1=\pm 2k\sqrt{\frac{\alpha_1}{3}},\ \text{and}\ \alpha_2=\frac{-3\lambda^2}{2k^4}. \tag{15}$$

Plugging (15) into Equation (14), we obtain the following solution for the traveling wave Equation (11):

$$\varphi(\zeta)=\frac{-\lambda}{k}\pm 2k\sqrt{\frac{\alpha_1}{3}}\mathcal{P}(\zeta). \tag{16}$$

Using Equation (10), we have

$$\psi(\zeta)=\frac{\lambda^2}{2k^2}-\frac{2k^2\alpha_1}{3}\mathcal{P}^2(\zeta). \tag{17}$$

Consequently, substituting Equations (16) and (17) into Equation (2), we have the solutions of the SWZS (1) as follows:

$$\begin{aligned}\Phi&=\left\{\tfrac{-\lambda}{k}\pm 2k\sqrt{\tfrac{\alpha_1}{3}}\mathcal{P}(\zeta)\right\}e^{\varpi\mathcal{B}-\frac{1}{2}\varpi^2t},\\ \Psi&=\left\{\tfrac{\lambda^2}{2k^2}-\tfrac{2k^2\alpha_1}{3}\mathcal{P}^2(\zeta)\right\}e^{\varpi\mathcal{B}-\frac{1}{2}\varpi^2t},\end{aligned} \tag{18}$$

where $\zeta=kx+\lambda t$.

There are many cases for the solutions of Equation (15) relying on α_1 as follows:

Case 1: If $\alpha_1 =ß^2$, $\alpha_2 = -\left(1+ß^2\right)$ and $\alpha_3 = 1$, then $\mathcal{P}(\zeta) = sn(\zeta)$, and Equation (18) takes the form

$$\Phi = \left\{\frac{-\lambda}{k} \pm 2k\sqrt{\frac{ß^2}{3}}sn(\zeta)\right\}e^{\varpi B-\frac{1}{2}\varpi^2 t}, \quad (19)$$

$$\Psi = \left\{\frac{\lambda^2}{2k^2} - \frac{2k^2ß^2}{3}sn^2(\zeta)\right\}e^{\varpi B-\frac{1}{2}\varpi^2 t}. \quad (20)$$

If ß→ 1, then Equations (19) and (20) become

$$\Phi = \left\{\frac{-\lambda}{k} \pm 2k\sqrt{\frac{1}{3}}\tanh(\zeta)\right\}e^{\varpi B-\frac{1}{2}\varpi^2 t}, \quad (21)$$

$$\Psi = \left\{\frac{\lambda^2}{2k^2} - \frac{2k^2}{3}\tanh^2(\zeta)\right\}e^{\varpi B-\frac{1}{2}\varpi^2 t}. \quad (22)$$

Case 2: If $\alpha_1 =ß^2$, $\alpha_2 = -\left(1+ß^2\right)$ and $\alpha_3 = 1$, then $\mathcal{P}(\zeta) = cd(\zeta)$, and Equation (18) takes the form

$$\Phi = \left\{\frac{-\lambda}{k} \pm 2k\sqrt{\frac{ß^2}{3}}cd(\zeta)\right\}e^{\varpi B-\frac{1}{2}\varpi^2 t}, \quad (23)$$

$$\Psi = \left\{\frac{\lambda^2}{2k^2} - \frac{2k^2ß^2}{3}cd^2(\zeta)\right\}e^{\varpi B-\frac{1}{2}\varpi^2 t}. \quad (24)$$

Case 3: If $\alpha_1 = 1$, $\alpha_2 = -\left(1+ß^2\right)$ and $\alpha_3 =ß^2$, then $\mathcal{P}(\zeta) = ns(\zeta)$, and Equation (18) takes the form

$$\Phi = \left\{\frac{-\lambda}{k} \pm 2k\sqrt{\frac{1}{3}}ns(\zeta)\right\}e^{\varpi B-\frac{1}{2}\varpi^2 t}, \quad (25)$$

$$\Psi = \left\{\frac{\lambda^2}{2k^2} - \frac{2k^2}{3}ns^2(\zeta)\right\}e^{\varpi B-\frac{1}{2}\varpi^2 t}. \quad (26)$$

If ß→ 1, then Equations (25) and (26) become

$$\Phi = \left\{\frac{-\lambda}{k} \pm 2k\sqrt{\frac{1}{3}}\coth(\zeta)\right\}e^{\varpi B-\frac{1}{2}\varpi^2 t}, \quad (27)$$

$$\Psi = \left\{\frac{\lambda^2}{2k^2} - \frac{2k^2}{3}\coth^2(\zeta)\right\}e^{\varpi B-\frac{1}{2}\varpi^2 t}. \quad (28)$$

However, if ß→ 0, then Equations (25) and (26) become

$$\Phi = \left\{\frac{-\lambda}{k} \pm 2k\sqrt{\frac{1}{3}}\csc(\zeta)\right\}e^{\varpi B-\frac{1}{2}\varpi^2 t}, \quad (29)$$

$$\Psi = \left\{\frac{\lambda^2}{2k^2} - \frac{2k^2}{3}\csc^2(\zeta)\right\}e^{\varpi B-\frac{1}{2}\varpi^2 t}. \quad (30)$$

Case 4: If $\alpha_1 = 1$, $\alpha_2 = -\left(1+ß^2\right)$ and $\alpha_3 =ß^2$, then $\mathcal{P}(\zeta) = dc(\zeta)$, and Equation (18) takes the form

$$\Phi = \left\{ \frac{-\lambda}{k} \pm 2k\sqrt{\frac{1}{3}} dc(\zeta) \right\} e^{\varpi B - \frac{1}{2}\varpi^2 t}, \tag{31}$$

$$\Psi = \left\{ \frac{\lambda^2}{2k^2} - \frac{2k^2}{3} dc^2(\zeta) \right\} e^{\varpi B - \frac{1}{2}\varpi^2 t}. \tag{32}$$

If ß→ 0, then Equations (31) and (32) become

$$\Phi = \left\{ \frac{-\lambda}{k} \pm 2k\sqrt{\frac{1}{3}} \sec(\zeta) \right\} e^{\varpi B - \frac{1}{2}\varpi^2 t}, \tag{33}$$

$$\Psi = \left\{ \frac{\lambda^2}{2k^2} - \frac{2k^2}{3} \sec^2(\zeta) \right\} e^{\varpi B - \frac{1}{2}\varpi^2 t}. \tag{34}$$

Case 5: If $\alpha_1 = 1 - ß^2$, $\alpha_2 = 2ß^2 - 1$ and $\alpha_3 = -ß^2$, then $\mathcal{P}(\zeta) = nc(\zeta)$, and Equation (18) takes the form

$$\Phi = \left\{ \frac{-\lambda}{k} \pm 2k\sqrt{\frac{1-ß^2}{3}} nc(\zeta) \right\} e^{\varpi B - \frac{1}{2}\varpi^2 t}, \tag{35}$$

$$\Psi = \left\{ \frac{\lambda^2}{2k^2} - \frac{2k^2(1-ß^2)}{3} nc^2(\zeta) \right\} e^{\varpi B - \frac{1}{2}\varpi^2 t}. \tag{36}$$

If ß→ 0, then Equations (35) and (36) become Equations (33) and (34), respectively.

Case 6: If $\alpha_1 = 1 - ß^2$, $\alpha_2 = 2 - ß^2$ and $\alpha_3 = 1$, then $\mathcal{P}(\zeta) = sc(\zeta)$, and Equation (18) takes the form

$$\Phi = \left\{ \frac{-\lambda}{k} \pm 2k\sqrt{\frac{1-ß^2}{3}} sc(\zeta) \right\} e^{\varpi B - \frac{1}{2}\varpi^2 t}, \tag{37}$$

$$\Psi = \left\{ \frac{\lambda^2}{2k^2} - \frac{2k^2(1-ß^2)}{3} sc^2(\zeta) \right\} e^{\varpi B - \frac{1}{2}\varpi^2 t}. \tag{38}$$

If ß→ 0, then Equations (37) and (38) become

$$\Phi = \left\{ \frac{-\lambda}{k} \pm 2k\sqrt{\frac{1}{3}} \tan(\zeta) \right\} e^{\varpi B - \frac{1}{2}\varpi^2 t}, \tag{39}$$

$$\Psi = \left\{ \frac{\lambda^2}{2k^2} - \frac{2k^2}{3} \tan^2(\zeta) \right\} e^{\varpi B - \frac{1}{2}\varpi^2 t}. \tag{40}$$

Case 7: If $\alpha_1 = 1$, $\alpha_2 = 2 - ß^2$ and $\alpha_3 = 1 - ß^2$, then $\mathcal{P}(\zeta) = cs(\zeta)$, and Equation (18) takes the form

$$\Phi = \left\{ \frac{-\lambda}{k} \pm 2k\sqrt{\frac{1}{3}} cs(\zeta) \right\} e^{\varpi B - \frac{1}{2}\varpi^2 t}, \tag{41}$$

$$\Psi = \left\{ \frac{\lambda^2}{2k^2} - \frac{2k^2}{3} cs^2(\zeta) \right\} e^{\varpi B - \frac{1}{2}\varpi^2 t}. \tag{42}$$

If ß→ 1, then Equations (41) and (42) become

$$\Phi = \left\{ \frac{-\lambda}{k} \pm 2k\sqrt{\frac{1}{3}} \operatorname{csch}(\zeta) \right\} e^{\varpi B - \frac{1}{2}\varpi^2 t}, \tag{43}$$

$$\Psi = \left\{ \frac{\lambda^2}{2k^2} - \frac{2k^2}{3} \operatorname{csch}^2(\zeta) \right\} e^{\varpi B - \frac{1}{2}\varpi^2 t}. \tag{44}$$

However, if ß→ 0, then Equations (41) and (42) become

$$\Phi = \left\{\frac{-\lambda}{k} \pm 2k\sqrt{\frac{1}{3}}\cot(\zeta)\right\}e^{\varpi B-\frac{1}{2}\varpi^2 t}, \tag{45}$$

$$\Psi = \left\{\frac{\lambda^2}{2k^2} - \frac{2k^2}{3}\cot^2(\zeta)\right\}e^{\varpi B-\frac{1}{2}\varpi^2 t}. \tag{46}$$

Case 8: If $\alpha_1 = 1$, $\alpha_2 = 2ß^2 - 1$ and $\alpha_3 = -ß^2(1-ß^2)$, then $\mathcal{P}(\zeta) = ds(\zeta)$, and Equation (18) takes the form

$$\Phi = \left\{\frac{-\lambda}{k} \pm 2k\sqrt{\frac{\alpha_1}{3}}ds(\zeta)\right\}e^{\varpi B-\frac{1}{2}\varpi^2 t}, \tag{47}$$

$$\Psi = \left\{\frac{\lambda^2}{2k^2} - \frac{2k^2\alpha_1}{3}ds^2(\zeta)\right\}e^{\varpi B-\frac{1}{2}\varpi^2 t}. \tag{48}$$

Case 9: If $\alpha_1 = \frac{1}{4}$, $\alpha_2 = \frac{1-2ß^2}{2}$ and $\alpha_3 = \frac{1}{4}$, then $\mathcal{P}(\zeta) = ns(\zeta) \pm cs(\zeta)$, and Equation (18) takes the form

$$\Phi = \left\{\frac{-\lambda}{k} \pm k\sqrt{\frac{1}{3}}(ns(\zeta) \pm cs(\zeta))\right\}e^{\varpi B-\frac{1}{2}\varpi^2 t}, \tag{49}$$

$$\Psi = \left\{\frac{\lambda^2}{2k^2} - \frac{k^2}{6}(ns(\zeta) \pm cs(\zeta))^2\right\}e^{\varpi B-\frac{1}{2}\varpi^2 t}. \tag{50}$$

Case 10: If $\alpha_1 = \frac{1}{4}$, $\alpha_2 = \frac{ß^2-2}{2}$ and $\alpha_3 = \frac{ß^2}{4}$, then $\mathcal{P}(\zeta) = ns(\zeta) \pm ds(\zeta)$, and Equation (18) takes the form

$$\Phi = \left\{\frac{-\lambda}{k} \pm k\sqrt{\frac{1}{3}}(ns(\zeta) \pm ds(\zeta))\right\}e^{\varpi B-\frac{1}{2}\varpi^2 t}, \tag{51}$$

$$\Psi = \left\{\frac{\lambda^2}{2k^2} - \frac{k^2}{6}(ns(\zeta) \pm ds(\zeta))^2\right\}e^{\varpi B-\frac{1}{2}\varpi^2 t}. \tag{52}$$

If ß→ 1, then Equations (49) and (50) [or Equations (51) and (52)] become

$$\Phi = \left\{\frac{-\lambda}{k} \pm k\sqrt{\frac{1}{3}}(\coth(\zeta) \pm \text{csch}(\zeta))\right\}e^{\varpi B-\frac{1}{2}\varpi^2 t}, \tag{53}$$

$$\Psi = \left\{\frac{\lambda^2}{2k^2} - \frac{k^2}{6}(\coth(\zeta) \pm \text{csch}(\zeta))^2\right\}e^{\varpi B-\frac{1}{2}\varpi^2 t}. \tag{54}$$

However, if ß→ 0, then Equations (49) and (50) [or Equations (51) and (52)] become

$$\Phi = \left\{\frac{-\lambda}{k} \pm k\sqrt{\frac{1}{3}}(\csc(\zeta) \pm \cot(\zeta))\right\}e^{\varpi B-\frac{1}{2}\varpi^2 t}, \tag{55}$$

$$\Psi = \left\{\frac{\lambda^2}{2k^2} - \frac{k^2}{6}(\csc(\zeta) \pm \cot(\zeta))^2\right\}e^{\varpi B-\frac{1}{2}\varpi^2 t}. \tag{56}$$

Case 11: If $\alpha_1 = \frac{1-ß^2}{4}$, $\alpha_2 = \frac{1+ß^2}{2}$ and $\alpha_3 = \frac{1-ß^2}{4}$, then $\mathcal{P}(\zeta) = nc(\zeta) \pm sc(\zeta)$, and Equation (18) takes the form

$$\Phi = \left\{\frac{-\lambda}{k} \pm k\sqrt{\frac{1-ß^2}{3}}(nc(\zeta) \pm sc(\zeta))\right\}e^{\varpi\mathcal{B}-\frac{1}{2}\varpi^2 t}, \quad (57)$$

$$\Psi = \left\{\frac{\lambda^2}{2k^2} - \frac{k^2(1-ß^2)}{6}(nc(\zeta) \pm sc(\zeta))^2\right\}e^{\varpi\mathcal{B}-\frac{1}{2}\varpi^2 t}. \quad (58)$$

If ß$\to 0$, then Equations (57) and (58) become

$$\Phi = \left\{\frac{-\lambda}{k} \pm k\sqrt{\frac{1}{3}}(\sec(\zeta) \pm \tan(\zeta))\right\}e^{\varpi\mathcal{B}-\frac{1}{2}\varpi^2 t}, \quad (59)$$

$$\Psi = \left\{\frac{\lambda^2}{2k^2} - \frac{k^2}{6}(\sec(\zeta) \pm \tan(\zeta))^2\right\}e^{\varpi\mathcal{B}-\frac{1}{2}\varpi^2 t}. \quad (60)$$

Case 12: If $\alpha_1 = \frac{ß^2}{4}$, $\alpha_2 = \frac{ß^2-2}{2}$ and $\alpha_3 = \frac{ß^2}{4}$, then $\mathcal{P}(\zeta) = \sqrt{1-ß^2}(sd(\zeta) \pm cd(\zeta))$, and Equation (18) takes the form

$$\Phi = \left\{\frac{-\lambda}{k} \pm k\sqrt{\frac{ß^2}{3}}\sqrt{1-ß^2}(sd(\zeta) \pm cd(\zeta))\right\}e^{\varpi\mathcal{B}-\frac{1}{2}\varpi^2 t}, \quad (61)$$

$$\Psi = \left\{\frac{\lambda^2}{2k^2} - \frac{k^2ß^2(1-ß^2)}{6}(sd(\zeta) \pm cd(\zeta))^2\right\}e^{\varpi\mathcal{B}-\frac{1}{2}\varpi^2 t}. \quad (62)$$

Case 13: If $\alpha_1 = \frac{ß^2}{4}$, $\alpha_2 = \frac{ß^2-2}{2}$ and $\alpha_3 = \frac{1}{4}$, then $\mathcal{P}(\zeta) = \frac{sn(\zeta)}{1\pm dn}$, and Equation (18) takes the form

$$\Phi = \left\{\frac{-\lambda}{k} \pm k\sqrt{\frac{ß^2}{3}}\left(\frac{sn(\zeta)}{1 \pm dn(\zeta)}\right)\right\}e^{\varpi\mathcal{B}-\frac{1}{2}\varpi^2 t}, \quad (63)$$

$$\Psi = \left\{\frac{\lambda^2}{2k^2} - \frac{k^2ß^2}{6}\left(\frac{sn(\zeta)}{1 \pm dn(\zeta)}\right)^2\right\}e^{\varpi\mathcal{B}-\frac{1}{2}\varpi^2 t}. \quad (64)$$

If ß$\to 1$, then Equations (63) and (64) become

$$\Phi = \left\{\frac{-\lambda}{k} \pm k\sqrt{\frac{1}{3}}\left(\frac{\tanh(\zeta)}{1 \pm \text{sech}(\zeta)}\right)\right\}e^{\varpi\mathcal{B}-\frac{1}{2}\varpi^2 t}, \quad (65)$$

$$\Psi = \left\{\frac{\lambda^2}{2k^2} - \frac{k^2}{6}\left(\frac{\tanh(\zeta)}{1 \pm \text{sech}(\zeta)}\right)^2\right\}e^{\varpi\mathcal{B}-\frac{1}{2}\varpi^2 t}. \quad (66)$$

Case 14: If $\alpha_1 = \frac{(1-ß^2)^2}{4}$, $\alpha_2 = \frac{ß^2+1}{2}$ and $\alpha_3 = \frac{1}{4}$, then $\mathcal{P}(\zeta) = (ds(\zeta) \pm cs(\zeta))$, and Equation (18) has the form

$$\Phi = \left\{\frac{-\lambda}{k} \pm k\left(1-ß^2\right)\sqrt{\frac{1}{3}}(ds(\zeta) \pm cs(\zeta))\right\}e^{\varpi\mathcal{B}-\frac{1}{2}\varpi^2 t}, \quad (67)$$

$$\Psi = \left\{\frac{\lambda^2}{2k^2} - \frac{k^2\left(1-ß^2\right)^2}{6}(ds(\zeta) \pm cs(\zeta))^2\right\}e^{\varpi\mathcal{B}-\frac{1}{2}\varpi^2 t}. \quad (68)$$

If ß$\to 0$, then Equations (67) and (68) become

$$\Phi = \left\{\frac{-\lambda}{k} \pm k\sqrt{\frac{1}{3}}(\sec(\zeta) \pm \tan(\zeta))\right\}e^{\varpi\mathcal{B}-\frac{1}{2}\varpi^2 t}, \quad (69)$$

$$\Psi = \left\{\frac{\lambda^2}{2k^2} - \frac{k^2}{6}(\sec(\zeta) \pm \tan(\zeta))^2\right\}e^{\varpi\mathcal{B}-\frac{1}{2}\varpi^2 t}. \quad (70)$$

Case 15: If $\alpha_1 = 1$, $\alpha_2 = 2 - 4ß^2$ and $\alpha_3 = 1$, then $\mathcal{P}(\zeta) = \frac{sn(\zeta)dn(\zeta)}{cn(\zeta)}$, and Equation (18) takes the form

$$\Phi = \left\{\frac{-\lambda}{k} \pm 2k\sqrt{\frac{1}{3}}\frac{sn(\zeta)dn(\zeta)}{cn(\zeta)}\right\}e^{\varpi\mathcal{B}-\frac{1}{2}\varpi^2 t}, \quad (71)$$

$$\Psi = \left\{\frac{\lambda^2}{2k^2} - \frac{2k^2}{3}\frac{sn^2(\zeta)dn^2(\zeta)}{cn^2(\zeta)}\right\}e^{\varpi\mathcal{B}-\frac{1}{2}\varpi^2 t}. \quad (72)$$

Case 16: If $\alpha_1 = ß^4$, $\alpha_2 = 2$ and $\alpha_3 = 1$, then $\mathcal{P}(\zeta) = \frac{sn(\zeta)cn(\zeta)}{dn(\zeta)}$, and Equation (18) takes the form

$$\Phi = \left\{\frac{-\lambda}{k} \pm 2k\sqrt{\frac{ß^4}{3}}\frac{sn(\zeta)cn(\zeta)}{dn(\zeta)}\right\}e^{\varpi\mathcal{B}-\frac{1}{2}\varpi^2 t}, \quad (73)$$

$$\Psi = \left\{\frac{\lambda^2}{2k^2} - \frac{2k^2ß^4}{3}\frac{sn^2(\zeta)cn^2(\zeta)}{dn^2(\zeta)}\right\}e^{\varpi\mathcal{B}-\frac{1}{2}\varpi^2 t}. \quad (74)$$

If $ß \to 1$, then Equations (73) and (74) become

$$\Phi = \left\{\frac{-\lambda}{k} \pm 2k\sqrt{\frac{1}{3}}\tanh(\zeta)\right\}e^{\varpi\mathcal{B}-\frac{1}{2}\varpi^2 t}, \quad (75)$$

$$\Psi = \left\{\frac{\lambda^2}{2k^2} - \frac{2k^2}{3}(\tanh(\zeta))^2\right\}e^{\varpi\mathcal{B}-\frac{1}{2}\varpi^2 t}. \quad (76)$$

Case 17: If $\alpha_1 = 1$, $\alpha_2 = ß^2 + 2$, and $\alpha_3 = 1 - 2ß^2 + ß^4$, then $\mathcal{P}(\zeta) = \frac{dn(\zeta)cn(\zeta)}{sn(\zeta)}$, and Equation (18) takes the form

$$\Phi = \left\{\frac{-\lambda}{k} \pm 2k\sqrt{\frac{1}{3}}\frac{dn(\zeta)cn(\zeta)}{sn(\zeta)}\right\}e^{\varpi\mathcal{B}-\frac{1}{2}\varpi^2 t}, \quad (77)$$

$$\Psi = \left\{\frac{\lambda^2}{2k^2} - \frac{2k^2dn^2(\zeta)cn^2(\zeta)}{3sn^2(\zeta)}\right\}e^{\varpi\mathcal{B}-\frac{1}{2}\varpi^2 t}. \quad (78)$$

If $ß \to 1$, then Equations (77) and (78) become

$$\Phi = \left\{\frac{-\lambda}{k} \pm 2k\sqrt{\frac{1}{3}}\text{sech}(\zeta)\text{csch}(\zeta)\right\}e^{\varpi\mathcal{B}-\frac{1}{2}\varpi^2 t}, \quad (79)$$

$$\Psi = \left\{\frac{\lambda^2}{2k^2} - \frac{2k^2}{3}(\text{sech}(\zeta)\text{csch}(\zeta))^2\right\}e^{\varpi\mathcal{B}-\frac{1}{2}\varpi^2 t}. \quad (80)$$

Case 18: If $\alpha_1 = \frac{1}{4}$, $\alpha_2 = \frac{1-2ß^2}{2}$ and $\alpha_3 = \frac{1}{4}$, then $\mathcal{P}(\zeta) = \frac{sn(\zeta)}{1 \pm cn(\zeta)}$, and Equation (18) takes the form

$$\Phi = \left\{\frac{-\lambda}{k} \pm k\sqrt{\frac{1}{3}}\frac{sn(\zeta)}{1 \pm cn(\zeta)}\right\}e^{\varpi\mathcal{B}-\frac{1}{2}\varpi^2 t}, \quad (81)$$

$$\Psi = \left\{\frac{\lambda^2}{2k^2} - \frac{k^2}{6}\frac{sn^2(\zeta)}{(1 \pm cn(\zeta))^2}\right\}e^{\varpi\mathcal{B}-\frac{1}{2}\varpi^2 t}. \quad (82)$$

If ß→ 0, then Equations (81) and (82) become

$$\Phi = \left\{\frac{-\lambda}{k} \pm k\sqrt{\frac{1}{3}}(\csc(\zeta) \pm \cot(\zeta))\right\}e^{\varpi\mathcal{B}-\frac{1}{2}\varpi^2 t}, \tag{83}$$

$$\Psi = \left\{\frac{\lambda^2}{2k^2} - \frac{k^2}{6}(\csc(\zeta) \pm \cot(\zeta))^2\right\}e^{\varpi\mathcal{B}-\frac{1}{2}\varpi^2 t}. \tag{84}$$

Case 19: If $\alpha_1 = \frac{1-ß^2}{4}$, $\alpha_2 = \frac{1+ß^2}{2}$ and $\alpha_3 = \frac{1-ß^2}{4}$, then $\mathcal{P}(\zeta) = \frac{cn(\zeta)}{1 \pm sn(\zeta)}$, and Equation (18) takes the form

$$\Phi = \left\{\frac{-\lambda}{k} \pm k\sqrt{\frac{1-ß^2}{3}\frac{cn(\zeta)}{1 \pm sn(\zeta)}}\right\}e^{\varpi\mathcal{B}-\frac{1}{2}\varpi^2 t}, \tag{85}$$

$$\Psi = \left\{\frac{\lambda^2}{2k^2} - \frac{k^2(1-ß^2)}{6}\frac{cn^2(\zeta)}{(1 \pm sn(\zeta))^2}\right\}e^{\varpi\mathcal{B}-\frac{1}{2}\varpi^2 t}. \tag{86}$$

If ß→ 0, then Equations (85) and (86) become

$$\Phi = \left\{\frac{-\lambda}{k} \pm k\sqrt{\frac{1}{3}}(\sec(\zeta) \pm \tan(\zeta))\right\}e^{\varpi\mathcal{B}-\frac{1}{2}\varpi^2 t}, \tag{87}$$

$$\Psi = \left\{\frac{\lambda^2}{2k^2} - \frac{k^2}{6}(\sec(\zeta) \pm \tan(\zeta))^2\right\}e^{\varpi\mathcal{B}-\frac{1}{2}\varpi^2 t}. \tag{88}$$

Remark 1. *If we substitute $\varpi = 0$, $k = 1$ and $\lambda = \pm\frac{1}{3}\sqrt{6}$ in (29), (30), (33), (34), (43), (44), (69), (70), (83) and (84), then we have the same trigonometric function solutions stated in [13], while if we substitute $\varpi = 0$, $k = 1$ and $\lambda = \frac{2}{3}\sqrt{3}$ in (21), (22), (27), (28), (39), (40), (59), and (60), then we have the same hyperbolic function solutions stated in [13].*

5. Physical Meaning and Effect of Noise

Physical meaning: Obtaining exact solutions for stochastic Wu–Zhang systems is of utmost importance as it enables us to accurately predict and control the behavior of these systems under uncertainty. Different types of exact solutions, including periodic solitons, kink solitons, bright soliton, dark soliton and singular solitons, for Equation (1) are obtained here. Solitons are self-reinforcing solitary waves that maintain their shape and speed as they propagate through a medium. By obtaining exact soliton solutions of the Wu–Zhang system, researchers can better understand the dynamics of these waves and how they interact with their environment.

Furthermore, exact soliton solutions of the Wu–Zhang system allow for the prediction and manipulation of wave behavior in various applications. For example, in the field of optics, solitons play a crucial role in maintaining the coherence and stability of light pulses in fiber optic communications. By studying the exact soliton solutions of the Wu–Zhang system, researchers can develop more efficient methods for transmitting and controlling light waves in optical devices. This knowledge can lead to advancements in areas such as telecommunications, laser technology, and imaging systems.

Effect of Noise: Noise plays an essential role in the dynamics of the Wu–Zhang system in quantum mechanics. By studying the effects of noise on the system's behavior, researchers can gain valuable insights into its properties and develop strategies to mitigate the impact of noise on its performance. Experimental studies have confirmed the theoretical predictions about the effects of noise on entanglement generation and quantum phase transitions in the Wu–Zhang system, highlighting the importance of noise in understanding and controlling quantum systems.

Now, let us show the effect of noise on the exact solution of the SWZS (1). To illustrate the behavior of some of the discovered solutions, many figures are provided, including Equations (19)–(22) as follows:

Now, Figures 1–4 show that there are several kinds of solutions, such as periodic solutions, kink solutions, singular solutions and so on, when the multiplicative noise is neglected (i.e., when $\varpi = 0$). The surface becomes flatter after brief transit patterns when noise is added, and its amplitude is raised by $\varpi = 0.1,\ 0.3,\ 1,\ 2$. This indicates that the solutions of SWZS (1) are influenced by multiplicative white noise and are kept stable around zero.

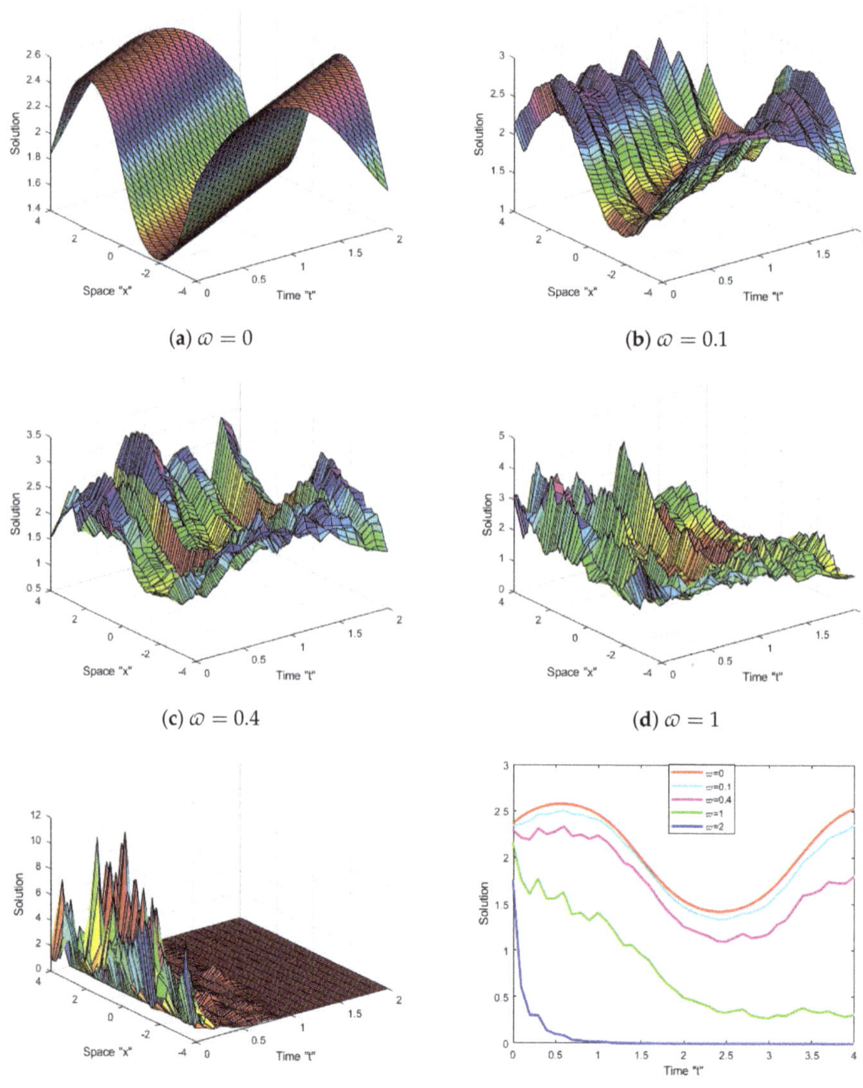

(**a**) $\varpi = 0$ (**b**) $\varpi = 0.1$

(**c**) $\varpi = 0.4$ (**d**) $\varpi = 1$

(**e**) $\varpi = 2$ (**f**) $\varpi = 0,\ 0.1,\ 0.3,\ 1,\ 2$

Figure 1. (**a**–**c**) display 3D shape of solution $\Phi(x,t)$ in Equation (19) with ß$= 0.5, k = 1,\ \lambda = -2,\ x \in [-4,4],\ t \in [0,2]$ and $\varpi = 0,\ 0.1,\ 0.3,\ 1,\ 2$ (**d**) shows 2D shape of Equation (19) with different ϖ.

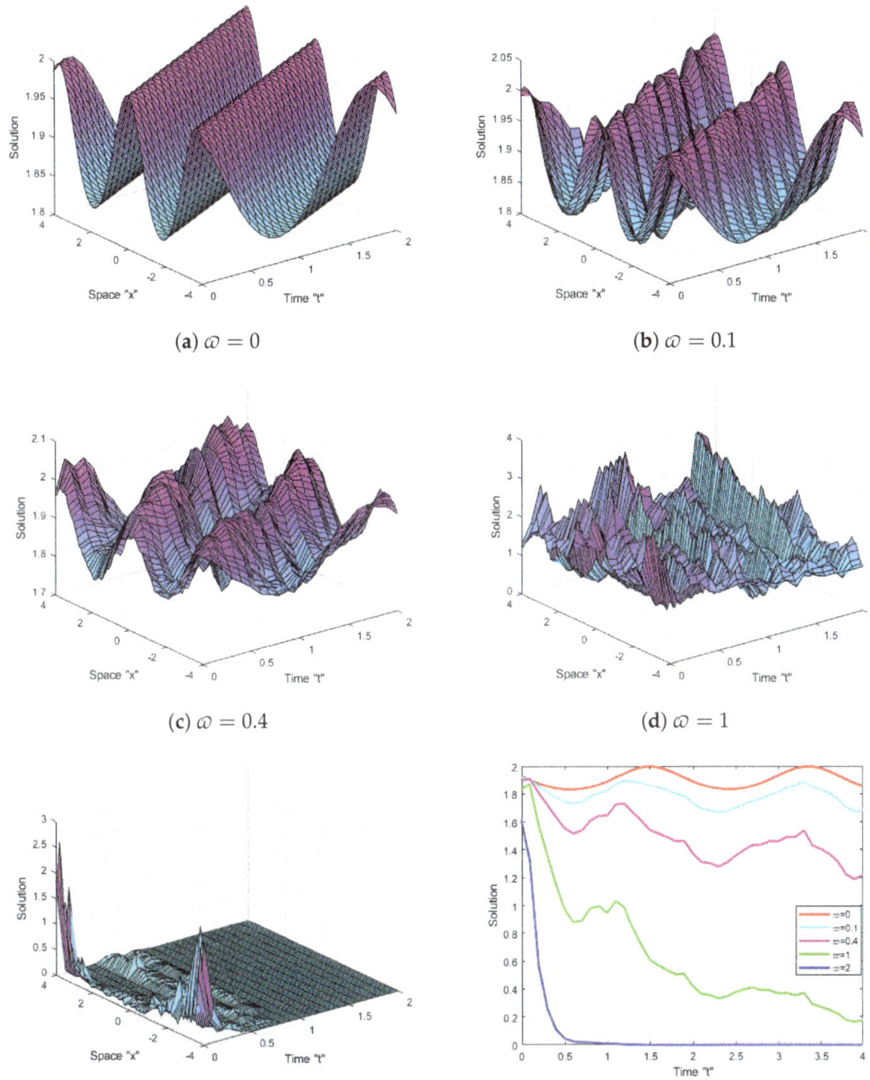

(**a**) $\varpi = 0$ (**b**) $\varpi = 0.1$

(**c**) $\varpi = 0.4$ (**d**) $\varpi = 1$

(**e**) $\varpi = 2$ (**f**) $\varpi = 0,\ 0.1,\ 0.3,\ 1,\ 2$

Figure 2. (**a**–**e**) display Figure 3D shape of solution $\Psi(x,t)$ in Equation (20) with ß= 0.5, $k = 1$, $\lambda = -2$, $x \in [-4,4]$, $t \in [0,2]$ and $\varpi = 0,\ 0.1,\ 0.3,\ 1,\ 2$ (**f**) shows 2D shape of Equation (20) with different ϖ.

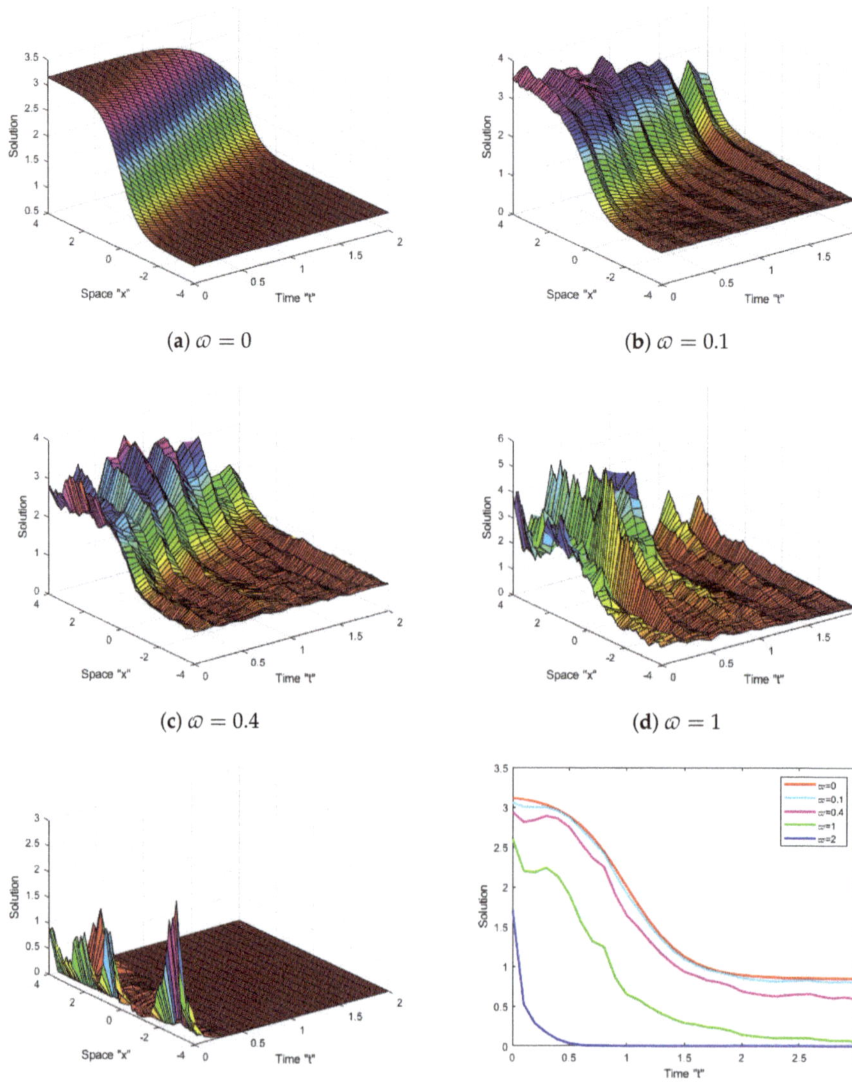

(**a**) $\varpi = 0$ (**b**) $\varpi = 0.1$

(**c**) $\varpi = 0.4$ (**d**) $\varpi = 1$

(**e**) $\varpi = 2$ (**f**) $\varpi = 0,\ 0.1,\ 0.3,\ 1,\ 2$

Figure 3. (**a**–**e**) display Figure 3D shape of solution $\Phi(x,t)$ in Equation (21) with $k = 1,\ \lambda = -2,\ x \in [-4,4]$, $t \in [0,2]$ and $\varpi = 0,\ 0.1,\ 0.3,\ 1,\ 2$ (**f**) shows 2D shape of Equation (21) with different ϖ.

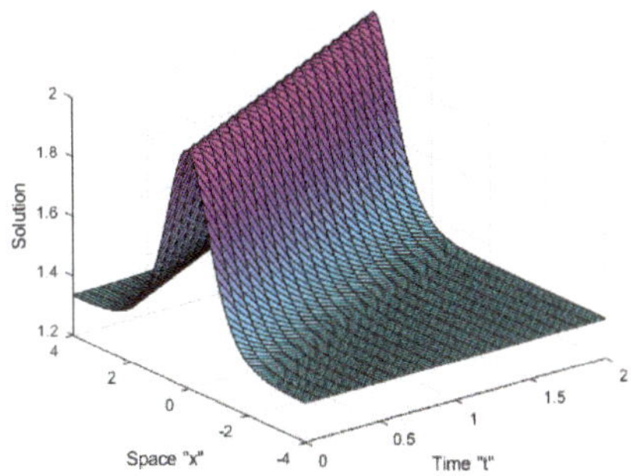

(**a**) $\varpi = 0$

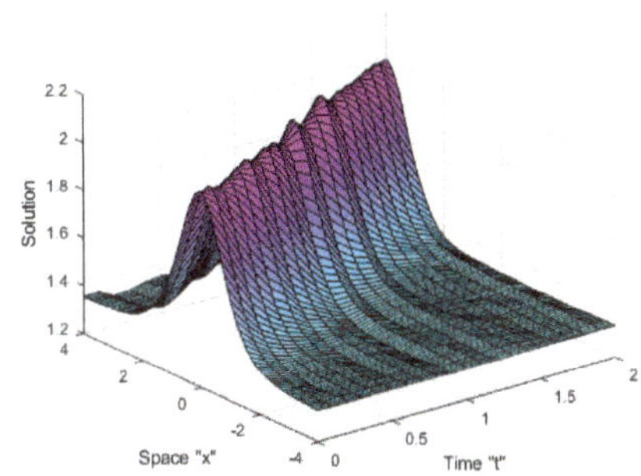

(**b**) $\varpi = 0.1$

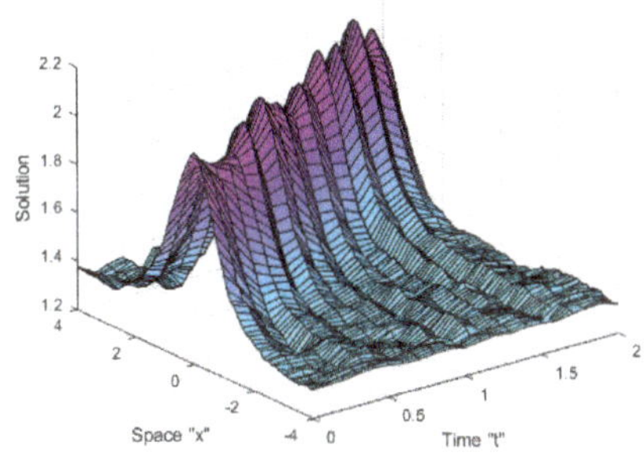

(**c**) $\varpi = 0.4$

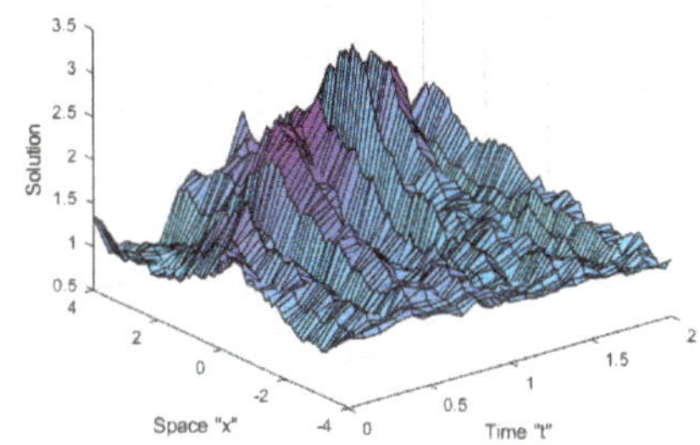

(**d**) $\varpi = 1$

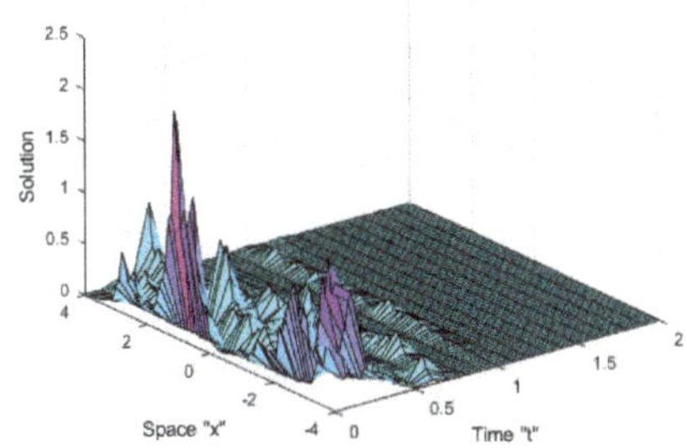

(**e**) $\varpi = 2$

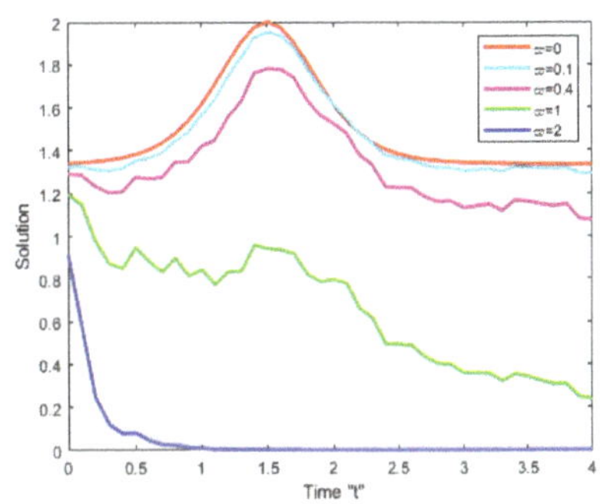

(**f**) $\varpi = 0,\ 0.1,\ 0.3,\ 1,\ 2$

Figure 4. (**a**–**c**) display Figure 3D shape of solution $\Psi(x,t)$ in Equation (22) with $k = 1$, $\lambda = -2$, $x \in [-4,4]$, $t \in [0,2]$ and $\varpi = 0,\ 0.1,\ 0.3,\ 1,\ 2$ (**d**) shows 2D shape of Equation (22) with different ϖ.

6. Conclusions

In this paper, the stochastic Wu–Zhang system (1) perturbed by multiplicative white noise in the Itô sense was considered. We obtained novel hyperbolic, trigonometric, and elliptic stochastic solutions by applying a mapping approach. In the absence of noise, we obtained some previously obtained solutions of SWZS (1) such as the solutions stated in [13]. Since the Wu–Zhang system has significant uses in quantum mechanics, these solutions may be used to analyze a wide range of significant physical phenomena. Additionally, the MATLAB program was used to demonstrate the effects of the noise term on the analytical solution of the SWZS (1). We showed that the solutions of SWZS (1) were stabilized at zero by multiplicative white noise. In further work, we can obtain the solutions for the Wu–Zhang system with different fractional derivative operators such as the Caputo fractional derivative, Riemann–Liouville fractional derivative and M-truncated derivative [25,26].

Author Contributions: Conceptualization, E.E.A., A.I.A. and M.E.; methodology, E.E.A., A.I.A. and M.E.; software, W.W.M.; validation, W.W.M., E.E.A., A.I.A. and M.E.; formal analysis, E.E.A., A.I.A. and M.E.; data curation, E.E.A., A.I.A. and M.E.; writing—original draft preparation, W.W.M., E.E.A., A.I.A. and M.E.; writing—review and editing, W.W.M.; visualization, E.E.A., A.I.A. and M.E.; supervision, W.W.M.; project administration, W.W.M.; funding acquisition, W.W.M. All authors have read and agreed to the published version of the manuscript.

Funding: This research has been funded by Scientific Research Deanship at the University of Ha'il-Saudi Arabia through project number RG-24065.

Informed Consent Statement: Not applicable.

Data Availability Statement: The original contributions presented in this study are included in this article; further inquiries can be directed to the corresponding author.

Acknowledgments: This research has been funded by Scientific Research Deanship at the University of Ha'il-Saudi Arabia through project number RG-24065.

Conflicts of Interest: The authors declare no conflicts of interest.

References

1. Khan, K.; Akbar, M.A. The $exp(-\phi(\varsigma))$-expansion method for finding travelling wave solutions of Vakhnenko-Parkes equation. *Int. J. Dyn. Syst. Differ. Equ.* **2014**, *5*, 72–83.
2. Yan, Z.L. Abunbant families of Jacobi elliptic function solutions of the dimensional integrable Davey-Stewartson-type equation via a new method. *Chaos Solitons Fractals* **2003**, *18*, 299–309. [CrossRef]
3. Baskonus, H.M.; Bulut, H.; Sulaiman, T.A. New complex hyperbolic structures to the lonngren-wave equation by using sine-gordon expansion method. *Appl. Math. Nonlinear Sci.* **2019**, *4*, 129–138. [CrossRef]
4. Lu, B. The first integral method for some time fractional differential equations. *J. Math. Anal. Appl.* **2012**, *395*, 684–693. [CrossRef]
5. Jiong, S. Auxiliary equation method for solving nonlinear partial differential equations. *Phys. Lett. A* **2003**, *309*, 387–396.
6. Wang, M.L.; Li, X.Z.; Zhang, J.L. The (G'/G)-expansion method and travelling wave solutions of nonlinear evolution equations in mathematical physics. *Phys. Lett. A* **2008**, *372*, 417–423. [CrossRef]
7. Zhang, H. New application of the (G'/G)-expansion method. *Commun. Nonlinear Sci. Numer. Simul.* **2009**, *14*, 3220–3225. [CrossRef]
8. He, J.H.; Wu X.H. Exp-function method for nonlinear wave equations. *Chaos Solitons Fractals* **2006**, *30*, 700–708. [CrossRef]
9. Wazwaz, A.M. The sine-cosine method for obtaining solutions with compact and noncompact structures. *Appl. Math. Comput.* **2004**, *159*, 559–576. [CrossRef]
10. Dong, W.B.; Wu, R.B.; Zhang, W.; Li, C.W.; Tarn, T.J. Spatial Control Model and Analysis of Quantum Fields in One-Dimensional Waveguides. *SIAM J. Control Optim.* **2016**, *54*, 1352–1377. [CrossRef]
11. Lin, J.; Ren, B.; Li, H.; Li, Y. Soliton solutions for two nonlinear partial differential equations using a Darboux transformation of the Lax pairs. *Phys. Rev. E* **2008**, *77*, 036605. [CrossRef] [PubMed]
12. Zheng, H.; Xia, Y.; Bai, Y.; Lei, G. Travelling Wave Solutions of Wu–Zhang System via Dynamic Analysis. *Discret. Dyn. Nat. Soc.* **2020**, *2020*, 2845841. [CrossRef]
13. Zheng, X.; Chen, Y.; Zhang, H. Generalized extended tanh-function method and its application to (1 +1)-dimensional dispersive long wave equation. *Phys. Lett. A* **2003**, *311*, 145–157. [CrossRef]
14. Awad, A.J.M.; Al-Azzawi, F.J.I. Soliton solutions of Wu–Zhang system of evolution equations. *Numer. Comput. Methods Sci. Eng.* **2019**, *1*, 1–11.
15. Inc, M.; Kilic, B.; Karatas, E.; Al Qurashi, M.M.; Baleanu, D.; Tchier, F. On soliton solutions of the Wu–Zhang system. *Open Phys.* **2016**, *14*, 76–80. [CrossRef]
16. Mirzazadeh, M.; Ekici, M.; Eslami, M.; Krishnan, E.V.; Kumar, S.; Biswas, A. Solitons and other solutions to Wu–Zhang system. *Nonlinear Anal. Model. Control* **2017**, *22*, 441–458. [CrossRef]
17. Khater, M. M. A.; Lu, D.; Attia, R. Dispersive long wave of nonlinear fractional Wu–Zhang system via a modified auxiliary equation method. *AIP Adv.* **2019**, *9*, 025003. [CrossRef]

18. Eslami, M.; Rezazadeh, H. The first integral method for Wu–Zhang system with conformable time-fractional derivative. *Calcolo* **2016**, *53*, 475. [CrossRef]
19. Liang, Y.H.; Wang, K.J. On a variational principle for the fractal Wu–Zhang system arising in shallow water. *Int. J. Geomath.* **2021**, *12*, 8. [CrossRef]
20. Kaur, B.; Gupta, R.K. Time fractional (2+1)-dimensional Wu–Zhang system: Dispersion analysis, similarity reductions, conservation laws, and exact solutions. *Comput. Math. Appl.* **2020**, *79*, 1031–1048. [CrossRef]
21. Yasmin, H.; Alderremy, A.A.; Shah, R.; Ganie, A.; Aly, S. Iterative solution of the fractional Wu–Zhang equation under Caputo derivative operator. *Front. Phys.* **2024**, *12*, 1333990. [CrossRef]
22. Peng, Y.Z. Exact periodic wave solutions to the coupled Schrödinger-KdV equation and DS equations. *Pramana-J. Phys.* **2004**, *62*, 933–941. [CrossRef]
23. Ahmed, A.I. Algolam, M.S.; Cesarano, C.; Rizk, D.; Gassem, F.; Mohammed, W.W. Dynamical behavior of the fractional generalized nonlinear Schrödinger equation of third-order. *Opt. Quantum Electron.* **2024**, *56*, 843. [CrossRef]
24. Liu, Q.; Zhu, J.M. Exact Jacobian elliptic function solutions and hyperbolic function solutions for Sawada-Kotere equation with variable coefficient. *Phys. Lett. A* **2006**, *352*, 233–238. [CrossRef]
25. He, J.H. A Tutorial Review on Fractal Spacetime and Fractional Calculus. *Int. J. Theor. Phys.* **2014**, *53*, 3698–3718. [CrossRef]
26. Lu, J.-F.; Ma, L. Analysis of a Fractal Modification of Attachment Oscillator. *Therm. Sci.* **2024**, *28*, 2153–2163. [CrossRef]

mathematics

Article

Novel Analytical Methods for and Qualitative Analysis of the Generalized Water Wave Equation

Haitham Qawaqneh [1], Abdulaziz S. Al Naim [2] and Abdulrahman Alomair [2,*]

[1] Department of Mathematics, Faculty of Science and Information Technology, Al-Zaytoonah University of Jordan, Amman 11733, Jordan; h.alqawaqneh@zuj.edu.jo
[2] Accounting Department, Business School, King Faisal University, Al-Ahsa 31982, Saudi Arabia; asaudalnaim@kfu.edu.sa
* Correspondence: aamalomair@kfu.edu.sa

Abstract

For a significant fluid model and the truncated M-fractional (1 + 1)-dimensional nonlinear generalized water wave equation, distinct types of truncated M-fractional wave solitons are obtained. Ocean waves, tidal waves, weather simulations, river and irrigation flows, tsunami predictions, and more are all explained by this model. We use the improved (G'/G) expansion technique and a modified extended direct algebraic technique to obtain these solutions. Results for trigonometry, hyperbolic, and rational functions are obtained. The impact of the fractional-order derivative is also covered. We use Mathematica software to verify our findings. Furthermore, we use contour graphs in two and three dimensions to illustrate some wave solitons that are obtained. The results obtained have applications in ocean engineering, fluid dynamics, and other fields. The stability analysis of the considered equation is also performed. Moreover, the stationary solutions of the concerning equation are studied through modulation instability. Furthermore, the used methods are useful for other nonlinear fractional partial differential equations in different areas of applied science and engineering.

Keywords: generalized water wave model; fractional derivative; analytical methods; exact solitons; stability analysis; modulation instability analysis

MSC: 35C07; 35C08; 83C15

1. Introduction

Fluid mechanics is an important branch of applied science and engineering. Many models in the field of fluid mechanics have been developed such as the unstable nonlinear Schrödinger model [1], nano-ionic currents model [2], Sharma–Tasso–Olver model [3], Cahn–Allen model [4], simplified modified Camassa–Holm model [5], improved Boussinesq model [6], Boussinesq–Burgers system [7], higher-order Schrödinger equation [8], Whitham–Broer–Kaup equations [9], and perturbed Schrödinger–Hirota equation [10]. Nowadays, fractional models have garnered interest among researchers, such as the generalized Korteweg–de Vries–Zakharov–Kuznetsov model [11], the single-joint robot arm model [12], the Westervelt model [13], the Pareto probability Shannon isotope model [14], the generalized coupled Helmholtz model [15], and the Estevez–Mansfield–Clarkson model [16]. Different methods have been developed to obtain different types of solutions such as the plane dynamic system method [17], the polynomial complete discriminant system method [18], and the auxiliary function method [19].

We use two simple yet effective methods in this work: the improved (G'/G) expansion and the modified extended direct algebraic method. There are several uses for these techniques. For instance, some new kinds of traveling wave solutions of the Hirota–Ramani model were obtained by using the modified extended direct algebraic technique [20]; distinct wave solutions of the concatenation model were achieved [21]. Many wave solitons of extended shallow water wave equations were obtained by applying the improved (G'/G) expansion method [22], and many exact traveling wave solutions of the Calogero–Bogoyavlenskii-Schiff equation were obtained by utilizing the improved (G'/G) expansion scheme [23].

The nonlinear (1 + 1)-dimensional generalized water wave equation is an important model among the mathematical fluid models. In fluid dynamics, engineering, and other domains, this model is highly significant. This model has been solved using various methods. For instance, the $(\frac{G'}{G'+G+A})$ expansion technique in [24] yielded some new exact wave solutions, while a class $f(G, G')$ expansion schemes in [25] yielded distinct types of exact wave solitons; the modified rational sine–cosine method in [26] provides breathing solutions, kink-singular solutions, and complex-valued solutions.

Our motivation was to study new types of truncated M-fractional exact solitons for the nonlinear (1 + 1)-dimensional generalized shallow water wave equation by using two effective techniques. Both the improved (G'/G) expansion technique and the modified extended direct algebraic technique provide different types of exact soliton solutions. These techniques have not been previously applied for this model. The truncated M-fractional derivative (TMFD) gives solutions closer to the numerical solutions. This fractional derivative satisfies the conditions of both fractional derivatives and integer-order derivatives. The impact of the TMFD on the achieved results is displayed. The truncated M-fractional generalized water wave equation is the more prominent form of the model and helps us to understand the model more clearly. Additionally, stability analysis was used to verify the stability of a relevant equation. Moreover, the stationary solutions of the concerning equation were studied through modulation instability.

This paper consists of several sections: Section 2 explains our techniques, Section 3 discusses the studied equation and its mathematical analysis, Section 4 provides exact solitons, Section 5 provides a graphic representation of some of the results obtained, Section 6 provides the stability analysis, Section 7 explains the modulation instability analysis, Section 8 explains the results and provides a discussion, and Section 9 concludes this paper.

2. Truncated M-Fractional Derivative

Definition 1. *Suppose $g(t) : [0, \infty) \to \Re$; then, the truncated M derivative of g of order α is given as [27]*

$$D^{\alpha,\Upsilon}_{M,t} g(t) = \lim_{\tau \to 0} \frac{g\,(t\, E_{\Upsilon}(\tau t^{1-\alpha})) - g(t)}{\tau}, \quad 0 < \alpha < 1, \ \ \Upsilon > 0,$$

where $E_{\Upsilon}(.)$ is the truncated Mittag–Leffler function of one parameter, which is defined as [28]

$$E_{\Upsilon}(z) = \sum_{j-0}^{\infty} \frac{z^j}{\Gamma(\Upsilon j + 1)}, \ \ \Upsilon > 0 \ \textit{and} \ z \in C.$$

Characteristics:

Let $\alpha \in (0, 1], \Upsilon > 0, r, s \in \Re$, and g, f are α- differentiable at a point $t > 0$; then, by [27]:

$$\text{(i) } D^{\alpha,\Upsilon}_{M,t}(rg(t) + sf(t)) = rD^{\alpha,\Upsilon}_{M,t} g(t) + sD^{\alpha,\Upsilon}_{M,t} f(t).$$

$$\text{(ii) } D^{\alpha,\Upsilon}_{M,t}(g(t).f(t)) = g(t)D^{\alpha,\Upsilon}_{M,t}f(t) + f(t)D^{\alpha,\Upsilon}_{M,t}g(t).$$

$$\text{(iii) } D^{\alpha,\Upsilon}_{M,t}\left(\frac{g(t)}{f(t)}\right) = \frac{f(t)D^{\alpha,\Upsilon}_{M,t}g(t) - g(t)D^{\alpha,\Upsilon}_{M,t}f(t)}{(f(t))^2}.$$

$$\text{(iv) } D^{\alpha,\Upsilon}_{M,t}(A) = 0, \ \textit{where } A \textit{ is a constant}.$$

$$\text{(v) } D^{\alpha,\Upsilon}_{M,t}g(t) = \frac{t^{1-\alpha}}{\Gamma(\Upsilon+1)}\frac{dg(t)}{dt}.$$

3. Description of Strategies

3.1. MEDA Technique

Here, we provide the main steps of the scheme [29]:

Step 1:

Assume a nonlinear partial fractional differential equation:

$$Y(g, D^{\epsilon,\varrho}_{M,t}g^2, g^2g_x, g_{xx}, g_{xt}, \ldots) = 0, \tag{1}$$

where a wave profile is represented by $g = g(x,t)$. Examine the following wave transformations:

$$g(x,t) = G(\Theta), \ \Theta = \frac{\Gamma(1+\Upsilon)}{\alpha}(x^\alpha + \lambda t^\alpha). \tag{2}$$

Here, λ represents the soliton velocity.

Putting Equation (2) into Equation (1) provides

$$Y(G, G^2G', G'', \ldots) = 0. \tag{3}$$

Step 2:

Assume the solution of Equation (3) is as follows:

$$G(\Theta) = \sum_{-m}^{m} \alpha_s \psi^s(\Theta). \tag{4}$$

Here, $\alpha_s(s = -m, \ldots, 0, 1, 2, 3, \ldots, m)$ are unknowns to be found, where $\alpha_s \neq 0$. A positive integer "m" can be obtained by balancing the highest-order term and the nonlinear term in Equation (3) according to the homogenous balance technique. A function $\psi(\Theta)$ fulfills the ordinary differential equation given as

$$\psi'(\Theta) = \log(d)\left(p + q\psi(\Theta) + r\psi(\Theta)^2\right). \tag{5}$$

Here, p, q, and r denote the constants, and $d \neq 0, 1$. Equation (5) provides the answers for the various situations listed below:

Type I: when $q^2 - 4pr < 0$ and r is nonzero, then

$$\psi_1(\Theta) = -\frac{q}{2r} + \frac{\sqrt{-(q^2-4pr)}\tan_B(\frac{1}{2}\sqrt{-(q^2-4pr)}\Theta)}{2r}. \tag{6}$$

$$\psi_2(\Theta) = -\frac{q}{2r} - \frac{\sqrt{4pr-q^2}\cot_B(\frac{1}{2}\sqrt{4pr-q^2}\Theta)}{2r}. \tag{7}$$

$$\psi_3(\Theta) = -\frac{q}{2r} + \frac{\sqrt{4pr-q^2}(\tan_B(\sqrt{4pr-q^2}\Theta) \pm (\sqrt{cf}\ \sec_B(\sqrt{4pr-q^2}\Theta)))}{2r}. \tag{8}$$

$$\psi_4(\Theta) = -\frac{q}{2r} - \frac{\sqrt{4pr - q^2}(\cot_B(\sqrt{4pr - q^2}\Theta) \pm (\sqrt{cf}\ \csc_B(\sqrt{4pr - q^2}\Theta)))}{2r}. \quad (9)$$

$$\psi_5(\Theta) = -\frac{q}{2r} + \frac{\sqrt{4pr - q^2}(\tan_B(\frac{1}{4}\sqrt{4pr - q^2}\Theta) - (\ \cot_B(\frac{1}{4}\sqrt{4pr - q^2}\Theta)))}{2r}. \quad (10)$$

Type II: when $q^2 - 4pr > 0$ and r is nonzero, we have

$$\psi_6(\Theta) = -\frac{q}{2r} - \frac{\sqrt{q^2 - 4pr}\tanh_B(\frac{1}{2}\sqrt{q^2 - 4pr}\Theta)}{2r}. \quad (11)$$

$$\psi_7(\Theta) = -\frac{q}{2r} - \frac{\sqrt{q^2 - 4pr}\coth_B(\frac{1}{2}\sqrt{q^2 - 4pr}\Theta)}{2r}. \quad (12)$$

$$\psi_8(\Theta) = -\frac{q}{2r} - \frac{\sqrt{q^2 - 4pr}(\tanh_B(\sqrt{q^2 - 4pr}\Theta) \pm (\sqrt{cf}\ sech_B(\sqrt{q^2 - 4pr}\Theta)))}{2r}. \quad (13)$$

$$\psi_9(\Theta) = -\frac{q}{2r} - \frac{\sqrt{q^2 - 4pr}(\coth_B(\sqrt{q^2 - 4pr}\Theta) \pm (\sqrt{cf}\ csch_B(\sqrt{q^2 - 4pr}\Theta)))}{2r}. \quad (14)$$

$$\psi_{10}(\Theta) = -\frac{q}{2r} - \frac{\sqrt{q^2 - 4pr}(\tanh_B(\frac{1}{4}\sqrt{q^2 - 4pr}\Theta) - (\ \coth_B(\frac{1}{4}\sqrt{q^2 - 4pr}\Theta)))}{2r}. \quad (15)$$

Type III: when $pr > 0$ and q is zero, then

$$\psi_{11}(\Theta) = \sqrt{\frac{p}{r}}\tan_B(\sqrt{pr}\Theta). \quad (16)$$

$$\psi_{12}(\Theta) = -\sqrt{\frac{p}{r}}\cot_B(\sqrt{pr}\Theta). \quad (17)$$

$$\psi_{13}(\Theta) = \sqrt{\frac{p}{r}}(\tan_B(2\sqrt{rp}\,\Theta) \pm (\sqrt{fc}\sec_B(2\sqrt{rp}\,\Theta))). \quad (18)$$

$$\psi_{14}(\Theta) = -\sqrt{\frac{p}{r}}(\cot_B(2\sqrt{rp}\,\Theta) \pm (\sqrt{fc}\csc_B(2\sqrt{rp}\,\Theta))). \quad (19)$$

$$\psi_{15}(\Theta) = \frac{1}{2}\sqrt{\frac{p}{r}}(\tan_B(\frac{1}{2}\sqrt{pr}\Theta) - \cot_B(\frac{1}{2}\sqrt{pr}\Theta)). \quad (20)$$

Type IV: when $pr < 0$ and q is zero, then

$$\psi_{16}(\Theta) = -\sqrt{-\frac{p}{r}}\tanh_B(\sqrt{-pr}\Theta). \quad (21)$$

$$\psi_{17}(\Theta) = -\sqrt{-\frac{p}{r}}\coth_B(\sqrt{-pr}\Theta). \quad (22)$$

$$\psi_{18}(\Theta) = -\sqrt{-\frac{p}{r}}(\tanh_B(2\sqrt{-pr}\Theta) \pm \iota\sqrt{cf}\,\mathrm{sech}_B(2\sqrt{-pr}\Theta)). \quad (23)$$

$$\psi_{19}(\Theta) = -\sqrt{-\frac{p}{r}}(\coth_B(2\sqrt{-pr}\Theta) \pm (\sqrt{cf}\,\mathrm{csch}_B(2\sqrt{-pr}\Theta))). \quad (24)$$

$$\psi_{20}(\Theta) = -\frac{1}{2}\sqrt{-\frac{p}{r}}(\tanh_B(\frac{1}{2}\sqrt{-pr}\Theta) + \coth_B(\frac{1}{2}\sqrt{-pr}\Theta)). \quad (25)$$

Type V: when $r = p$ and $q = 0$, we attain

$$\psi_{21}(\Theta) = \tan_B(p\Theta). \quad (26)$$

$$\psi_{22}(\Theta) = -\cot_B(p\Theta). \quad (27)$$

$$\psi_{23}(\Theta) = \tan_B(2p\Theta) \pm \sqrt{cf}\sec_B(2p\Theta). \tag{28}$$

$$\psi_{24}(\Theta) = -\cot_B(2p\Theta) \pm \sqrt{cf}\csc_B(2p\Theta). \tag{29}$$

$$\psi_{25}(\Theta) = \frac{1}{2}\tan_B(\frac{1}{2}p\Theta) - \frac{1}{2}\cot_B(\frac{1}{2}p\Theta). \tag{30}$$

Type VI: when $r = -p$ and q is zero, we have

$$\psi_{26}(\Theta) = -\tanh_B(p\Theta). \tag{31}$$

$$\psi_{27}(\Theta) = -\coth_B(p\Theta). \tag{32}$$

$$\psi_{28}(\Theta) = -\tanh_B(2p\Theta) \pm \imath\sqrt{cf}\,\mathrm{sech}_B(2p\Theta). \tag{33}$$

$$\psi_{29}(\Theta) = -\coth_B(2p\Theta) \pm \sqrt{cf}\,\mathrm{csch}_B(2p\Theta). \tag{34}$$

$$\psi_{30}(\Theta) = -\frac{1}{2}\tanh_B(\frac{1}{2}p\Theta) - \frac{1}{2}\coth_B(\frac{1}{2}p\Theta). \tag{35}$$

Type VII: when $q^2 - 4pr = 0$, then

$$\psi_{31}(\Theta) = -2\frac{p(q\Theta\log(d) + 2)}{q^2\Theta\log(d)}. \tag{36}$$

Type VIII: when $q = \rho$, $p = m\rho$ $(m \neq 0)$ and r is zero, one has

$$\psi_{32}(\Theta) = d^{\rho\Theta} - m. \tag{37}$$

Type IX: if $q = r = 0$, we have

$$\psi_{33}(\Theta) = p\,\Theta\,\log(d). \tag{38}$$

Type X: if $p = q = 0$, we have

$$\psi_{34}(\Theta) = -\frac{1}{\Theta\,\log(d)\,r}. \tag{39}$$

Type XI: when p is zero while q and r are nonzero, we have

$$\psi_{35}(\Theta) = -\frac{cq}{r(\cosh_B(q\Theta) - \sinh_B(q\Theta) + c)}. \tag{40}$$

$$\psi_{36}(\Theta) = -\frac{q(\cosh_B(q\Theta) + \sinh_B(q\Theta))}{r(\cosh_B(q\Theta) + \sinh_B(q\Theta) + f)}. \tag{41}$$

Type XII: when $q = \rho$, $r = m\rho$ $(m \neq 0)$, and p is zero, then

$$\psi_{37}(\Theta) = \frac{cd^{\rho\Theta}}{c - mfd^{\rho\Theta}}. \tag{42}$$

where the deformation parameters are represented by $c, f > 0$.

Step 3:

Enter Equations (4) and (5) into Equation (3) to start this step. The system of equations in $\alpha_s(s = -m, \ldots, 1, 2, 3, \ldots, m)$ and λ can then be obtained by adding the coefficients of every $\psi^s(s = -m, \ldots, 1, 2, 3, \ldots, m)$ term and setting the coefficients of the same power to 0. The results for the unknowns can be obtained by adjusting this collection of equations.

Step 4:

Now that we know the values of $\alpha_s(s = -m, \ldots, 1, 2, 3, \ldots, m)$ and λ, we can insert Equation (4) into Equation (1). The solutions to Equation (1) can be obtained from Equation (3).

The generalized trigonometric and hyperbolic functions are described as follows:

$$\begin{aligned} \cos_B(\Theta) &= \frac{cB^{\iota\Theta}+fB^{-\iota\Theta}}{2}, & \sin_B(\Theta) &= \frac{cB^{\iota\Theta}-fB^{-\iota\Theta}}{2\iota}, \\ \cot_B(\Theta) &= \iota\frac{cB^{\iota\Theta}+fB^{-\iota\Theta}}{cB^{\iota\Theta}-fB^{-\iota\Theta}}, & \tan_B(\Theta) &= -\iota\frac{cB^{\iota\Theta}-fB^{-\iota\Theta}}{cB^{\iota\Theta}+fB^{-\iota\Theta}}, \\ \csc_B(\Theta) &= \frac{2\iota}{cB^{\iota\Theta}-fB^{-\iota\Theta}}, & \sec_B(\Theta) &= \frac{2}{cB^{\iota\Theta}+fB^{-\iota\Theta}}. \end{aligned}$$

Similarly,

$$\begin{aligned} \cosh_B(\Theta) &= \frac{cB^{\Theta}+fB^{-\Theta}}{2}, & \sinh_B(\Theta) &= \frac{cB^{\Theta}-fB^{-\Theta}}{2}, \\ \coth_B(\Theta) &= \frac{cB^{\Theta}+fB^{-\Theta}}{cB^{\Theta}-fB^{-\Theta}}, & \tanh_B(\Theta) &= \frac{cB^{\Theta}-fB^{-\Theta}}{cB^{\Theta}+fB^{-\Theta}}, \\ \mathrm{csch}_B(\Theta) &= \frac{2}{cB^{\Theta}-fB^{-\Theta}}, & \mathrm{sech}_B(\Theta) &= \frac{2}{cB^{\Theta}+fB^{-\Theta}}. \end{aligned}$$

The modified extended direct algebraic method (mEDAM), while powerful for finding the soliton solutions of nonlinear equations, has limitations, particularly when the highest derivative and nonlinear terms are not well balanced, and it might not be applicable to all types of nonlinear equations, especially those with complex structures or non-standard forms.

3.2. The Improved (G'/G) Expansion Method

This subsection briefs the basic steps for the method shown as [30].

Step 1:

Consider a partial fractional nonlinear differential equation:

$$Y(h, D^{\alpha,\Upsilon}_{M,t}h, h^2h_x, h_y, h_{yy}, h_{xx}, h_{xy}, \ldots) = 0. \tag{43}$$

Step 2:

Assume the following transformation:

$$h(x,y,t) = H(\Theta), \;\; \Theta = x - \nu y + \kappa\frac{\Gamma(1+\Upsilon)}{\alpha}t^{\alpha}, \tag{44}$$

Here, ν and κ denote the constants. Using Equation (44) in Equation (43) provides a nonlinear ordinary differential equation:

$$Z(H, H^2H', H'', \ldots) = 0. \tag{45}$$

Step 3:

Suppose the solution to Equation (45) is given as

$$H(\Theta) = \sum_{j=0}^{m} \alpha_j \left(\frac{G'(\Theta)}{G(\Theta)}\right)^j. \tag{46}$$

In Equation (46), α_0 and $\alpha_j, (j = 1, 2, 3, \ldots, m)$ are to found. By utilizing the homogenous balance method in Equation (45), we obtain m. The profile $G = G(\Theta)$ satisfies the equation below:

$$GG'' - \kappa_1 G^2 - \kappa_2 GG' - \kappa_3 (G')^2 = 0, \tag{47}$$

where κ_1, κ_2, and κ_3 are constants.

Step 4:

Consider a solution to Equation (47) that is given as

Type I: when $\kappa_2 \neq 0$ and $\pi = \kappa_2^2 + 4\kappa_1 - 4\kappa_1\kappa_3 > 0$, we have

$$\frac{G'(\Theta)}{G(\Theta)} = \frac{\kappa_2\sqrt{\pi}\left(C_1 \exp\left(\frac{1}{2}\Theta\sqrt{\pi}\right) + C_2 \exp\left(\frac{1}{2}\Theta(-\sqrt{\pi})\right)\right)}{(2(1-\kappa_3))\left(C_1 \exp\left(\frac{1}{2}\Theta\sqrt{\pi}\right) - C_2 \exp\left(\frac{1}{2}\Theta(-\sqrt{\pi})\right)\right)} + \frac{\kappa_2}{2(1-\kappa_3)}. \tag{48}$$

Type II: if $\kappa_2 \neq 0$ and $\pi = \kappa_2^2 + 4\kappa_1 - 4\kappa_1\kappa_3 < 0$, then

$$\frac{G'(\Theta)}{G(\Theta)} = \frac{\kappa_2\sqrt{-\pi}(C_1\iota\cos(\frac{1}{2}\Theta\sqrt{-\pi}) - C_2\sin(\frac{1}{2}\Theta\sqrt{-\pi}))}{(2(1-\kappa_3))(C_1\iota\sin(\frac{1}{2}\Theta\sqrt{-\pi}) + C_2\cos(\frac{1}{2}\Theta\sqrt{-\pi}))} + \frac{\kappa_2}{2(1-\kappa_3)}. \tag{49}$$

Type III: if $\kappa_2 = 0$ and $\kappa_1 - \kappa_1\kappa_3 \geq 0$, we have

$$\frac{G'(\Theta)}{G(\Theta)} = \frac{\sqrt{\kappa_1 - \kappa_1\kappa_3}(C_2\sin(\Theta\sqrt{\kappa_1 - \kappa_1\kappa_3}) + C_1\cos(\Theta\sqrt{\kappa_1 - \kappa_1\kappa_3}))}{(1-\kappa_3)(C_1\sin(\Theta\sqrt{\kappa_1 - \kappa_1\kappa_3}) - C_2\cos(\Theta\sqrt{\kappa_1 - \kappa_1\kappa_3}))}. \tag{50}$$

Type IV: if $\kappa_2 = 0$ and $\kappa_1 - \kappa_1\kappa_3 < 0$, we have

$$\frac{G'(\Theta)}{G(\Theta)} = \frac{\sqrt{\kappa_1\kappa_3 - \kappa_1}(C_1\iota\cosh(\Theta\sqrt{\kappa_1\kappa_3 - \kappa_1}) - C_2\sinh(\Theta\sqrt{\kappa_1\kappa_3 - \kappa_1}))}{(1-\kappa_3)(C_1\iota\sinh(\Theta\sqrt{\kappa_1\kappa_3 - \kappa_1}) - C_2\cosh(\Theta\sqrt{\kappa_1\kappa_3 - \kappa_1}))}. \tag{51}$$

Here, κ_1, κ_2, κ_3, C_1, and C_2 are constants.

Step 5:

Equations (46) and (47) are combined into Equation (45), and the coefficients of each power of $\left(\frac{G'(\Theta)}{G(\Theta)}\right)$ are obtained. The system of algebraic equations is obtained by setting every coefficient to 0.

Step 6:

By utilizing the Mathematica tool to simplify the system mentioned above, we obtain different solitons to the NLPD Equation (43).

The limitations of the improved (G′/G) expansion method, while offering advantages in finding traveling-wave solutions for nonlinear evolution equations, include the potential for complex algebraic manipulations and the need for specialized software like Maple 17 or Mathematica 11 to handle the resulting equations.

4. Model Description

In 1967, Gardner, Greene, Kruskal, and Miura discovered the generalized shallow water wave equation. The generalized shallow water wave equation is a generalization of the Korteweg–de Vries (KdV) equation, which is a well-known model for water waves. The generalized water wave equation includes higher-order, nonlinear, and dispersive terms, making it a more accurate model for certain types of water waves.

The (1 + 1)-dimensional generalized shallow water wave equation given in [24] is considered by replacing the ordinary derivative with a truncated M-fractional derivative as follows:

$$D_{M,t}^{\alpha,\Upsilon}(D_{M,x}^{3\alpha,\Upsilon}h) + a(D_{M,x}^{\alpha,\Upsilon}h)(D_{M,xt}^{2\alpha,\Upsilon}h) + b(D_{M,t}^{\alpha,\Upsilon}h)(D_{M,x}^{2\alpha,\Upsilon}h) - D_{M,xt}^{2\alpha,\Upsilon}h - D_{M,x}^{2\alpha,\Upsilon}h = 0. \tag{52}$$

Assume the following wave transformations:

$$v = V(\xi); \qquad \xi = \frac{\Gamma(1+\Upsilon)}{u}(x^\alpha - \lambda t^\alpha), \tag{53}$$

Here, λ is a wave speed. Putting Equation (53) into Equation (52) produces

$$\lambda(a+b)\left(H'\right)^2+2\lambda H'''+2(1-\lambda)H'=0. \quad (54)$$

We obtain the natural number $m=1$ with the use of the homogenous balance technique in Equation (54). We now use two distinct approaches to solve Equation (54).

5. Different Types of Wave Solitons

5.1. Through Modified Extended Direct Algebraic Technique

For our case, Equation (4) reduces to this form:

$$H(\xi)=\alpha_{-1}(\psi(\xi))^{-1}+\alpha_0+\alpha_1\psi(\xi). \quad (55)$$

Using Equations (55) and (5) in Equation (54) provides the given sets:
Set 1:

$$\left\{\alpha_{-1}=\frac{12p\log(d)}{a+b},\alpha_0=\alpha_0,\alpha_1=0,\lambda=\frac{1}{4p\ r\log^2(d)-q^2\log^2(d)+1}\right\}. \quad (56)$$

When $q^2-4pr<0$ and r is nonzero, then we have the following by using Equations (6)–(10):

$$h(x,t)=\alpha_0+\frac{12p\log(d)}{a+b}\left(-\frac{q}{2r}+\frac{\sqrt{4p\ r-q^2}\tan_B\left(\frac{1}{2}\sqrt{4p\ r-q^2}\xi\right)}{2r}\right)^{-1}. \quad (57)$$

$$h(x,t)=\alpha_0+\frac{12p\log(d)}{a+b}\left(-\frac{q}{2r}-\frac{\sqrt{4p\ r-q^2}\cot_B\left(\frac{1}{2}\sqrt{4p\ r-q^2}\xi\right)}{2r}\right)^{-1}. \quad (58)$$

$$h(x,t)=\alpha_0+\frac{12p\log(d)}{a+b}\Big(-\frac{q}{2r}+\Big(\sqrt{4p\ r-q^2}\Big(\tan_B\Big(\sqrt{4p\ r-q^2}\xi\Big)\pm \Big(\sqrt{c\ f}\ \sec_B\Big(\sqrt{4p\ r-q^2}\xi\Big)\Big)\Big)\Big)/(2r)\Big)^{-1}. \quad (59)$$

$$h(x,t)=\alpha_0+\frac{12p\log(d)}{a+b}\Big(-\frac{q}{2r}-\Big(\sqrt{-(q^2-4p\ r)}\Big(\cot_B\Big(\sqrt{-(q^2-4p\ r)}\xi\Big)\pm \Big(\sqrt{c\ f}\ \csc_B\Big(\sqrt{-(q^2-4p\ r)}\xi\Big)\Big)\Big)\Big)/(2r)\Big)^{-1}. \quad (60)$$

$$h(x,t)=\alpha_0+\frac{12p\log(d)}{a+b}\Big(-\frac{q}{2r}+\Big(\sqrt{-(q^2-4p\ r)}\Big(\tan_B\Big(\frac{1}{4}\sqrt{-(q^2-4p\ r)}\xi\Big)- \Big(\ \cot_B\Big(\frac{1}{4}\sqrt{-(q^2-4p\ r)}\xi\Big)\Big)\Big)\Big)/(2r)\Big)^{-1}. \quad (61)$$

When $q^2-4pr>0$ and r is nonzero, we obtain the following solutions by using Equations (11)–(15):

$$h(x,t)=\alpha_0+\frac{12p\log(d)}{a+b}\left(-\frac{q}{2r}-\frac{\sqrt{(q^2-4p\ r)}\tanh_B\left(\frac{1}{2}\sqrt{(q^2-4p\ r)}\xi\right)}{2r}\right)^{-1}. \quad (62)$$

$$h(x,t)=\alpha_0+\frac{12p\log(d)}{a+b}\left(-\frac{q}{2r}-\frac{\sqrt{(q^2-4p\ r)}\coth_B\left(\frac{1}{2}\sqrt{(q^2-4p\ r)}\xi\right)}{2r}\right)^{-1}. \quad (63)$$

$$h(x,t) = \alpha_0 + \frac{12p\log(d)}{a+b}(-\frac{q}{2r} - (\sqrt{q^2-4p\ r}(\tanh_B(\sqrt{q^2-4p\ r}\xi)\pm (\sqrt{c\ f}\, sech_B(\sqrt{q^2-4pr}\xi))))/(2r))^{-1}. \quad (64)$$

$$h(x,t) = \alpha_0 + \frac{12p\log(d)}{a+b}(-\frac{q}{2r} - (\sqrt{q^2-4p\ r}(\coth_B(\sqrt{q^2-4p\ r}\xi)\pm (\sqrt{c\ f}\, csch_B(\sqrt{q^2-4p\ r}\xi))))/(2r))^{-1}. \quad (65)$$

$$h(x,t) = \alpha_0 + \frac{12p\log(d)}{a+b}(-\frac{q}{2r} - (\sqrt{q^2-4p\ r}(\tanh_B(\frac{1}{4}\sqrt{q^2-4p\ r}\xi)- (\ \coth_B(\frac{1}{4}\sqrt{q^2-4p\ r}\xi))))/(2r))^{-1}. \quad (66)$$

where $\xi = \frac{\Gamma(1+\Upsilon)}{\alpha}(x^\alpha - \frac{t^\alpha}{4p\ r\log^2(d)-q^2\log^2(d)+1})$.

When $pr > 0$ and q is zero, then we have the following solutions by using Equations (16)–(20):

$$h(x,t) = \alpha_0 + \frac{12p\log(d)}{a+b}(\sqrt{\frac{p}{r}}\tan_B(\sqrt{p\ r}\frac{\Gamma(1+\Upsilon)}{\alpha}(x^\alpha - \frac{t^\alpha}{4p\ r\log^2(d)+1})))^{-1}. \quad (67)$$

$$h(x,t) = \alpha_0 + \frac{12p\log(d)}{a+b}(-\sqrt{\frac{p}{r}}\cot_B(\sqrt{p\ r}\frac{\Gamma(1+\Upsilon)}{\alpha}(x^\alpha - \frac{t^\alpha}{4p\ r\log^2(d)+1})))^{-1}. \quad (68)$$

$$h(x,t) = \alpha_0 + \frac{12p\log(d)}{a+b}(\sqrt{\frac{p}{r}}(\tan_B(2\sqrt{p\ r}\frac{\Gamma(1+\Upsilon)}{\alpha}(x^\alpha - \frac{t^\alpha}{4p\ r\log^2(d)+1}))\pm (\sqrt{cf}\sec_B(2\sqrt{p\ r}\frac{\Gamma(1+\Upsilon)}{\alpha}(x^\alpha - \frac{t^\alpha}{4pr\log^2(d)+1})))))^{-1}. \quad (69)$$

$$h(x,t) = \alpha_0 + \frac{12p\log(d)}{a+b}(-\sqrt{\frac{p}{r}}(\cot_B(2\sqrt{p\ r}\frac{\Gamma(1+\Upsilon)}{\alpha}(x^\alpha - \frac{t^\alpha}{4p\ r\log^2(d)+1}))\pm (\sqrt{c\ f}\csc_B(2\sqrt{p\ r}\frac{\Gamma(1+\Upsilon)}{\alpha}(x^\alpha - \frac{t^\alpha}{4p\ r\log^2(d)+1})))))^{-1}. \quad (70)$$

$$h(x,t) = \alpha_0 + \frac{12p\log(d)}{a+b}(\frac{1}{2}\sqrt{\frac{p}{r}}(\tan_B(\frac{1}{2}\sqrt{p\ r}\frac{\Gamma(1+\Upsilon)}{\alpha}(x^\alpha - \frac{t^\alpha}{4p\ r\log^2(d)+1}))- \cot_B(\frac{1}{2}\sqrt{p\ r}\frac{\Gamma(1+\Upsilon)}{\alpha}(x^\alpha - \frac{t^\alpha}{4p\ r\log^2(d)+1}))))^{-1}. \quad (71)$$

When $pr < 0$ and q is zero, then we obtain the following solutions by using Equations (21)–(25):

$$h(x,t) = \alpha_0 + \frac{12p\log(d)}{a+b}(-\sqrt{-\frac{p}{r}}\tanh_B(\sqrt{-p\ r}\frac{\Gamma(1+\Upsilon)}{\alpha}(x^\alpha - \frac{t^\alpha}{4p\ r\log^2(d)+1})))^{-1}. \quad (72)$$

$$h(x,t) = \alpha_0 + \frac{12p\log(d)}{a+b}(-\sqrt{-\frac{p}{r}}\coth_B(\sqrt{-p\ r}\frac{\Gamma(1+\Upsilon)}{\alpha}(x^\alpha - \frac{t^\alpha}{4p\ r\log^2(d)+1})))^{-1}. \quad (73)$$

$$h(x,t) = \alpha_0 + \frac{12p\log(d)}{a+b}(-\sqrt{-\frac{p}{r}}(\tanh_B(2\sqrt{-p\ r}\frac{\Gamma(1+\Upsilon)}{\alpha}(x^\alpha - \frac{t^\alpha}{4p\ r\log^2(d)+1}))\pm (\iota\sqrt{cf}sech_B(2\sqrt{-p\ r}\frac{\Gamma(1+\Upsilon)}{\alpha}(x^\alpha - \frac{t^\alpha}{4p\ r\log^2(d)+1})))))^{-1}. \quad (74)$$

$$h(x,t) = \alpha_0 + \frac{12p\log(d)}{a+b}(-\sqrt{-\frac{p}{r}}(\coth_B(2\sqrt{-p\ r}\frac{\Gamma(1+\Upsilon)}{\alpha}(x^\alpha - \frac{t^\alpha}{4p\ r\log^2(d)+1}))\pm (\sqrt{cf}csch_B(2\sqrt{-p\ r}\frac{\Gamma(1+\Upsilon)}{\alpha}(x^\alpha - \frac{t^\alpha}{4p\ r\log^2(d)+1})))))^{-1}. \quad (75)$$

$$h(x,t) = \alpha_0 + \frac{12p\log(d)}{a+b}(-\frac{1}{2}\sqrt{-\frac{p}{r}}(\tanh_B(\frac{1}{2}\sqrt{-p\ r}\frac{\Gamma(1+\Upsilon)}{\alpha}(x^\alpha - \frac{t^\alpha}{4p\ r\log^2(d)+1}))+ \coth_B(\frac{1}{2}\sqrt{-p\ r}\frac{\Gamma(1+\Upsilon)}{\alpha}(x^\alpha - \frac{t^\alpha}{4p\ r\log^2(d)+1}))))^{-1}. \quad (76)$$

When $r = p$ and $q = 0$, we attain the following solutions by using Equations (26)–(30):

$$h(x,t) = \alpha_0 + \frac{12p\log(d)}{a+b}(\tan_B(p\frac{\Gamma(1+\Upsilon)}{\alpha}(x^\alpha - \frac{t^\alpha}{4p^2\log^2(d)+1})))^{-1}. \quad (77)$$

$$h(x,t) = \alpha_0 + \frac{12p\log(d)}{a+b}(-\cot_B(p\frac{\Gamma(1+\Upsilon)}{\alpha}(x^\alpha - \frac{t^\alpha}{4p^2\log^2(d)+1})))^{-1}. \quad (78)$$

$$h(x,t) = \alpha_0 + \frac{12p\log(d)}{a+b}(\tan_B(2p\frac{\Gamma(1+\Upsilon)}{\alpha}(x^\alpha - \frac{t^\alpha}{4p^2\log^2(d)+1}))\pm (\sqrt{cf}\sec_B(2p\frac{\Gamma(1+\Upsilon)}{\alpha}(x^\alpha - \frac{t^\alpha}{4p^2\log^2(d)+1}))))^{-1}. \quad (79)$$

$$h(x,t) = \alpha_0 + \frac{12p\log(d)}{a+b}(-\cot_B(2p\frac{\Gamma(1+\Upsilon)}{\alpha}(x^\alpha - \frac{t^\alpha}{4p^2\log^2(d)+1}))\pm (\sqrt{cf}\csc_B(2p\frac{\Gamma(1+\Upsilon)}{\alpha}(x^\alpha - \frac{t^\alpha}{4p^2\log^2(d)+1}))))^{-1}. \quad (80)$$

$$h(x,t) = \alpha_0 + \frac{12p\log(d)}{a+b}(\frac{1}{2}\tan_B(\frac{1}{2}p\frac{\Gamma(1+\Upsilon)}{\alpha}(x^\alpha - \frac{t^\alpha}{4p^2\log^2(d)+1}))- \frac{1}{2}\cot_B(\frac{1}{2}p\frac{\Gamma(1+\Upsilon)}{\alpha}(x^\alpha - \frac{t^\alpha}{4p^2\log^2(d)+1})))^{-1}. \quad (81)$$

When $r = -p$ and q is zero, we obtain the following solutions by utilizing Equations (31)–(35):

$$h(x,t) = \alpha_0 + \frac{12p\log(d)}{a+b}(-\tanh_B(p\frac{\Gamma(1+\Upsilon)}{\alpha}(x^\alpha - \frac{t^\alpha}{-4p^2\log^2(d)+1})))^{-1}. \quad (82)$$

$$h(x,t) = \alpha_0 + \frac{12p\log(d)}{a+b}(-\coth_B(p\frac{\Gamma(1+\Upsilon)}{\alpha}(x^\alpha - \frac{t^\alpha}{-4p^2\log^2(d)+1})))^{-1}. \quad (83)$$

$$h(x,t)=\alpha_0+\frac{12p\log(d)}{a+b}(-\tanh_B(2p\frac{\Gamma(1+\Upsilon)}{\alpha}(x^\alpha-\frac{t^\alpha}{-4p^2\log^2(d)+1}))\pm$$
$$(\iota\sqrt{c\ f}sech_B(2p\frac{\Gamma(1+\Upsilon)}{\alpha}(x^\alpha-\frac{t^\alpha}{-4p^2\log^2(d)+1}))))^{-1}. \quad (84)$$

$$h(x,t)=\alpha_0+\frac{12p\log(d)}{a+b}(-\coth_B(2p\frac{\Gamma(1+\Upsilon)}{\alpha}(x^\alpha-\frac{t^\alpha}{-4p^2\log^2(d)+1}))\pm$$
$$(\sqrt{c\ f}csch_B(2p\frac{\Gamma(1+\Upsilon)}{\alpha}(x^\alpha-\frac{t^\alpha}{-4p^2\log^2(d)+1}))))^{-1}. \quad (85)$$

$$h(x,t)=\alpha_0+\frac{12p\log(d)}{a+b}(-\frac{1}{2}\tanh_B(\frac{1}{2}p\frac{\Gamma(1+\Upsilon)}{\alpha}(x^\alpha-\frac{t^\alpha}{-4p^2\log^2(d)+1}))-$$
$$\frac{1}{2}\coth_B(\frac{1}{2}p\frac{\Gamma(1+\Upsilon)}{\alpha}(x^\alpha-\frac{t^\alpha}{-4p^2\log^2(d)+1})))^{-1}. \quad (86)$$

when $q^2-4pr=0$, then we obtain the following solution by using Equation (36),

$$h(x,t)=\alpha_0+\frac{12p\log(d)}{a+b}(-2\frac{p(q\xi\log(d)+2)}{q^2\frac{\Gamma(1+\Upsilon)}{\alpha}(x^\alpha-t^\alpha)\log(d)})^{-1}. \quad (87)$$

When $q=\rho$, $p=m\rho$ $(m\neq 0)$ and r is zero, we obtain the following solution by utilizing Equation (37):

$$h(x,t)=\alpha_0+\frac{12m\rho\log(d)}{a+b}(d^{\rho\frac{\Gamma(1+\Upsilon)}{\alpha}(x^\alpha-\frac{t^\alpha}{-\rho^2\log^2(d)+1})}-m)^{-1}. \quad (88)$$

if $q=r=0$, we obtain the following solution by using Equation (38):

$$h(x,t)=\alpha_0+\frac{12p\log(d)}{a+b}(p\frac{\Gamma(1+\Upsilon)}{\alpha}(x^\alpha-t^\alpha)\log(d))^{-1}. \quad (89)$$

Set 2:

$$\left\{\alpha_{-1}=0,\alpha_1=-\frac{12r\log(d)}{a+b},\lambda=\frac{1}{4p\ r\log^2(d)-q^2\log^2(d)+1}\right\}. \quad (90)$$

When $q^2-4pr<0$ and r is nonzero, then we have the following by using Equations (6)–(10):

$$h(x,t)=\alpha_0-\frac{12r\log(d)}{a+b}(-\frac{q}{2r}+\frac{\sqrt{-(q^2-4p\ r)}\tan_B(\frac{1}{2}\sqrt{-(q^2-4p\ r)}\xi)}{2r}). \quad (91)$$

$$h(x,t)=\alpha_0-\frac{12r\log(d)}{a+b}(-\frac{q}{2r}-\frac{\sqrt{-(q^2-4p\ r)}\cot_B(\frac{1}{2}\sqrt{-(q^2-4p\ r)}\xi)}{2r}). \quad (92)$$

$$h(x,t)=\alpha_0-\frac{12r\log(d)}{a+b}(-\frac{q}{2r}+\frac{\sqrt{4p\ r-q^2}(\tan_B(\sqrt{4p\ r-q^2}\xi)\pm(\sqrt{c\ f}\ \sec_B(\sqrt{4p\ r-q^2}\xi)))}{2r}). \quad (93)$$

$$h(x,t)=\alpha_0-\frac{12r\log(d)}{a+b}(-\frac{q}{2r}-\frac{\sqrt{4p\ r-q^2}(\cot_B(\sqrt{4p\ r-q^2}\xi)\pm(\sqrt{cf}\ \csc_B(\sqrt{4p\ r-q^2}\xi)))}{2r}). \quad (94)$$

$$h(x,t)=\alpha_0-\frac{12r\log(d)}{a+b}(-\frac{q}{2r}+\frac{\sqrt{4p\ r-q^2}(\tan_B(\frac{1}{4}\sqrt{4p\ r-q^2}\xi)-(\ \cot_B(\frac{1}{4}\sqrt{4p\ r-q^2}\xi)))}{2r}). \quad (95)$$

When $q^2 - 4pr > 0$ and r is nonzero, we obtain the following solutions by using Equations (11)–(15):

$$h(x,t) = \alpha_0 - \frac{12r\log(d)}{a+b}\left(-\frac{q}{2r} - \frac{\sqrt{(q^2-4p\,r)}\tanh_B(\frac{1}{2}\sqrt{(q^2-4p\,r)}\xi)}{2r}\right). \quad (96)$$

$$h(x,t) = \alpha_0 - \frac{12r\log(d)}{a+b}\left(-\frac{q}{2r} - \frac{\sqrt{(q^2-4p\,r)}\coth_B(\frac{1}{2}\sqrt{(q^2-4p\,r)}\xi)}{2r}\right). \quad (97)$$

$$h(x,t) = \alpha_0 - \frac{12r\log(d)}{a+b}\left(-\frac{q}{2r} - \frac{\sqrt{q^2-4p\,r}(\tanh_B(\sqrt{q^2-4p\,r}\xi) \pm (\sqrt{c\,f}\ \mathrm{sech}_B(\sqrt{q^2-4p\,r}\xi)))}{2r}\right). \quad (98)$$

$$h(x,t) = \alpha_0 - \frac{12r\log(d)}{a+b}\left(-\frac{q}{2r} - \frac{\sqrt{q^2-4p\,r}(\coth_B(\sqrt{q^2-4p\,r}\xi) \pm (\sqrt{c\,f}\ \mathrm{csch}_B(\sqrt{q^2-4p\,r}\xi)))}{2r}\right). \quad (99)$$

$$h(x,t) = \alpha_0 - \frac{12r\log(d)}{a+b}\left(-\frac{q}{2r} - \frac{\sqrt{q^2-4p\,r}(\tanh_B(\frac{1}{4}\sqrt{q^2-4p\,r}\xi) - (\ \coth_B(\frac{1}{4}\sqrt{q^2-4p\,r}\xi)))}{2r}\right). \quad (100)$$

where $\xi = \frac{\Gamma(1+\Upsilon)}{\alpha}(x^\alpha - \frac{t^\alpha}{4p\,r\log^2(d) - q^2\log^2(d)+1})$.

When $pr > 0$ and q is zero, then we obtain the following solutions by using Equations (16)–(20):

$$h(x,t) = \alpha_0 - \frac{12r\log(d)}{a+b}\left(\sqrt{\frac{p}{r}}\tan_B(\sqrt{p\,r}\frac{\Gamma(1+\Upsilon)}{\alpha}(x^\alpha - \frac{t^\alpha}{4p\,r\log^2(d)+1}))\right). \quad (101)$$

$$h(x,t) = \alpha_0 - \frac{12r\log(d)}{a+b}\left(-\sqrt{\frac{p}{r}}\cot_B(\sqrt{p\,r}\frac{\Gamma(1+\Upsilon)}{\alpha}(x^\alpha - \frac{t^\alpha}{4p\,r\log^2(d)+1}))\right). \quad (102)$$

$$\begin{aligned} h(x,t) = \alpha_0 - \frac{12r\log(d)}{a+b}(\sqrt{\frac{p}{r}}(\tan_B(2\sqrt{p\,r}\frac{1}{\alpha}\Gamma(1+\Upsilon)(x^\alpha - \frac{t^\alpha}{4p\,r\log^2(d)+1}))\pm \\ (\sqrt{c\,f}\sec_B(2\sqrt{p\,r}\frac{1}{\alpha}\Gamma(1+\Upsilon)(x^\alpha - \frac{t^\alpha}{4p\,r\log^2(d)+1}))))). \quad (103) \end{aligned}$$

$$\begin{aligned} h(x,t) = \alpha_0 - \frac{12r\log(d)}{a+b}(-\sqrt{\frac{p}{r}}(\cot_B(2\sqrt{p\,r}\frac{1}{\alpha}\Gamma(1+\Upsilon)(x^\alpha - \frac{t^\alpha}{4p\,r\log^2(d)+1}))\pm \\ (\sqrt{c\,f}\csc_B(2\sqrt{p\,r}\frac{1}{\alpha}\Gamma(1+\Upsilon)(x^\alpha - \frac{t^\alpha}{4p\,r\log^2(d)+1}))))). \quad (104) \end{aligned}$$

$$\begin{aligned} h(x,t) = \alpha_0 - \frac{12r\log(d)}{a+b}(\frac{1}{2}\sqrt{\frac{p}{r}}(\tan_B(\frac{1}{2}\sqrt{p\,r}\frac{\Gamma(1+\Upsilon)}{\alpha}(x^\alpha - \frac{t^\alpha}{4p\,r\log^2(d)+1}))- \\ \cot_B(\frac{1}{2}\sqrt{p\,r}\frac{\Gamma(1+\Upsilon)}{\alpha}(x^\alpha - \frac{t^\alpha}{4p\,r\log^2(d)+1})))). \quad (105) \end{aligned}$$

When $pr < 0$ and q is zero, then we obtain the following solutions by using Equations (21)–(25),

$$h(x,t) = \alpha_0 - \frac{12r\log(d)}{a+b}\left(-\sqrt{-\frac{p}{r}}\tanh_B(\sqrt{-p\,r}\frac{\Gamma(1+\Upsilon)}{\alpha}(x^\alpha - \frac{t^\alpha}{4p\,r\log^2(d)+1}))\right). \quad (106)$$

$$h(x,t) = \alpha_0 - \frac{12r\log(d)}{a+b}\left(-\sqrt{-\frac{p}{r}}\coth_B(\sqrt{-p\,r}\frac{\Gamma(1+\Upsilon)}{\alpha}(x^\alpha - \frac{t^\alpha}{4p\,r\log^2(d)+1}))\right). \quad (107)$$

$$h(x,t)=\alpha_0-\frac{12r\log(d)}{a+b}(-\sqrt{-\frac{p}{r}}(\tanh_B(2\sqrt{-p\,r}\frac{\Gamma(1+\Upsilon)}{\alpha}(x^{\alpha}-\frac{t^{\alpha}}{4p\,r\log^2(d)+1}))\pm (\iota\sqrt{c\,f}\,\mathrm{sech}_B(2\sqrt{-p\,r}\frac{\Gamma(1+\Upsilon)}{\alpha}(x^{\alpha}-\frac{t^{\alpha}}{4p\,r\log^2(d)+1}))))). \quad (108)$$

$$h(x,t)=\alpha_0-\frac{12r\log(d)}{a+b}(-\sqrt{-\frac{p}{r}}(\coth_B(2\sqrt{-p\,r}\frac{\Gamma(1+\Upsilon)}{\alpha}(x^{\alpha}-\frac{t^{\alpha}}{4p\,r\log^2(d)+1}))\pm (\sqrt{c\,f}\mathrm{csch}_B(2\sqrt{-p\,r}\frac{\Gamma(1+\Upsilon)}{\alpha}(x^{\alpha}-\frac{t^{\alpha}}{4p\,r\log^2(d)+1}))))). \quad (109)$$

$$h(x,t)=\alpha_0-\frac{12r\log(d)}{a+b}(-\frac{1}{2}\sqrt{-\frac{p}{r}}(\tanh_B(\frac{1}{2}\sqrt{-pr}\frac{\Gamma(1+\Upsilon)}{\alpha}(x^{\alpha}-\frac{t^{\alpha}}{4p\,r\log^2(d)+1}))+ \coth_B(\frac{1}{2}\sqrt{-p\,r}\frac{\Gamma(1+\Upsilon)}{\alpha}(x^{\alpha}-\frac{t^{\alpha}}{4pr\log^2(d)+1})))). \quad (110)$$

When $r=p$ and $q=0$, we obtain the following solutions by using Equations (26)–(30):

$$h(x,t)=\alpha_0-\frac{12p\log(d)}{a+b}(\tan_B(p\frac{\Gamma(1+\Upsilon)}{\alpha}(x^{\alpha}-\frac{t^{\alpha}}{4p^2\log^2(d)+1}))). \quad (111)$$

$$h(x,t)=\alpha_0-\frac{12p\log(d)}{a+b}(-\cot_B(p\frac{1}{\alpha}\Gamma(1+\Upsilon)(x^{\alpha}-\frac{t^{\alpha}}{4p^2\log^2(d)+1}))). \quad (112)$$

$$h(x,t)=\alpha_0-\frac{12p\log(d)}{a+b}(\tan_B(2p\frac{1}{\alpha}\Gamma(1+\Upsilon)(x^{\alpha}-\frac{t^{\alpha}}{4p^2\log^2(d)+1}))\pm (\sqrt{c\,f}\sec_B(2p\frac{1}{\alpha}\Gamma(1+\Upsilon)(x^{\alpha}-\frac{t^{\alpha}}{4p^2\log^2(d)+1})))). \quad (113)$$

$$h(x,t)=\alpha_0-\frac{12p\log(d)}{a+b}(-\cot_B(2p\frac{1}{\alpha}\Gamma(1+\Upsilon)(x^{\alpha}-\frac{t^{\alpha}}{4p^2\log^2(d)+1}))\pm (\sqrt{c\,f}\csc_B(2p\frac{\Gamma(1+\Upsilon)}{\alpha}(x^{\alpha}-\frac{t^{\alpha}}{4p^2\log^2(d)+1})))). \quad (114)$$

$$h(x,t)=\alpha_0-\frac{12p\log(d)}{a+b}(\frac{1}{2}\tan_B(\frac{1}{2}p\frac{\Gamma(1+\Upsilon)}{\alpha}(x^{\alpha}-\frac{t^{\alpha}}{4p^2\log^2(d)+1}))- \frac{1}{2}\cot_B(\frac{1}{2}p\frac{\Gamma(1+\Upsilon)}{\alpha}(x^{\alpha}-\frac{t^{\alpha}}{4p^2\log^2(d)+1}))). \quad (115)$$

When $r=-p$ and q is zero, we achieve the following solutions by utilizing Equations (31)–(35):

$$h(x,t)=\alpha_0+\frac{12p\log(d)}{a+b}(-\tanh_B(p\frac{\Gamma(1+\Upsilon)}{\alpha}(x^{\alpha}-\frac{t^{\alpha}}{-4p^2\log^2(d)+1}))). \quad (116)$$

$$h(x,t)=\alpha_0+\frac{12p\log(d)}{a+b}(-\coth_B(p\frac{1}{\alpha}\Gamma(1+\Upsilon)(x^{\alpha}-\frac{t^{\alpha}}{-4p^2\log^2(d)+1}))). \quad (117)$$

$$h(x,t) = \alpha_0 + \frac{12p\log(d)}{a+b}(-\tanh_B(2p\frac{1}{\alpha}\Gamma(1+\Upsilon)(x^\alpha - \frac{t^\alpha}{-4p^2\log^2(d)+1}))\pm (\iota\sqrt{c\ f}sech_B(2p\frac{1}{\alpha}\Gamma(1+\Upsilon)(x^\alpha - \frac{t^\alpha}{-4p^2\log^2(d)+1})))). \quad (118)$$

$$h(x,t) = \alpha_0 + \frac{12p\log(d)}{a+b}(-\coth_B(2p\frac{\Gamma(1+\Upsilon)}{\alpha}(x^\alpha - \frac{t^\alpha}{-4p^2\log^2(d)+1}))\pm (\sqrt{c\ f}csch_B(2p\frac{\Gamma(1+\Upsilon)}{\alpha}(x^\alpha - \frac{t^\alpha}{-4p^2\log^2(d)+1})))). \quad (119)$$

$$h(x,t) = \alpha_0 + \frac{12p\log(d)}{a+b}(-\frac{1}{2}\tanh_B(\frac{1}{2}p\frac{\Gamma(1+\Upsilon)}{\alpha}(x^\alpha - \frac{t^\alpha}{-4p^2\log^2(d)+1}))- \frac{1}{2}\coth_B(\frac{1}{2}p\frac{\Gamma(1+\Upsilon)}{\alpha}(x^\alpha - \frac{t^\alpha}{-4p^2\log^2(d)+1}))). \quad (120)$$

when $q^2 - 4pr = 0$, then we obtain the following solution by using Equation (36):

$$h(x,t) = \alpha_0 - \frac{12r\log(d)}{a+b}(-2\frac{p(q\frac{\Gamma(1+\Upsilon)}{\alpha}(x^\alpha - t^\alpha)\log(d)+2)}{q^2\frac{\Gamma(1+\Upsilon)}{\alpha}(x^\alpha - t^\alpha)\log(d)}). \quad (121)$$

When $p = q = 0$, we obtain the following solution by using the Equation (39),

$$h(x,t) = \alpha_0 - \frac{12r\log(d)}{a+b}(-\frac{1}{r\,\frac{\Gamma(1+\Upsilon)}{\alpha}(x^\alpha - t^\alpha)\log(d)}). \quad (122)$$

When p is zero while q and r are nonzero, we obtain the following solutions by using Equations (40)–(41):

$$h(x,t) = \alpha_0 - \frac{12r\log(d)}{a+b}(-(cq)/(r(\cosh_B(q\frac{\Gamma(1+\Upsilon)}{\alpha}(x^\alpha - \frac{t^\alpha}{-q^2\log^2(d)+1}))- \sinh_B(q\frac{\Gamma(1+\Upsilon)}{\alpha}(x^\alpha - \frac{t^\alpha}{-q^2\log^2(d)+1}))+c))). \quad (123)$$

$$h(x,t) = \alpha_0 - \frac{12r\log(d)}{a+b}(-(q(\cosh_B(q\frac{\Gamma(1+\Upsilon)}{\alpha}(x^\alpha - \frac{t^\alpha}{-q^2\log^2(d)+1}))+ \sinh_B(q\frac{\Gamma(1+\Upsilon)}{\alpha}(x^\alpha - \frac{t^\alpha}{-q^2\log^2(d)+1}))))/(r(\cosh_B(q\frac{\Gamma(1+\Upsilon)}{\alpha}(x^\alpha - \frac{t^\alpha}{-q^2\log^2(d)+1})) + \sinh_B(q\frac{\Gamma(1+\Upsilon)}{\alpha}(x^\alpha - \frac{t^\alpha}{-q^2\log^2(d)+1}))+f))). \quad (124)$$

If $q = \rho$, $r = m\rho$ $(m \neq 0)$ and $p = 0$, then we obtain the following solution by using Equation (42):

$$h(x,t) = \alpha_0 - \frac{12m\rho\log(d)}{a+b}(\frac{cd^{\rho\frac{\Gamma(1+\Upsilon)}{\alpha}(x^\alpha - \frac{t^\alpha}{-\rho^2\log^2(d)+1})}}{c - mfd^{\rho\frac{\Gamma(1+\Upsilon)}{\alpha}(x^\alpha - \frac{t^\alpha}{-\rho^2\log^2(d)+1})}}). \quad (125)$$

5.2. Exact Solitons via Improved (G'/G) Expansion Scheme

For $m = 1$, Equation (46) reduces to the given form:

$$H(\xi) = \alpha_0 + \alpha_1 \left(\frac{G'(\xi)}{G(\xi)} \right). \tag{126}$$

Here, α_0 and α_1 are undetermined.

By putting Equations (126) and (47) in Equation (54), one obtains the given solution set:

Set:

$$\left\{ \alpha_1 = -\frac{12(\kappa_3 - 1)}{a+b}, \lambda = \frac{1}{-\kappa_2^2 + 4\kappa_1(\kappa_3 - 1) + 1} \right\}. \tag{127}$$

When $\kappa_2 \neq 0$ and $\pi = \kappa_2^2 + 4\kappa_1 - 4\kappa_1\kappa_3 > 0$, we obtain the following solution by using Equation (48):

$$\begin{aligned} h(x,t) = \alpha_0 - \frac{12(\kappa_3 - 1)}{a+b}((\kappa_2\sqrt{\pi}(C_1 \exp(\frac{1}{2}\frac{\Gamma(1+\Upsilon)}{\alpha}(x^\alpha - \frac{t^\alpha}{-\kappa_2^2 + 4\kappa_1(\kappa_3 - 1) + 1}) \\ \sqrt{\pi}) + C_2 \exp(\frac{1}{2}\frac{\Gamma(1+\Upsilon)}{\alpha}(x^\alpha - \frac{t^\alpha}{-\kappa_2^2 + 4\kappa_1(\kappa_3 - 1) + 1})(-\sqrt{\pi}))))/((2(1-\kappa_3)) \\ (C_1 \exp(\frac{1}{2}\frac{\Gamma(1+\Upsilon)}{\alpha}(x^\alpha - \frac{t^\alpha}{-\kappa_2^2 + 4\kappa_1(\kappa_3 - 1) + 1})\sqrt{\pi}) - C_2 \exp(\frac{1}{2}\frac{\Gamma(1+\Upsilon)}{\alpha}(x^\alpha \\ - \frac{t^\alpha}{-\kappa_2^2 + 4\kappa_1(\kappa_3 - 1) + 1})(-\sqrt{\pi})))) + \frac{\kappa_2}{2(1-\kappa_3)}). \end{aligned} \tag{128}$$

if $\kappa_2 \neq 0$ and $\pi = \kappa_2^2 + 4\kappa_1 - 4\kappa_1\kappa_3 < 0$, then we obtain the following solution by using Equation (49):

$$\begin{aligned} h(x,t) = \alpha_0 - \frac{12(\kappa_3 - 1)}{a+b}((\kappa_2\sqrt{-\pi}(C_1\iota \cos(\frac{1}{2}\frac{\Gamma(1+\Upsilon)}{\alpha}(x^\alpha - \frac{t^\alpha}{-\kappa_2^2 + 4\kappa_1(\kappa_3 - 1) + 1}) \\ \sqrt{-\pi}) - C_2 \sin(\frac{1}{2}\frac{\Gamma(1+\Upsilon)}{\alpha}(x^\alpha - \frac{t^\alpha}{-\kappa_2^2 + 4\kappa_1(\kappa_3 - 1) + 1})\sqrt{-\pi})))/((2(1-\kappa_3)) \\ (C_1\iota \sin(\frac{1}{2}\frac{\Gamma(1+\Upsilon)}{\alpha}(x^\alpha - \frac{t^\alpha}{-\kappa_2^2 + 4\kappa_1(\kappa_3 - 1) + 1})\sqrt{-\pi}) + C_2 \cos(\frac{1}{2}\frac{\Gamma(1+\Upsilon)}{\alpha}(x^\alpha - \\ \frac{t^\alpha}{-\kappa_2^2 + 4\kappa_1(\kappa_3 - 1) + 1})\sqrt{-\pi}))) + \frac{\kappa_2}{2(1-\kappa_3)}). \end{aligned} \tag{129}$$

if $\kappa_2 = 0$ and $\kappa_1 - \kappa_1\kappa_3 \geq 0$, then we achieve the following solution by utilizing Equation (50):

$$\begin{aligned} h(x,t) = \alpha_0 - \frac{12(\kappa_3 - 1)}{a+b}((\sqrt{\kappa_1 - \kappa_1\kappa_3}(C_2 \sin(\frac{\Gamma(1+\Upsilon)}{\alpha}(x^\alpha - \frac{t^\alpha}{4\kappa_1(\kappa_3 - 1) + 1}) \\ \sqrt{\kappa_1 - \kappa_1\kappa_3}) + C_1 \cos(\frac{\Gamma(1+\Upsilon)}{\alpha}(x^\alpha - \frac{t^\alpha}{4\kappa_1(\kappa_3 - 1) + 1})\sqrt{\kappa_1 - \kappa_1\kappa_3})))/((1-\kappa_3) \\ (C_1 \sin(\frac{\Gamma(1+\Upsilon)}{\alpha}(x^\alpha - \frac{t^\alpha}{4\kappa_1(\kappa_3 - 1) + 1})\sqrt{\kappa_1 - \kappa_1\kappa_3}) - C_2 \cos(\frac{\Gamma(1+\Upsilon)}{\alpha}(x^\alpha \\ - \frac{t^\alpha}{4\kappa_1(\kappa_3 - 1) + 1})\sqrt{\kappa_1 - \kappa_1\kappa_3})))). \end{aligned} \tag{130}$$

if $\kappa_2 = 0$ and $\kappa_1 - \kappa_1\kappa_3 < 0$, we obtain the following solution by using Equation (51):

$$h(x,t) = \alpha_0 - \frac{12(\kappa_3 - 1)}{a+b}((\sqrt{\kappa_1\kappa_3 - \kappa_1}(C_1\iota\cosh(\frac{\Gamma(1+\Upsilon)}{\alpha}(x^\alpha - \frac{t^\alpha}{4\kappa_1(\kappa_3-1)+1}) \\ \sqrt{\kappa_1\kappa_3-\kappa_1}) - C_2\sinh(\frac{\Gamma(1+\Upsilon)}{\alpha}(x^\alpha - \frac{t^\alpha}{4\kappa_1(\kappa_3-1)+1})\sqrt{\kappa_1\kappa_3-\kappa_1})))/((1-\kappa_3) \\ (C_1\iota\sinh(\frac{\Gamma(1+\Upsilon)}{\alpha}(x^\alpha - \frac{t^\alpha}{4\kappa_1(\kappa_3-1)+1})\sqrt{\kappa_1\kappa_3-\kappa_1}) - C_2\cosh(\frac{\Gamma(1+\Upsilon)}{\alpha}(x^\alpha \\ - \frac{t^\alpha}{4\kappa_1(\kappa_3-1)+1})\sqrt{\kappa_1\kappa_3-\kappa_1})))). \quad (131)$$

6. Graphical Representation

Here, we use contour, 3D, and 2D graphs to illustrate some of our solutions. The graphs for $\alpha = 0.5$, $\alpha = 0.7$, and $\alpha = 1.0$ are also used to illustrate the impact of fractional derivatives in the following Figures 1–6. Graphs are drawn for different values of the involved parameters. Mathematica software 11 was used for drawing the following graphs.

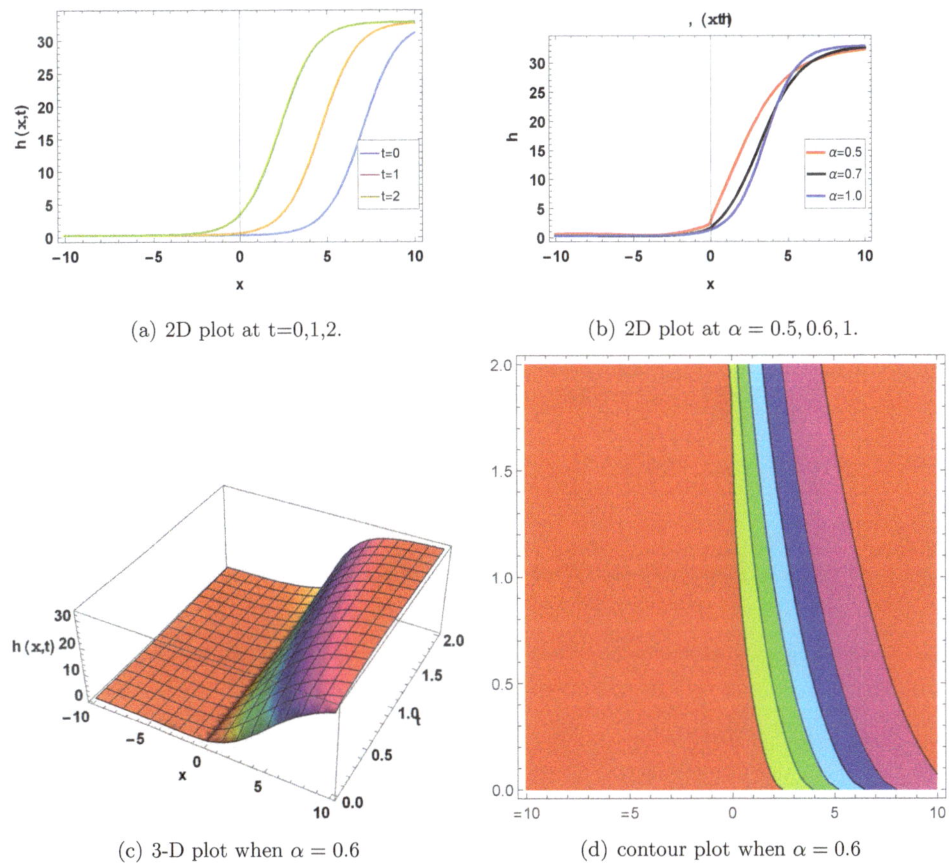

(a) 2D plot at t=0,1,2.

(b) 2D plot at $\alpha = 0.5, 0.6, 1$.

(c) 3-D plot when $\alpha = 0.6$

(d) contour plot when $\alpha = 0.6$

Figure 1. Periodic wave solution. A graph of (x,t) in Equation (57) for $\alpha_0 = 0.01$, $a = 1, b = -0.5, p = 0.01, q = -1, r = 1, d = 4$, and $\Upsilon = 1$. (**a**) displays a two-dimensional plot for $x \in (-10, 10)$ and $\alpha = 1$, with the blue indicating $t = 0$, the orange indicating $t = 1$, and the green indicating $t = 2$. We can observe that the wave repeats in shape and travels along x over time. The shape is not a single localized hump but shows wave-like oscillations, indicating periodicity.

(**b**) displays a two-dimensional plot at $x \in (-10, 10)$ and $t \in (0, 2)$, where the red indicates $\alpha = 0.5$, the black indicates $\alpha = 0.7$, and the blue indicates $\alpha = 1$. It can be observed that the variation in sharpness and spread with increases in α suggests a solution with internal oscillatory behavior. (**c**) shows a 3D plot at $\alpha = 0.6$ for $t \in [0, 2]$. (**d**) shows a contour graph for $\alpha = 0.6$ when $0 < t < 2$. The 3D and contour plots further emphasize a wave repeating in space and time, consistent with a periodic wave solution. Periodic solitons have applications in physics, mathematics, and engineering for explaining water waves, model wave propagation, mechanical systems, etc.

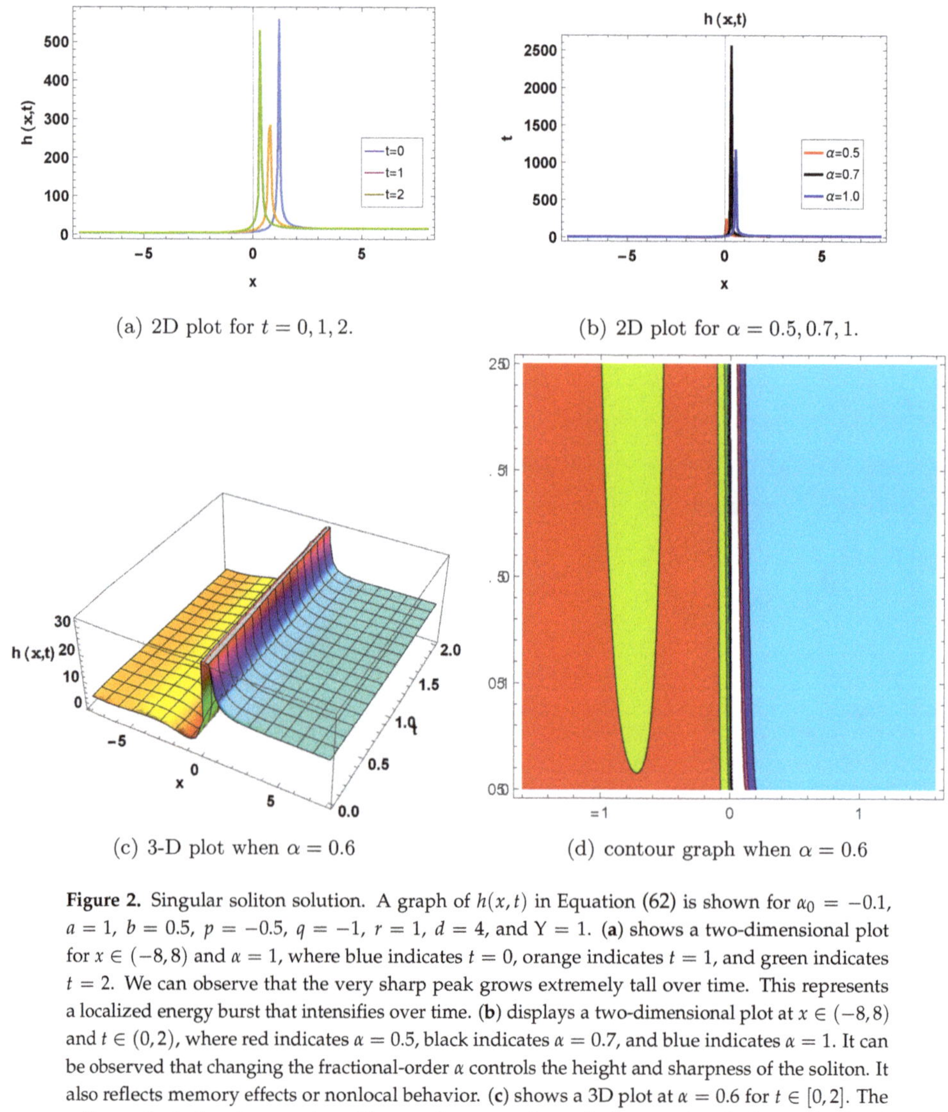

(a) 2D plot for $t = 0, 1, 2$.

(b) 2D plot for $\alpha = 0.5, 0.7, 1$.

(c) 3-D plot when $\alpha = 0.6$

(d) contour graph when $\alpha = 0.6$

Figure 2. Singular soliton solution. A graph of $h(x,t)$ in Equation (62) is shown for $\alpha_0 = -0.1$, $a = 1$, $b = 0.5$, $p = -0.5$, $q = -1$, $r = 1$, $d = 4$, and $\Upsilon = 1$. (**a**) shows a two-dimensional plot for $x \in (-8, 8)$ and $\alpha = 1$, where blue indicates $t = 0$, orange indicates $t = 1$, and green indicates $t = 2$. We can observe that the very sharp peak grows extremely tall over time. This represents a localized energy burst that intensifies over time. (**b**) displays a two-dimensional plot at $x \in (-8, 8)$ and $t \in (0, 2)$, where red indicates $\alpha = 0.5$, black indicates $\alpha = 0.7$, and blue indicates $\alpha = 1$. It can be observed that changing the fractional-order α controls the height and sharpness of the soliton. It also reflects memory effects or nonlocal behavior. (**c**) shows a 3D plot at $\alpha = 0.6$ for $t \in [0, 2]$. The soliton spike is sharply concentrated in space but grows dramatically over time. It shows a localized singular behavior that propagates and intensifies. (**d**) shows a contour graph at $\alpha = 0.6$ when $0 < t < 2$. Extremely tight contours can be seen near the origin, indicating a sudden sharp increase in $h(x,t)$. It confirms local singularities in both x and t. Singular solitons have been studied in various nonlinear evolution equations, including those describing optical fibers, quantum gases, and other physical systems.

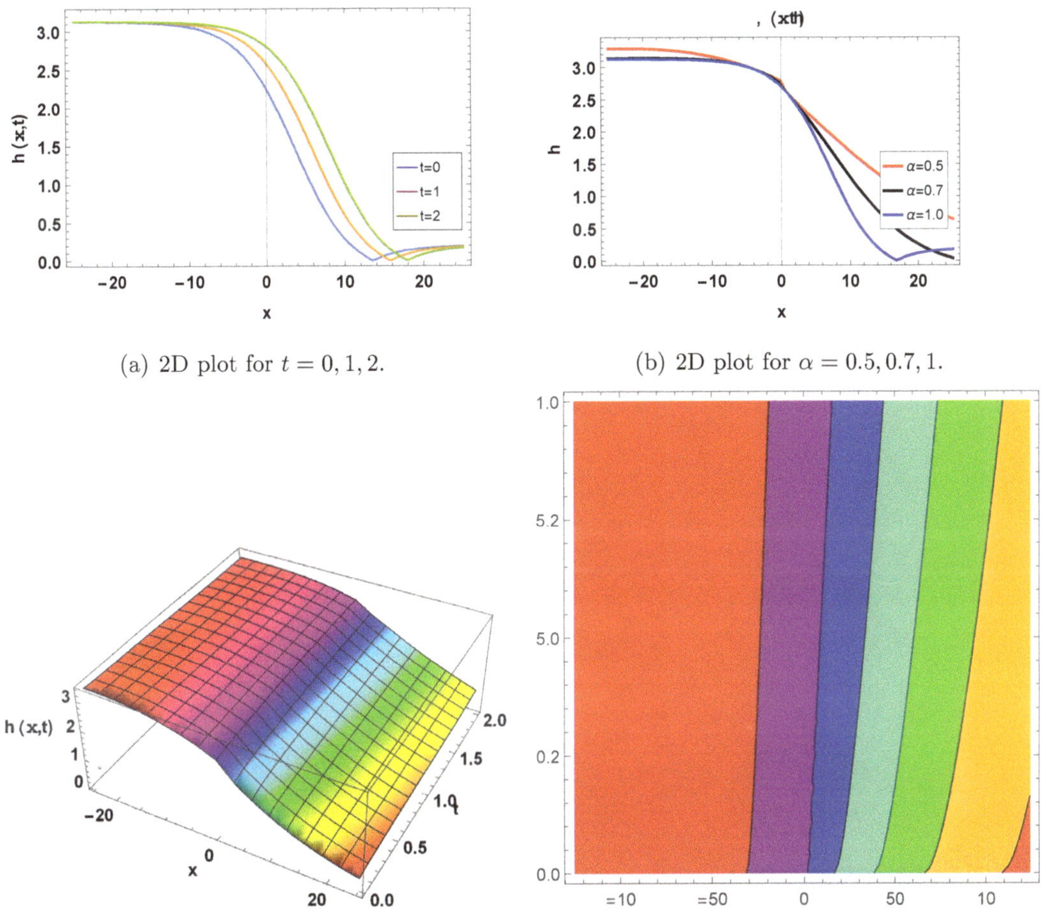

(a) 2D plot for $t = 0, 1, 2$.

(b) 2D plot for $\alpha = 0.5, 0.7, 1$.

(c) 3-D plot when $\alpha = 0.6$

(d) contour plot at $\alpha = 0.6$

Figure 3. Rational soliton. A graph of $h(x,t)$ in Equation (88) for $\alpha_0 = 0.2, a = 0.5$, $b = 0.5$, $\rho = 0.2$, $m = -5$, $r = 1$, $d = 4$, and $\Upsilon = 1$. (**a**) shows a two-dimensional plot for $x \in (-25, 25)$ and $\alpha = 1$, where blue indicates $t = 0$, orange indicates $t = 1$, green indicates $t = 2$. It can be observed that the soliton preserves its structure but shifts in amplitude or position over time. This persistence suggests a stable traveling wave, typical of soliton behavior. (**b**) displays a two-dimensional plot at $x \in (-25, 25)$ and $t \in (0, 2)$, where red indicates $\alpha = 0.5$, black indicates $\alpha = 0.7$, and blue indicates $\alpha = 1$. The parameter α likely controls the nonlinearity or dispersion strength. The variations in shape and height suggest that changing the system parameters can control the wave amplitude or width. (**c**) shows a 3D plot where $\alpha = 0.6$ at $\in [0, 2]$. It provides a comprehensive picture of wave evolution, emphasizing the localized and non-dispersive nature of the rational soliton. (**d**) shows a contour graph at $\alpha = 0.6$ when $0 < t < 2$. The contour pattern illustrates the trajectory of the soliton and how it propagates steadily through space–time. Rational solitons can be found in various fields, including nonlinear optics, water waves, and other areas where nonlinear wave phenomena are studied.

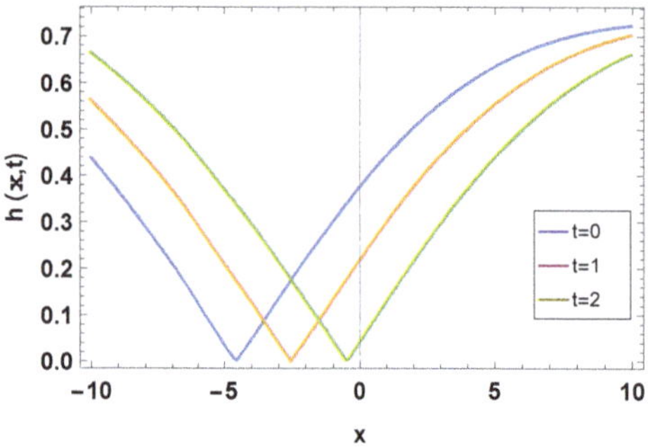

(a) 2D plot when $t = 0, 1, 2$.

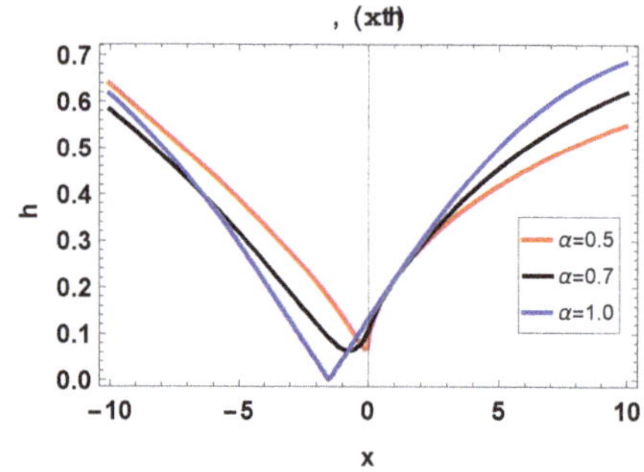

(b) 2D plot when $\alpha = 0.5, 0.7, 1$.

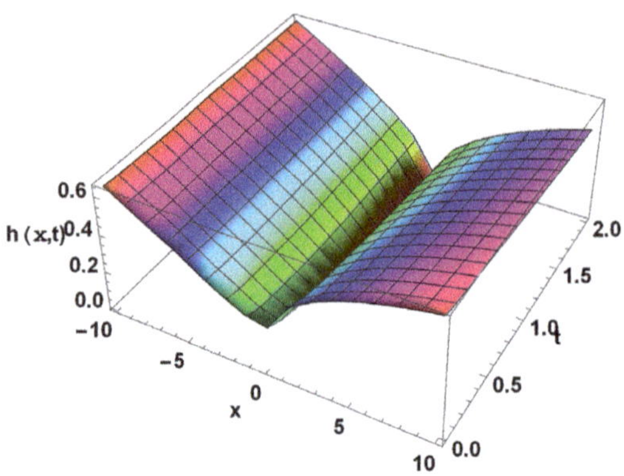

(c) 3-D plot when $\alpha = 0.6$

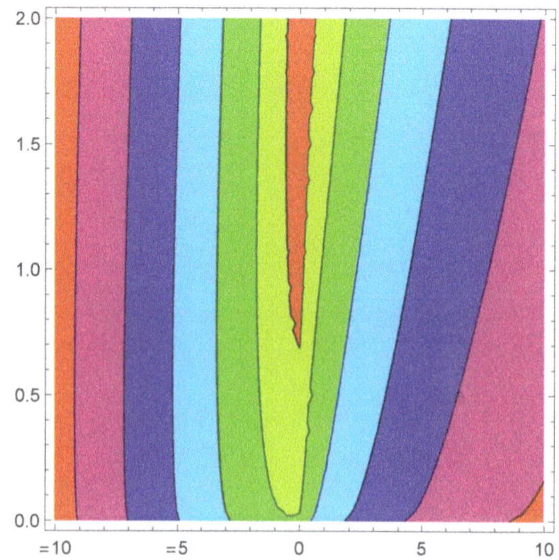

(d) contour plot when $\alpha = 0.6$

Figure 4. Bright–dark soliton solution. Graph of $h(x,t)$ in Equation (118) for $\alpha_0 = 0.2, a = 0.5$, $b = 0.5$, $c = 0.5$, $f = 0.5$, $p = 0.05$, $d = 4$, and $\Upsilon = 1$. (**a**) shows a two-dimensional plot for $x \in [-10, 10]$ and $\alpha = 1$; blue indicates $t = 0$, orange indicates $t = 1$, and green indicates $t = 2$. We can observe that the phases of the wave shift with time. So, the waves are time-dependent. (**b**) displays a two-dimensional plot at $x \in (-10, 10)$ and $t \in (0, 2)$; red indicates $\alpha = 0.5$, black indicates $\alpha = 0.7$, and blue indicates $\alpha = 1$. It can be observed that the phases shift with the increase in the value of α. (**c**) shows a 3D plot at $\alpha = 0.6$, where $t \in [0, 2]$. A sharp transition is shown in both directions. It shows the symmetric property of the wave. (**d**) shows a contour graph at $\alpha = 0.6$ when $0 < t < 2$. Bright–dark solitons are used in the fields of optical communication, optical sensing, and nonlinear optics.

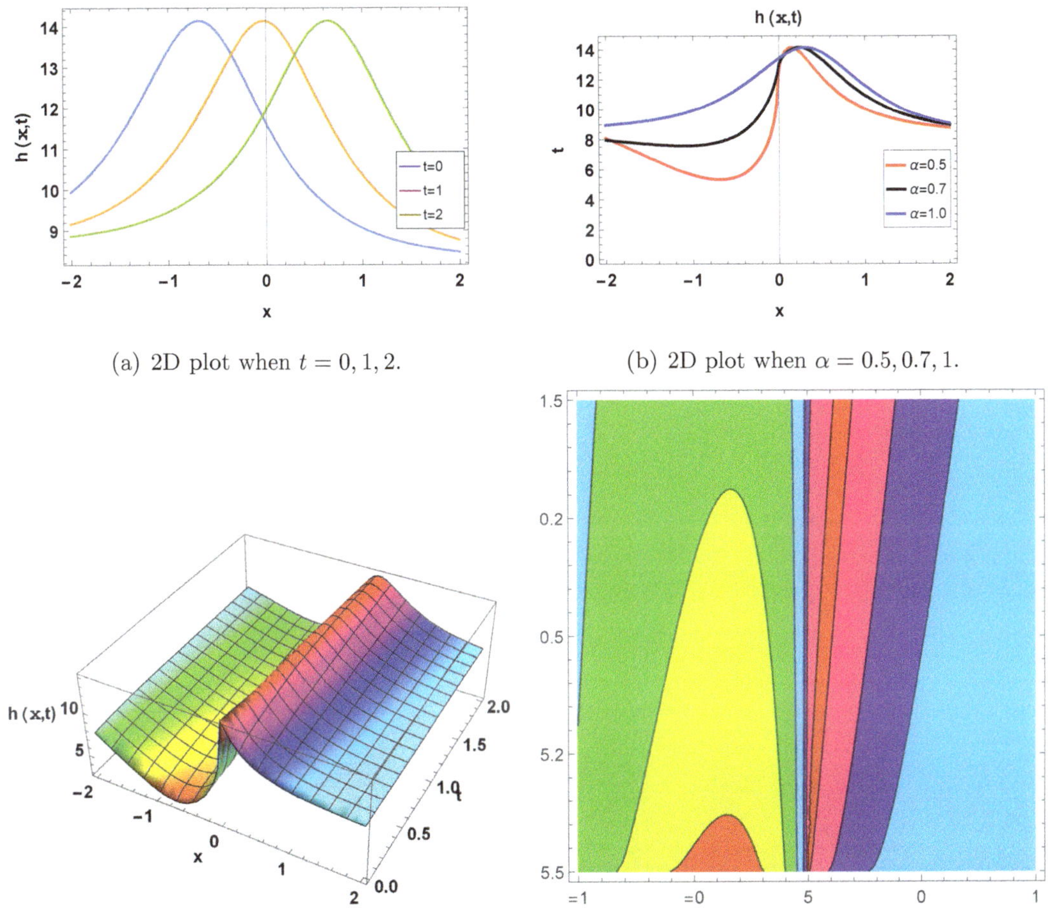

(a) 2D plot when $t = 0, 1, 2$.

(b) 2D plot when $\alpha = 0.5, 0.7, 1$.

(c) 3-D plot when $\alpha = 0.6$

(d) contour plot when $\alpha = 0.6$

Figure 5. Periodic soliton. A graph of $h(x,t)$ in Equation (130) for $\alpha_0 = -0.2, a = 0.5$, $b = 0.5$, $c_1 = 0.5$, $c_2 = 0.3$, $\kappa_1 = 1$, $\kappa_3 = 1.5$, and $\Upsilon = 1$. (**a**) shows a two-dimensional graph, where $x \in [-2, 2]$ for $\alpha = 1$; blue indicates $t = 0$, orange indicates $t = 1$, and green indicates $t = 2$. The phases of the waves change with the change in time. It shows the waves are time-dependent. (**b**) displays a two-dimensional plot at $x \in [-2, 2]$ and $t \in [0, 2]$; red indicates $\alpha = 0.5$, black indicates $\alpha = 0.7$, and blue indicates $\alpha = 1$. The phase of the wave changes with the change in the value of the fractional derivative parameter α. It shows that the phase of the wave is also α-dependent. (**c**) shows a 3D plot at $\alpha = 0.6$ for $t \in [0, 2]$. It shows a wave-like pole in both directions. (**d**) shows a contour graph for $\alpha = 0.6$ when $0 < t < 2$.

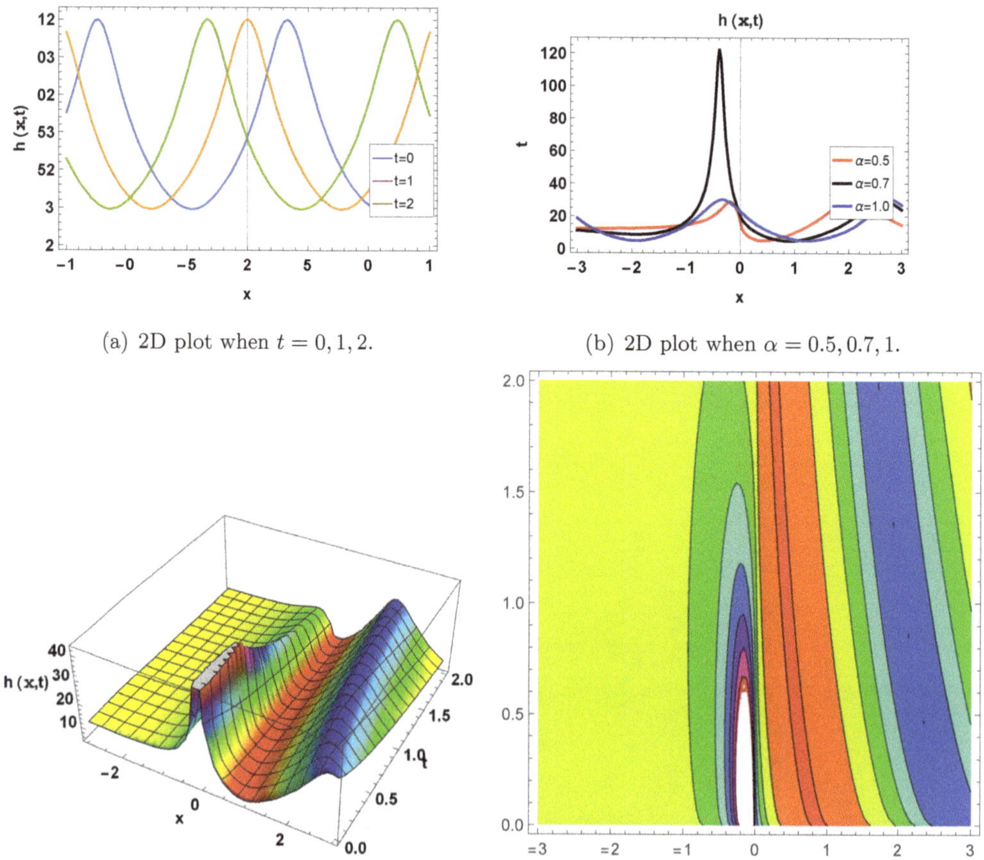

(a) 2D plot when $t = 0, 1, 2$.

(b) 2D plot when $\alpha = 0.5, 0.7, 1$.

(c) 3-D plot when $\alpha = 0.6$

(d) contour plot when $\alpha = 0.6$

Figure 6. Kink-singular soliton. Graph of $h(x,t)$ in Equation (131) for $\alpha_0 = -0.2, a = 0.5$, $b = 0.5$, $c_1 = -0.5$, $c_2 = -0.2$, $\kappa_1 = -1$, $\kappa_3 = 2$, and $\Upsilon = 1$. (**a**) shows a two-dimensional plot for $x \in (-3,3)$ when $\alpha = 1$; blue indicates $t = 0$, orange indicates $t = 1$, and green indicates $t = 2$. It shows that the phases of the wave shift with time. So, the waves are time-dependent. (**b**) displays a two-dimensional plot at $x \in (-3,3)$ and $t \in (0,2)$; red indicates $\alpha = 0.5$, black indicates $\alpha = 0.7$, and blue indicates $\alpha = 1$. It shows that the phases of the waves also change with the change in α. (**c**) shows a 3D plot for $\alpha = 0.6$ at $t \in [0,2]$. It shows wave-like poles. (**d**) shows a contour graph for $\alpha = 0.6$ when $0 < t < 2$. Kink-singular solitons are used to explain models' phenomena in nerve fibers, liquid crystals, etc.

7. The Stability Analysis (SA)

Stability analysis was employed to describe how the system reacts over time and how it acts in response to outside influences. In order to describe the stability of an equation in applications, SA is carried out by testing some obtained solutions and applying the characteristics of the Hamiltonian system. The stability of various models has been analyzed in the literature, including [31,32]. Let us examine the selected equation. We define the Hamiltonian transformation for the stability of Equation (1) as [33,34]

$$\mathcal{S} = \frac{1}{2} \int_{-\infty}^{\infty} h^2 \, dx. \tag{132}$$

where $h(x,t)$ denotes the possibility of power, and $\mathcal{S}$ denotes the momentum factor. We now present a prerequisite for stable soliton solutions.

$$\frac{\partial \mathcal{S}}{\partial \lambda} > 0, \tag{133}$$

where λ indicates the wave speed. Using Equation (88) in Equation (132) provides

$$\mathcal{S} = \frac{1}{2}\int_{-6}^{6}(\alpha_0 + \frac{12m\rho\log(d)}{a+b}(d^{\rho^{\frac{\Gamma(1+Y)}{\alpha}(x^\alpha - \frac{t^\alpha}{-\rho^2\log^2(d)+1})}} - m)^{-1})^2 dx, \tag{134}$$

Equation (134) provides the solution:

$$\begin{aligned}\mathcal{S} = {} & (6(\alpha_0^2(a+b)^2 - 2\alpha_0 m(a+b)(d^{\rho^{\frac{\Gamma(1+Y)}{\alpha}(-\lambda t^\alpha - 6)}} - d^{\rho^{\frac{\Gamma(1+Y)}{\alpha}(6-\lambda t^\alpha)}} + 12m\rho\log(d)) \\ & +6m^2\rho\log(d)(24m^2\rho\log(d) - (d^{\rho^{\frac{\Gamma(1+Y)}{\alpha}(-\lambda t^\alpha-6)}} - d^{\rho^{\frac{\Gamma(1+Y)}{\alpha}(6-\lambda t^\alpha)}})(d^{\rho^{\frac{\Gamma(1+Y)}{\alpha}(-\lambda t^\alpha-6)}} \\ & +d^{\rho^{\frac{\Gamma(1+Y)}{\alpha}(6-\lambda t^\alpha)}} - 4m))))/((a+b)^2).\end{aligned} \tag{135}$$

where $\frac{1}{-\rho^2\log^2(d)+1} = \lambda$.

By putting the result given in Equation (135) into Equation (133) and using $\lambda = \frac{1}{-\rho^2\log^2(d)+1}$, we obtain the following:

$$\begin{aligned} & (6(6m^2\rho\log(d)((\rho t\log(d)d^{\rho^{\frac{\Gamma(1+Y)}{\alpha}(\frac{t^\alpha}{\rho^2\log^2(d)-1}+6)}} - \rho t\log(d)d^{\rho^{\frac{\Gamma(1+Y)}{\alpha}(\frac{t^\alpha}{\rho^2\log^2(d)-1}-6)}}) \\ & (d^{\rho^{\frac{\Gamma(1+Y)}{\alpha}(\frac{t^\alpha}{\rho^2\log^2(d)-1}-6)}} + d^{\rho^{\frac{\Gamma(1+Y)}{\alpha}(\frac{t^\alpha}{\rho^2\log^2(d)-1}+6)}} - 4m) + (d^{\rho^{\frac{\Gamma(1+Y)}{\alpha}(\frac{t^\alpha}{\rho^2\log^2(d)-1}+6)}} - \\ & d^{\rho^{\frac{\Gamma(1+Y)}{\alpha}(\frac{t^\alpha}{\rho^2\log^2(d)-1}-6)}})(\rho t\log(d)d^{\rho^{\frac{\Gamma(1+Y)}{\alpha}(\frac{t^\alpha}{\rho^2\log^2(d)-1}-6)}} + \rho t\log(d)d^{\rho^{\frac{\Gamma(1+Y)}{\alpha}(\frac{t^\alpha}{\rho^2\log^2(d)-1}+6)}}))- \\ & 2\alpha_0 m(a+b)(\rho t\log(d)d^{\rho^{\frac{\Gamma(1+Y)}{\alpha}(\frac{t^\alpha}{\rho^2\log^2(d)-1}-6)}} - \rho t\log(d)d^{\rho^{\frac{\Gamma(1+Y)}{\alpha}(\frac{t^\alpha}{\rho^2\log^2(d)-1}+6)}})))/((a+b)^2) > 0.\end{aligned} \tag{136}$$

By using the values $Y = 1, \alpha_0 = 0.2, a = 0.5, b = 0.5, m = -5, \rho = 0.2, d = 4, t = 1$ in the above expression (136), we ob tain the solution: $14626.2 > 0$.

Hence, Equation (88) satisfies the given condition. So, Equation (88) is a stable solution. Similarly, we can check the stability of the other solutions.

8. Modulation Instability (MI) Analysis

A steady-state method for solving the generalized shallow water wave equation model is [35,36]

$$h(x,t) = (H(x,t) + \sqrt{\tau})e^{\iota\tau t}. \tag{137}$$

where τ is the optical power of normalizing.

Insert Equation (137) into Equation (1). Using linearity, one gets

$$-\iota\tau H_x - H_{xt} - H_{xx} + \iota\tau H_{xxx} + H_{xxxt} = 0. \tag{138}$$

Suppose the solution of Equation (138) is

$$H(x,t) = H_1 e^{\iota(\rho x - \omega t)} + H_2 e^{-\iota(\rho x - \omega t)}. \tag{139}$$

Here, ρ and ω are constants. Equation (139) is substituted into Equation (138). After solving the determinant of the coefficient matrix, we obtain the dispersion relation by adding the coefficients of $e^{\iota(\rho x-\omega t)}$ and $e^{-\iota(\rho x-\omega t)}$.

$$-\rho^6\tau^2 + \rho^6\omega^2 - 2\rho^5\omega - 2\rho^4\tau^2 + 2\rho^4\omega^2 + \rho^4 - 2\rho^3\omega - \rho^2\tau^2 + \rho^2\omega^2 = 0. \tag{140}$$

The dispersion relation can be found in Equation (140) for q, which results in

$$\omega = \pm\tau + \frac{\sqrt{\rho^2}}{\rho^2+1}. \tag{141}$$

The steady-state stability is demonstrated by the obtained dispersion relation. The steady-state outcome is not stable when the wave number ω is not real because the perturbation increases exponentially. However, a steady state becomes stable against minor perturbations if ω is not imaginary. The result is an unstable steady state if

$$\rho^2 < 0. \tag{142}$$

It is possible to acquire the MI gain spectrum $G(p)$ as follows:

$$G(\rho) = 2Im(\omega) = \pm\tau + \frac{\sqrt{\rho^2}}{\rho^2+1}. \tag{143}$$

9. Findings and Analysis

Now, we compare our solutions with the existing solutions to the considered model. By using the $(\frac{G'}{G'+G+A})$ expansion technique in [24], distinct types of periodic and singular wave solutions are obtained. By applying the class $f(G, G')$ expansion scheme in [25], different kinds of traveling wave solutions are obtained. By utilizing the modified rational sine–cosine method in [26], many explicit wave solutions are obtained. Similar models are discussed in [37,38] through the modified auxiliary equation, (G'/G) expansion, and the improved (G'/G) expansion techniques. We studied the fractional form of the considered equation to understand the phenomena. We utilized effective techniques: the improved (G'/G) expansion technique and the modified extended direct algebraic technique. As a result, we obtained various exact solitons, including periodic, singular, bright–dark, kink-singular, rational solitons, and many others. The impact of the fractional derivative on the obtained solutions is also shown through 2D graphs in Figures 1–6. The validity of the obtained solutions was checked by putting them back into the considered model. By comparing the obtained results with the existing results, we validated our results. Moreover, the stability of the obtained solutions was also checked. Further, the modulation instability is explained with two-dimensional, three-dimensional, and contour graphs as shown in Figure 7. The achieved solutions are useful for future studies of the considered model. Furthermore, the effect of the following terms can be discussed in future studies of the model.

(i) A body force term, representing the applied force or flow;

(ii) A density gradient term, representing the effect of density variations on the wave;

(iii) A viscosity term, representing the effect of friction or dissipation on the wave.

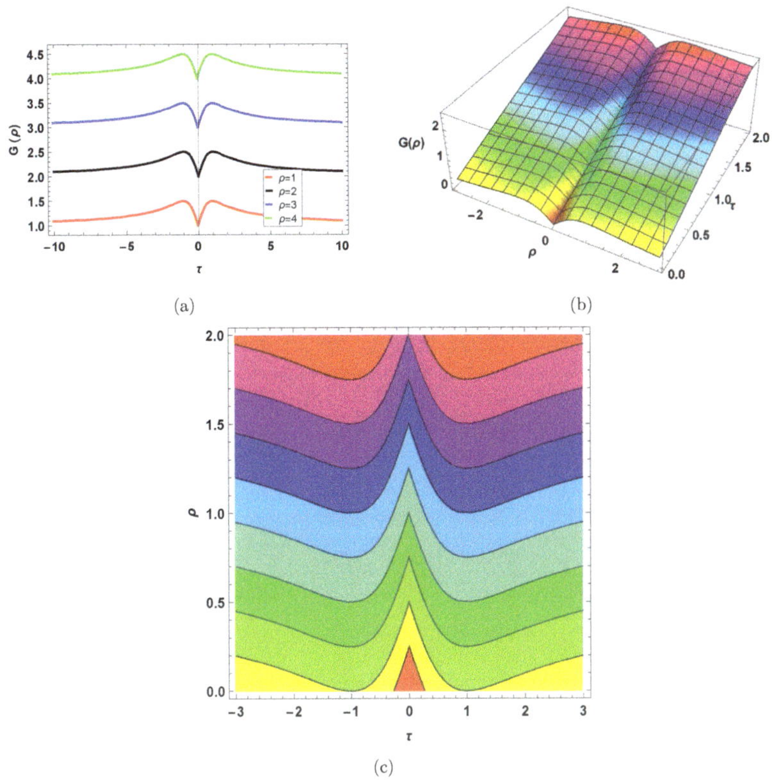

Figure 7. MI gain spectrum. This figure is drawn for the Equation (143). (**a**) represents the two-dimensional graph for $\tau \in (-10, 10)$. (**b**) shows the three-dimensional graph for $\tau \in (0, 2)$ and $\rho \in (-3, 3)$. (**c**) represents the contour graph for $\tau \in (0, 2)$ and $\rho \in (-3, 3)$.

10. Conclusions

This paper successfully obtained diverse exact soliton solutions for a truncated M-fractional nonlinear (1 + 1)-dimensional generalized shallow water wave equation. We employed two efficient techniques: the improved (G'/G) expansion technique and the modified extended direct algebraic technique. The obtained solutions included kink, dark–bright, periodic, and various other wave solitons. We examined the impact of the fractional derivative. Mathematica software was utilized to obtain and validate our results. Additionally, in Figures 1–6, we used 2D, 3D, and contour graphs to visualize some of the obtained wave solitons. Our results can be applied in ocean engineering, fluid dynamics, and other fields. The stability of the governing model was also investigated. In conclusion, these methods are simple and very efficient when applied for solving nonlinear fractional models.

Author Contributions: Conceptualization, H.Q., A.S.A.N. and A.A.; Methodology, A.S.A.N. and A.A.; Formal analysis, A.S.A.N.; Writing—original draft, H.Q.; Writing—review & editing, H.Q.; Supervision, H.Q. and A.A.; Project administration, H.Q.; Funding acquisition, A.A. All authors have read and agreed to the published version of the manuscript.

Funding: This work was supported by the Deanship of Scientific Research, Vice Presidency for Graduate Studies and Scientific Research, King Faisal University, Saudi Arabia [KFU252576].

Data Availability Statement: The datasets used and/or analyzed during the current study are available from the corresponding author upon reasonable request.

Acknowledgments: This work was supported by the Deanship of Scientific Research, Vice Presidency for Graduate Studies and Scientific Research, King Faisal University, Saudi Arabia [KFU252576].

Conflicts of Interest: The authors declare that there are no conflicts of interest.

References

1. Khan, M.I.; Farooq, A.; Nisar, K.S.; Shah, N.A. Unveiling new exact solutions of the unstable nonlinear Schrödinger equation using the improved modified Sardar sub-equation method. *Results Phys.* **2024**, *59*, 107593. [CrossRef]
2. Islam, S.M.R. Bifurcation analysis and exact wave solutions of the nano-ionic currents equation: Via two analytical techniques. *Results Phys.* **2024**, *58*, 107536. [CrossRef]
3. Mehdi, K.B.; Mehdi, Z.; Samreen, S.; Siddique, I.; Elmandouh, A.A.; Elbrolosy, M.E.; Osman, M.S. Novel exact traveling wave solutions of the space-time fractional Sharma Tasso-Olver equation via three reliable methods. *Partial. Differ. Equ. Appl. Math.* **2024**, *11*, 100784. [CrossRef]
4. Hashemi, M.S.; Bayram, M.; Riaz, M.B.; Baleanu, D. Bifurcation analysis, and exact solutions of the two-mode Cahn–Allen equation by a novel variable coefficient auxiliary equation method. *Results Phys.* **2024**, *64*, 107882. [CrossRef]
5. Akram, G.; Sadaf, M.; Arshed, S.; Iqbal, M.A.B. Simulations of exact explicit solutions of simplified modified form of Camassa–Holm equation. *Opt. Quantum Electron.* **2024**, *56*, 1037. [CrossRef]
6. Bilal, M.; Ren, J.; Alsubaie, A.S.A.; Mahmoud, K.H.; Inc, M. Dynamics of nonlinear diverse wave propagation to Improved Boussinesq model in weakly dispersive medium of shallow waters or ion acoustic waves using efficient technique. *Opt. Quantum Electron.* **2024**, *56*, 21. [CrossRef]
7. Qawaqneh, H.; Jari, H.A.; Altalbe, A.; Bekir, A. Stability analysis, modulation instability, and the analytical wave solitons to the fractional Boussinesq-Burgers system. *Phys. Scr.* **2024**, *99*, 125235. [CrossRef]
8. Zhao, X.H.; Li, S. Dark soliton solutions for a variable coefficient higher-order Schrödinger equation in the dispersion decreasing fibers. *Appl. Math. Lett.* **2022**, *132*, 108159. [CrossRef]
9. Fan, L.; Bao, T. Similarity wave solutions of Whitham–Broer–Kaup equations in the oceanic shallow water. *Phys. Fluids* **2024**, *36*, 072110. [CrossRef]
10. Han, T.; Liang, Y.; Fan, W. Dynamics and soliton solutions of the perturbed Schrödinger-Hirota equation with cubic-quintic-septic nonlinearity in dispersive media. *AIMS Math.* **2025**, *10*, 754–776. [CrossRef]
11. Zhao, S. Multiple solutions and dynamical behavior of the periodically excited beta-fractional generalized KdV-ZK system. *Phys. Scr.* **2025**, *100*, 045244. [CrossRef]
12. Batiha, I.M.; Njadat, S.A.; Batyha, R.M.; Zraiqat, A.; Dababneh, A.; Momani, S. Design fractional-order PID controllers for single-joint robot arm model. *Int. J. Adv. Soft Comput. Appl.* **2022**, *14*, 96–114. [CrossRef]
13. Qawaqneh, H.; Zafar, A.; Raheel, M.; Zaagan, A.A.; Zahran, E.H.; Cevikel, A.; Bekir, A. New soliton solutions of M-fractional Westervelt model in ultrasound imaging via two analytical techniques. *Opt. Quantum Electron.* **2024**, *56*, 737. [CrossRef]
14. Judeh, D.A.; Hammad, M.M. Applications of Conformable Fractional Pareto Probability Distribution. *Int. J. Adv. Soft Comput. Appl.* **2022**, *14*, 115–124.
15. Zhang, K.; Cao, J. Dynamic behavior and modulation instability of the generalized coupled fractional nonlinear Helmholtz equation with cubic–quintic term. *Open Phys.* **2025**, *23*, 20250144. [CrossRef]
16. Qawaqneh, H.; Alrashedi, Y. Mathematical and physical analysis of fractional Estevez–Mansfield–Clarkson equation. *Fractal Fract.* **2024**, *8*, 467. [CrossRef]
17. Han, T.; Zhao, L. Bifurcation, sensitivity analysis and exact traveling wave solutions for the stochastic fractional Hirota–Maccari system. *Results Phys.* **2023**, *47*, 106349. [CrossRef]
18. Adeyemo, O.D. Real-world applications of analytic travelling wave solutions of a (3 + 1)-dimensional Hirota–Satsuma–Ito-Like system via polynomial complete discriminant system and elementary integral technique. *Int. J. Appl. Comput. Math.* **2025**, *11*, 23. [CrossRef]
19. Al Nuwairan, M.; Elmandouh, A. Modification to an auxiliary function method for solving space-fractional Stochastic Regularized Long-Wave equation. *Fractal Fract.* **2025**, *9*, 298. [CrossRef]
20. Ashraf, F.; Ashraf, R.; Akgül, A. Traveling waves solutions of Hirota–Ramani equation by modified extended direct algebraic method and new extended direct algebraic method. *Int. J. Mod. Phys. B* **2024**, *38*, 2450329. [CrossRef]
21. Shehab, M.F.; El-Sheikh, M.; Ahmed, H.M.; El-Gaber, A.A.; Mirzazadeh, M.; Eslami, M. Extraction new solitons and other exact solutions for nonlinear stochastic concatenation model by modified extended direct algebraic method. *Opt. Quantum Electron.* **2024**, *56*, 1166. [CrossRef]

22. Hawlader, F.; Kumar, D. A variety of exact analytical solutions of extended shallow water wave equations via improved (G'/G)-expansion method. *Int. J. Phys. Res.* **2017**, *5*, 21–27. [CrossRef]
23. Shakeel, M.; Mohyud-Din, S.T. Improved (G'/G)-expansion and extended tanh methods for (2+1)-dimensional Calogero–Bogoyavlenskii–Schiff equation. *Alex. Eng. J.* **2015**, *54*, 27–33. [CrossRef]
24. Mia, R.; Paul, A.K. New exact solutions to the generalized shallow water wave equation. *arXiv* **2024**, arXiv:2401.01098. [CrossRef]
25. Wang, X. New Explicit Exact Solutions for the (1 + 1)-Dimensional Generalized Shallow Water Wave Equation. *Adv. Appl. Math.* **2017**, *6*, 787–794. [CrossRef]
26. Li, W.; Zuo, H. New Explicit Exact Solutions for the (1 + 1) Dimensional Generalized Shallow Water Wave Equation. *Asian Res. J. Math.* **2024**, *20*, 163–176. [CrossRef]
27. Sulaiman, T.A.; Yel, G.; Bulut, H. M-fractional solitons and periodic wave solutions to the Hirota–Maccari system. *Mod. Phys. Lett. B* **2019**, *33*, 1950052. [CrossRef]
28. Sousa, J.V.D.A.C.; Oliveira, E.C.D. A new truncated M-fractional derivative type unifying some fractional derivative types with classical properties. *Int. J. Anal. Appl.* **2018**, *16*, 83–96. [CrossRef]
29. Bilal, M.; Iqbal, J.; Ali, R.; Awwad, F.A.; Ismail, E.A.A. Exploring Families of Solitary Wave Solutions for the Fractional Coupled Higgs System Using Modified Extended Direct Algebraic Method. *Fractal Fract.* **2023**, *7*, 653. [CrossRef]
30. Sahoo, S.; Ray, S.S.; Abdou, M.A. New exact solutions for time-fractional Kaup-Kupershmidt equation using improved (G'/G)-expansion and extended (G'/G)-expansion methods. *Alex. Eng. J.* **2020**, *59*, 3105–3110. [CrossRef]
31. Tariq, K.U.; Wazwaz, A.-M.; Javed, R. Construction of different wave structures, stability analysis and modulation instability of the coupled nonlinear Drinfel'd–Sokolov–Wilson model. *Chaos Solitons Fractals* **2023**, *166*, 112903. [CrossRef]
32. Zulfiqar, H.; Aashiq, A.; Tariq, K.U.; Ahmad, H.; Almohsen, B.; Aslam, M.; Rehman, H.U. On the solitonic wave structures and stability analysis of the stochastic nonlinear Schrödinger equation with the impact of multiplicative noise. *Optik* **2023**, *289*, 171250. [CrossRef]
33. Altalbe, A.; Taishiyeva, A.; Myrzakulov, R.; Bekir, A.; Zaagan, A.A. Effect of truncated M-fractional derivative on the new exact solitons to the Shynaray-IIA equation and stability analysis. *Results Phys.* **2024**, *57*, 107422. [CrossRef]
34. Qawaqneh, H.; Manafian, J.; Alsubaie, A.S.; Ahmad, H. Investigation of exact solitons to the quartic Rosenau-Kawahara-Regularized-Long-Wave fluid model with fractional derivative and qualitative analysis. *Phys. Scr.* **2024**, *100*, 015270. [CrossRef]
35. Rehman, S.; Ahmad, J. Modulation instability analysis and optical solitons in birefringent fibers to RKL equation without four wave mixing. *Alex. Eng. J.* **2021**, *60*, 1339–1354. [CrossRef]
36. Alomair, A.; Al Naim, A.S.; Bekir, A. Exploration of Soliton Solutions to the Special Korteweg–De Vries Equation with a Stability Analysis and Modulation Instability. *Mathematics* **2024**, *13*, 54. [CrossRef]
37. Sahoo, S.; Ray, S.S. Solitary wave solutions for time fractional third order modified KdV equation using two reliable techniques (G'/G)-expansion method and improved (G'/G)-expansion method. *Phys. A* **2016**, *448*, 265–282. [CrossRef]
38. Ali, K.K.; Alotaibi, M.F.; Omri, M.; Mehanna, M.S.; Abdel-Aty, A.-H. Some Traveling Wave Solutions to the Fifth-Order Nonlinear Wave Equation Using Three Techniques: Bernoulli Sub-ODE, Modified Auxiliary Equation, and (G'/G)-Expansion Methods. *J. Math.* **2023**, *2023*, 7063620. [CrossRef]

mathematics

MDPI

Article

Very Large Angular Oscillations (Up to 3π/4) of the Physical Pendulum—A Simple Trigonometric Analytical Solution

Joao C. Fernandes

Physics Department, Instituto Superior Técnico, Av. Rovisco Pais, 1049-001 Lisboa, Portugal; joao.ferreira.fernandes@tecnico.ulisboa.pt

Abstract

The oscillatory properties of pendular motion, along with the associated energetic conditions, are used to induce analytical functions capable of simultaneously describing the angular position and velocity. To describe the angular position of a generic pendulum, for very large amplitudes of oscillation, we used the numerical solutions obtained from the numerical resolution of the differential equation of motion. The solver software needed was built using the LabView 2019 platform, but any other ODE solver containing peak and valley detectors can be used. The fitting software and plots were performed with the ORIGIN 7.0 program, but also other equivalent programs can be used. For a non-damped pendulum, an analytical model is proposed, built from simple trigonometric functions, but containing the important physical information of the dependence between the period and amplitude of oscillation. The application of the proposed model, using the numerical solutions of the non-approximated differential equation of motion, shows very good agreement, less than 0.01%, for large amplitudes, up to $3\pi/4$.

Keywords: undamped pendulum; very large angular oscillations; friction; damped oscillator

MSC: 70-10

1. Introduction

When pendula motion is studied in university graduate courses large angle oscillations are usually omitted.

Two reasons contribute to that omission; the period is amplitude-dependent and there is a lack of simple periodic functions able to reproduce correctly the angular dislocation.

The period amplitude dependence problem can be removed because there is an analytical solution, a function involving the first kind complete elliptical integral that is well known by academics, with calculation nowadays simplified as it is included in several mathematical software packages used widely.

The second problem, a periodic function to describe $\theta(t)$ is more paradigmatic because the usual function $\cos(\omega t)$ is inaccurate for large angle oscillations, even when the frequency amplitude dependence $\omega(\theta_0)$ is correctly introduced (Figures 1–3).

For these reasons, most of the referenced authors, and we cite several [1–13], seek analytical solutions in the form of a sum of sinusoidal functions, truncating this sum when the error is acceptable.

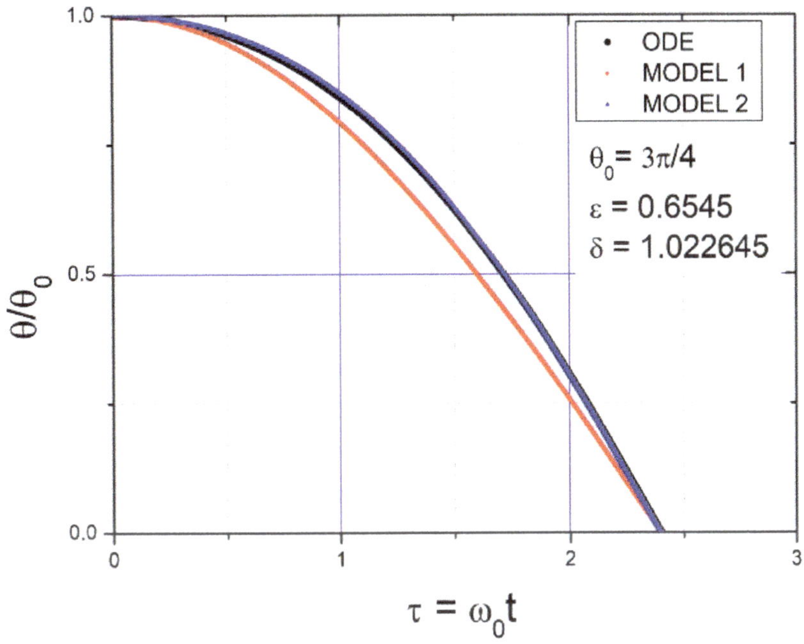

Figure 1. ODE are numerical data. Relative angle, for the initial quarter period of a pendulum dropping from an initial angle $\theta_0 = \frac{3\pi}{4}$.

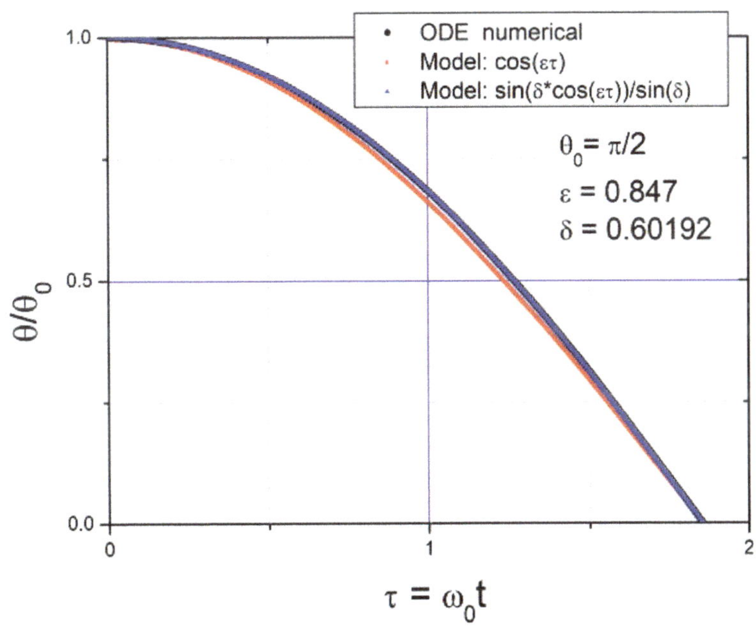

Figure 2. ODE are numerical data. Relative angle, for the initial quarter period of a pendulum dropping from an initial angle $\theta_0 = \frac{\pi}{2}$.

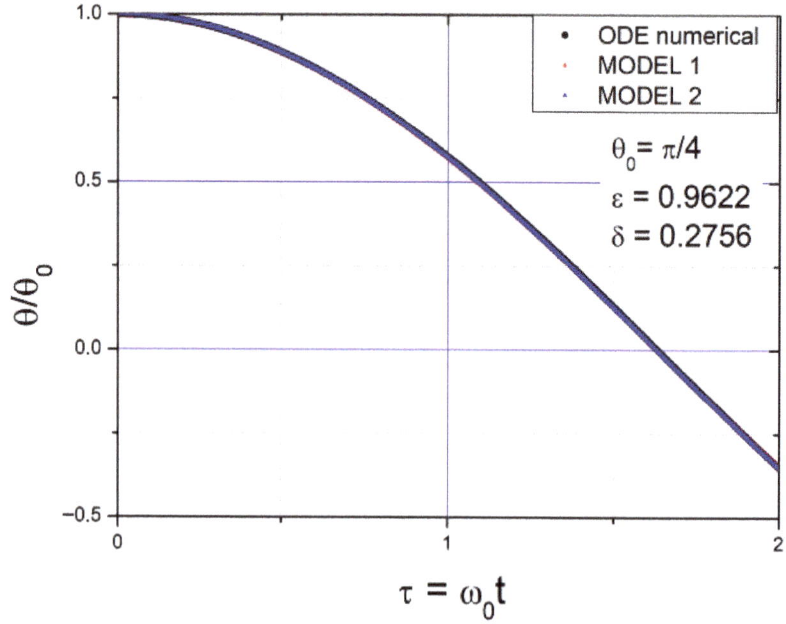

Figure 3. ODE are numerical data. Both models describe very well the relative deviation during the initial quarter period of a pendulum dropping from an initial angle: $\theta_0 = \frac{\pi}{4}$.

What we propose in this article is different, a simple trigonometric analytical solution, of the type $\frac{\sin(\delta\cos(\omega t))}{\sin(\delta)}$ for the angular deviation of a pendulum without damping, up to an initial angle of 135°.

We also showed that its derivative, the angular velocity, also satisfies the data obtained in the numerical solution of the oscillation ODE.

The letters introduced follow the usual nomenclature: $\theta(t)$ stands for angle deviation, θ_0 is the initial angle, and $\omega = \frac{2\pi}{T}$ is the angular frequency (T is period, time between three consecutive zeros of the speed). It is assumed in all examples that the pendulum is released at the initial time t = 0 from angle θ_0.

The results presented are valid for any physical pendulum of mass m, inertia moment I, and distance L from pivot to the center of mass. The natural frequency is therefore $\omega_0^2 = \frac{mgL}{I}$.

In the following section, we will focus our attention on the frictionless pendulum.

The traditional Model 1 is presented, which, as we already know, does not provide an adequate response, either for the amplitude or for the velocity, for large initial angles.

We then develop our proposed Model 2, which, as will be shown in Figures 1–6, describes amplitude and velocity along the entire path with great accuracy. This section may be useful in teaching pendulum motion at engineering universities, without worrying about friction forces.

In Section 3, we will address the pendulum with friction, the damped pendulum. The introduction of friction forces in our pendulum requires special care with the solution of the new ODE. For this reason, we consider that Section 3 can be considered as an extra of the Appendix type. As such, it may only be of interest to those who wish to study pendulum situations with various friction forces.

In this article, we will introduce three types of frictional forces: constant, proportional to velocity, and proportional to the square of velocity. In a recent article [14], the author addresses this theme without concern for describing large initial angles.

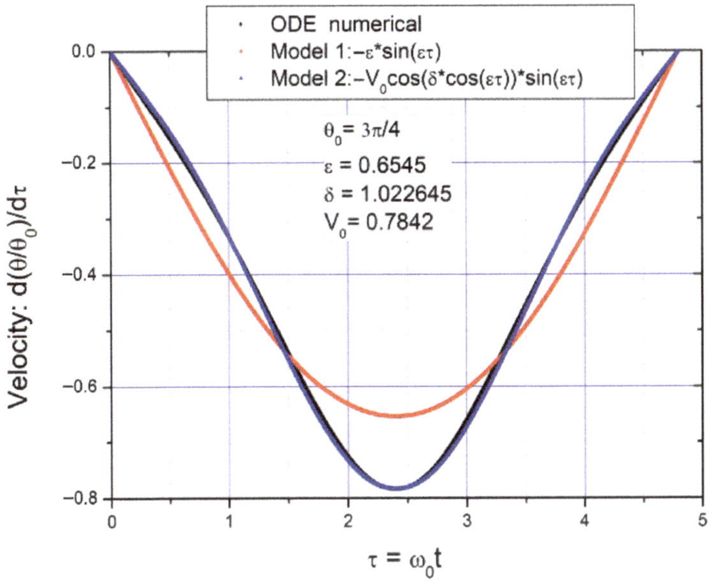

Figure 4. ODE are numerical data. Velocity evolution, for the initial half period of a pendulum dropping from an initial angle $\theta_0 = \frac{3\pi}{4}$.

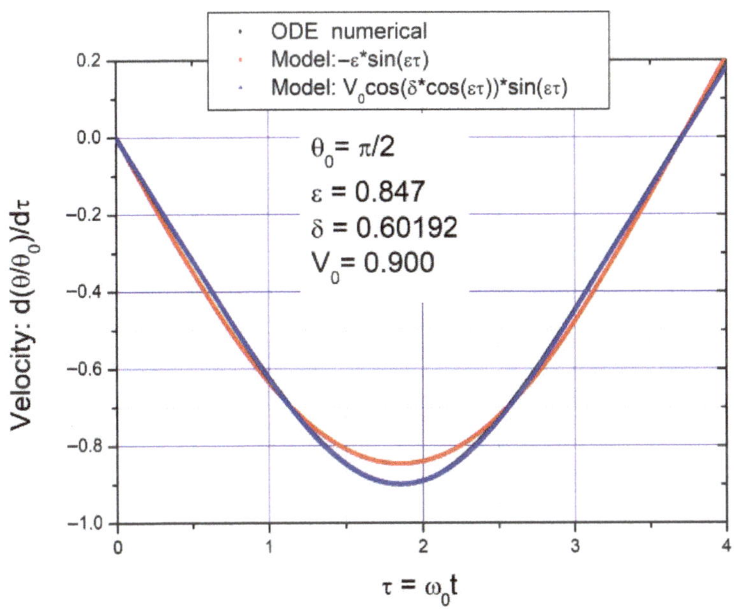

Figure 5. ODE are numerical data. Velocity evolution for the initial half period of a pendulum dropping from an initial angle $\theta_0 = \frac{\pi}{2}$.

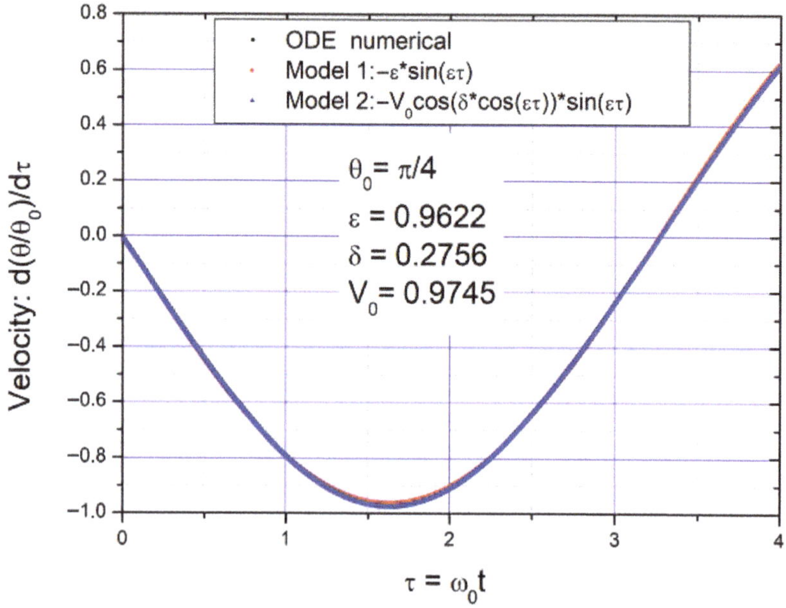

Figure 6. ODE are numerical data. Velocity evolution for the initial half period of a pendulum dropping from an initial angle $\theta_0 = \frac{\pi}{4}$.

2. The Undamped Pendulum

2.1. Differential Equations and Period

The fundamental equations governing motion and energy of a generic undamped physical pendulum are simpler to write:

$$I\frac{d^2\theta}{dt^2} = -mgL\sin(\theta) \Leftrightarrow \frac{d^2\theta}{dt^2} = -\omega_0^2\sin(\theta) \quad (1)$$

$$\frac{1}{2}I\left(\frac{d\theta}{dt}\right)^2 - mgL\cos(\theta) = -mgL \Leftrightarrow \left(\frac{d\theta}{dt}\right)^2 = 2\omega_0^2(\cos(\theta) - \cos(\theta_0)) \quad (2)$$

The extrema of $\theta(t)$ are the nulls of velocity: $\frac{d\theta}{dt} = 0 \Rightarrow \theta_{extrema} = \pm\theta_0$.

The extrema of velocity are nulls of acceleration:

$$\sin(\theta) = 0 \Rightarrow \left(\frac{d\theta}{dt}\right)_{extrema} = 2\omega_0\sin\left(\frac{\theta_0}{2}\right) \quad (3)$$

Notice that Equation (2) can be easily obtained by multiplying Equation (1) by $d\theta$ and integrating once.

To obtain information about the period, it is necessary to solve Equation (2) to time.

Assuming that the pendulum falls from the maximum angle,

$$dt = -\frac{d\theta}{\omega_0\sqrt{2(\cos(\theta) - \cos(\theta_0))}} \Rightarrow t = -\int_{\theta_0}^{\theta}\frac{d\theta}{\omega_0\sqrt{2(\cos(\theta) - \cos(\theta_0))}} \quad (4)$$

Using transformation to the semi angles, Equation (4) writes

$$t = -\int_{\theta_0}^{\theta}\frac{d\theta}{2\omega_0\sqrt{\sin^2\left(\frac{\theta_0}{2}\right) - \sin^2\left(\frac{\theta}{2}\right)}} \quad (5)$$

This integral can be again transformed, using $\sin\left(\frac{\theta}{2}\right) = \sin\left(\frac{\theta_0}{2}\right)\sin(\varphi)$. Note that when θ is maximum $\varphi = \frac{\pi}{2}$ and when θ is minimum $\varphi = -\frac{\pi}{2}$. When θ is null $\varphi = 0$. When it starts from the maximum,

$$t = -\int_{\frac{\pi}{2}}^{\varphi} \frac{d\varphi}{\omega_0\sqrt{1 - \sin^2\left(\frac{\theta_0}{2}\right)\sin^2\varphi}}$$

The quarter period is reached when $\theta = 0$, that is $\varphi = 0$,

$$\frac{T}{4} = \frac{1}{\omega_0}\int_0^{\frac{\pi}{2}} \frac{d\varphi}{\sqrt{1 - \sin^2\left(\frac{\theta_0}{2}\right)\sin^2\varphi}} \tag{6}$$

This integral is the complete first order elliptic integral $K\left(\sin^2\left(\frac{\theta_0}{2}\right); \frac{\pi}{2}\right)$, tabulated and found in mathematical packages as a predefined function. The expression for the period is

$$T = \frac{4}{\omega_0}K\left(\sin^2\left(\frac{\theta_0}{2}\right); \frac{\pi}{2}\right) = T_0\frac{2}{\pi}K\left(\sin^2\left(\frac{\theta_0}{2}\right)\right) \tag{7}$$

The ratio between frequencies will be widely used and is designated by $\varepsilon(\theta_0)$,

$$\varepsilon(\theta_0) = \frac{\omega}{\omega_0} = \frac{T_0}{T} = \frac{\pi}{2K\left(\sin^2\left(\frac{\theta_0}{2}\right)\right)} \tag{8}$$

2.2. Solutions for Angle and Velocity

2.2.1. Model 1

Knowing the period we concentrate our attention into the periodic analytical function able to reproduce the angular dislocation. The simpler choice is the usual trigonometric $\cos(\omega t)$, that is, the exact solution for the common harmonic oscillator:

$$\begin{cases} \theta(t) = \theta_0\cos(\omega(\theta_0)t) \\ \frac{d\theta}{dt} = -\omega\theta_0\sin(\omega(\theta_0)t) \end{cases} \tag{9}$$

This choice seems to be not accurate for large initial angles.

The comparison with the numerical results obtained from the solution of differential Equation (1), (Figures 1–3), presents significant differences for large angles.

However, the worst problem comes from the velocity Equation (9), (Figures 4–6).

This sinusoidal function predicts a maximum velocity $\left(\frac{d\theta}{dt}\right)_{max} = \omega\theta_0$ and we know that maximum velocity should be, by expression (3), $\left(\frac{d\theta}{dt}\right)_{max} = 2\omega_0\sin\left(\frac{\theta_0}{2}\right)$.

Equating the two, a condition is obtained: $\frac{\omega}{\omega_0} = \frac{\sin(\theta_0/2)}{\theta_0/2}$.

This ratio was calculated in the last section for a period and depends on the elliptical integral

$$\varepsilon(\theta_0) = \frac{\omega}{\omega_0} = \frac{\pi}{2K\left(\sin^2\left(\frac{\theta_0}{2}\right)\right)}.$$

The two results are incompatible.

As an example, for $\theta_0 = \frac{\pi}{2} \Rightarrow \frac{\sin(\theta_0/2)}{\theta_0/2} = 0.9003$ and $\frac{\omega}{\omega_0} = \varepsilon(\theta_0) = 0.847$, the difference is obvious.

2.2.2. Model 2

We need a different function, whose derivative should lead to the right velocity amplitude:

$$\begin{cases} \theta(t) = \theta_0 f(u) \text{ with } u = \cos(\omega t) \\ \frac{d\theta}{dt} = -\theta_0 \omega \frac{df}{du} \sin(\omega t) \end{cases} \tag{10}$$

with the conditions

$$f(\pm 1) = \pm 1 \tag{11}$$

and

$$\left(\frac{df}{du}\right)_{u=0} = \frac{\omega_0}{\omega} \frac{\sin(\theta_0/2)}{\theta_0/2} \tag{12}$$

A good candidate is

$$f(u) = \frac{\sin(\delta \cos(\omega t))}{\sin(\delta)} = \frac{\sin(\delta u)}{\sin(\delta)} \tag{13}$$

A parameter δ was introduced. This function always satisfies condition (11) for every δ.

Its derivative is as follows:

$$\frac{df}{du} = \frac{\delta \cos(\delta u)}{\sin(\delta)} \tag{14}$$

To satisfy condition (12), Equation (14) imposes a definition of parameter δ:

$$\left(\frac{df}{du}\right)_{u=0} = \frac{\delta}{\sin(\delta)} = \frac{\omega_0}{\omega} \frac{\sin(\theta_0/2)}{\theta_0/2} = \frac{1}{\varepsilon} \frac{\sin(\theta_0/2)}{\theta_0/2} \tag{15}$$

Parameter $\delta(\theta_0)$ can be extracted from the knowledge of θ_0 and $\varepsilon(\theta_0)$;

$$\frac{\sin(\delta)}{\delta} \frac{\sin(\theta_0/2)}{\theta_0/2} = \frac{\pi}{2K(\theta_0)} \tag{16}$$

The transcendent Equation (16) can be solved numerically, using for instance the Newton–Raphson method, to extract the solution $\delta(\theta_0)$.

Now we have system (10) completely defined:

$$\begin{cases} \theta(t) = \theta_0 \frac{\sin(\delta \cos(\varepsilon \omega_0 t))}{\sin(\delta)} \\ \frac{d\theta}{dt} = -2\omega_0 \sin(\theta_0/2) \cos(\delta \cos(\varepsilon \omega_0 t)) \sin(\varepsilon \omega_0 t) \end{cases} \tag{17}$$

The pendulum physical characteristics appear in these equations only in parameter ω_0.

To obtain a system independent of these characteristics, it is enough to change from variable t to variable τ ($\tau = \omega_0 t$). Furthermore, to compare the different examples in this study, we used relative angular dislocation θ/θ_0, instead of the absolute value. The system used, named Model 2, was

$$\begin{cases} \frac{\theta(\tau)}{\theta_0} = \frac{\sin(\delta \cos(\varepsilon \tau))}{\sin(\delta)} \\ \frac{d(\theta/\theta_0)}{d\tau} = -\frac{\sin(\theta_0/2)}{\theta_0/2} \cos(\delta \cos(\varepsilon \tau)) \sin(\varepsilon \tau) \end{cases} \tag{18}$$

Parameter $\varepsilon(\theta_0)$ is given by expression (8) and $\delta(\theta_0)$ is the solution of Equation (16).

We chose three standard initial angles $\left\{\frac{3\pi}{4};\ \frac{\pi}{2};\ \frac{\pi}{4}\right\}$ to compare the results obtained by the numerical solution of the motion differential Equation (1), with Model 1 (system 9) and Model 2 (system 18).

In Figures 1–3, the results for the three angles are presented and in Figures 4–6 the respective velocities are presented.

The simpler Model 1 is not appropriate, but Model 2 adjusts very well the numeric data.

The simpler Model 1 begins to show a disagreement with the numerical solution, especially halfway, because the predicted minima differ from the numerical ODE solution. Model 2 adjusts very well all the way.

Both models describe well the evolution of the velocity during the initial half period, although Model 2 shows a better agreement.

2.3. Conclusions for the Undamped Pendulum

This work shows that the large angle oscillations of an undamped pendulum can be suitably characterized using a simple and univocal composed sinusoidal function. The introduction of an amplitude dependent parameter allows the correct angular description. The correct angular velocity is obtained by simple differentiation of the angular function.

We can conclude that, up to 130°, Model 2 is always much superior to the traditional model.

The exploration for higher angles begins to show divergences, and we would have to develop more complex analytical functions that are not the more didactic objective of this article.

3. The Damped Pendulum

Let us accept that the main forces of friction acting on our pendulum can be of three types: constant, proportional to velocity, and proportional to the square of velocity.

In a recent article [14], the author explains these three types of friction acting in pendular motion and modulating its extremes. The constant is of the Coulomb type, the one proportional to velocity is the traditional viscous, and the one proportional to the square of velocity is related to high speeds.

One of the fundamental reasons why Model 2 succeeds where Model 1 does not function is that the average value of the quantities, especially the velocity, is different in the two cases.

Now, with the different types of friction forces depending on speed, we will need to calculate these average values.

For this reason, we anticipate the calculation of these average values right away. We will see that the results will be important later for Equation (28).

The Expressions (19), (21), and (22) represent, respectively, the average values of speed, the square of speed, and the cube of speed for the pendulum:

$$\overline{\left|\dot{\theta}\right|} = \frac{\omega_0\theta_0}{K(\theta_0)} \qquad \overline{\left|\dot{\theta}^2\right|} = \dot{\theta}^2_{\max}\left(1 - \frac{1 - \frac{E(\theta_0)}{K(\theta_0)}}{\sin^2\left(\frac{\theta_0}{2}\right)}\right) \qquad \overline{\left|\dot{\theta}^3\right|} = \frac{2\omega_0^3}{K(\theta_0)}(\sin\theta_0 - \theta_0\cos\theta_0)$$

Using the new differential equation of motion (23), we were able to derive differential Equation (30) for the angular amplitude. To obtain analytical solutions, it is preferable to transform it into a velocity, Equation (31).

We found that there are three functions f_μ, f_λ, and f_β that completely affect and dominate each of the friction coefficients. These three functions are calculated in Figures 7–9, adjusting to the numerical data. It was found that, for angles up to 90°, each of the functions can be defined by a third-degree polynomial, thus obtaining a matrix (34).

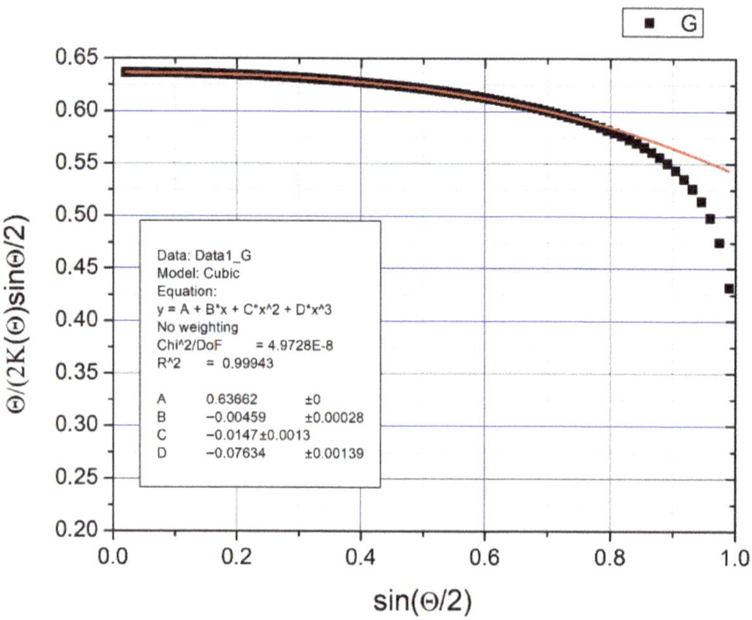

Figure 7. Function f_μ and the adjusting third order polynomial.

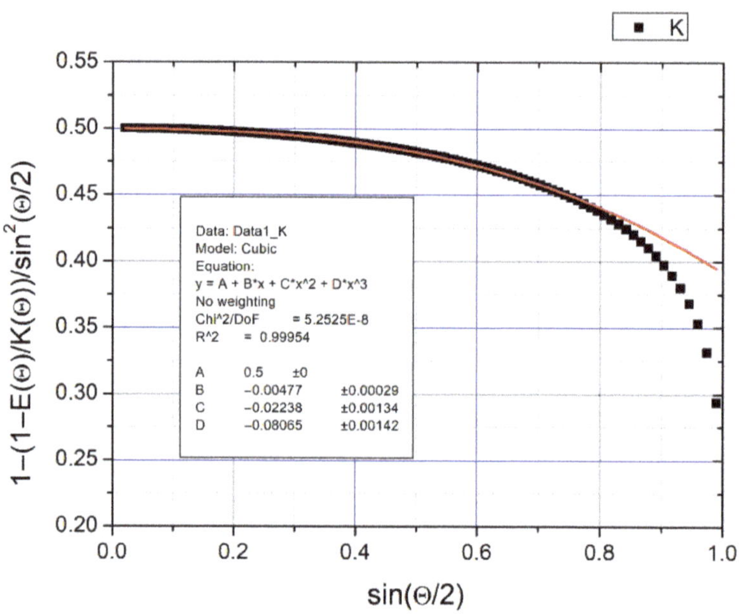

Figure 8. Function f_λ and the adjusting third order polynomial.

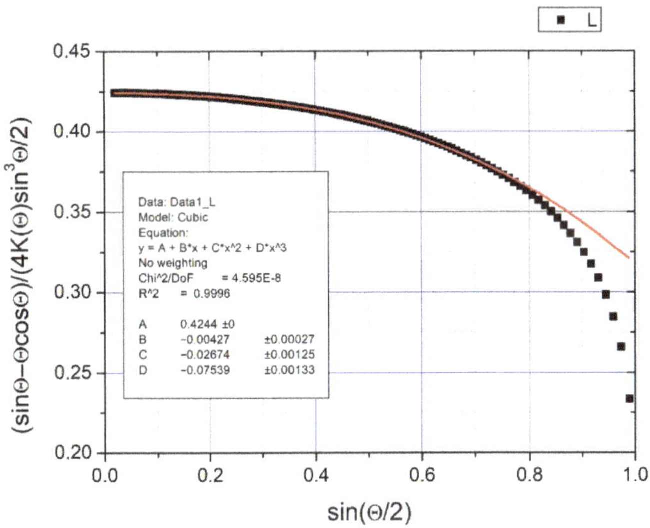

Figure 9. Function f_β and the adjusting third order polynomial.

Substituting into the initial Equation (31) we obtain an ODE (35) for the speed, linear of the 5th degree.

To achieve some practical results, we assume that the terms of the speed with a degree higher than quadratic can be neglected, and we obtain a much-simplified ODE (36), where there are only three constant coefficients: a, b, and c, which depend only on the friction coefficients expression (37).

In Section 4, we will verify Equation (36) with the numerical data from the solution of the equation using LabView software [15,16]. Three practical examples of different forces were made.

In the first case, the pendulum only contains the force of viscous friction and two different friction coefficients, λ = 0.008 in Figure 10 and λ = 0.08 in Figure 11.

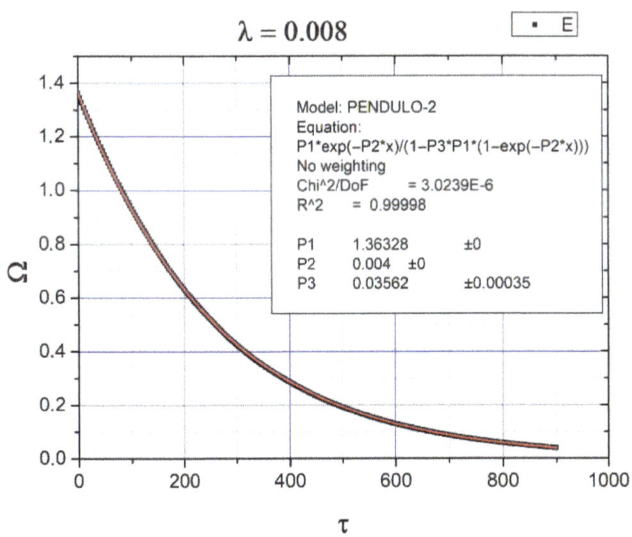

Figure 10. Pendulum dropped from 1.5 rad and acted on by a viscous force with coefficient $\lambda = 0.008$.

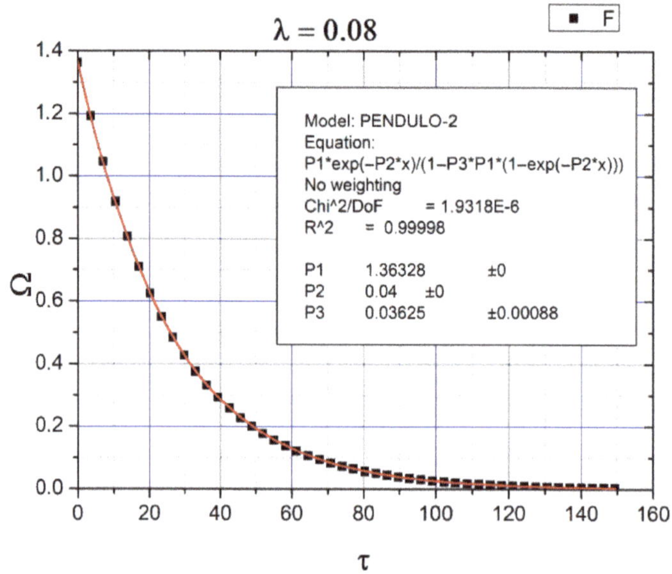

Figure 11. Pendulum dropped from 1.5 rad and acted on by a viscous force with coefficient λ = 0.08.

In the second example, the pendulum contains only the constant friction force and two different coefficients of friction, μ = 0.002 in Figure 12 and μ = 0.008 in Figure 13.

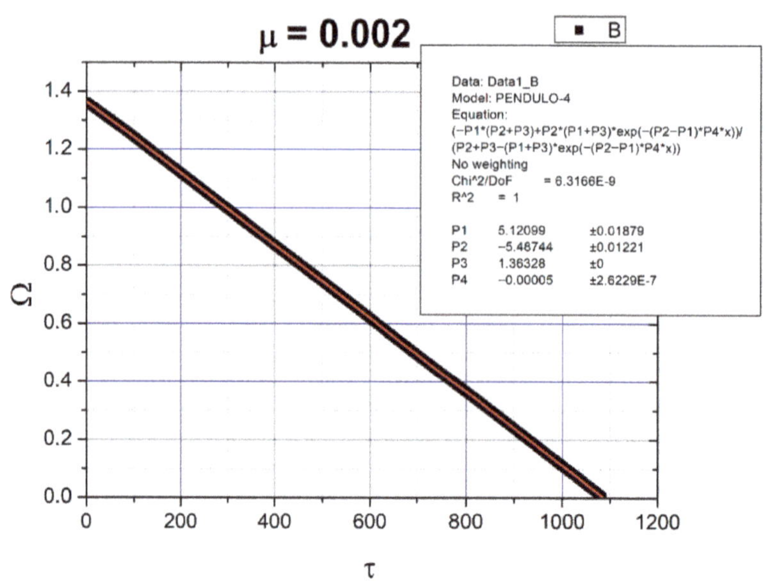

Figure 12. Pendulum acted on only by a Coulomb constant drag force with coefficient $\mu = 0.002$.

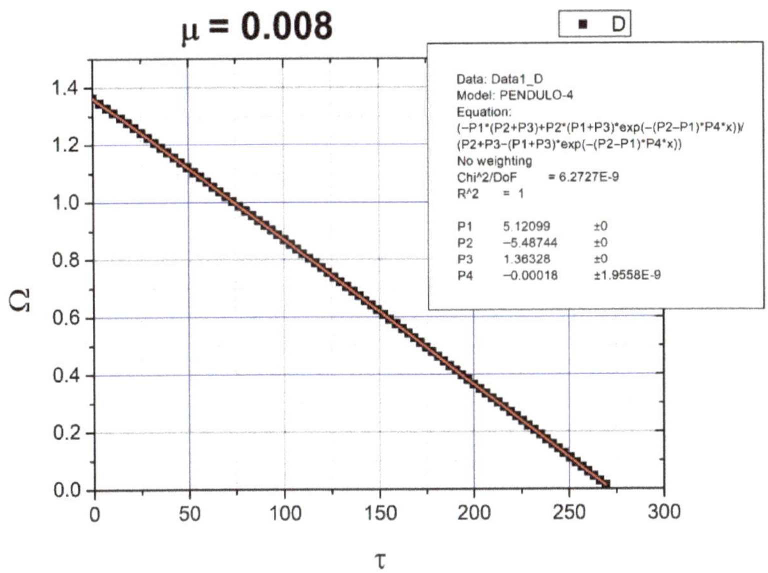

Figure 13. Pendulum acted on only by a Coulomb constant drag force with coefficient $\mu = 0.008$.

In the third example, the pendulum contains only the force of quadratic turbulent friction and three different friction coefficients; b = 0.04 in Figure 14, b = 0.08 in Figure 15, and b = 0.008 in Figure 16.

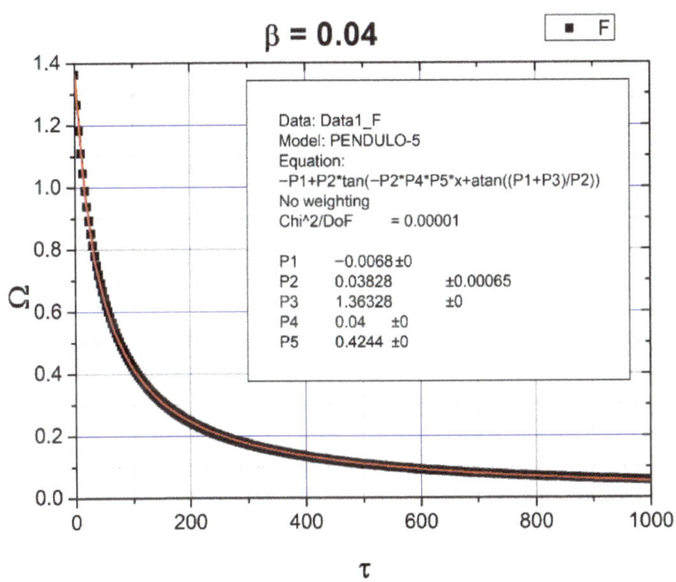

Figure 14. Pendulum acted on only by a turbulent quadratic drag force with $\beta = 0.04$.

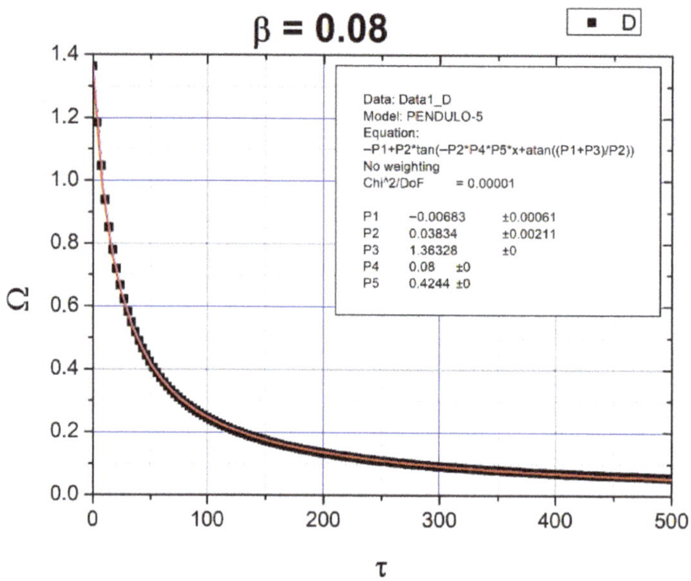

Figure 15. Pendulum acted on only by a turbulent quadratic drag force with $\beta = 0.08$.

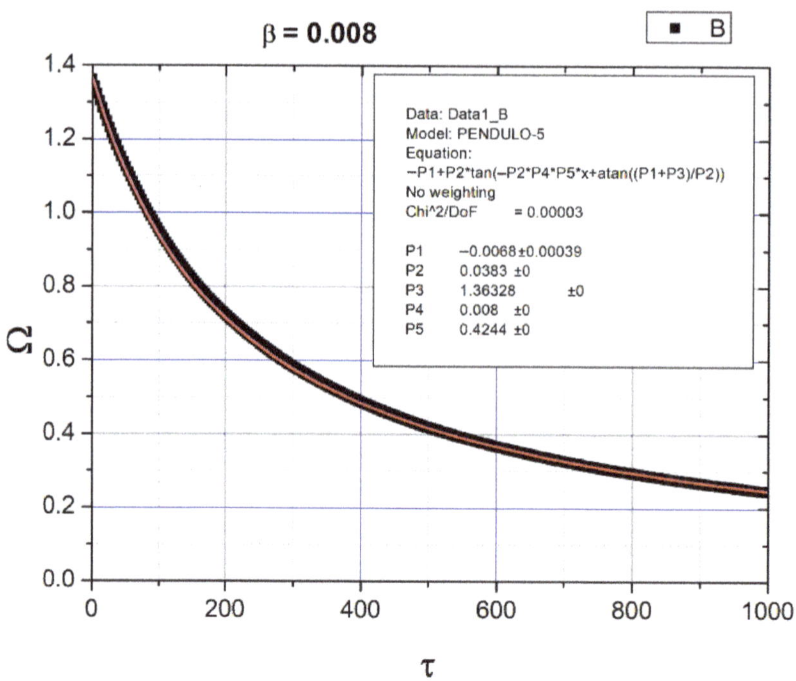

Figure 16. Pendulum acted on only by a turbulent quadratic drag force with $\beta = 0.008$.

3.1. Average Values of Velocity

3.1.1. Half Period Velocity Average Value $\left|\bar{\dot{\theta}}\right|$

There are some important physical consequences of the period amplitude dependence found in (7). The average value of velocity in each half cycle depends not only on the extrema angle but also on the half period.

The harmonic oscillator has an average velocity $\frac{4\theta_0}{T_0} = \frac{2\omega_0\theta_0}{\pi}$ and the value for the pendulum is

$$\left|\bar{\dot{\theta}}\right| = \frac{4\theta_0}{T_0}\frac{\pi}{2K(\theta_0)} = \frac{\omega_0\theta_0}{K(\theta_0)} \tag{19}$$

Only for small values of amplitude they are similar. For instance, if

$$\theta_0 = \frac{\pi}{2} \Rightarrow K\left(\sin^2\left(\frac{\pi}{4}\right)\right) = 1.85407,$$

meaning that the pendulum average velocity is 15.3% lower than a linear oscillator.

3.1.2. Half Period Square Velocity Average Value $\left|\bar{\dot{\theta}}^2\right|$

The square velocity given by (2) changes signal each half cycle;

$$\frac{d\theta}{dt} = \pm 2\omega_0\sqrt{\sin^2\left(\frac{\theta}{2}\right) - \sin^2\left(\frac{\theta_0}{2}\right)} \tag{20}$$

To obtain the average value we integrate over half a period:

$$\left|\overline{\dot{\theta}^2}\right| = \frac{\int_0^{T/2}\left(\frac{d\theta}{dt}\right)^2 dt}{T/2} = \frac{\int_{\theta_0}^{-\theta_0}\frac{d\theta}{dt}d\theta}{T_0\frac{K(\theta_0)}{\pi}} = \frac{\omega_0^2}{K(\theta_0)}\int_{\theta_0}^{-\theta_0}\sqrt{\sin^2\left(\frac{\theta}{2}\right) - \sin^2\left(\frac{\theta_0}{2}\right)}d\theta$$

Using, as before, $\sin\left(\frac{\theta}{2}\right) = \sin\left(\frac{\theta_0}{2}\right)\sin(\varphi)$, we obtain

$$\left|\overline{\dot{\theta}^2}\right| = \frac{4\omega_0^2}{K(\theta_0)}\sin^2\left(\frac{\theta_0}{2}\right)\int_0^{\pi/2}\frac{\cos^2\varphi}{\sqrt{1-\sin^2\left(\frac{\theta_0}{2}\right)\sin^2\varphi}}d\varphi = \frac{4\omega_0^2}{K(\theta_0)}\int_0^{\pi/2}\left[\frac{-\cos^2\left(\frac{\theta_0}{2}\right)}{\sqrt{1-\sin^2\left(\frac{\theta_0}{2}\right)\sin^2\varphi}} + \sqrt{1-\sin^2\left(\frac{\theta_0}{2}\right)\sin^2\varphi}\right]d\varphi$$

The first integral gives the elliptic integral of first kind $K\left(\sin^2\left(\frac{\theta_0}{2}\right)\right)$ and the second the elliptic integral of second kind $E\left(\sin^2\left(\frac{\theta_0}{2}\right)\right)$.

$$\left|\overline{\dot{\theta}^2}\right| = \frac{4\omega_0^2}{K(\theta_0)}\left(-\cos^2\left(\frac{\theta_0}{2}\right)K(\theta_0) + E(\theta_0)\right) = 4\omega_0^2\left(\sin^2\left(\frac{\theta_0}{2}\right) - 1 + \frac{E(\theta_0)}{K(\theta_0)}\right)$$

Using the maximum velocity, the expression is

$$\left|\overline{\dot{\theta}^2}\right| = 4\omega_0^2\sin^2\left(\frac{\theta_0}{2}\right)\left(1 - \frac{1-\frac{E(\theta_0)}{K(\theta_0)}}{\sin^2\left(\frac{\theta_0}{2}\right)}\right) = \dot{\theta}^2_{\max}\left(1 - \frac{1-\frac{E(\theta_0)}{K(\theta_0)}}{\sin^2\left(\frac{\theta_0}{2}\right)}\right) \tag{21}$$

The corrective term inside parentheses is a characteristic of pendulum motion.

For small amplitudes, the ratio of the two elliptic integrals is $\frac{E(\theta_0)}{K(\theta_0)} \approx 1 - \frac{1}{2}\sin^2\left(\frac{\theta_0}{2}\right)$ and this term is close to ½ the average value of the quadratic sinusoidal functions, characteristic of a linear oscillator.

In fact, for a linear oscillator, the calculation is simple:

$$\overline{\left|\dot{\theta}^2\right|} = \frac{\int_0^{T/2}\left(\frac{d\theta}{dt}\right)^2 dt}{T_0/2} = \frac{\int_{\theta_0}^{-\theta_0}\frac{d\theta}{dt}d\theta}{T_0/2} = \frac{2\omega_0}{T_0}\int_{\theta_0}^{-\theta_0}\sqrt{\theta_0^2-\theta^2}d\theta = \frac{\omega_0^2\theta_0^2}{2}$$

3.1.3. Half Period Cubic Velocity Average Value $\left|\bar{\dot{\theta}}^3\right|$

To obtain the average value we integrate over half a period;

$$\overline{\left|\dot{\theta}^3\right|} = \frac{\int_0^{T/2}\left(\frac{d\theta}{dt}\right)^3 dt}{T/2} = \frac{\int_{\theta_0}^{-\theta_0}\left(\frac{d\theta}{dt}\right)^2 d\theta}{T_0\frac{K(\theta_0)}{\pi}} = \frac{\omega_0^3}{K(\theta_0)}\int_{-\theta_0}^{\theta_0}(-\cos\theta_0+\cos\theta)d\theta$$

This is a direct integration:

$$\overline{\left|\dot{\theta}^3\right|} = \frac{2\omega_0^3}{K(\theta_0)}(\sin\theta_0 - \theta_0\cos\theta_0) \tag{22}$$

For small angles, $\sin\theta_0 \approx \theta_0 - \frac{\theta_0^3}{6}$, $\cos\theta_0 \approx 1 - \frac{\theta_0^2}{2}$ and $K(\theta_0) \approx \frac{\pi}{2}$. The average value rests $\overline{\left|\dot{\theta}^3\right|} \approx \frac{4\omega_0^3\theta_0^3}{3\pi} = \frac{4}{3\pi}\dot{\theta}^3_{\max}$.

For a linear oscillator the calculation is

$$\overline{\left|\dot{\theta}^3\right|} = \frac{\int_0^{T/2}\left(\frac{d\theta}{dt}\right)^3 dt}{T_0/2} = \frac{\int_{\theta_0}^{-\theta_0}\left(\frac{d\theta}{dt}\right)^2 d\theta}{T_0/2} = \frac{2\omega_0^2}{T_0}\int_{\theta_0}^{-\theta_0}\left(\theta_0^2-\theta^2\right)d\theta = \frac{4\omega_0^3\theta_0^3}{3\pi}$$

3.2. Differential Equations and Amplitude

Fundamental equation governing motion of a generic damped physical pendulum is, instead of (1),

$$I\frac{d^2\theta}{dt^2} = -mgL\sin\theta - \mu_R L\frac{\dot{\theta}}{\left|\dot{\theta}\right|} - \lambda_R L\dot{\theta} - \beta_R L\dot{\theta}\left|\dot{\theta}\right| \tag{23}$$

Three types of generic torques are included. A constant torque associated to pivot rotation, a viscous torque due to solid fluid flow, and a quadratic term usually associated with turbulent flow. The coefficients used have index R because they are real force coefficients: $[\mu_R \equiv [N] \quad \lambda_R \equiv [kg/s] \quad \beta_R \equiv [kg/m]]$.

Dividing by inertia (I) we obtain the equation for acceleration:

$$\frac{d^2\theta}{dt^2} = -\omega_0^2\sin(\theta) - \mu_A\frac{\dot{\theta}}{\left|\dot{\theta}\right|} - \lambda_A\dot{\theta} - \beta_A\dot{\theta}\left|\dot{\theta}\right| \text{ with } \left[\mu_A = \frac{\mu_R L}{I} \quad \lambda_A = \frac{\lambda_R L}{I} \quad \beta_A = \frac{\beta_R L}{I}\right]$$

The coefficients used now have index A because they are acceleration coefficients.

This equation can be made independent of the proper frequency by changing time to phase time $\tau = \omega_0 t$:

$$\frac{d^2\theta}{d\tau^2} = -\sin(\theta) - \mu\frac{\dot{\theta}}{\left|\dot{\theta}\right|} - \lambda\dot{\theta} - \beta\dot{\theta}\left|\dot{\theta}\right| \text{ with } \left[\mu = \frac{\mu_R}{mg} \quad \lambda = \frac{\lambda_R}{mg}\omega_0 \quad \beta = \frac{\beta_R}{mg}\omega_0^2\right] \tag{24}$$

Now all differentiation is for τ and the coefficients have lost the index.

This is the equation that must be solved to obtain the angle deviation and the angular velocity.

To obtain the energy equation we multiply Equation (23) by $\frac{d\theta}{dt}$:

$$\frac{d}{dt}\left(\frac{1}{2}I\left|\frac{d\theta}{dt}\right|^2\right)+\frac{d}{dt}\left(2mgL\sin^2\left(\frac{\theta}{2}\right)\right)=-\left(\mu_R+\lambda_R\left|\frac{d\theta}{dt}\right|+\beta_R\left|\frac{d\theta}{dt}\right|^2\right)L\left|\frac{d\theta}{dt}\right|$$

The left side represents the instant power and the right side contains the instant dissipated power.

As before, this equation can be made independent of the proper frequency by changing time to phase time $\tau=\omega_0 t$:

$$\frac{d}{d\tau}\left(\dot{\theta}^2+4\sin^2\left(\frac{\theta}{2}\right)\right)=-2\left(\mu\left|\dot{\theta}\right|+\lambda\left|\dot{\theta}\right|^2+\beta_R\left|\dot{\theta}\right|^3\right) \tag{25}$$

This is the energy ODE equation that will be used simultaneously with Equation (24) to obtain angle, angular velocity, and total energy.

To obtain information about the amplitude function, it is important to follow the instants of null velocity from Equation (25). We will follow these points $(\tau_i \quad \theta_{extrema})_{\dot{\theta}=0}$ by using the amplitude function $\Theta(\tau_i)=|\theta_{extrema}(\tau_i)|_{\dot{\theta}=0}$. This function is the tail of the angular amplitude.

From energy in Equation (25) we obtain important information; the velocity amplitude and the angular amplitude are related through a simple function $\left|\dot{\theta}_{extrema}\right|=2\sin\left(\frac{\Theta}{2}\right)$.

Of course they do not occur at the same instant, but the continuous angular amplitude function $\Theta(\tau)$ enables us to obtain the continuous velocity amplitude function $\Omega(\tau)=2\sin\left(\frac{\Theta(\tau)}{2}\right)$.

The total energy variation in each half period can be evaluated by integrating (25) between two successive instants of null velocity:

$$\Delta\left(4\sin^2\left(\frac{\Theta}{2}\right)\right)=-2\int_{\tau_i}^{\tau_{i+1}}\left(\mu\left|\dot{\theta}\right|+\lambda\left|\dot{\theta}\right|^2+\beta_R\left|\dot{\theta}\right|^3\right)d\tau \tag{26}$$

The time interval is $\Delta\tau=\tau_{i+1}-\tau_i=\omega_0\frac{T(\Theta)}{2}=\pi\frac{T(\Theta)}{T_0}$.

This ratio was evaluated in (8) and allows a univocal expression for the time interval:

$$\Delta\tau=2K\left(\sin^2\left(\frac{\Theta}{2}\right)\right) \tag{27}$$

The average power loss in each half cycle is therefore the ratio of (26) and (27):

$$\frac{\Delta\left(4\sin^2\left(\frac{\Theta}{2}\right)\right)}{\Delta\tau}=-2\frac{\int_{\tau_i}^{\tau_{i+1}}\left(\mu\left|\dot{\theta}\right|+\lambda\left|\dot{\theta}\right|^2+\beta\left|\dot{\theta}\right|^3\right)d\tau}{\Delta\tau}=-2\left(\mu\overline{\left|\dot{\theta}\right|}+\lambda\overline{\left|\dot{\theta}^2\right|}+\beta\overline{\left|\dot{\theta}^3\right|}\right) \tag{28}$$

The result shows that the average power loss in each half cycle is proportional to the velocity, square velocity, and cubic velocity, during that half cycle.

These average values were evaluated in Sections 3.1.1–3.1.3, Expressions (19), (21), and (22).

These expressions must be corrected because we change from time t to the phase time τ:

$$\overline{\left|\dot{\theta}\right|} = \frac{\Theta}{K(\Theta)}\ ;\quad \overline{\left|\dot{\theta}^2\right|} = 4\sin^2\left(\frac{\Theta}{2}\right)\left(1 - \frac{1-\frac{E(\Theta)}{K(\Theta)}}{\sin^2\left(\frac{\Theta}{2}\right)}\right)\ ;\quad \overline{\left|\dot{\theta}^3\right|} = \frac{2}{K(\Theta)}(\sin\Theta - \Theta\cos\Theta) \tag{29}$$

If we assume that the average power loss in each half cycle can be substituted by the instant power, an equation for the angular amplitude is found:

$$\frac{d\left(4\sin^2\left(\frac{\Theta}{2}\right)\right)}{d\tau} = 2\sin\Theta\frac{d\Theta}{d\tau} = -2\left(\mu\frac{\Theta}{K(\Theta)} + 4\lambda\left(\sin^2\left(\frac{\Theta}{2}\right) - 1 + \frac{E(\Theta)}{K(\Theta)}\right) + 2\beta\frac{\sin\Theta - \Theta\cos\Theta}{K(\Theta)}\right) \tag{30}$$

To obtain analytical solutions of this equation it is necessary to find analytic expressions for the elliptic integrals.

Using velocity instead of angle we transform this equation into

$$\frac{d\Omega}{d\tau} = -\left(\mu\frac{\Theta}{2K(\Theta)\sin\left(\frac{\Theta}{2}\right)} + \lambda\Omega\left(1 - \frac{1-\frac{E(\Theta)}{K(\Theta)}}{\sin^2\left(\frac{\Theta}{2}\right)}\right) + \beta\Omega^2\frac{\sin\Theta - \Theta\cos\Theta}{4K(\Theta)\sin^3\left(\frac{\Theta}{2}\right)}\right) \tag{31}$$

Analyzing individually the three functions affecting the three drag coefficients, we find

$$f_\mu = \frac{\Theta}{2K(\Theta)\sin\left(\frac{\Theta}{2}\right)}$$

in Figure 7,

$$f_\lambda = 1 - \frac{1-\frac{E(\Theta)}{K(\Theta)}}{\sin^2\left(\frac{\Theta}{2}\right)}$$

in Figure 8

$$f_\beta = \frac{\sin\Theta - \Theta\cos\Theta}{4K(\Theta)\sin^3\left(\frac{\Theta}{2}\right)}$$

in Figure 9.

We conclude that, apart from the very large angles, they could be adjusted using polynomials of $\sin\left(\frac{\Theta}{2}\right)$.

A third-degree polynomial seems to be enough for angles as high as $\frac{\pi}{2}$.

The results are presented in the same Figures 7–9.

$$\begin{cases} f_\mu = \frac{\Theta}{2K(\Theta)\sin\left(\frac{\Theta}{2}\right)} = \frac{2}{\pi} + A_1\sin\left(\frac{\Theta}{2}\right) + A_2\sin^2\left(\frac{\Theta}{2}\right) + A_3\sin^3\left(\frac{\Theta}{2}\right) \\ f_\lambda = 1 - \frac{1-\frac{E(\Theta)}{K(\Theta)}}{\sin^2\left(\frac{\Theta}{2}\right)} = \frac{1}{2} + B_1\sin\left(\frac{\Theta}{2}\right) + B_2\sin^2\left(\frac{\Theta}{2}\right) + B_3\sin^3\left(\frac{\Theta}{2}\right) \\ f_\beta = \frac{\sin\Theta - \Theta\cos\Theta}{4K(\Theta)\sin^3\left(\frac{\Theta}{2}\right)} = \frac{4}{3\pi} + C_1\sin\left(\frac{\Theta}{2}\right) + C_2\sin^2\left(\frac{\Theta}{2}\right) + C_3\sin^3\left(\frac{\Theta}{2}\right) \end{cases} \tag{32}$$

The adjusting matrix found was

$$\begin{bmatrix} A_1 & A_2 & A_3 \\ B_1 & B_2 & B_3 \\ C_1 & C_2 & C_3 \end{bmatrix} = \begin{bmatrix} -0.00459 & -0.01470 & -0.07630 \\ -0.00477 & -0.02238 & -0.08065 \\ -0.00427 & -0.02674 & -0.07539 \end{bmatrix} \tag{33}$$

The three functions can be written in terms of a velocity polynomial:

$$\begin{cases} f_\mu = \frac{2}{\pi} + \frac{A_1}{2}\Omega + \frac{A_2}{4}\Omega^2 + \frac{A_3}{8}\Omega^3 \\ f_\lambda = \frac{1}{2} + \frac{B_1}{2}\Omega + \frac{B_2}{4}\Omega^2 + \frac{B_3}{8}\Omega^3 \\ f_\beta = \frac{4}{3\pi} + \frac{C_1}{2}\Omega + \frac{C_2}{4}\Omega^2 + \frac{C_3}{8}\Omega^3 \end{cases} \tag{34}$$

Notice that the independent terms are the same as those found for the linear oscillator. Equation (31) can now be rewritten as a first order ODE function of Ω:

$$\begin{aligned} &\frac{d\Omega}{d\tau} = -(\mu f_\mu + \lambda\Omega f_\lambda + \beta f_\beta) = \\ &-\frac{2}{\pi}\mu - \left(\frac{A_1}{2}\mu + \frac{1}{2}\lambda\right)\Omega - \left(\frac{A_2}{4}\mu + \frac{B_1}{2}\lambda + \frac{4}{3\pi}\beta\right)\Omega^2 - \left(\frac{A_3}{8}\mu + \frac{B_2}{4}\lambda + \frac{C_1}{2}\beta\right)\Omega^3 - \left(\frac{B_3}{8}\lambda + \frac{C_2}{4}\beta\right)\Omega^4 - \frac{C_3}{8}\beta\Omega^5 \end{aligned} \tag{35}$$

To obtain analytical solutions we assume that the third degree and higher terms can be neglected.

This should be true for amplitudes lower than $\Theta < \frac{\pi}{2}$.

Equation (35) takes the form

$$\frac{d\Omega}{a\Omega^2 + b\Omega + c} = -d\tau \tag{36}$$

Coefficients a, b, and c depend only on the drag coefficients:

$$\begin{cases} c = \frac{2}{\pi}\mu \\ b = \frac{A_1}{2}\mu + \frac{1}{2}\lambda = -2.295 * 10^{-3}\mu + \frac{1}{2}\lambda \\ a = \frac{A_2}{4}\mu + \frac{B_1}{2}\lambda + \frac{4}{3\pi}\beta = -3.675 * 10^{-3}\mu - 2.385 * 10^{-3}\lambda + \frac{4}{3\pi}\beta \end{cases} \tag{37}$$

The solution of (36) depends on the type, real or complex, of the second-degree polynomial roots.

When the discriminant is positive, $b^2 > 4ac$, the two roots are real, and the decay is of an exponential type.

We call this case viscous oscillation.

When the discriminant is negative, $b^2 < 4ac$, the two roots are complex, and the decay is of a tangent type.

We call this case turbulent type oscillation.

4. Results from Numerical Data

The coefficients obtained in Equation (35) must be tested using numeric data.

We do not know if the non-dominant terms represent univocally the best approach to the third order polynomial itself and the best choice when reduced to the second order.

In order to obtain the coefficients from numeric data we must solve the ODE containing one of the forces at a time, pick the oscillation extrema, and fit to the corresponding mathematical model.

4.1. Pendulum Acted on Only by the Viscous Drag Force

This is the most academic case but the analytical function available for amplitude decay is valid only for the very small angles.

From (34) the polynomial coefficients are

$$\left[a = B_1\frac{\lambda}{2} \quad b = \frac{\lambda}{2} \quad c = 0\right]$$

The solution and predicted adjust parameters of function (35) are

$$\Omega = \frac{Z_0 e^{-\frac{\lambda}{2}\tau}}{1 - B_1 Z_0 e^{-\frac{\lambda}{2}\tau}} \text{ where } Z_0 = \frac{\Omega_0}{1 + B_1 \Omega_0} \tag{38}$$

In order to obtain univocal parameter dependence we change Formula (30) to

$$\Omega = \frac{\Omega_0 e^{-\frac{\lambda}{2}\tau}}{1 + B_1 \Omega_0 \left(1 - e^{-\frac{\lambda}{2}\tau}\right)} \text{ used } \Theta_0 = 1.5$$

Figures 10 and 11 contain numeric data and adjusting parameters for two cases of a pendulum dropped from an angle of 1.5 rad and acted on only by a viscous force with coefficients $\lambda = 0.008$ and $\lambda = 0.08$, respectively.

The velocity amplitude is very well described with the same parameter $B_1 = -0.036$. This value is lower than the one predicted by our polynomial ($B_1 = -0.00477$) indicating a wrong choice.

We conclude that the viscous force can be represented by the three-component vector:

$$\left[a_\lambda = -0.018\lambda \quad b_\lambda = \tfrac{\lambda}{2} \quad c_\lambda = 0\right] \tag{39}$$

4.2. Pendulum Acted on Only by the Coulomb Constant Drag Force

This case is important to check the adjusting polynomial coefficients. From (33) and (34) the polynomial coefficients are

$$\left[a = -0.0037\mu \quad b = -0.0023\mu \quad c = \tfrac{2}{\pi}\mu\right]$$

The solution predicted is again of viscous type due to the presence of the negative coefficient a.

To adjust data we used a complete model designated by PENDULO-4:

$$\Omega = \frac{-P_1(P_2 + P_3) + P_2(P_1 + P_3)e^{-(P_2 - P_1)P_4\tau}}{(P_2 + P_3) - (P_1 + P_3)e^{-(P_2 - P_1)P_4\tau}} \tag{40}$$

The coefficients P1 and P2 are the real roots of the polynomial, P3 is the initial velocity, and P4 is the constant a.

$$\left[P_1 = \tfrac{b - \sqrt{\Delta}}{2a} \quad P_2 = \tfrac{b + \sqrt{\Delta}}{2a} \quad P_3 = \Omega_0 \quad P_4 = a\right] \Rightarrow \left[a = P_4 \quad \tfrac{b}{a} = P_1 + P_2 \quad \tfrac{c}{a} = P_1 P_2\right]$$

Figures 12 and 13 contain numeric data and adjusting parameters for two cases of a pendulum dropped from an angle of 1.5 rad and acted on only by the constant drag force with coefficients $\mu = 0.002$ and $\mu = 0.008$, respectively.

We conclude that the Coulomb force can be represented by the three-component vector:

$$\left[a_\mu = -0.02265\mu \quad b_\mu = 0.0083\mu \quad c_\mu = \tfrac{2}{\pi}\mu\right] \tag{41}$$

4.3. Pendulum Acted on Only by the Turbulent Quadratic Drag Force

This is the third case we must solve, to check the adjusting polynomial coefficients. From (33) and (34) the polynomial coefficients are

$$\left[a = \tfrac{4}{3\pi}\beta \quad b = 0 \quad c = 0\right]$$

The solution predicted is of the turbulent type.

The polynomial $a\Omega^2 + b\Omega + c$ has complex roots because $\Delta = b^2 - 4ac < 0$.

The solution of Equation (36) is now of the tangent type

$$\Omega = -\frac{b}{2a} + \frac{\sqrt{\Delta}}{2a}\tan\left(-\frac{\sqrt{\Delta}}{2} + Z_0\right) \text{ where } \tan(Z_0) = \frac{2a\Omega_0 + b}{\sqrt{\Delta}} \text{ and } \Delta = 4ac - b^2 \quad (42)$$

To adjust data we used a complete model designated by PENDULO-5 with five parameters:

$$\Omega = -P_1 + P_2 tg\left(-P_2P_4P_5\tau + arctg\left(\frac{P_1 + P_3}{P_2}\right)\right) \quad (43)$$

The coefficient P3 is initial velocity, P4 is β, and P5 is β coefficient, expected to be $\frac{4}{3\pi}$.

$$\left[P_1 = \frac{b}{2a} \quad P_2 = \frac{\sqrt{\Delta}}{2a} \quad P_3 = \Omega_0 \quad P_4 = \beta\right] \Rightarrow \left[a = P_5\beta \quad \frac{b}{a} = 2P_1 \quad \frac{c}{a} = \left(P_1^2 + P_2^2\right)\right]$$

Figures 14–16 contain numeric data and adjusting parameters for three cases of a pendulum dropped from an angle of 1.5 rad and acted on only by a turbulent drag force with coefficients β = 0.04, 0.08, and 0.008, respectively.

We conclude that the turbulent force can be represented by the three-component vector:

$$\left[a_\beta = \frac{4}{3\pi}\beta \quad b_\beta = -0.0058\beta \quad c_\beta = 0.00064\beta\right] \quad (44)$$

As expected, the *b* and *c* components are very small and can be neglected in usual calculations.

4.4. Conclusions for the Pendulum with Friction

The seven examples used in the last seven figures show that it is possible to univocally fit the obtained functions to the numerical data for angles much higher than those traditionally used in the approximation. $\sin(\theta)$ approximately equal to θ.

Funding: This research received no external funding.

Data Availability Statement: The original contributions presented in this study are included in the article. Further inquiries can be directed to the corresponding author.

Conflicts of Interest: The authors declare no conflict of interest.

References

1. Kidd, R.B.; Fogg, S.L. A simple formula for the large-angle pendulum period. *Phys. Teach.* **2002**, *40*, 81–83. [CrossRef]
2. Parwani, R.R. An approximate expression for the large angle period of a simple pendulum. *Eur. J. Phys.* **2003**, *25*, 37. [CrossRef]
3. Belendez, A.; Hernandez, A.; Marquez, A.; Beléndez, T.; Neipp, C. Analytical approximations for the period of a nonlinear pendulum. *Eur. J. Phys.* **2006**, *27*, 539–551. [CrossRef]
4. Lima, F.M.S. Simple 'log formulae' for pendulum motion valid for any amplitude. *Eur. J. Phys.* **2008**, *29*, 1091–1098. [CrossRef]
5. Beléndez, A.; Rodes, J.J.; Beléndez, T.; Hernández, A. Approximation for a large-angle simple pendulum period. *Eur. J. Phys.* **2009**, *30*, L25. [CrossRef]
6. Johannessen, K. An approximate solution to the equation of motion for large-angle oscillations of the simple pendulum with initial velocity. *Eur. J. Phys.* **2010**, *31*, 511–518. [CrossRef]
7. Butikov, E.I. Oscillations of a simple pendulum with extremely large amplitudes. *Eur. J. Phys.* **2012**, *33*, 1555–1563. [CrossRef]
8. Benacka, J. Fast converging exact power series for the time and period of the simple pendulum. *Eur. J. Phys.* **2017**, *38*, 025004. [CrossRef]
9. Lima, F.M.S. Simple but accurate periodic solutions for the nonlinear pendulum equation. *Revis Bras. Ensino Física* **2019**, *41*, e20180201–e20180202. [CrossRef]
10. Abdulkareem, S.S.; Akgül, A.; Jalal, V.J.; Faraj, B.M.; Abdulla, O.G. Numerical solution for time period of simple pendulum with large angle. *Therm. Sci.* **2020**, *24*, 25–30. [CrossRef]
11. Big-Alabo, A. Approximate periodic solution for the large-amplitude oscillations of a simple pendulum. *Int. J. Mech. Eng. Educ.* **2020**, *48*, 335–350. [CrossRef]

12. Big-Alabo, A. Fifth-order AGM-formula for the period of a large-angle pendulum. *Rev. Bras. Ensino Física* **2023**, *45*, e20230014. [CrossRef]
13. Erol, M.; Oğur, M. Teaching large angle pendulum via Arduino based STEM education material. *Phys. Educ. IOP Publ.* **2023**, *58*, 045001. [CrossRef]
14. Fernandes, J.C. The Characterization of the Mechanical Harmonic Oscillator Extremum Envelope Shape According to Different Friction Types. *Axioms* **2025**, *14*, 554. [CrossRef]
15. LabVIEW™ 2019 Is a Product from National Instruments. Available online: http://www.ni.com (accessed on 29 August 2025).
16. ORIGIN™ 7.0 Is a Product from Origin Lab—Data Analysis and Graphical Software. Available online: http://www.originlab.com (accessed on 29 August 2025).

mathematics

MDPI

Article

Solutions for Linear Fractional Differential Equations with Multiple Constraints Using Fractional B-Poly Bases

Md. Habibur Rahman, Muhammad I. Bhatti * and Nicholas Dimakis

Department of Physics and Astronomy, University of Texas Rio Grande Valley, Edinburg, TX 78539, USA; habiburrahmanphy42@gmail.com (M.H.R.); nicholas.dimakis@utrgv.edu (N.D.)
* Correspondence: muhammad.bhatti@utrgv.edu

Abstract

This study presents an innovative numerical method for solving linear fractional differential equations (LFDEs) using modified Bernstein polynomial bases. The proposed approach effectively addresses the challenges posed by the nonlocal nature of fractional derivatives, providing a robust framework for handling multiple initial and boundary value constraints. By integrating the LFDEs and approximating the solutions with modified fractional-order Bernstein polynomials, we derive operational matrices to solve the resulting system numerically. The method's accuracy is validated through several examples, showing excellent agreement between numerical and exact solutions. Comparative analysis with existing data further confirms the reliability of the approach, with absolute errors ranging from 10^{-18} to 10^{-4}. The results highlight the method's efficiency and versatility in modeling complex systems governed by fractional dynamics. This work offers a computationally efficient and accurate tool for fractional calculus applications in science and engineering, helping to bridge existing gaps in numerical techniques.

Keywords: Bernstein polynomials; operational matrices; initial and boundary value problems; fractional differential equations; numerical approximation; Caputo derivative

MSC: 12-XX; 32-XX; 41-XX

1. Introduction

This paper introduces a novel numerical method addressing key limitations in existing approaches for solving linear fractional differential equations (LFDEs). Fractional calculus is pivotal for modeling anomalous transport and memory-dependent phenomena in physics, engineering, biology, and finance [1–5]. Linear fractional partial differential equations (LFPDEs) are indispensable for modeling nonlocal and memory-driven phenomena. However, their analytical intractability frequently necessitates robust numerical frameworks [6,7]. The nonlocal nature of fractional derivatives presents specific challenges, such as disrupting the periodicity of periodic functions [8]. This poses a critical challenge for analyzing dynamical systems governed by such operators [9]. The absence of a systematic stability framework for fractional-order delay systems contrasted with mature theories for integer-order systems reflects unresolved challenges posed by memory effects and power-law kernels [10]. By integrating Genocchi polynomials with semi-orthogonal bases, this study develops operational matrices tailored for solving fractional differential equations, bridging gaps in handling nonlinearity and nonlocality [11]. Fractional models better capture nonlocal effects and memory phenomena in complex systems (e.g., fractal geometries, turbulent flow) [1,12]. Unlike integer-order derivatives, fractional derivatives are nonlocal, enabling accurate modeling of irregular or discontinuous dynamics [13,14]. Extending the proposed error estimation method to time fractional PDEs and exploring applications in multi-physics systems [15,16]. The work underscores the need for robust numerical frameworks to handle the singularity and complexity of linear and nonlinear FDEs [17–19].

There are various existing methods for solving linear and nonlinear fractional differential equation (FDE) problems [20–23], but many of these techniques have limitations. Therefore, a new approach is needed. This study introduces a novel procedure for solving linear fractional differential equations using an integral method. While exploring different solution strategies, we identified several drawbacks in existing methods, reinforcing the need for our proposed approach [24–30].

For the reasons mentioned above, fractional calculus is a key tool for modeling modern complex systems and is also indispensable for capturing nonlocal and memory-driven phenomena in various fields, including physics, engineering, biology, and finance [1–5]. Although several existing methods have been implemented, many of these techniques still possess significant limitations, and most methods are analytical methods. Although several methods exist for solving fractional differential equations (FDEs), such as the Runge–Kutta method, Taylor series expansions, and finite difference methods, they often struggle with complex or nonlinear problems [31]. For instance, techniques that combine Sawi with iterative methods still face limitations inherent to these traditional approaches [31].

Another author uses finite difference schemes and spectral methods to solve FDEs [32]. It has limitations due to Numerical methods for fractional calculus, such as finite difference and spectral schemes, which face significant challenges, including poor error control, high computational costs for multidimensional data, and inefficiency with complex geometries. These difficulties are compounded by the nonlocal nature of fractional operators, which leads to theoretical complexity and practical issues like numerical instability and uncertain convergence. Furthermore, the absence of a standardized methodology for choosing between fractional operators that yield different results remains a significant obstacle in the field [32].

Another study uses the shifted Jacobi method, which employs Jacobi polynomials within a conformable fractional derivative framework to solve second-order singular periodic boundary value problems [33]. The method can be computationally intensive and complex to implement compared to simpler polynomial bases, and may converge slowly, particularly for large systems or matrices with poorly scaled elements [33]. Another study proposes a meshless Generalized Finite Difference Method (GFDM) for discretizing spatial derivatives, which uses moving least squares and a weight function to optimize a weighted Taylor series based on node distance for approximating Caputo and Riemann–Liouville fractional derivatives [34]. The method proves "conditional convergence", which means its convergence depends on certain conditions [34].

The Tantawy Technique is a fast, computationally efficient method that uses direct compensation for high accuracy [35]. In contrast, the Variational Iteration Transform Method (VITM) employs correction functionals to solve nonlinear differential equations without linearization [35]. The Variational Iteration Transform Method (VITM) requires expertise in variational calculus to identify the Lagrange multiplier effectively [35]. Another study employs a hybrid method combining a finite difference L1 scheme on a graded mesh for temporal discretization of the Caputo derivative and a Generalized Jacobi Petrov–Galerkin spectral approach with non-smooth basis functions for spatial discretization, effectively handling non-smooth solutions [36]. Achieving high-order accuracy in finite difference/spectral methods relies on often unrealistic smoothness assumptions, facing spatial challenges with non-guaranteed smoothness in spectral methods and temporal limitations in handling non-smooth solutions on uniform meshes, as hybrid approaches generally presume smoothness in at least one dimension [36]. Given these persistent challenges and limitations across existing numerical approaches, the development of novel, more versatile numerical techniques remain essential to accurately and efficiently solve fractional differential equations.

To address these challenges and numerical gaps, we outline a new computational technique to solve fractional differential equations. We begin by introducing the classical Bernstein polynomials and subsequently extend them into fractional Bernstein polynomials through the application of Caputo's fractional derivative. The structure of the method begins by integrating the linear fractional differential equation and applying the initial and boundary conditions as integration limits. We assume an approximate solution as a linear combination of modified fractional B-polys, called Bhatti fractional B-polys. This approximation is then substituted into the integral form of the linear fractional differential equation. The resulting equation is solved using an operational matrix approach, and the unknown coefficients are determined to obtain the final solution. To gauge the accuracy of our method, we apply it to three examples of linear fractional differential equations in this study. We then perform an error analysis to demonstrate the accuracy and efficiency of the proposed method.

This study is structured as follows. First, the Introduction establishes the necessity for a novel numerical technique by discussing the limitations of existing methods in solving fractional differential equations. Next, the Methodology section details the theoretical foundation of the proposed approach, including the construction of fractional Bernstein polynomial bases and operational matrices. The Implementation section describes the application of this method to specific problem types, followed by Numerical Examples, where the method is tested on several benchmark problems. Error Analysis is then performed to evaluate the accuracy and robustness of the solutions. Finally, the Conclusion summarizes the findings, highlights the advantages of the proposed technique, and suggests potential directions for future research.

2. Fractional-Order Bernstein Polynomials Basis

The generalized form of fractional B-polys $B_{i,n}(\alpha, x)$, expressed in terms of the variable x or t over the interval $[0,\ R]$ or $[0,\ T]$, is defined in the referenced sources [26,37],

$$B_{i,n}(\alpha, x) = \sum_{k=0}^{n} \beta_{i,k} \left(\frac{x}{R}\right)^{\alpha k}. \tag{1}$$

where α represents the fractional order of B-polys. In this equation, $\beta_{i,k}$ is described as,

$$\beta_{i,k} = (-1)^{i-k} \binom{n}{k} \binom{k}{i}. \tag{2}$$

The coefficient of binomial is expressed as $\binom{n}{k} = \frac{n!}{k!(n-k)!}$.

3. Caputo's Fractional Derivative

We compute fractional derivatives using Caputo's operator. Fractional derivatives are computed via Caputo's operator [38], formulated as:

$${}^{C}D^{\gamma}_{a^+} f(t) = \frac{1}{\Gamma(n-\alpha)} \int_a^t \frac{f^{(n)}}{(t-\tau)^{\alpha-n+1}} d\tau \;\; for \; n-1 < \alpha < n, \tag{3}$$

where γ denotes the fractional order, Γ represents the gamma function, and $f^{(n)}$ is the nth integer-order derivative of f. The Caputo derivative D^γ notably facilitates direct incorporation of initial and boundary conditions, making it consistent with physical systems [38]. The Caputo derivative D^γ of polynomial is given by

$$D^\gamma x^\alpha = \begin{cases} 0 & for\ \alpha \in N_o\ and\ \ \alpha < |\gamma| \\ \frac{\Gamma(\alpha+1)x^{\alpha-\gamma}}{\Gamma(\alpha+1-\gamma)} & otherwise. \end{cases} \tag{4}$$

where α denotes the fractional order function. The one-dimensional approximate solution $y(x)$ is represented as a series expansion in terms of fractional-order B-polys $B_{i,n}(\alpha, x)$. Specifically, the estimated solution to the linear fractional differential equation is expressed in the form:

$$y(x) = \sum_{i=0}^{n} c_i\ B_{i,n}(\alpha, x). \tag{5}$$

where c_i are the expansion coefficients in Equation (5). Let us examine a canonical linear fractional differential equation (FDE) of order γ, expressed in the form, ref. [30]:

$$\frac{\partial^\gamma y(x)}{\partial x^\gamma} + a_1 \frac{\partial y(x)}{\partial x} + a_2 g(x) y(x) = f(x). \tag{6}$$

Integrating both sides with respect to the variable x, where a_1, a_2 are constants. Applying the initial $y(0) = 1$ and boundary conditions to the equation, we obtain [30,39]:

$$\begin{aligned} &\int_0^x \frac{\partial y(x)}{\partial x} dx + \int_0^x \frac{\partial^\gamma y(x)}{\partial x^\gamma} dx + \int_0^x g(x)y(x)dx = \int_0^x f(x)dx \\ &\Rightarrow y(x) + \int_0^x \frac{\partial^\gamma y(x)}{\partial x^\gamma} dx + \int_0^x g(x)y(x)dx = \int_0^x f(x)dx + 1. \end{aligned} \tag{7}$$

By substituting the approximate solution $y(x) = \sum_{i=0}^{n} c_i\ B_{i,n}(\alpha, x)$, Equation (5) into Equation (7) in above equation. We then separate the coefficient term c_i as vector C, and represent the remaining terms as a matrix X on the left-hand side, while denoting the right-hand side as column matrix W. This leads to the operational matrix equation $X\,C = W$. This equation is solved numerically to determine the unknown coefficients c_i. Substituting these coefficients back into the approximate solution then yields the approximated numerical solution. We evaluated our method's accuracy by solving various linear fractional equations and calculating absolute errors.

4. Examples

In this section, we present three illustrative examples to thoroughly evaluate the accuracy and effectiveness of the proposed method. These examples are carefully chosen to represent a diverse set of fractional differential equations involving various initial and boundary conditions. The goal is to demonstrate the method's robustness and adaptability in handling complex problems across different scenarios. Due to its flexible framework, the method is expected to be highly versatile, capable of addressing both linear and nonlinear cases with high precision. Through these examples, we aim to showcase not only the accuracy of numerical results but also the method's potential as a reliable tool for solving a wide class of problems in the field of fractional calculus.

Example 1: As a first example, we consider solving a one-dimensional linear fractional differential equation that incorporates both integer-order and non-integer (fractional) derivatives. The equation is given by [40]:

$$\frac{d^2y(x)}{dx^2} + 3\left(\frac{dy(x)}{dx}\right) + 2\left(\frac{d^{0.1379}y(x)}{dx^{0.1379}}\right) + \left(\frac{d^{0.0159}y(x)}{dx^{0.0159}}\right) + 5y(x) = f(x). \tag{8}$$

where $f(x)$ is given by,

$$\begin{aligned} f(x) = 6 + 3x + \tfrac{5x^2}{2} + 2\left(\tfrac{0.908102}{x^{0.1379}} + 0.565684\, x^{1.8621}\right) \\ + \left(\tfrac{0.990657}{x^{0.0159}} + 0.507365\, x^{1.9841}\right). \end{aligned} \tag{9}$$

where the terms fractional $\left(\frac{d^{0.1379}y(x)}{dx^{0.1379}}\right)$ and $\left(\frac{d^{0.0159}y(x)}{dx^{0.0159}}\right)$ represent derivatives of the function $y(x)$ with respect to x. These fractional derivatives are typically interpreted in the Caputo or Riemann–Liouville sense, depending on the context and required initial/boundary conditions. This equation serves as a benchmark problem to test the accuracy and efficiency of our proposed numerical method. By including derivatives of both integer and low-order fractional degrees, the equation simulates scenarios found in physical systems with memory or hereditary properties, such as anomalous diffusion, porous media flow, or viscoelastic materials. This example illustrates the method's robustness in handling mixed-order differential operators and its capability to produce highly accurate results even when fractional orders are very small and close to zero.

Employing the initial conditions $y(0) = 1$, $y'(0) = 0$, we numerically solve the equation over the interval $0 \le x \le 1$. The exact solution to Equation (8) is given by

$$y_{exact}(x) = \left(1 + \frac{x^2}{2}\right). \tag{10}$$

We perform double integration of the equation on both sides as follows:

$$\begin{aligned} &\Rightarrow I^2(D^2(y(x))) + 3I^2(D(y(x))) + 2\, I^2(D^{0.1379}(y(x))) + I^2(D^{0.0159}(y(x))) + I^2(5\, y(x)) = I^2(f(x)) \\ &\Rightarrow I^2(y''(x)) + 3I^2(D(y(x))) + 2\, I^2(D^{0.1379}(y(x))) + I^2(D^{0.0159}(y(x))) + I^2(5\, y(x)) = I^2(f(x)). \end{aligned} \tag{11}$$

Twice integration (I^2) of both terms with respect to x, subject to the given initial condition, produces [30,39]

$$\begin{aligned} &\Rightarrow I(y'(x) - y'(0)) + 3I^2(D(y(x))) + 2\, I^2(D^{0.1379}(y(x))) + I^2(D^{0.0159}(y(x))) + I^2(5\, y(x)) = I^2(f(x)) \\ &\Rightarrow I(y'(x) - 0) + 3I^2(D(y(x))) + 2\, I^2(D^{0.1379}(y(x))) + I^2(D^{0.0159}(y(x))) + I^2(5\, y(x)) = I^2(f(x)) \\ &\Rightarrow y(x) - y(0) + 3I^2(D(y(x))) + 2\, I^2(D^{0.1379}(y(x))) + I^2(D^{0.0159}(y(x))) + I^2(5\, y(x)) = I^2(f(x)) \\ &\Rightarrow y(x) - 1 + I^2(5\, y(x)) + 3I^2(D(y(x))) + 2\, I^2(D^{0.1379}(y(x))) + I^2(D^{0.0159}(y(x))) = I^2(f(x)). \end{aligned} \tag{12}$$

A simplified representation of this equation is obtained as

$$\Rightarrow y(x) + 3I^2(D(y(x))) + 5I^2(\, y(x)) + 2\, I^2\left(D^{0.1379}(y(x))\right) + I^2\left(D^{0.0159}(y(x))\right) = I^2(f(x) + 1). \tag{13}$$

The solution to Equation (8) can be approximated using a fractional B-polynomial expansion in the x variable:

$$y(x) = \sum_i^n c_i\, B_i(x), \tag{14}$$

where c_i represents the unknown expansion coefficient. Substituting these fractional B-polys into Equation (13) and $W = I^2(f(x) + 1)$ and applying the Galerkin minimization procedure yields [38]

$$\begin{aligned} &\Rightarrow \sum c_i\, B_i(x) + 3I^2(D(\sum c_i\, B_i(x))) + 5I^2(\sum c_i\, B_i(x)) + 2I^2(D^{0.1379}(\sum c_i\, B_i(x))) + I^2(D^{0.0159}(\sum c_i\, B_i(x))) = W \\ &\Rightarrow c_i\, [\langle B_i|B_l\rangle + \langle 3\, I^2(D(B_i))|B_l\rangle + \langle 5\, I^2(B_i)|B_l\rangle + \langle 2\, I^2(D^{0.1379}(B_i))|B_l\rangle + \langle I^2(D^{0.0159}(B_i))|B_l\rangle] = W \\ &\Rightarrow C\,[M + N + R + P + Q] = W, \end{aligned} \tag{15}$$

where M, N, P, Q denote the corresponding matrix operators with elements,

$$\begin{gathered} Let, X = [M + N + R + P + Q] \\ M = \langle B_i | B_l \rangle \\ N = \langle 3I^2(D(B_i)) | B_l \rangle \\ R = \langle 5I^2(B_i) | B_l \rangle \\ P = \langle 2I^2(D^{0.1379}(B_i)) | B_l \rangle \\ Q = \langle I^2(D^{0.0159}(B_i)) | B_l \rangle \\ W = \langle\, I^2(f+1) |\, B_l \rangle. \end{gathered} \tag{16}$$

This equation can be expressed in matrix form as

$$\begin{gathered} \Rightarrow C[M + N + R + P + Q] = W \\ \Rightarrow C\, X = W \end{gathered} \tag{17}$$

This formulation yields an $(n+1)$ by $(n+1)$ system of equations $X\, C = W$, which is solved numerically for the unknown coefficients C as column matrix; these coefficients are then substituted into Equation (14) to obtain the complete solution. Matrices X and W in Equations (15) and (17) are constructed from inner products of fractional B-polys, computed numerically. The coefficient vector C is determined by solving the linear system derived from Equation (17). The final numerical solution to the fractional differential equation is given by

$$\begin{gathered} y_{appr.}(x) = \sum c_i B_i(x) \\ = 0.9999999999999991 \; + 3.552713678800501 \times 10^{-15} x + 0.4999999999999556 x^2 \end{gathered} \tag{18}$$

The numerical solution demonstrates excellent agreement with the exact solution $y_{exact}(x) = \left(1 + \frac{x^2}{2}\right)$. For this computation, the fractional B-polynomials $n = 3$ in Equation (1) were employed in the x variables to solve the linear fractional differential Equation (8). As shown in Figure 1, the numerical and exact solutions coincide within machine precision, confirming the high accuracy of the method.

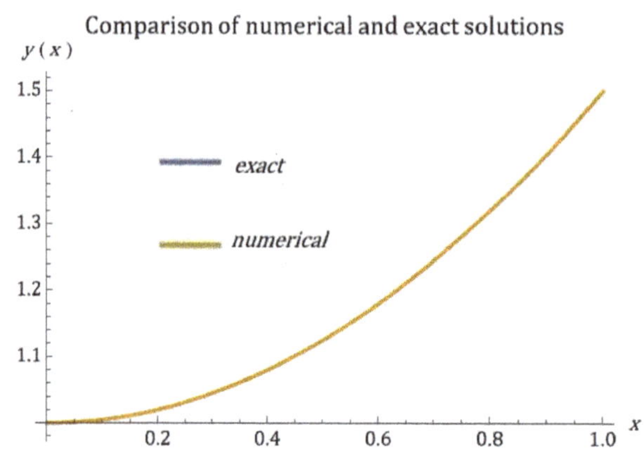

Figure 1. The approximate solution, $y(x)$, and the exact solutions are depicted in Figure 1. This visual simulation highlights the significant overlap between the two solutions.

Example 2: We now consider solving a third one-dimensional linear fractional differential equation of the form:

$$\frac{d^2y(x)}{dx^2} - 2\left(\frac{d^{0.75}y(x)}{dx^{0.75}}\right) + y(x) = f(x) \tag{19}$$

where $f(x)$ is given by

$$f(x) = x^3 + 6x + \frac{128}{15\Gamma\left(\frac{1}{4}\right)}x^{2.25} \tag{20}$$

where $\frac{d^2y(x)}{dx^2}$ represents the classical second-order derivative, and $\frac{d^{0.75}y(x)}{dx^{0.75}}$ denotes the fractional derivative of order 3/4 = 0.75, which can be interpreted using either the Caputo or Riemann–Liouville definition depending on the initial and boundary conditions.

This equation is particularly interesting because it combines local (integer-order) and nonlocal (fractional-order) differential operators, modeling systems where both instantaneous and memory-dependent behaviors are present. The fractional term introduces a nonlocal influence, capturing effects such as historical dependence or anomalous transport, which are common in complex physical and engineering systems.

The main objective here is to assess how well our numerical method handles the interaction between different derivative orders, especially when fractional orders are less than one, as is the case here. This type of mixed-order equation is more challenging to solve due to the presence of the fractional term, which requires careful numerical treatment.

By applying our proposed method to this problem, we aim to demonstrate its robustness, flexibility, and accuracy in solving fractional differential equations of mixed order across the domain $0 \leq x \leq 1$ under appropriate boundary conditions $y(0) = 0$ and $y'(0) = 0$. This example serves as a further test of the proposed numerical method's effectiveness in handling equations involving both integer- and non-integer-order derivatives, particularly when initial-value conditions are prescribed. The inclusion of a fractional derivative of order 3/4 = 0.75 poses additional challenges due to the nonlocal nature of fractional operators, which depend on the entire history of the solution up to a given point.

We utilize the initial conditions $y(0) = 0$, $y'(0) = 0$, and the numerical solution of this equation is sought out in intervals $0 \leq x \leq 1$. The exact solution which satisfies initial conditions and Equation (19) is given by

$$y_{exact}(x) = x^3. \tag{21}$$

Let us twice integrate the equation on both sides as given below:

$$\Rightarrow I^2\left(D^2(y(x))\right) - 2I^2\left(D^{0.75}(y(x))\right) + I^2(y(x)) = I^2(f(x)) \tag{22}$$

The integration twice (I^2) of both terms with respect to variable x is provided with two initial conditions implemented [30,39],

After first integration of the first term in Equation (22),

$$\Rightarrow I(y'(x) - y'(0)) - 2I^2\left(D^{0.75}(y(x))\right) + I^2(y(x)) = I^2(f(x)) \tag{23}$$

After second integration and implementing the initial conditions,

$$\Rightarrow y(x) - y(0) - 2I^2\left(D^{0.75}(y(x))\right) + I^2(y(x)) = I^2(f(x)).$$

A simplified representation of this equation is obtained:

$$\Rightarrow y(x) - 2I^2\left(D^{0.75}(y(x))\right) + I^2(y(x)) = I^2(f(x)). \tag{24}$$

We approximate that the solution of Equation (19) can be expressed in terms of the fractional B-polys expansion in variable x:

$$y\,(x) = \sum_{i}^{n} c_i\; B_i(x)\,. \tag{25}$$

where c_i are the unknown expansion coefficients in Equation (23). After substituting these fractional B-polys into Equation (22) using the Galerkin method for minimization [38], we obtain the following expression,

$$\begin{gathered}\Rightarrow \sum c_i\; B_i(x) \; - 2I^2\big(D^{0.75}(\sum c_i\; B_i(x)\;)\big) + I^2(\sum c_i\; B_i(x)\;) = I^2(f(x)) \\ \Rightarrow c_i\;\left[\langle B_i|B_l\rangle - \langle 2\;I^2\big(D^{0.75}(B_i)\;\big)|B_l\rangle + \langle I^2(B_i)|B_l\rangle\right] = \langle I^2(f)|B_l\;\rangle \\ \Rightarrow C\;[M - N + P] = W\end{gathered} \tag{26}$$

where matrices M, N, P, W are represented by matrix elements

$$\begin{gathered}Let,\; M = \langle B_i|B_l\rangle \\ N = \langle 2\;I^2\big(D^{0.75}(B_i)\;\big)|B_l\rangle \\ P = \langle I^2(B_i)|B_l\rangle \\ W = \langle\; I^2(f)|\;B_l\;\rangle \\ X = [M - N + P].\end{gathered} \tag{27}$$

We can arrange this equation in terms of matrices so that

$$X\,C = W. \tag{28}$$

This formulation results in an $(n\;+\;1)$ by $(n\;+\;1)$ linear system $X\;C\;=\;W$, which is solved numerically for the expansion coefficients c_i in Equation (34). These coefficients are then substituted into Equation (22) to construct the approximate solution. Matrices X and W in Equations (24) and (25) are defined through inner products of fractional B-polys, computed numerically. The coefficient vector C is determined by solving the linear system derived from Equation (26). The final numerical solution is given by

$$\begin{gathered}y_{appr.}(x) = \sum c_i\; B_i(x) \\ = 0.\times 10^{-30} + 0.\times 10^{-29}x + 0.\times 10^{-28}x^2 + 1.0x^3 \\ y_{appr.}(x) = 1.0x^3.\end{gathered} \tag{29}$$

The above result is highly accurate and matches the exact solution $y_{exact}(x) = x^3$. The B-polys with $n = 3$ have been employed in x variables in order to solve the linear fractional Equation (26). The perfect agreement between the two results, exact and numerical solutions, at the level of machine accuracy is demonstrated in Figure 2. This solution precisely matches the exact solution, illustrating the effectiveness of the current approach. For this example, we also present a graph to compare the exact solution of the example. The comparative plot visually validates this exact correspondence, demonstrating the approach's effectiveness.

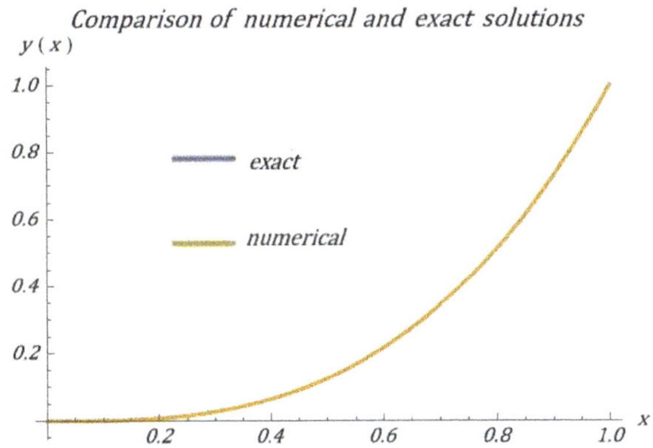

Figure 2. The approximate solution, $y(x)$, and the exact solutions are depicted in Figure 2. This visual simulation highlights the significant overlap between the two solutions.

Example 3: We now consider a second example involving the solution of a one-dimensional linear fractional differential equation of the form [40]:

$$\frac{d^{1.5}y(x)}{dx^{1.5}} + y(x) = f(x), \tag{30}$$

where $\frac{d^{1.5}y(x)}{dx^{1.5}}$ denotes the fractional derivative of order 1.5 with respect to x, typically interpreted in the Caputo or Riemann–Liouville sense. This equation is representative of systems exhibiting super-diffusive behavior, where the dynamics are governed by nonlocal and memory-dependent effects. The inclusion of a non-integer derivative of order greater than one introduces both fractional integration and differentiation into the model, reflecting more complex physical phenomena than traditional integer-order models can capture. This example is used to further validate the proposed numerical method's ability to handle fractional orders beyond the first derivative and to demonstrate its effectiveness in providing accurate solutions for equations involving higher-order fractional operators.

The function $f(x)$ on the right-hand side of Equation (30) is given by

$$f(x) = x^5 - x^4 + \frac{128}{7\sqrt{\pi}}x^{3.5} - \frac{64}{5\sqrt{\pi}}x^{2.5}. \tag{31}$$

Subject to the boundary conditions, $y(0) = 0$ and $y(1) = 0$, we seek a numerical solution to this fractional differential equation over the interval $0 \leq x \leq 1$. These conditions ensure a well-posed boundary value problem and allow for a meaningful comparison between the numerical and exact solutions. The purpose of this example is to assess the accuracy of the proposed method when applied to a fractional differential equation involving a non-integer derivative of order 1.5. The exact analytical solution of Equation (30) is given by:

$$y_{exact}(x) = x^4(x-1), \tag{32}$$

which satisfies the boundary conditions and serves as a benchmark for evaluating the performance of the numerical approach. Applying double integration with respect to x to both sides of Equation (30), yields an equivalent integral form that can be more suitable for certain numerical methods. Specifically, integrating both sides twice reduces the fractional derivative order and helps in transforming the problem into a form that is more amenable to approximation techniques. Both terms are integrated with respect to x while incorporating two initial conditions, yielding the resulting expression is:

$$\Rightarrow I^2\left(D^{1.5}(y(x))\right) + I^2(y(x)) = I^2(f(x)). \quad (33)$$

This transformation can facilitate the construction of numerical schemes by replacing fractional derivatives with their corresponding integral representations, allowing the use of standard quadrature or interpolation-based methods.

The approximate solution to Equation (30) takes the form of a fractional-order Bernstein polynomial expansion in the spatial variable x:

$$y\,(x) = \sum_{i}^{n} c_i\, B_i(x), \quad (34)$$

where c_i denotes the expansion coefficient. Substituting the fractional B-polynomial expansion into Equation (33) and applying the Galerkin minimization procedure to Equation (33) yields [38]

$$\Rightarrow I^2\left(D^{1.5}(\sum c_i\, B_i(x)\,)\right) + I^2(\sum c_i\, B_i(x)) = I^2(f(x)). \quad (35)$$

This equation can be expressed in matrix form as

$$\begin{gathered} \Rightarrow c_i\left[\left\langle I^2(D^{1.5}(B_i))\,\middle|B_l\right\rangle + \langle I^2(B_i)|B_l\rangle\right] = \langle I^2 f|\, B_l\,\rangle \\ \Rightarrow [M+\ N]C = W \\ \Rightarrow X\,C = W. \end{gathered} \quad (36)$$

where matrices M, N, and W are represented by matrix elements.

Let

$$\begin{gathered} X = [M+N] \\ M = \left\langle\, I^2(D^{1.5}(B_i))\,\middle|B_l\right\rangle \\ N = \langle I^2(B_i)|B_l\rangle \\ W = \langle I^2(f)|\,B_l\rangle \\ C = \sum_{i}^{n} c_i \end{gathered} \quad (37)$$

The formulation reduces to an $(n\,+\,1)$ by $(n\,+\,1)$ linear system $X\,C\;=\;W$, which is solved numerically for the coefficient of vector C. These coefficients are then substituted into Equation (33) to construct the complete solution. The matrices X and W in Equations (36) and (37) are defined through inner products of fractional B-polynomials, computed numerically. The coefficients c_i are obtained by solving the linear system derived from Equation (36). The final numerical solution is given by

$$\begin{gathered} y_{estimate}(x) = \sum c_i\, B_i(x) \\ = -2.942091015256665\times 10^{-15} + 1.110500580381312\times 10^{-12}x \\ -1.201538868400575\times 10^{-11}x^2 + 3.955114014075889\times 10^{-11}x^3 \\ -1.0000000000506684x^4 + 1.0000000000222073x^5 \end{gathered} \quad (38)$$

The numerical solution exhibits excellent agreement with the exact solution $y_{exact}(x) = x^4(x-1)$. Using fractional B-polynomials $n = 5$ in x variables, we solved the linear fractional Equation (30). Figures 3 and 4 show perfect convergence between the numerical and exact solutions at machine precision level, confirming the method's accuracy. The exact correspondence between both solutions validates the effectiveness of our approach. For clarity, we include a comparative visualization of the exact and numerical solutions.

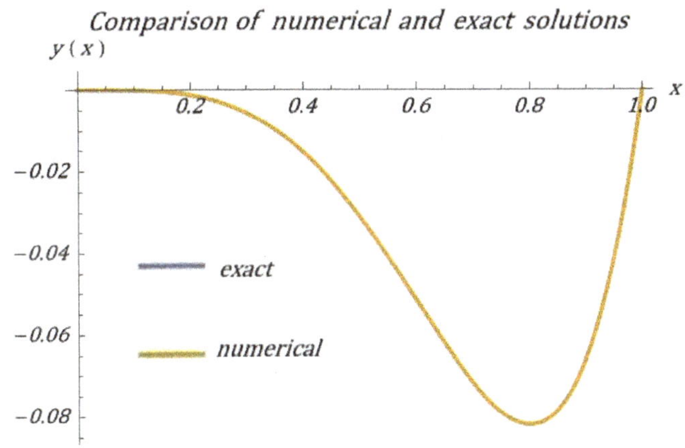

Figure 3. The approximate solution, $y(x)$, and the exact solutions are depicted in Figure 2. This visual simulation highlights the significant overlap between the two solutions.

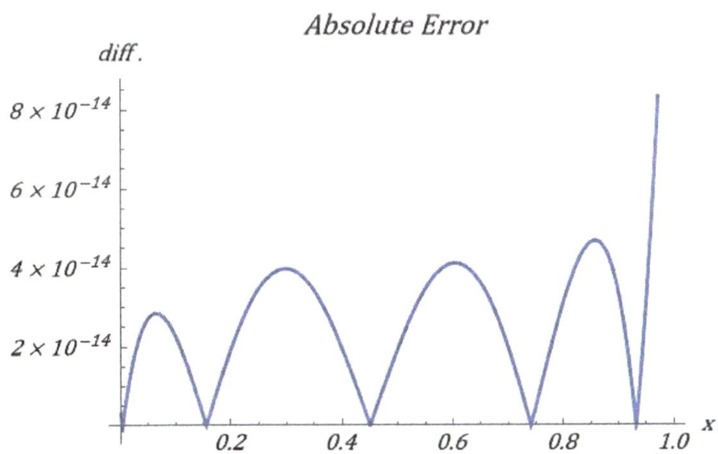

Figure 4. The picture above presents the absolute error between the exact and approximate solutions for example 3. Notably, the absolute error is on the order of 10^{-14}, indicating an extremely high degree of accuracy in the approximation. This level of precision suggests that the approximate solution closely aligns with the exact solution, making it a reliable choice for further analysis or applications.

5. Error Analysis

In this section, we perform an error analysis of examples considered in this study. Table 1 presents a comparison between the exact and the approximate solutions for Example 1 at various values of x within the interval $[0,\ 1]$. The approximate results were obtained using the proposed numerical method, and the absolute error was calculated as the absolute difference between the exact and numerical solutions divided by a hundred. As shown in Table 1, the error is exceptionally small at the lower end of the interval 1.0×10^{-10} at $x = 0$ and increases gradually with larger values of x. The maximum absolute error remains below 4×10^{-4} at $x = 1$, indicating a high level of accuracy across the domain. When compared to the results reported in [40], our method demonstrates significantly improved precision, particularly in the early and mid-range values of x. These results validate the effectiveness and reliability of the proposed approach in solving linear fractional differential equations.

Table 1. For Example, 1, at different values of x, we compare our calculated solution $y_{appr.}(x)$ with those from another study [40]. The exact solution is $y_{exact}(x) = \left(1 + \frac{x^2}{2}\right)$.

x	Our Result	Reference Result [40]	Absolute Error
0	1.00000	1.00000	1.0×10^{-10}
0.1	1.00500	1.00482	1.7×10^{-6}
0.2	1.02	1.01955	4.4×10^{-6}
0.3	1.045	1.04456	4.4×10^{-6}
0.4	1.08	1.08021	2.2×10^{-6}
0.5	1.125	1.12689	1.89×10^{-5}
0.6	1.18000	1.18495	4.96×10^{-5}
0.7	1.24500	1.25479	9.79×10^{-5}
0.8	1.32000	1.33676	1.67×10^{-4}
0.9	1.40500	1.43125	2.62×10^{-4}
1.0	1.50000	1.53863	3.86×10^{-4}

Table 2 presents a comparison between the exact and approximate solutions for Example 2 at various values of x within the interval [0, 1]. The approximate values were obtained using the proposed numerical method, and the absolute error was calculated as the absolute difference between the exact and approximate solutions divided by a hundred. As shown in the table, the error is exceptionally small at all values of x, indicating a high level of accuracy across the domain. These results validate the effectiveness and reliability of the proposed approach in solving linear fractional differential equations.

Table 2. For Example 2, at different values of x, we compare our calculated solution $y_{appr.}(x)$ with those from another study [40]. The exact solution is $y_{exact}(x) = x^3$.

x	Our Result	Reference Result [40]	Absolute Error
0	0	0	0
0.1	0.00100	0.00100	1.105×10^{-19}
0.2	0.00800	0.00800	2.255×10^{-19}
0.3	0.02700	0.02700	3.469×10^{-19}
0.4	0.06400	0.06400	4.163×10^{-19}
0.5	0.125	0.12500	5.551×10^{-19}
0.6	0.21600	0.21600	5.551×10^{-19}
0.7	0.34300	0.34300	5.551×10^{-19}
0.8	0.51200	0.51200	1.110×10^{-18}
0.9	0.72900	0.72900	1.110×10^{-18}
1.0	1.0	1.0	0

Table 3 below presents a comparison between the exact and approximate solutions for Example 3 at various values of x within the interval $[0, 1]$. The approximate values were obtained using the proposed numerical method, and the absolute error was calculated as the absolute difference between the exact and approximate solutions divided by 100. As shown in the table, the error is exceptionally small at the lower end of the interval 2.2×10^{-9} at $x = 0$ and increases gradually with larger values of x. The maximum absolute error remains below 3.2×10^{-9} at $x = 1$, indicating a high level of accuracy across the domain. When compared to the results reported in [40], our method demonstrates significantly improved precision at values of x. These results validate the effectiveness and reliability of the proposed approach in solving linear fractional differential equations.

Table 3. For Example, 3, at different values of x, we compare our calculated solution $y_{appr.}(x)$ with those from another study [40]. The exact solution is $y_{exact}(x) = x^4(x-1)$.

x	Our Result	Reference Result [40]	Absolute Error
0	0	2.19999×10^{-7}	2.199×10^{-9}
0.1	−0.00009	−0.00008	1.964×10^{-9}
0.2	−0.00128	−0.00127	2.131×10^{-9}
0.3	−0.00567	−0.00566	2.544×10^{-9}
0.4	−0.01536	−0.01535	3.079×10^{-9}
0.5	−0.03125	−0.03124	3.637×10^{-9}
0.6	−0.05184	−0.05183	4.124×10^{-9}
0.7	−0.07203	−0.07202	4.447×10^{-9}
0.8	−0.08191	−0.08191	4.497×10^{-9}
0.9	−0.06561	−0.06560	4.139×10^{-9}
1.0	0	3.20000×10^{-7}	3.200×10^{-9}

To quantitatively assess the performance of our technique, we compare its results against those of a previously established method [40]. As detailed in Tables 1–3, the numerical approximations $y_{appr.}(x)$ generated by our method for different problems are in significantly closer agreement with the benchmark solutions than the values reported in [40]. This comparative analysis clearly indicates the enhanced precision and reliability of our proposed approach.

Table 4 demonstrates the convergence properties of the proposed method for Example 3, where the exact solution is given by $y_{exact}(x) = x^5 - x^4 = x^4(x-1)$ [40]. The table lists the absolute error $|y_{appr.}(x) - y_{exact}(x)| \times 10^{-2}$ at various points x for an increasing number of fractional B-polynomial basis functions n. The results clearly show that the accuracy of the approximation improves significantly as the size of the basis set n is increased, albeit with a corresponding increase in computational cost, as indicated by the CPU time provided in the last row of Table 4. The absolute error approaches zero for the basis set $n = 5$ and $n = 6$ as shown in the last two columns of Table 4.

Table 5 shows that the absolute error in Example 1 depends on the fractional order α of the basis set. Although the exact solution in this case is of integer order, the method's inherent tunability offers a promising direction for future research into problems governed by fractional-order dynamics. It is evident that for $\alpha = 0.9$ and 0.75, the absolute error is significantly higher, indicating that a greater number of fractional basis functions are required to improve the accuracy of the solution. At the same time, the computational cost increases significantly. Therefore, in these cases, $\alpha = 1$ was selected for comparison with the exact solutions.

Table 4. For various values of x, we evaluate the absolute error between the approximate solution $y_{appr.}(x)$ and the exact solution $y_{exact}(x)$, considering different numbers of basis functions and corresponding CPU times.

x	Absolute Error Between Exact and Approximate Solutions at Various Values of x and the Number of Basis Used in This Study				
	n = 2	n = 3	n = 4	n = 5	n = 6
0	10.6104	1.93419	0.77274	0	0
0.1	17.8211	4.83627	4.00420	0	0
0.2	24.5130	7.59033	7.10768	0	0
0.3	30.6883	10.180380	10.046122	0	0
0.4	36.3492	12.590412	12.791602	0	0
0.5	41.4964	14.805625	15.324165	0	0
0.6	46.1284	16.813614	17.630604	0	0
0.7	50.2403	18.605579	19.703266	0	0
0.8	53.8221	20.177514	21.53885	0	0
0.9	56.8578	21.531418	23.13722	0	0
1.0	59.3244	22.676487	24.50017	0	0
CPU time	8.83 s	10.39 s	19.91 s	34.88 s	56.25 s

Table 5. In example 1 the exact solution to the fractional differential equation is $y(x) = 1 + \frac{x^2}{2}$. The method's sensitivity to fractional order values α near 0 and 1 is illustrated using absolute error presented in each column. The number of fractional B-polynomials was fixed at $n = 4$, while the fractional order α was varied between 0 and 1.

x	α=1 Absolute Error	α=0.9 Absolute Error	$\alpha=\frac{3}{4}$ Absolute Error	$\alpha=\frac{1}{2}$ Absolute Error
0	8.29336×10^{-14}	0.00028	0.00027	1.39976×10^{-12}
0.1	1.55431×10^{-15}	0.00020	0.00019	7.91366×10^{-13}
0.2	2.22044×10^{-15}	0.00051	0.00053	1.63069×10^{-12}
0.3	4.15223×10^{-14}	0.00105	0.00104	2.65631×10^{-12}
0.4	7.90478×10^{-14}	0.00173	0.00159	3.71058×10^{-12}
0.5	9.28146×10^{-14}	0.00240	0.00208	4.65338×10^{-12}
0.6	7.68274×10^{-14}	0.00299	0.00247	5.37525×10^{-12}
0.7	3.99680×10^{-14}	0.00344	0.00274	5.78692×10^{-12}
0.8	7.99360×10^{-15}	0.00377	0.00292	5.81734×10^{-12}
0.9	2.10942×10^{-14}	0.00406	0.00305	5.40567×10^{-12}
1	1.36335×10^{-13}	0.00442	0.00321	4.50128×10^{-12}

6. Conclusions

Our current methodology effectively solves linear fractional differential equations, extending its previous application to linear and nonlinear ordinary differential equations. This study specifically addresses higher-order fractional differential equations subject to multiple initial and boundary conditions. The method offers high accuracy, with solutions for most fractional equations aligning exactly with known analytical solutions. For the remaining cases, absolute errors, defined as the difference between exact and numerical solutions, are typically on the order of 10^{-14} (see Figure 4 and example 3). Solution accuracy is directly influenced by the size of the fractional B-poly basis set employed. Larger basis sets yield more accurate solutions but necessitate more iterations to achieve coefficient convergence, consequently increasing computational time and cost. A notable advantage of our approach is its relative simplicity and accessibility. It avoids grid representation by utilizing a fractional B-polys basis set (Equations (1)–(5)), which reduces the number of iterations needed for coefficient convergence compared to some alternative numerical approaches. This straightforward implementation was realized using the symbolic programming language Mathematica [41].

This study presented an innovative numerical technique for solving linear fractional differential equations (LFDEs) using modified fractional B-polys. The proposed method demonstrated high accuracy and efficiency in handling fractional-order derivatives, as evidenced by the close agreement between numerical and exact solutions across multiple examples. Comparison analyses of all results are provided in four tables in Section 5. Key findings include the following.

The method achieved solutions with absolute errors on the order of 10^{-14}, shown in example 3 in Figure 4, showcasing its capability to approximate fractional differential equations with excellent precision. The graphical comparisons further validated the method's effectiveness, with near-perfect overlaps between exact and numerical solutions. By leveraging fractional B-poly bases and operational matrices, the approach simplified the integration and differentiation processes inherent in fractional calculus. This framework reduced computational complexity while maintaining robustness, even for higher-order fractional derivatives. The computational time for all examples considered here was less than 1–2 min of CPU time. More details on CPU time with respect to the basis set are provided in Table 4.

The technique successfully addresses various LFDEs, including those with multiple initial and boundary conditions, demonstrating its adaptability to diverse problems. The examples spanned different fractional orders and functional forms, underscoring the method's broad applicability. The study bridged gaps in existing numerical methods by offering a systematic approach to handle nonlocality and memory effects in fractional models. This advancement has potential applications in physics, engineering, and other fields where fractional calculus is pivotal. While the method excels in accuracy, larger basis sets may increase computational costs. Future research could explore optimizations for computational efficiency, extensions to nonlinear fractional equations, and applications in multi-physics systems.

In summary, this work contributes a reliable and accessible numerical framework for solving LFDEs, combining theoretical rigor with practical utility. The results affirm the potential of B-poly bases in fractional calculus, paving the way for further innovations in computational mathematics.

Author Contributions: Conceptualization: M.I.B., Software: M.I.B., Methodology: M.I.B. and N.D., Formal Analysis: M.I.B., N.D. and M.H.R., Validation: M.I.B., N.D. and M.H.R., Data Curation: M.I.B., N.D. and M.H.R., Resources: M.I.B., Project Administration: M.I.B., Investigation: M.I.B., N.D. and M.H.R., Supervision: M.I.B., Writing—Original Draft: M.I.B. and M.H.R., Writing—Review and Editing: M.I.B., N.D. and M.H.R. All authors have read and agreed to the published version of the manuscript.

Funding: This research received no external funding.

Data Availability Statement: The data supporting the findings of this study are available within the article.

Acknowledgments: The authors gratefully acknowledge the use of departmental computing resources for this study.

Conflicts of Interest: The authors declare no competing financial or personal interests that could influence this work.

References

1. Sun, H.G.; Zhang, Y.; Baleanu, D.; Chen, W.; Chen, Y.Q. A new collection of real world applications of fractional calculus in science and engineering. *Commun. Nonlinear Sci. Numer. Simul.* **2018**, *64*, 213–231. [CrossRef]
2. Iqbal, M.A.B.; Raza, M.Z.; Khan, A.; Abdeljawad, T.; Almutairi, D.K. Advanced wave dynamics in the STF-mBBM equation using fractional calculus. *Sci. Rep.* **2025**, *15*, 1–24. [CrossRef]
3. Birs, I.; Muresan, C. Fractional-Order Event-Based Control Meets Biomedical Applications. In *Computational and Mathematical Models in Biology*; Springer: Cham, Switzerland, 2023; pp. 281–304. [CrossRef]
4. Tien, D.N. Fractional stochastic differential equations with applications to finance. *J. Math. Anal. Appl.* **2013**, *397*, 334–348. [CrossRef]
5. Najafi, A.; Taleghani, R. Fractional Liu uncertain differential equation and its application to finance. *Chaos Solitons Fractals* **2022**, *165*, 112875. [CrossRef]
6. Al-Refai, M.; Baleanu, D.; Al-Refai, M.; Baleanu, D. Comparison principles of fractional differential equations with non-local derivative and their applications. *AIMS Math.* **2021**, *6*, 1443–1451. [CrossRef]
7. Derakhshan, M.H.; Ordokhani, Y. Numerical and stability analysis of linear B-spline and local radial basis functions for solving two-dimensional distributed-order time-fractional telegraph models. *J. Appl. Math. Comput.* **2025**, *71*, 2859–2887. [CrossRef]
8. Tavazoei, M.S. A note on fractional-order derivatives of periodic functions. *Automatica* **2010**, *46*, 945–948. [CrossRef]
9. Singh, M.; Singh, M.P.; Tamsir, M.; Asif, M. Analysis of Fractional-Order Nonlinear Dynamical Systems by Using Different Techniques. *Int. J. Appl. Comput. Math.* **2025**, *11*, 47. [CrossRef]
10. Du, F.; Lu, J.G. New criterion for finite-time stability of fractional delay systems. *Appl. Math. Lett.* **2020**, *104*, 106248. [CrossRef]
11. Baishya, C.; Veeresha, P. Laguerre polynomial-based operational matrix of integration for solving fractional differential equations with non-singular kernel. *Proc. R. Soc. A* **2021**, *477*, 86–90. [CrossRef]
12. Luchko, Y.F.; Rivero, M.; Trujillo, J.J.; Velasco, M.P. Fractional models, non-locality, and complex systems. *Comput. Math. Appl.* **2010**, *59*, 1048–1056. [CrossRef]
13. Abu-Ghuwaleh, M.; Saadeh, R. New definitions of fractional derivatives and integrals for complex analytic functions. *Arab. J. Basic. Appl. Sci.* **2023**, *30*, 675–690. [CrossRef]
14. de Oliveira, E.C. Fractional Derivatives. *Stud. Syst. Decis. Control* **2019**, *240*, 169–222. [CrossRef]
15. Kopteva, N. Pointwise-in-time a posteriori error control for time-fractional parabolic equations. *Appl. Math. Lett.* **2022**, *123*, 107515. [CrossRef]
16. Mohammad, M.; Trounev, A. Computational precision in time fractional PDEs: Euler wavelets and novel numerical techniques. *Partial. Differ. Equ. Appl. Math.* **2024**, *12*, 100918. [CrossRef]
17. Zhang, D.; Wang, Y.; Jiang, K.; Liang, L. Safe optimal robust control of nonlinear systems with asymmetric input constraints using reinforcement learning. *Appl. Intell.* **2024**, *54*, 1–13. [CrossRef]
18. Liu, P.; Meeker, W.Q. Robust Numerical Methods for Nonlinear Regression. 2024. Available online: https://arxiv.org/abs/2403.12759v1 (accessed on 9 April 2025).
19. Zhang, S.; Jia, R.; He, D.; Chu, F.; Mao, Z. A general data-driven nonlinear robust optimization framework based on statistic limit and principal component analysis. *Comput. Chem. Eng.* **2022**, *160*, 107707. [CrossRef]
20. Momani, S.; Odibat, Z. Numerical comparison of methods for solving linear differential equations of fractional order. *Chaos Solitons Fractals* **2007**, *31*, 1248–1255. [CrossRef]
21. Rodríguez-Rozas, Á.; Acebrón, J.A.; Spigler, R. The PDD Method for Solving Linear, Nonlinear, and Fractional PDEs Problems. In *Nonlocal and Fractional Operators*; Springer: Cham, Switzerland, 2021; Volume 26, pp. 239–273. [CrossRef]
22. AlAhmad, R.; Al-Khaleel, M.; Almefleh, H. On solutions of linear and nonlinear fractional differential equations with application to fractional order RC type circuits. *J. Comput. Appl. Math.* **2024**, *438*, 115507. [CrossRef]
23. Ali, H.M.; Ameen, I.G. Application of various methods to solve some fractional differential equations in different fields. In *Fractional Differential Equations*; Elsevier: Amsterdam, The Netherlands, 2024. [CrossRef]
24. Bhatti, M.; Bracken, P.; Dimakis, N.; Herrera, A. Solution of mathematical model for gas solubility using fractional-order Bhatti polynomials. *J. Phys. Commun.* **2018**, *2*, 085013. [CrossRef]
25. Bhatti, M.I.; Bhatta, D.D. Numerical solutions of Burgers' equation in a B-polynomial basis. *Phys. Scr.* **2006**, *73*, 539. [CrossRef]
26. Bhatti, M.I.; Bracken, P. Solutions of differential equations in a Bernstein polynomial basis. *J. Comput. Appl. Math.* **2007**, *205*, 272–280. [CrossRef]
27. Bhatti, M.I.; Hinojosa, E. 26 results of hyperbolic partial differential equations in B-poly basis. *J. Phys. Commun.* **2020**, *4*, 095010. [CrossRef]

28. Bhatti, M.I.; Rahman, M.H. Technique to Solve Linear Fractional Differential Equations Using B-Polynomials Bases. *Fractal Fract.* **2021**, *5*, 208. [CrossRef]
29. Rahman, M.H.; Bhatti, M.I.; Dimakis, N. Employing a Fractional Basis Set to Solve Nonlinear Multidimensional Fractional Differential Equations. *Mathematics* **2023**, *11*, 4604. [CrossRef]
30. Bhatti, M.I.; Rahman, M.H. A B-Polynomial Approach to Approximate Solutions of PDEs with Multiple Initial Conditions. *Axioms* **2024**, *13*, 833. [CrossRef]
31. Saadeh, R.; Al-Wadi, A.; Qazza, A. Advancing Solutions for Fractional Differential Equations: Integrating the Sawi Transform with Iterative Methods. *Eur. J. Pure Appl. Math.* **2025**, *18*, 5583. [CrossRef]
32. Hafez, M.; Alshowaikh, F.; Voon, B.W.N.; Alkhazaleh, S.; Al-Faiz, H. Review on Recent Advances in Fractional Differentiation and its Applications. *Prog. Fract. Differ. Appl.* **2025**, *11*, 245–261. [CrossRef]
33. Al-Nana, A.; Batiha, I.M.; Jebril, I.H.; Al Khazaleh, S.; Abdeljawad, T. Numerical Solution of Conformable Fractional Periodic Boundary Value Problems by Shifted Jacobi Method. *Int. J. Math. Eng. Manag. Sci.* **2024**, *10*, 189–206. [CrossRef]
34. García, A.; Negreanu, M.; Ureña, F.; Vargas, A.M. On the numerical solution to space fractional differential equations using meshless finite differences. *J. Comput. Appl. Math.* **2025**, *457*, 116322. [CrossRef]
35. El-Tantawy, S.A.; Al-Johani, A.S.; Almuqrin, A.H.; Khan, A.; El-Sherif, L.S. Novel approximations to the fourth-order fractional Cahn–Hillard equations: Application to the Tantawy Technique and other two techniques with Yang transform. *J. Low. Freq. Noise Vib. Act. Control* **2025**, *44*, 14613484251322240. [CrossRef]
36. Chao, Z.; Wang, X.-S.; Zaky, M.A. Finite Difference/Fractional Pertrov–Galerkin Spectral Method for Linear Time-Space Fractional Reaction–Diffusion Equation. *Mathematics* **2025**, *13*, 1864. [CrossRef]
37. Bhatti, M.I. Solutions of the harmonic oscillator equation in a B-polynomial basis. *Adv. Stud. Theor. Phys.* **2009**, *3*, 451–460.
38. Podlubny, I. *Fractional Differential Equations: An Introduction to Fractional Derivatives, Fractional Differential Equations, to Methods of Their Solution and Some of Their Applications*; Mathematics in Science and Engineering; Academic Press: Cambridge, MA, USA, 1999; Volume 198.
39. Al-Mazmumy, M.; Alsulami, M. Utilization of the Modified Adomian Decomposition Method on the Bagley-Torvik Equation Amidst Dirichlet Boundary Conditions. *Eur. J. Pure Appl. Math.* **2024**, *17*, 546–568. [CrossRef]
40. Kawala, A.M. Numerical Solution for Initial and Boundary Value Problems of Fractional Order. *Adv. Pure Math.* **2018**, *8*, 831. [CrossRef]
41. Wolfram Research, Inc. *Mathematica 14.1*, Version 14.1; Wolfram Research, Inc.: Champaign, IL, USA, 2024.

mathematics

MDPI

Article

Nonlinear Wave Structures, Multistability, and Chaotic Behavior of Quantum Dust-Acoustic Shocks in Dusty Plasma with Size Distribution Effects

Huanbin Xue and Lei Zhang *

School of Mathematics and Statistics, Hanshan Normal University, Chaozhou 521041, China; hbxue@hstc.edu.cn
* Correspondence: zhangl399@hstc.edu.cn

Abstract

This paper presents a detailed study of the $(3+1)$-dimensional Zakharov–Kuznetsov–Burgers equation to investigate shock-wave phenomena in dusty plasmas with quantum effects. The model provides significant physical insight into nonlinear dispersive and dissipative structures arising in charged-dust–ion environments, corresponding to both laboratory and astrophysical plasmas. We then perform a qualitative, numerically assisted dynamical analysis using bifurcation diagrams, multistability checks, return maps, Poincaré sections, and phase portraits. For both the unperturbed and a perturbed system, we identify chaotic, quasi-periodic, and periodic regimes from these numerical diagnostics; accordingly, our dynamical conclusions are qualitative. We also examine frequency-response and time-delay sensitivity, providing a qualitative classification of nonlinear behavior across a broad parameter range. After establishing the global dynamical picture, traveling-wave solutions are obtained using the Paul–Painlevé approach. These solutions represent shock and solitary structures in the plasma system, thereby bridging the analytical and dynamical perspectives. The significance of this study lies in combining a detailed dynamical framework with exact traveling-wave solutions, allowing a deeper understanding of nonlinear shock dynamics in quantum dusty plasmas. These results not only advance theoretical plasma modeling but also hold potential applications in plasma-based devices, wave propagation in optical fibers, and astrophysical plasma environments.

Keywords: Zakharov–Kuznetsov–Burgers equation; shock waves; bifurcation analysis; Lyapunov exponents; chaotic attractors; multistability; Poincaré maps; Paul–Painlevé approach

MSC: 35C07; 35C08; 37G35

1. Introduction

Nonlinear partial differential equations (NLPDEs) serve as significant tools for modeling collective processes in complex plasmas, specifically in systems where dust particles play an essential role [1,2]. In dusty plasmas, the distribution of dust grain sizes has a profound influence on the dynamics of nonlinear wave propagation [3]. In contrast to idealized models that assume uniform dust particles, realistic plasmas contain grains of varying sizes and charges, which modify both the dispersion and dissipation properties of the medium [4]. This variation directly affects the stability and structure of shock waves, leading to broadened wavefronts, modified amplitudes, and in certain regimes, the emergence of new nonlinear characteristics such as precursor solitons or attenuated shocks [5].

In the context of quantum dusty plasmas, the importance of NLPDEs becomes even more pronounced. Quantum effects introduce additional pressure-like terms arising from tunneling and degeneracy, which, when combined with dust size distribution, create a extremely nonlinear environment for wave propagation [6]. NLPDE-based models such as Zakharov–Kuznetsov (ZK) or Burgers-type equations presents an effective mathematical framework to capture these complexities by incorporating dissipation, dispersion, and nonlinear interactions in a unified manner [7]. Through such formulations, one can observe how different dust size distributions alter shock profiles, potentially trigger instabilities, and modulate energy transport [8]. These insights are relevant not only for laboratory plasmas but also for astrophysical environments, where dust size variation is a natural characteristic and shock waves play a critical role in structure formation and energy dissipation [9].

Solitons and exact solutions to NLPDEs are of great significance in comprehending the role of dust size distribution on shock-wave dynamics in quantum dusty plasmas [10,11]. Dust grains of different sizes modify the charge-to-mass ratio and consequently alter the dissipative and dispersive properties of the medium, which directly influences the shape, amplitude, and stability of solitons and shock profiles [12]. Exact solutions allow for a precise characterization of how dust size variation can lead to broadened shocks, attenuated fronts, or the coexistence of solitary and oscillatory behaviors, which are crucial in describing energy transport and nonlinear interactions in such plasmas [13]. Recently, many scholars have focused on deriving solitons and exact solutions to NLPDEs using a variety of analytical techniques, including Painlevé analysis [14], the Hirota bilinear method [15], the extended tanh-function method [16], the (G'/G)-expansion method [17], the exp-function method [18], the variational iteration method [19], Backlund transformation [20], the modified Jacobi elliptic expansion method [21], the improved F-expansion method [22], and the inverse scattering method [23]. These techniques not only provide explicit solitary and shock-wave solutions but also shed light on their stability, bifurcation properties, and possible chaotic transitions in dusty-plasma environments. Such studies are valuable in both laboratory plasma experiments and astrophysical scenarios, where dust size distribution plays a significant role in the propagation of nonlinear waves and the formation of shock structures [24].

The $(3+1)$-dimensional ZK–Burgers equation presents a compact yet physically rich framework for explaining shock-wave phenomena in plasmas containing dust-charged particles with quantum effects [25]. By combining the ZK dispersion (capturing oblique, multidimensional propagation and transverse modulation) with Burgers-type dissipation (modeling viscosity, dust–neutral drag, and charge-fluctuation damping), the ZK–Burgers model embeds the essential steepening–dispersion–dissipation balance that governs the emergence of monotonic and solitary structures, oscillatory shocks, and their interactions [26]. Quantum corrections typically entering through a Bohm-type potential and degeneracy (Fermi) pressure renormalize the dispersive scale and, together with dust charging and amplitude, modify shock width and admissibility conditions. In realistic dusty plasmas, the dust-size distribution further alters the effective inertia and charging dynamics, thereby reshaping the nonlinear and dispersive coefficients of the reduced model and yeilding to broadened fronts, precursor oscillations, or attenuated (under/overcompressive) shocks [27].

From a literature standpoint, lower-dimensional ZK- or Burgers-type reductions have long been used to observe ion-acoustic and dust-acoustic structures; however, many classic treatments either neglect quantum contributions or restrict attention to $(1+1)$ or $(2+1)$ geometries, limiting their capacity to capture transverse effects, filamentation, and oblique-shock formation. The $(3+1)$-D ZK–Burgers formulation addresses these gaps by (i) accommodating fully three-dimensional geometries relevant to laboratory devices, microgravity dusty-plasma experiments, and space/astrophysical environments (e.g., cometary tails, planetary rings); (ii) incorporating dust charging, drag, and grain-size dispersion into the dissipation and nonlinearity; and (iii) including quantum dispersion, which is crucial in dense or degenerate plasmas. In this setting, exact and traveling-wave solutions (bright, periodic, hybrid, dark–bright) characterize coherent behaviors and shock profiles, while complementary dynamical bifurcation analysis, multistability, Poincaré maps, and return maps reveals parameter regimes of periodic, quasi-periodic, and chaotic responses.

Overall, the $(3+1)$-D ZK–Burgers equation serves as a unifying asymptotic model that links microphysics (dust charging, quantum pressure, grain-size effects) to macroscopic observables (shock morphology, stability, and coherence). It thus provides a rigorous basis for predicting shock thickness, front oscillations, and transition thresholds, and for designing diagnostics and control strategies in dusty quantum plasmas across laboratory and astrophysical settings.

Although different studies have investigated shock and soliton structures in plasmas using ZK and Burgers-type equations, most of the available literature is limited to lower-dimensional $(1+1)$ or $(2+1)$ frameworks and frequently neglects essential physical effects such as dust grain charging, quantum corrections, and grain-size distribution [28]. In particular, the majority of earlier works considered either classical dusty plasmas or weakly nonlinear regimes, without incorporating quantum effects or external magnetic fields. Such simplifications restrict their applicability to realistic plasma environments, where dust dynamics, multidimensionality, and quantum contributions play a central role in shaping shock morphology and stability [29–31].

In the present work, we address these gaps by focusing on quantum dust-acoustic (QDA) shock waves in collisionless dusty plasma under the influence of an external magnetic field. The system is modeled through the $(3+1)$-dimensional ZKB equation, which simultaneously accounts for dissipation, dispersion, and nonlinear steepening in dusty quantum plasmas. Our main motivation is twofold: (i) to construct exact solitary and shock-type solutions (bright, periodic, combo, dark–bright) using the Paul–Painlevé approach, and (ii) to perform a comprehensive dynamical analysis applying chaos-identification tools such as Lyapunov exponents, bifurcation diagrams, return maps, multistability, and basin attractors. This dual framework allows us to uncover the rich nonlinear dynamics of QDA shock waves and to emphasize the influence of dust size distribution and quantum effects, thereby extending the scope of previous studies.

Figure 1 provides a complete flowchart of the methodology and analysis applied in this study. The remainder of this paper is structured as follows. Section 2 outlines the formulation of the $(3+1)$-dimensional ZKB model describing dusty plasma with quantum effects. In Section 3, the dynamical properties of the system are observed through bifurcation theory. Section 5 introduces a range of chaos-identification tools that are used to classify the nonlinear regimes, including periodic, quasi-periodic, and chaotic behaviors. Section 6 describes the construction of exact solutions using the Paul–Painlevé approach together with their physical interpretations. Finally, Section 7 summarizes our main findings and outlines possible directions for future research.

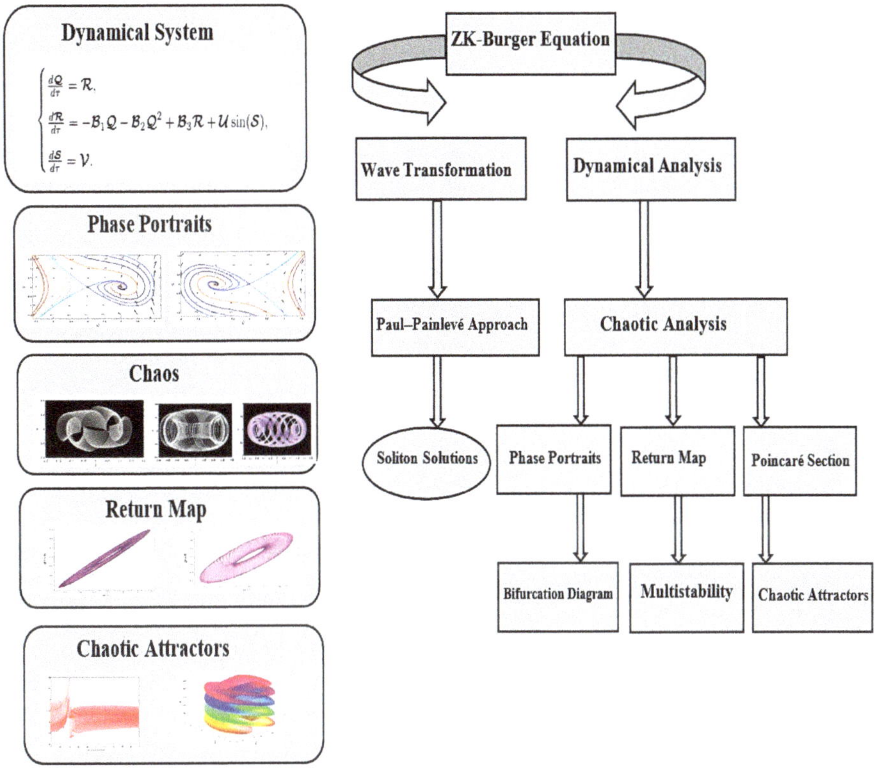

Figure 1. Graphical abstract illustrating the methodological framework for the ZK-Burger equation, integrating soliton solutions via wave transformation with dynamical and chaotic analyses through phase portraits, return maps, bifurcation diagrams, and attractors. .

2. Formulation of Model

In this study, we consider a three-dimensional dusty-plasma system incorporating quantum effects. The plasma comprises inertia-less ions and electrons, along with negatively charged dust particles [32]. The pressure for a given species l is modeled as [33–35]

$$E_\ell = \frac{m_\ell W_{F\ell}^2}{3G_{\ell 0}^2} G_l^3, \tag{1}$$

where G_l denotes the number density of species l, and G_{l0} represents its corresponding equilibrium value. Here, $\ell = ds$ refers to the sth dust species, while $\ell = e$ and $\ell = i$ correspond to electrons and ions, respectively. The mass of the species is indicated by m_ℓ, and the Fermi thermal speed is given by $W_{Fl} = \sqrt{2S_B H_{F\ell}/m_\ell}$, where S_B is the Boltzmann constant and $H_{F\ell}$ is the Fermi temperature.

The overall charge balance in the plasma system satisfies the following condition:

$$G_{k0} = G_{e0} + \sum_{s=1}^{M} Y_{ds} G_{ds0}, \tag{2}$$

where G_{ds0}, G_{e0}, and G_{i0} refer to the equilibrium number densities of the sth dust population, electrons, and ions, respectively. Furthermore, the behavior of shock structures in a quantum plasma system characterized by a spatially varying density $G(r)$ is described in detail in [36–38].

$$\frac{\partial G_{ds}}{\partial t} + \nabla \cdot (G_{ds}\mathbf{v}_{ds}) = 0, \tag{3}$$

$$\frac{\partial G_{ds}}{\partial t} + G_{ds}(\nabla \cdot (G_{ds}\mathbf{v}_{ds})) = \frac{Y_{ds}}{m_{ds}}\nabla\Psi - \frac{\epsilon_d}{m_{ds}}G_{ds}\mathbf{\Theta}(\mathbf{v}_{ds} \times \mathbf{x}) + \frac{\rho}{m_{ds}}\nabla^2\mathbf{v}_{ds} + \frac{K_d^2}{2m_{ds}^2}\nabla\left(\frac{\nabla^2\sqrt{G_{ds}}}{\sqrt{G_{ds}}}\right), \tag{4}$$

$$\nabla^2\Psi = \eta_e G_e - \eta_i G_i + \sum_{q=1}^{M} Y_{ds}G_{ds}, \tag{5}$$

$$\nabla\Psi - \epsilon_e G_e \nabla G_e + \frac{K_e^2}{2}\nabla\left(\frac{\nabla^2\sqrt{G_e}}{\sqrt{G_e}}\right) = 0, \tag{6}$$

$$-\nabla\Psi - \epsilon_i G_i \nabla G_i + \frac{K_i^2}{2}\nabla\left(\frac{\nabla^2\sqrt{G_i}}{\sqrt{G_i}}\right) = 0. \tag{7}$$

The parameters η_i and η_e are defined as $\eta_i = \frac{G_{i0}}{\bar{Y}_{d0}G_{\text{tot}}}, \quad \eta_e = \frac{G_{e0}}{\bar{Y}_{d0}G_{\text{tot}}}$, while the normalized temperature ratios are given by $\epsilon_e = \frac{H_e}{H_{\text{eff}}}, \quad \epsilon_i = \frac{H_i}{H_{\text{eff}}}, \quad \epsilon_d = \frac{H_{Fd}}{\bar{Y}_{d0}H_{\text{eff}}}$, and the quantum diffraction parameters take the form $K_e^2 = \frac{\hbar^2\bar{Y}_{d0}\omega_{pd}^2}{m_e c_d^4}, \quad K_i^2 = \frac{\hbar^2\bar{Y}_{d0}\omega_{pd}^2}{m_i c_d^4}, \quad H_d^2 = \frac{\hbar\bar{Z}_{d0}\omega_{pd}^2}{\bar{m}_d c_d^4}$. Here, H_{eff} represents the effective temperature, defined as $H_{\text{eff}} = \frac{H_i H_e}{\eta_i H_i + \eta_e H_e}$, with H_i and H_e being the ion and electron temperatures, respectively. Here, $\mathbf{v}_{ds}$ denotes the velocity vector of the s-th dust species, m_{ds} is the mass of a dust grain in that species, and Y_{ds} is the number of elementary charges associated with the surface of the sth dust grain. The total equilibrium number density of particles is denoted by G_{tot} and is given by $G_{\text{tot}} = \sum_{s=1}^{M} G_{ds}$, while $\bar{Y}_{d0}$ denotes the average charge number over all dust species. The average charge-weighted number density is expressed as

$$\bar{Y}_{d0}G_{\text{tot}} = \sum_{m=1}^{M} m_{ds}G_{ds}, \tag{8}$$

where m_d denotes the average mass of the dust particles, defined by

$$\bar{m}_d = \frac{1}{G_{\text{tot}}}\sum_{s=1}^{G} m_{ds}G_{ds}. \tag{9}$$

The dust-acoustic speed c_d is determined using the relation $c_d = \sqrt{\frac{2\bar{Y}_{d0}H_{\text{eff}}}{\bar{m}_d}}$, while the dust plasma frequency is given by $\omega_{pd} = \sqrt{\frac{4\pi e^2\bar{Y}_{d0}^2 G_{\text{tot}}}{\bar{m}_d}}$. The magnetization parameter is defined as $\Theta = \frac{e\bar{Y}_{d0}B_0}{\bar{m}_d c_d \omega_{pd}}$, and ρ denotes the viscosity of the dust species. The number densities of the sth dust particle, electrons, and ions are denoted by n_{ds}, n_e, and n_i, respectively. The velocity vector corresponding to the sth dust component is represented by $\mathbf{v}_{ds}$.

$$\mathbf{v}_{ds} = v_{dsx}\,\mathbf{i} + v_{dsy}\,\mathbf{j} + v_{dsz}\,\mathbf{k}. \tag{10}$$

The electrostatic potential is denoted by Ψ. By introducing dimensionless variables and applying the reductive perturbation technique [39], the potential Ψ can be expanded as a power series in the small parameter ϵ. As a result, we obtain the following expression:

$$\sum_{s=1}^{M} \frac{Y_{ds}^2 G_{ds0}}{\lambda^2 m_{ds} - \epsilon G_{ds0}^2} = 1. \tag{11}$$

Considering that the temperature H of the dust fluid is typically low while the mass is relatively large [40], the above reduces to:

$$\lambda^2 = \sum_{s=1}^{M} \frac{G_{ds}^2 Y_{ds}^2}{m_{dj}}. \tag{12}$$

Here, λ is the phase-speed parameter of the dust–acoustic mode for the ratio of the wave phase speed to the dust–acoustic speed; Equation (11) is the compatibility relation that determines λ^2 from G_{ds}, Y_{ds}, and m_{ds}. Next, by matching the coefficients of ϵ^4 in the y- and z-directional equations, we obtain additional conditions.

$$w_{dsy2} = -\frac{\lambda m_{ds}}{\Theta^2 Y_{ds}}\left(1 + \frac{Y_{ds}G_{ds0}}{\epsilon_d G_{ds0}^2 - \lambda^2 m_{ds}}\right)\frac{\partial^2 \mathcal{R}}{\partial x \partial y}, \tag{13}$$

$$w_{dsz2} = -\frac{\lambda m_{ds}}{\Theta^2 Y_{ds}}\left(1 + \frac{Y_{ds}G_{ds0}}{\epsilon_d G_{ds0}^2 - \lambda^2 m_{ds}}\right)\frac{\partial^2 \mathcal{R}}{\partial x \partial z}. \tag{14}$$

Thus, by considering terms in the power series expansion of ϵ up to an order of less than four, and incorporating Equations (11)–(14), we arrive at the ZK–Burgers equation.

$$\boldsymbol{\mathcal{M}}_t + \Pi_1 \boldsymbol{\mathcal{M}}\boldsymbol{\mathcal{M}}_x + \Pi_2 \boldsymbol{\mathcal{M}}_{xxx} + \Pi_3(\boldsymbol{\mathcal{M}}_{xyy} + \boldsymbol{\mathcal{M}}_{xzz}) - \Pi_4 \boldsymbol{\mathcal{M}}_{xx} = 0. \tag{15}$$

The coefficients involved are given by

$$\Pi_1 = -\frac{3}{2\lambda^3}\sum_{s=1}^{M}\frac{Y_{ds}^3 G_{ds0}}{m_{ds}^2} + \frac{1}{2\lambda}\sum_{s=1}^{M}\frac{\epsilon_d}{\mu_{ds}} \cdot \frac{Y_{ds}G_{ds0}^2}{\epsilon_d G_{ds0}^2 - \lambda^2 m_{ds0}} + \frac{\lambda}{2}\left(\frac{\eta_e}{\epsilon_e^2} - \frac{\eta_i}{\epsilon_i^2}\right), \tag{16}$$

$$\Pi_2 = \frac{\lambda}{2} - \frac{1}{2\lambda}\sum_{s=1}^{M}\frac{K_d^2}{4m_{ds}^2} - \frac{\lambda}{2}\left(\frac{\eta_e K_e^2}{4\epsilon_e^2} + \frac{\eta_i K_i^2}{4\epsilon_i^2}\right), \tag{17}$$

$$\Pi_3 = \frac{\lambda}{2}\sum_{s=1}^{M}\frac{m_{ds}n_{ds0}}{\Theta^2}\left(1 + \frac{\epsilon_d G^2}{\lambda^2 m_{ds} - \epsilon_d G_{ds0}^2}\right) + \Pi_2, \tag{18}$$

$$\Pi_4 = \frac{\rho'}{2\lambda^2}\sum_{s=1}^{M}\frac{Y_{ds}^2 G_{ds0}}{m_{ds}^2}. \tag{19}$$

To study the propagation of shock structures within a quantum dusty-plasma framework, we derive the ZK–Burgers equation as depicted in Equation (15). This approach enables the analysis of solitary-wave solutions under the influence of a quantum plasma environment, particularly when dust particle distributions follow a power-law.

3. Conversion of Proposed Model into ODE

To obtain traveling-wave solutions to the ZK–Burgers Equation (15), we introduce the traveling–wave transformation:

$$\boldsymbol{\mathcal{M}}(x,y,z,t) = \boldsymbol{\mathcal{Q}}(\tau),\ \tau = \mathfrak{z}_1 x + \mathfrak{z}_2 y + \mathfrak{z}_3 z - \omega t. \tag{20}$$

Plugging Equation (20) together with its various derivatives into Equation (15), we obtain

$$\omega\boldsymbol{\mathcal{Q}}' + \Pi_1\mathfrak{z}_1\boldsymbol{\mathcal{Q}}\boldsymbol{\mathcal{Q}}' + [\Pi_2\mathfrak{z}_1^3 + \Pi_3(\mathfrak{z}_1\mathfrak{z}_2^2 + \mathfrak{z}_1\mathfrak{z}_3^2)]\boldsymbol{\mathcal{Q}}''' - \Pi_4\mathfrak{z}_1^2\boldsymbol{\mathcal{Q}}'' = 0. \tag{21}$$

After performing integration once with regard to τ, Equation (21) reduces to

$$\omega\boldsymbol{\mathcal{Q}} + \frac{\Pi_1\mathfrak{z}_1}{2}\boldsymbol{\mathcal{Q}}^2 + [\Pi_2\mathfrak{z}_1^3 + \Pi_3(\mathfrak{z}_1\mathfrak{z}_2^2 + \mathfrak{z}_1\mathfrak{z}_3^2)]\boldsymbol{\mathcal{Q}}'' - \Pi_4\mathfrak{z}_1^2\boldsymbol{\mathcal{Q}}' = 0. \tag{22}$$

4. Dynamical Investigation of Unperturbed System

In this section, we conduct a comprehensive dynamical investigation of the $(3+1)$-dimensional ZK–Burgers equation through detailed bifurcation analysis [41,42]. Particular emphasis is placed on exploring the transitions between stable, quasi-periodic, and chaotic regimes, thereby uncovering the rich nonlinear behavior of the system.

Bifurcation Analysis

In this section, we investigate the dynamical consequences of Equation (22) through the lens of bifurcation theory. As a first step, we apply a Galilean transformation to the ordinary differential equation given in Equation (22), reformulating it into the following system of equations:

$$\begin{cases} \frac{d\mathcal{Q}}{d\tau} = \mathcal{R}, \\ \frac{d\mathcal{R}}{d\tau} = -\mathcal{B}_1\mathcal{Q} - \mathcal{B}_2\mathcal{Q}^2 + \mathcal{B}_3\mathcal{R}. \end{cases} \tag{23}$$

Here, $\mathcal{B}_1 = \frac{\omega}{[\Pi_2\mathfrak{z}_1^3+\Pi_3(\mathfrak{z}_1\mathfrak{z}_2^2+\mathfrak{z}_1\mathfrak{z}_3^2)]}$, $\mathcal{B}_2 = \frac{\Pi_1\mathfrak{z}_1}{2[\Pi_2\mathfrak{z}_1^3+\Pi_3(\mathfrak{z}_1\mathfrak{z}_2^2+\mathfrak{z}_1\mathfrak{z}_3^2)]}$, $\mathcal{B}_3 = \frac{\Pi_4\mathfrak{z}_1^2}{[\Pi_2\mathfrak{z}_1^3+\Pi_3(\mathfrak{z}_1\mathfrak{z}_2^2+\mathfrak{z}_1\mathfrak{z}_3^2)]}$.

Remark 1. *System (23) is inherently dissipative when $\mathcal{B}_3 < 0$, since the phase-space divergence equals $\mathcal{B}_3$. This dissipation governs the emergence of attractors and underpins the chaotic dynamics analyzed in subsequent sections.*

To find the equilibrium points of the dynamical system (23), we need to solve the following system of equations:

$$\begin{cases} \mathcal{R} = 0, \\ -\mathcal{B}_1\mathcal{Q} - \mathcal{B}_2\mathcal{Q}^2 + \mathcal{B}_3\mathcal{R} = 0. \end{cases} \tag{24}$$

System (24) is solved, and the resulting equilibrium points are as follows:

$$\mathcal{E}_1 = (0,0), \quad \mathcal{E}_2 = (-\frac{\mathcal{B}_1}{\mathcal{B}_2}, 0). \tag{25}$$

For system (23) at an equilibrium of $\mathcal{E}^* = (\mathcal{Q}^*, 0)$, the linearized matrix is

$$\mathcal{A} = \begin{pmatrix} 0 & 1 \\ -(\mathcal{B}_1 + 2\mathcal{B}_2\mathcal{Q}^*) & \mathcal{B}_3 \end{pmatrix},$$

with the characteristic polynomial

$$\lambda^2 - \mathcal{B}_3\lambda + (\mathcal{B}_1 + 2\mathcal{B}_2\mathcal{Q}^*) = 0.$$

Let $\Delta = \mathcal{B}_1 + 2\mathcal{B}_2\mathcal{Q}^*$. The eigenvalues are

$$\lambda_{1,2} = \frac{\mathcal{B}_3 \pm \sqrt{\mathcal{B}_3^2 - 4\Delta}}{2}.$$

Proposition 1. *The type of equilibrium point $\mathcal{E}^*$ is determined as follows:*

1. *If $\Delta < 0$, $\mathcal{E}^*$ is a **saddle**.*
2. *If $\Delta > 0$ and $\mathcal{B}_3^2 > 4\Delta$, $\mathcal{E}^*$ is a node: it is stable if $\mathcal{B}_3 < 0$, and unstable if $\mathcal{B}_3 > 0$.*
3. *If $\Delta > 0$ and $\mathcal{B}_3^2 < 4\Delta$, $\mathcal{E}^*$ is a spiral (focus): it is stable if $\mathcal{B}_3 < 0$, and unstable if $\mathcal{B}_3 > 0$.*

   Since $\mathcal{B}_3 \neq 0$ in the dissipative case, centers do not occur.

Applying this to system (23), we obtain

$$\mathcal{E}_1 = (0,0) : \Delta = \mathcal{B}_1, \qquad \mathcal{E}_2 = \left(-\frac{\mathcal{B}_1}{\mathcal{B}_2}, 0\right) : \Delta = -\mathcal{B}_1.$$

Thus, $\mathcal{E}_1$ is a saddle if $\mathcal{B}_1 < 0$, and $\mathcal{E}_2$ is a saddle if $\mathcal{B}_1 > 0$; otherwise they are stable/unstable nodes or foci depending on $\mathcal{B}_3$ and the discriminant. The various outcomes that arise from varying the involved parameters in system (23) are presented in Table 1.

Table 1. Classification of equilibrium points (EPs) under different parameter cases with the parameter values used to compute $(\mathcal{B}_1, \mathcal{B}_2, \mathcal{B}_3)$.

Case	Parameter Conditions	Parameter Values Used	Equilibrium Points and Nature	Figure
(i)	$\mathcal{B}_1 > 0,\ \mathcal{B}_2 > 0,\ \mathcal{B}_3 < 0$	$\mathfrak{z}_1 = 1,\ \mathfrak{z}_2 = 1,\ \mathfrak{z}_3 = 1, \omega = 3,$ $\Pi_1 = 6,\ \Pi_2 = 1,\ \Pi_3 = 1,\ \Pi_4 = -3$	$EP_1 = (-1,0)$ (Saddle) $EP_2 = (0,0)$ (Unstable focus)	Figure 2a
(ii)	$\mathcal{B}_1 < 0,\ \mathcal{B}_2 > 0,\ \mathcal{B}_3 < 0$	$\mathfrak{z}_1 = 1,\ \mathfrak{z}_2 = 1,\ \mathfrak{z}_3 = 1, \omega = -3,$ $\Pi_1 = 6,\ \Pi_2 = 1,\ \Pi_3 = 1,\ \Pi_4 = -3$	$EP_1 = (0,0)$ (Unstable focus) $EP_2 = (-1,0)$ (Saddle)	Figure 2b
(iii)	$\mathcal{B}_1 < 0,\ \mathcal{B}_2 < 0,\ \mathcal{B}_3 < 0$	$\mathfrak{z}_1 = 1,\ \mathfrak{z}_2 = 1,\ \mathfrak{z}_3 = 1, \omega = -3,$ $\Pi_1 = -6,\ \Pi_2 = 1,\ \Pi_3 = 1,\ \Pi_4 = -3$	$EP_1 = (0,0)$ (Saddle) $EP_2 = (1,0)$ (Unstable focus)	Figure 3a
(iv)	$\mathcal{B}_1 > 0,\ \mathcal{B}_2 < 0,\ \mathcal{B}_3 < 0$	$\mathfrak{z}_1 = 1,\ \mathfrak{z}_2 = 1,\ \mathfrak{z}_3 = 1, \omega = 3,$ $\Pi_1 = -6,\ \Pi_2 = 1,\ \Pi_3 = 1,\ \Pi_4 = -3$	$EP_1 = (-1,0)$ (Unstable focus) $EP_2 = (0,0)$ (Saddle)	Figure 3b

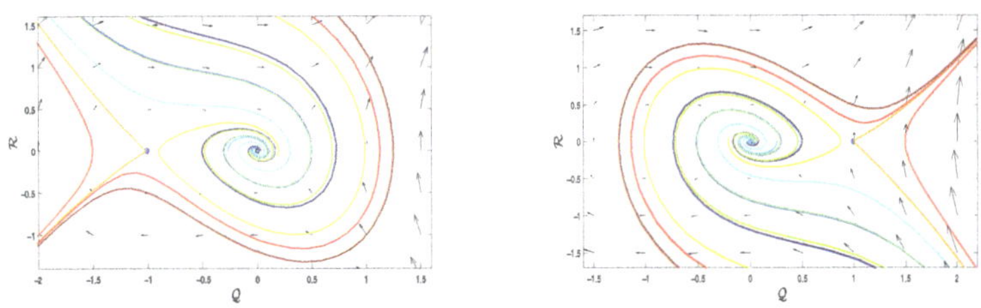

(a) $\mathcal{B}_1 > 0,\ \mathcal{B}_2 > 0,\ \mathcal{B}_3 < 0$ **(b)** $\mathcal{B}_1 < 0,\ \mathcal{B}_2 > 0,\ \mathcal{B}_3 < 0$

Figure 2. Phase portraits of the unperturbed system illustrating spiral and saddle-type behaviors for selected parameter cases $(\mathcal{B}_1, \mathcal{B}_2, \mathcal{B}_3)$, corresponding to Table 1.

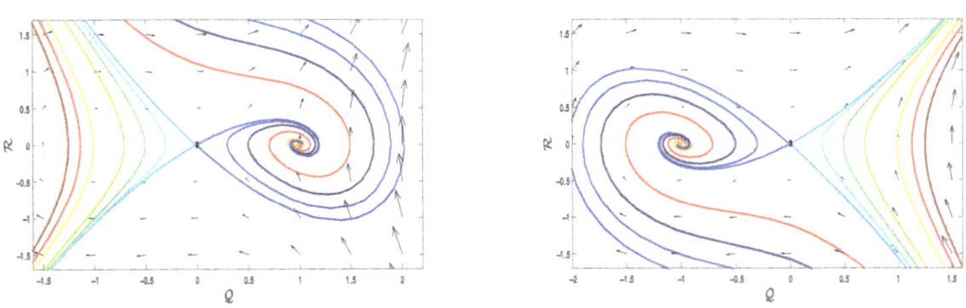

(a) $\mathcal{B}_1 < 0,\ \mathcal{B}_2 < 0,\ \mathcal{B}_3 < 0$ **(b)** $\mathcal{B}_1 > 0,\ \mathcal{B}_2 < 0,\ \mathcal{B}_3 < 0$

Figure 3. Phase portraits of the unperturbed system showing variations in stability patterns under alternative parameter choices $(\mathcal{B}_1, \mathcal{B}_2, \mathcal{B}_3)$, corresponding to Table 1.

The classification of equilibrium points summarized in Table 1 highlights the influence of parameter signs on the qualitative dynamics of the system. When the characteristic equation yields real eigenvalues of opposite signs, the corresponding equilibrium behaves as a saddle, indicating divergence along the unstable manifold and convergence along the stable one. When the eigenvalues are complex with a negative real part, the equilibrium appears as a stable spiral (focus), consistent with the trajectories spiraling inward in Figures 2 and 3. Since system (23) is dissipative, genuine centers do not occur, and thus, no closed neutral orbits are displayed in the phase portraits. This classification explains the coexistence of saddles and stable spirals under different parameter regimes, which provides the foundation for richer nonlinear dynamics, including multistability and transitions to chaos.

5. Chaotic Phenomena with Various Chaos-Identification Tools

In this section, we analyze the chaotic dynamics of the system using a range of diagnostic techniques, including return maps, multistability analysis, and chaotic attractors, as well as time series of the perturbed dynamical system. These tools allow us to systematically distinguish between chaotic, quasi-periodic, and periodic behaviors across different parameter regimes.

5.1. Detection of Chaos

To study the chaotic behavior of the model, an external forcing term $\mathcal{U}\sin(\mathcal{S})$ was introduced into the unperturbed dynamical system (23), thereby yielding a perturbed system.

$$\begin{cases} \frac{d\mathcal{Q}}{d\tau} = \mathcal{R}, \\ \frac{d\mathcal{R}}{d\tau} = -\mathcal{B}_1\mathcal{Q} - \mathcal{B}_2\mathcal{Q}^2 + \mathcal{B}_3\mathcal{R} + \mathcal{U}\sin(\mathcal{S}), \\ \frac{d\mathcal{S}}{d\tau} = \mathcal{V}. \end{cases} \tag{26}$$

Here, $\mathcal{S} = \mathcal{V}\tau$. System (23) corresponds to the unperturbed dynamical reduction of the ZK–Burgers equation, obtained through a traveling-wave transformation and subsequent Galilean reduction. While this system captures essential dissipative and dispersive interactions, it remains autonomous and therefore cannot display externally driven oscillations. To investigate the onset of more complex dynamics, we extended system (23) by incorporating the forcing term $\mathcal{U}\sin(\mathcal{S})$ and the auxiliary phase relation $\frac{d\mathcal{S}}{d\tau} = \mathcal{V}$. This yields system (26), a non-autonomous dynamical system capable of exhibiting richer behaviors, including bifurcations, quasi-periodicity, and chaos, thereby providing deeper insight into the nonlinear responses of dusty-plasma shocks. It is worth clarifying the physical motivation behind the introduction of the oscillatory forcing term in system (26). In realistic dusty-plasma environments, external periodic perturbations naturally arise from oscillatory electric or magnetic fields, fluctuations in dust charging, or background wave–particle interactions. The term $\mathcal{U}\sin(\mathcal{S})$ therefore models the action of an external driver that continuously injects energy into the plasma system. Such perturbations are known to induce transitions among periodic, quasi-periodic, and chaotic responses, which are frequently observed in both laboratory dusty-plasma experiments and astrophysical-plasma settings. Thus, the forcing term reflects physically relevant excitations that enrich the dynamical behavior of the dusty-plasma model. The trajectories depicted in Figure 4 illustrate the diverse dynamical responses of the perturbed ZK–Burgers system under different parameter regimes. For $\mathcal{U} = 3.4$ and $\mathcal{V} = -8.89$ (Figure 4a), the solution exhibits a closed-loop structure, indicating a stable periodic orbit. When the parameters are adjusted to $\mathcal{U} = 2.6$ and $\mathcal{V} = -8.4$ (Figure 4b), the trajectories evolve into nested patterns with slight variations, a hallmark of quasi-periodic motion where multiple incommensurate frequencies coexist. A further small change to $\mathcal{U} = 2.6$ and $\mathcal{V} = -8.9$ (Figure 4c) also produces toroidal structures, which correspond to quasi-periodic invariant tori rather than chaotic attractors. These observations demonstrate how subtle parameter variations can drive the system through periodic and quasi-periodic regimes, highlighting its sensitivity and complex oscillatory behavior.

The dynamical responses demonstrated in Figure 5 further illustrate the diverse behaviors of the perturbed ZK–Burgers system under different parameter values. For $\mathcal{U} = 0.9$ and $\mathcal{V} = -6.91$ (Figure 5a), the trajectories form regular, repeating loops, reflecting that the system is in a periodic state. When the parameters are changed to $\mathcal{U} = 1.1$ and

$\mathcal{V} = -6.91$ (Figure 5b), the orbit evolves into more intricate nested patterns, indicating a quasi-periodic regime characterized by oscillations with incommensurate frequencies. Finally, for $\mathcal{U} = 0.92$ and $\mathcal{V} = -4.4$ (Figure 5c), the solution develops into a more complex toroidal structure, which corresponds to a quasi-periodic invariant torus rather than a chaotic attractor. These results highlight the sensitivity of the model to small parameter variations and confirm the existence of transitions between periodic and quasi-periodic behaviors within the same physical framework.

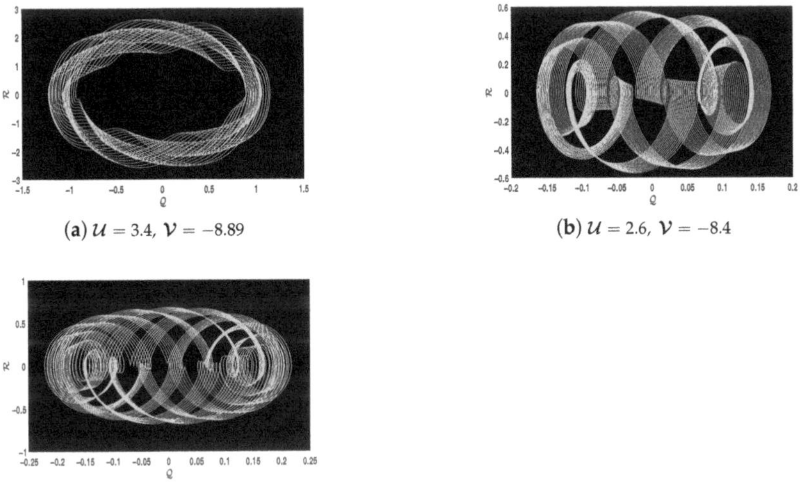

(a) $\mathcal{U} = 3.4$, $\mathcal{V} = -8.89$

(b) $\mathcal{U} = 2.6$, $\mathcal{V} = -8.4$

(c) $\mathcal{U} = 2.6$, $\mathcal{V} = -8.9$

Figure 4. Periodic and quasi-periodic trajectories of the perturbed system (26) under varying $(\mathcal{U}, \mathcal{V})$: highlighting the transition from simple loops to nested invariant tori.

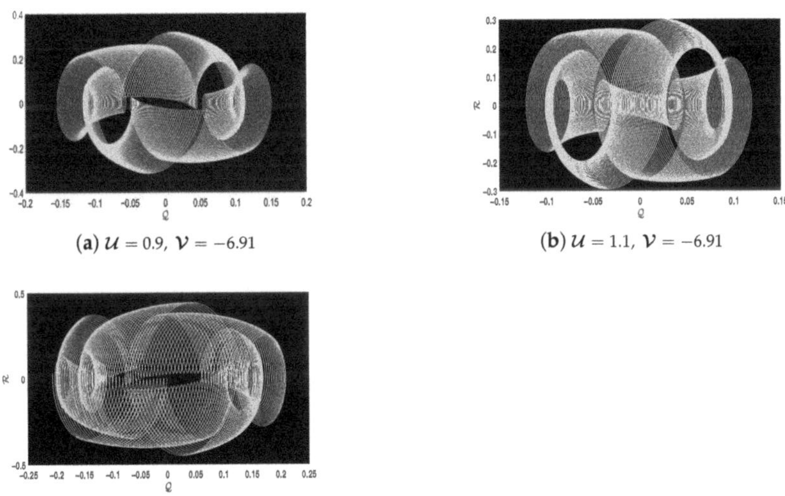

(a) $\mathcal{U} = 0.9$, $\mathcal{V} = -6.91$

(b) $\mathcal{U} = 1.1$, $\mathcal{V} = -6.91$

(c) $\mathcal{U} = 0.92$, $\mathcal{V} = -4.4$

Figure 5. Evolution of the perturbed system (26) under different $(\mathcal{U}, \mathcal{V})$: values, showing the emergence of quasi-periodic structures with increasingly intricate toroidal patterns.

The phase trajectories depicted in Figure 6 highlight the emergence of periodic and quasi-periodic behaviors in the perturbed ZK–Burgers system. In Figure 6a, corresponding to $\mathcal{U} = 1.07$

and $\mathcal{V} = -3.89$, the system evolves into smooth and repeating loops, characteristic of a periodic regime. As the parameters shift to $\mathcal{U} = 1.5$ and $\mathcal{V} = -3.9$ (Figure 6b), the trajectories develop into more intricate nested patterns, reflecting quasi-periodic motion where multiple oscillatory modes interact. Finally, for $\mathcal{U} = 0.92$ and $\mathcal{V} = -4.4$ (Figure 6c), the orbits also form complex toroidal structures, which correspond to quasi-periodic invariant tori rather than chaotic attractors. These results once again highlight the sensitivity of the system to parameter variations, where small changes can shift the dynamics from order to quasi-periodicity.

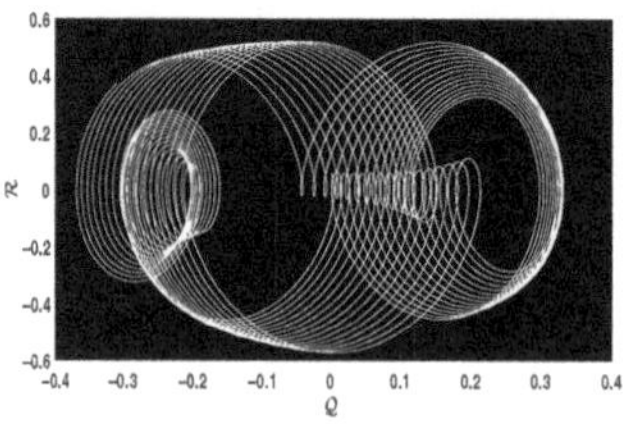

(**a**) $\mathcal{U} = 1.07$, $\mathcal{V} = -3.89$

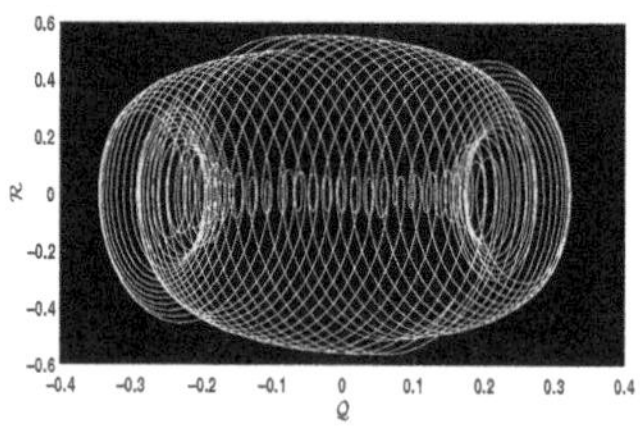

(**b**) $\mathcal{U} = 1.5$, $\mathcal{V} = -3.9$

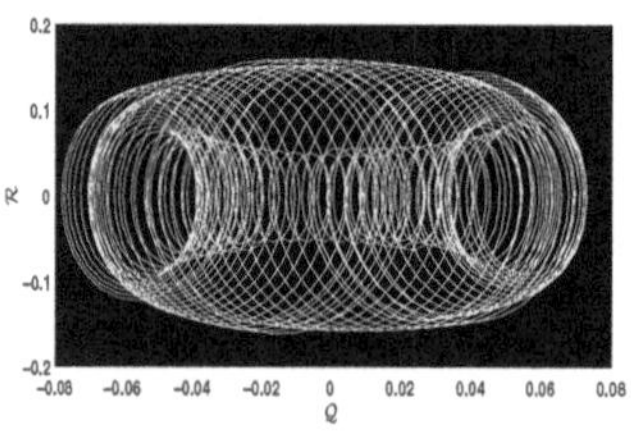

(**c**) $\mathcal{U} = 0.92$, $\mathcal{V} = -4.4$

Figure 6. Phase trajectories of the perturbed system (26) illustrating transitions from periodic motion to quasi-periodic regimes characterized by multi-frequency oscillations.

5.2. Multistability Analysis

In this subsection, we study the chaotic behavior of the perturbed ZK–Burgers system through the phenomenon of multistability. For the parameter set $\mathcal{B}_1 = 0.94$, $\mathcal{B}_2 = 0.4$, $\mathcal{B}_3 = -0.004$, $\mathcal{U} = 2.5$, $\mathcal{V} = 14.97$, the system represents multiple coexisting attractors when initialized with distinct starting conditions. As shown in Figure 7a, distinct trajectories emerge for the initial states $(\mathcal{Q}, \mathcal{R}, \mathcal{S}) = (-0.10, 0.10, 0)$, $(-0.20, 0.20, 0)$, and $(-0.25, 0.23, 0)$, despite identical governing equations and parameters. This coexistence of attractors confirms the system's strong sensitivity to initial conditions, a defining feature of multistability. To further examine this phenomenon, the corresponding Poincaré section is presented in Figure 7b. The scattered and irregular distribution of points reflects the chaotic nature of the multistable states, verifying that small perturbations in initial conditions can drive the system toward qualitatively distinct yet coexisting chaotic responses. These findings underscore the inherent complexity of the model, where multiple chaotic solutions can coexist under the same physical setting.

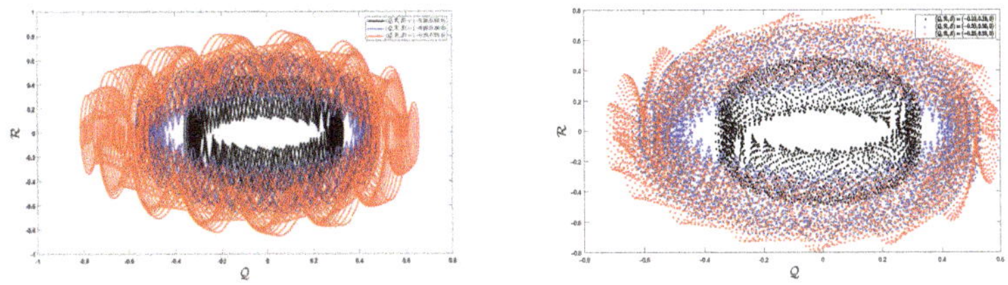

(**a**) (**b**)

Figure 7. Multistability analysis of the perturbed system (26) for the parameter values $\boldsymbol{\mathcal{B}}_1 = 0.94$, $\boldsymbol{\mathcal{B}}_2 = 0.4$, $\boldsymbol{\mathcal{B}}_3 = 0.004$, $\boldsymbol{\mathcal{U}} = 2.5$, $\boldsymbol{\mathcal{V}} = 14.97$.

5.3. Return Map Analysis

In this subsection, we examine the dynamical responses of the perturbed ZK–Burgers system via return map analysis. Figure 8 displays the return maps for different values of $\Re$ with fixed parameters $\boldsymbol{\mathcal{B}}_1 = 3.94$, $\boldsymbol{\mathcal{B}}_2 = 0.4$, $\boldsymbol{\mathcal{B}}_3 = -0.0004$, $\boldsymbol{\mathcal{U}} = 2.5$, $\boldsymbol{\mathcal{V}} = 2.97$ and the initial condition $(0.39, 0.22, -0.92)$. For $\Re = 0.1$ (Figure 8a), the points are distributed along a nearly smooth curve, indicating periodic behavior. As $\Re$ increases to 0.3 (Figure 8b), the return map develops more intricate loops, which correspond to quasi-periodic oscillations. When $\Re = 0.6$ (Figure 8c) and $\Re = 0.8$ (Figure 8d), the point distributions form increasingly complex toroidal patterns that reflect quasi-periodic invariant tori rather than chaotic attractors. These results confirm that return maps provide a useful diagnostic tool for distinguishing periodic and quasi-periodic regimes within the system.

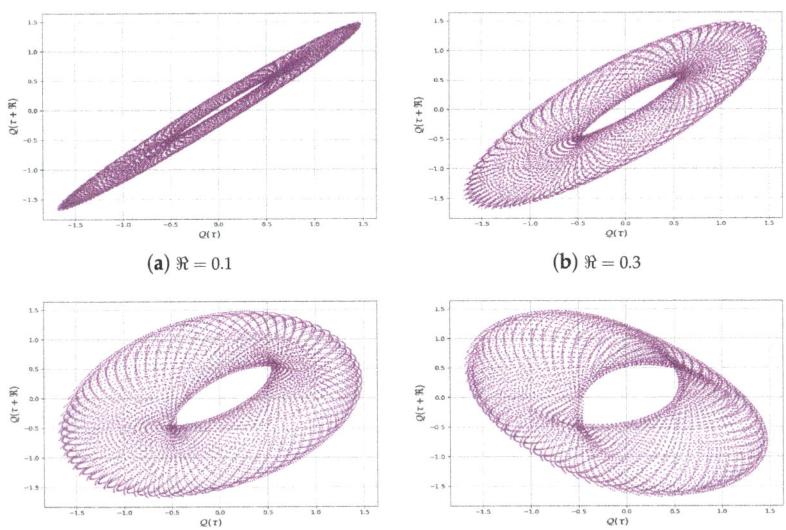

(**a**) $\Re = 0.1$ (**b**) $\Re = 0.3$

(**c**) $\Re = 0.6$ (**d**) $\Re = 0.8$

Figure 8. Return map analysis of the perturbed system (26) for varying $\Re$, illustrating transitions from periodic to quasi-periodic regimes.

5.4. Chaotic Attractors

In this subsection, we examine the dynamics of the perturbed ZK–Burgers system through 3D attractor plots. Figure 9 demonstrates the trajectories in $(\boldsymbol{\mathcal{Q}}, \boldsymbol{\mathcal{R}}, \boldsymbol{\mathcal{S}})$-space for distinct choices of the parameters $(\boldsymbol{\mathcal{U}}, \boldsymbol{\mathcal{V}})$. For $\boldsymbol{\mathcal{U}} = 2.5$, $\boldsymbol{\mathcal{V}} = 5.9$ (Figure 9b) and $\boldsymbol{\mathcal{U}} = 2.5$, $\boldsymbol{\mathcal{V}} = 7.9$ (Figure 9d), the attractors form relatively smooth layered structures, which are associated with quasi-periodic behavior. When $\mathcal{U} = 2.5$, $\mathcal{V} = 6.97$ (Figure 9a), the trajectories show irregular folding patterns and stretching, indicating fully developed chaotic motion. Finally, for $\mathcal{U} = 2.5$, $\mathcal{V} = 8.9$ (Figure 9c), the attractor maintains more regularity with repeating layers, suggesting a transition toward periodic behavior. These observations confirm that the system can switch between periodic, quasi-periodic, and chaotic regimes depending on parameter variations, reinforcing the richness of its nonlinear structure.

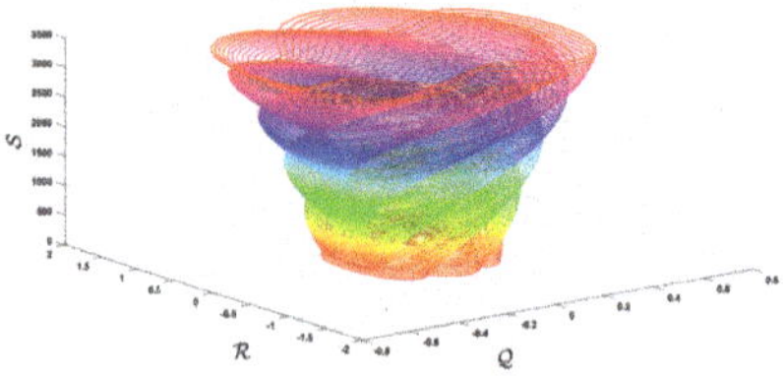

(a) $\mathcal{U} = 2.5$, $\mathcal{V} = 6.97$

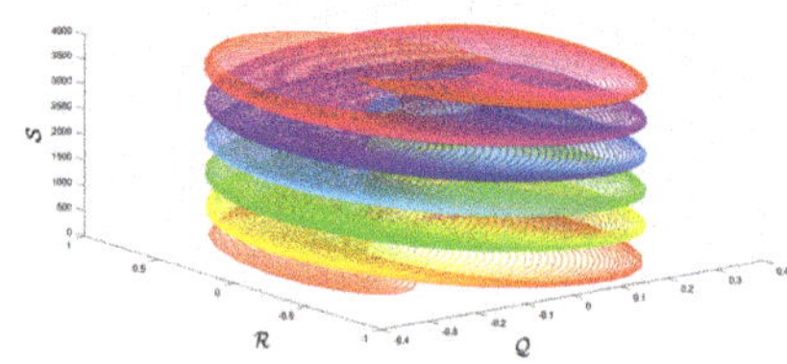

(b) $\mathcal{U} = 2.5$, $\mathcal{V} = 5.9$

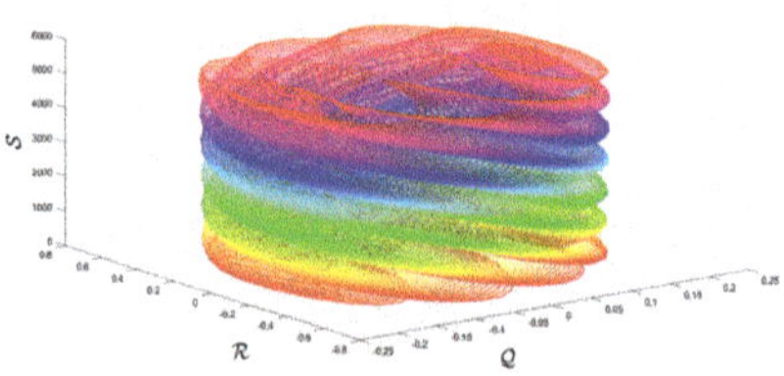

(c) $\mathcal{U} = 2.5$, $\mathcal{V} = 8.9$

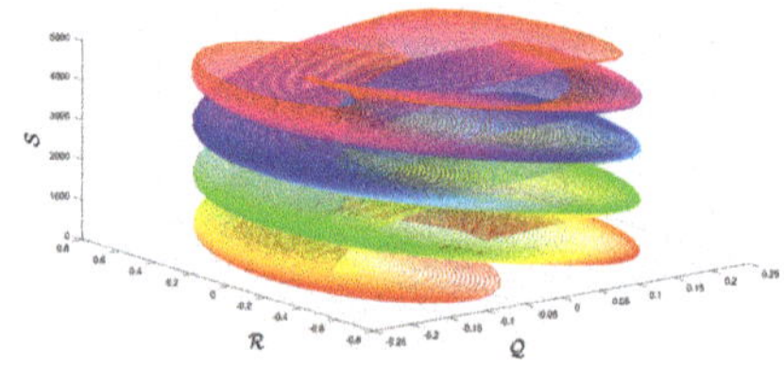

(d) $\mathcal{U} = 2.5$, $\mathcal{V} = 7.9$

Figure 9. Chaotic attractors of the perturbed system (26) for varying $(\mathcal{U}, \mathcal{V})$, showing transitions among periodic, quasi-periodic, and chaotic regimes.

5.5. Bifurcation Diagram Analysis

In this subsection, we examine the dynamical transitions of the perturbed ZK–Burgers system by constructing bifurcation diagrams with respect to different parameters. Figure 10 signifies how the qualitative behavior of the system evolves as the bifurcation parameters are varied. In Figure 10a, when the bifurcation parameter $\mathcal{M}$ increases from 0 to 2, the system initially demonstrates stable periodic states, represented by a single smooth branch. As $\mathcal{M}$ grows, the system undergoes a series of bifurcations that generate multiple branches, yielding to quasi-periodic oscillations. For larger values of $\mathcal{M}$ (around $\mathcal{M} \approx 1.5$), the branches become scattered and irregular, highlighting chaotic behavior. In Figure 10b, the bifurcation is plotted with respect to $\mathcal{B}_1$. For $3 \leq \mathcal{B}_1 \leq 3.3$, the system remains periodic, but around $\mathcal{B}_1 \approx 3.4$ a sudden bifurcation occurs, producing a dense web of points characteristic of chaos. As $\mathcal{B}_1$ increases further ($\mathcal{B}_1 \geq 4.2$), the system regains partial regularity with quasi-periodic structures. A similar scenario is analyzed in Figure 10c, where variations in $\mathcal{B}_2$ produce alternating windows of periodic, quasi-periodic, and chaotic regimes. Particularly, for $3 \leq \mathcal{B}_2 \leq 3.2$ the system shows periodic oscillations, whereas in the interval $3.3 \leq \mathcal{B}_2 \leq 3.8$ the dynamics become chaotic. Beyond this range, the system again shows quasi-periodic responses interspersed with narrow chaotic bands. The bifurcation diagrams confirm that the perturbed ZK–Burgers system is highly sensitive to parameter variations, showing transitions from periodic motion to quasi-periodic oscillations and ultimately to chaos, depending on the chosen bifurcation parameter values.

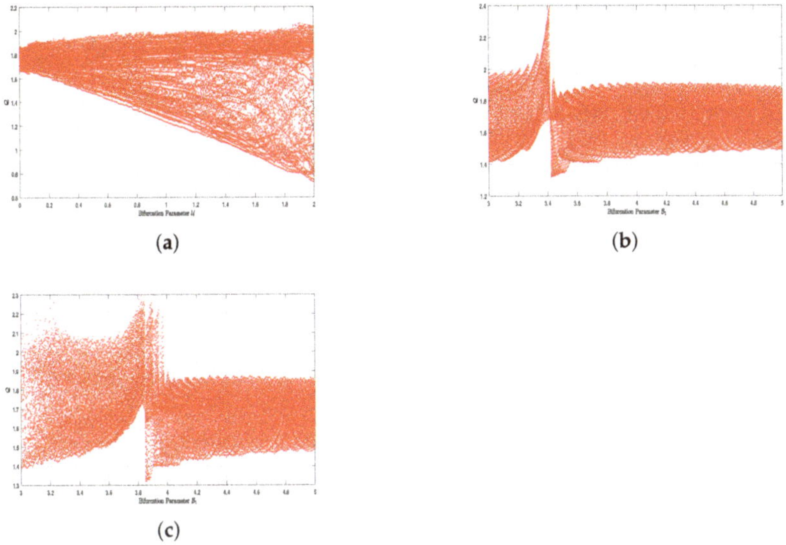

Figure 10. Bifurcation diagrams of the perturbed system (26) showing periodic states for small parameter values, quasi-periodic transitions at intermediate ranges, and chaotic behavior around $\mathcal{U} \approx 1.5$, $\mathcal{B}_1 \approx 3.4$, and $\mathcal{B}_2 \approx 3.8$.

Remark 2. *System (26) is directly connected to the ZK–Burgers Equation (15). Through the traveling-wave transformation (Equation (20)), Equation (15) reduces to the ODE (21), which, after integration, gives Equation (22). By setting* $\frac{d\mathcal{Q}}{d\tau} = \mathcal{R}$ *this yields system (23), and the addition of the external forcing* $\mathcal{U}\sin(\mathcal{S})$ *with* $\frac{d\mathcal{S}}{d\tau} = \mathcal{V}$ *leads to system (26). Hence, the forced system studied here is a natural extension of the reduced plasma model.*

Remark 3. *System (26) can be regarded as a three-dimensional autonomous system in the evolving variables* $(\mathcal{Q}, \mathcal{R}, \mathcal{S})$, *with* $\dot{\mathcal{S}} = V$ *representing a constant phase velocity. In some treatments, however, the pair* $(\mathcal{S}, \dot{\mathcal{S}})$ *is counted separately, leading to the description of a four-dimensional autonomous system. Such systems are known to exhibit both two-dimensional and three-dimensional invariant tori, whose detection requires analysis through first or second Poincaré sections. In the present study, Poincaré maps (Figure 7), together with return maps (Figure 8), provide the main evidence for distinguishing periodic and quasi-periodic regimes from chaotic ones. This ensures that the dynamical features illustrated in Figures 4–8 are quantitatively supported and consistently interpreted.*

6. Solitary-Wave Solutions to the Proposed Model

In this section, we investigate additional solitary-wave solutions using the Paul–Painlevé approach. The general framework of this method is outlined in Appendix A, while here we focus on its direct application to the present model to derive explicit solution structures.

6.1. Application of Paul–Painlevé Approach

This section presents the application of the Paul–Painlevé approach to the proposed nonlinear model given by Equation (15). After reducing the system to the single ODE in Equation (22), a balancing procedure is applied by comparing the highest-order nonlinear term with the highest-order derivative, which yields $M = 2$. By substituting $M = 2$ into Equation (A4), we obtain the following results:

$$\mathcal{Q} = \mathfrak{P}_0 + \mathfrak{P}_1 \mathcal{P}(\mathfrak{G}) e^{-n\tau} + \mathfrak{P}_2 \mathcal{P}(\mathfrak{G})^2 e^{-2n\tau}. \tag{27}$$

After substituting the solution (27) into Equation (22), a system of algebraic equations is derived by collecting terms corresponding to distinct powers of $\mathcal{P}(\mathfrak{G})$. This system is then solved using Mathematica, yielding the following solution set:

Set-1

$$\left\{\mathfrak{P}_0 = -\frac{2\sqrt{n}\sqrt{\Pi_4}\sqrt{\omega}}{\Pi_1},\ \mathfrak{P}_1 = \frac{2k\sqrt{\Pi_4}\sqrt{\omega}}{\sqrt{n}\Pi_1},\ \mathfrak{P}_2 = 0,\ \mathfrak{z}_1 = \frac{\sqrt{\omega}}{\sqrt{n}\sqrt{\Pi_4}},\ \mathfrak{z}_3 = -\frac{\sqrt{\mathfrak{z}_2^2(-n)\Pi_3\Pi_4 - \Pi_2\omega}}{\sqrt{n}\sqrt{\Pi_3}\sqrt{\Pi_4}}.\right. \tag{28}$$

By inserting the previously specified parameter values into Equation (27), we obtain

$$\mathcal{M}_1(x,y,z,t) = \frac{2\sqrt{\Pi_4}\sqrt{\omega}\left(d_0 n + k\left(e^{\left(-n\left(\frac{x\sqrt{\omega} - \frac{z\sqrt{\mathfrak{z}_2^2(-n)\Pi_3\Pi_4 - \Pi_2\omega}}{\sqrt{\Pi_3}}}{\sqrt{n}\sqrt{\Pi_4}} + t\omega + \mathfrak{z}_2 y\right)\right)} - n\mathfrak{Q}\right)\right)}{\sqrt{n}\Pi_1(k\mathfrak{Q} - d_0)}. \tag{29}$$

Set-2

$$\begin{cases} \mathfrak{P}_0 = \dfrac{2\sqrt{\frac{6}{5}}\sqrt{n}\sqrt{\Pi_4}\sqrt{\omega}}{\Pi_1},\ \mathfrak{P}_1 = -\dfrac{4\sqrt{\frac{6}{5}}k\sqrt{\Pi_4}\sqrt{\omega}}{\sqrt{n}\Pi_1},\ \mathfrak{P}_2 = \dfrac{2\sqrt{\frac{6}{5}}k^2\sqrt{\Pi_4}\sqrt{\omega}}{n^{3/2}\Pi_1},\ \mathfrak{z}_1 = -\dfrac{\sqrt{\frac{5}{6}}\sqrt{\omega}}{\sqrt{n}\sqrt{\Pi_4}}, \\ \mathfrak{z}_3 = \dfrac{\sqrt{\omega^2\left(-30\mathfrak{z}_2^2\Pi_3 - \frac{\sqrt{30}\sqrt{\Pi_4}\sqrt{\omega}}{n^{3/2}} - \frac{25\Pi_2\omega}{n\Pi_4}\right)}}{\sqrt{30}\sqrt{\Pi_3}\omega}. \end{cases}$$

By inserting the previously specified parameter values into Equation (27), we obtain

$$\begin{aligned}\mathcal{M}_2(x,y,z,t) = \frac{1}{n^{3/2}\Pi_1(d_0 - k\mathfrak{Q})^2}\Bigg[&2\sqrt{\frac{6}{5}}e^{\left(-2n\left(\frac{z\sqrt{\omega^2\left(-30\mathfrak{z}_2^2\Pi_3 - \frac{\sqrt{30}\sqrt{\Pi_4}\sqrt{\omega}}{n^{3/2}} - \frac{25\Pi_2\omega}{n\Pi_4}\right)}}{\sqrt{30}\sqrt{\Pi_3}\omega} - \frac{\sqrt{\frac{5}{6}}x\sqrt{\omega}}{\sqrt{n}\sqrt{\Pi_4}} + t\omega + \mathfrak{z}_2 y\right)\right)} \\ &\sqrt{\Pi_4}\sqrt{\omega}\left(k - n(k\mathfrak{Q} - d_0)e^{\left(n\left(\frac{z\sqrt{\omega^2\left(-30\mathfrak{z}_2^2\Pi_3 - \frac{\sqrt{30}\sqrt{\Pi_4}\sqrt{\omega}}{n^{3/2}} - \frac{25\Pi_2\omega}{n\Pi_4}\right)}}{\sqrt{30}\sqrt{\Pi_3}\omega} - \frac{\sqrt{\frac{5}{6}}x\sqrt{\omega}}{\sqrt{n}\sqrt{\Pi_4}} + t\omega + \mathfrak{z}_2 y\right)\right)}\right)^2\Bigg].\end{aligned} \tag{30}$$

Set-3

$$\begin{cases} \mathfrak{P}_0 = 0,\ \mathfrak{P}_1 = 0,\ \mathfrak{P}_2 = \dfrac{6k^2\Pi_4\left(\sqrt{\lambda_4^2 - 100\mathfrak{z}_2^2\Pi_2\Pi_3 n^2 - 100\mathfrak{z}_3^2\Pi_2\Pi_3 n^2} - \Pi_4\right)}{25\Pi_1\Pi_2 n^2}, \\ \mathfrak{z}_1 = \dfrac{\sqrt{\Pi_4^2 - 100(\mathfrak{z}_2^2 + \mathfrak{z}_3^2)\Pi_2\Pi_3 n^2} - \Pi_4}{10\Pi_2 n}, \\ \omega = \dfrac{3\Pi_4\left(50\mathfrak{z}_2^2\Pi_2\Pi_3 n^2 + 50\mathfrak{z}_3^2\Pi_2\Pi_3 n^2 + \Pi_4\left(\sqrt{\Pi_4^2 - 100\mathfrak{z}_2^2\Pi_2\Pi_3 n^2 - 100\mathfrak{z}_3^2\Pi_2\Pi_3 n^2} - \Pi_4\right)\right)}{125\Pi_2^2 n}. \end{cases} \tag{31}$$

By inserting the previously specified parameter values into Equation (27), we obtain

$$\begin{aligned}\mathcal{M}_3(x,y,z,t) = \frac{1}{25\Pi_1\Pi_2 n^2(d_0 - k\mathfrak{Q})^2}\Bigg[&e^{\left(-\frac{12\mathfrak{z}_2^2\Pi_3\Pi_4 n^2 t}{5\Pi_2} - \frac{12\mathfrak{z}_3^2\Pi_3\Pi_4 n^2 t}{5\Pi_2} - \frac{\left(\sqrt{\Pi_4^2 - 100(\mathfrak{z}_2^2 + \mathfrak{z}_3^2)\Pi_2\Pi_3 n^2} - \lambda_4\right)(6\Pi_4^2 t + 25\Pi_2 x)}{125\Pi_2^2} - 2\mathfrak{z}_2 n y - 2\mathfrak{z}_3 n z\right)} \\ &k^2\Pi_4\left(\sqrt{\Pi_4^2 - 100(\mathfrak{z}_2^2 + \mathfrak{z}_3^2)\Pi_2\Pi_3 n^2} - \Pi_4\right)\Bigg].\end{aligned} \tag{32}$$

Set-4

$$
\begin{cases}
\mathfrak{P}_0 = \frac{2i\sqrt{\mathfrak{z}_2^2+\mathfrak{z}_3^2}n\sqrt{\Pi_3}\Pi_4}{\Pi_1\sqrt{\Pi_2}}, \; \mathfrak{P}_1 = -\frac{2i\sqrt{\mathfrak{z}_2^2+\mathfrak{z}_3^2}k\sqrt{\Pi_3}\Pi_4}{\Pi_1\sqrt{\Pi_2}}, \; \mathfrak{P}_2 = 0, \; \mathfrak{z}_1 = -\frac{i\sqrt{\mathfrak{z}_2^2+\mathfrak{z}_3^2}\sqrt{\Pi_3}}{\sqrt{\Pi_2}}, \\
\omega = -\frac{\left(\mathfrak{z}_2^2+\mathfrak{z}_3^2\right)n\Pi_3\Pi_4}{\Pi_2}.
\end{cases}
\tag{33}
$$

By inserting the previously specified parameter values into Equation (27), we obtain

$$
\mathcal{M}_4(x,y,z,t) = \frac{2i\sqrt{\mathfrak{z}_2^2+\mathfrak{z}_3^2}\sqrt{\Pi_3}\Pi_4\left(n - \frac{ke^{\left(-n\left(-\frac{\left(\mathfrak{z}_2^2+\mathfrak{z}_3^2\right)n\Pi_3\Pi_4 t}{\Pi_2} - \frac{i\sqrt{\mathfrak{z}_2^2+\mathfrak{z}_3^2}\sqrt{\Pi_3}x}{\sqrt{\Pi_2}} + \mathfrak{z}_2 y + \mathfrak{z}_3 z\right)\right)}}{k\mathfrak{Q}-d_0}\right)}{\Pi_1\sqrt{\Pi_2}}.
\tag{34}
$$

Set-5

$$
\begin{cases}
\mathfrak{P}_0 = -\frac{12\Pi_4\left(-50\mathfrak{z}_2^2n^2\Pi_2\Pi_3-50\mathfrak{z}_3^2n^2\Pi_2\Pi_3+\Pi_4\left(\Pi_4+\sqrt{-100\mathfrak{z}_2^2n^2\Pi_2\Pi_3-100\mathfrak{z}_3^2n^2\Pi_2\Pi_3+\Pi_4^2}\right)\right)}{25\Pi_1\Pi_2\left(\Pi_4+\sqrt{-100\mathfrak{z}_2^2n^2\Pi_2\Pi_3-100\mathfrak{z}_3^2n^2\Pi_2\Pi_3+\Pi_4^2}\right)}, \\
\mathfrak{P}_1 = \frac{24k\Pi_4\left(-50\mathfrak{z}_2^2n^2\Pi_2\Pi_3-50\mathfrak{z}_3^2n^2\Pi_2\Pi_3+\Pi_4\left(\Pi_4+\sqrt{-100\mathfrak{z}_2^2n^2\Pi_2\Pi_3-100\mathfrak{z}_3^2n^2\Pi_2\Pi_3+\Pi_4^2}\right)\right)}{25n\Pi_1\Pi_2\left(\Pi_4+\sqrt{-100\mathfrak{z}_2^2n^2\Pi_2\Pi_3-100\mathfrak{z}_3^2n^2\Pi_2\Pi_3+\Pi_4^2}\right)}, \\
\mathfrak{P}_2 = -\frac{6k^2\Pi_4\left(\Pi_4+\sqrt{-100\mathfrak{z}_2^2n^2\Pi_2\Pi_3-100\mathfrak{z}_3^2n^2\Pi_2\Pi_3+\Pi_4^2}\right)}{25n^2\Pi_1\Pi_2}, \\
\mathfrak{z}_1 = \frac{\Pi_4+\sqrt{-100\mathfrak{z}_2^2n^2\Pi_2\Pi_3-100\mathfrak{z}_3^2n^2\Pi_2\Pi_3+\Pi_4^2}}{10n\Pi_2}, \\
\omega = \frac{3\Pi_4\left(-50\mathfrak{z}_2^2n^2\Pi_2\Pi_3-50\mathfrak{z}_3^2n^2\Pi_2\Pi_3+\Pi_4\left(\Pi_4+\sqrt{-100\mathfrak{z}_2^2n^2\Pi_2\Pi_3-100\mathfrak{z}_3^2n^2\Pi_2\Pi_3+\Pi_4^2}\right)\right)}{125n\Pi_2^2}.
\end{cases}
\tag{35}
$$

By inserting the previously specified parameter values into Equation (27), we obtain

$$
\begin{cases}
\mathcal{M}_5(x,y,z,t) = -\frac{1}{25n^2\Pi_1\Pi_2(d_0-k\mathfrak{Q})^2}\Bigg[6e^{-2\mathfrak{z}_2ny-2\mathfrak{z}_3nz-\frac{\left(25\Pi_2x+6t\Pi_4^2\right)\left(\Pi_4+\sqrt{-100\left(\mathfrak{z}_2^2+\mathfrak{z}_3^2\right)n^2\Pi_2\Pi_3+\Pi_4^2}\right)}{125\Pi_2^2}} \\
\Bigg(ke^{\frac{6\left(\mathfrak{z}_2^2+\mathfrak{z}_3^2\right)n^2\Pi_3\Pi_4t}{5\Pi_2}} - e^{\mathfrak{z}_2ny+\mathfrak{z}_3nz+\frac{\left(25\Pi_2x+6t\Pi_4^2\right)\left(\Pi_4+\sqrt{-100\left(\mathfrak{z}_2^2+\mathfrak{z}_3^2\right)n^2\Pi_2\Pi_3+\Pi_4^2}\right)}{250\Pi_2^2}} kn\mathfrak{Q} \\
+e^{\mathfrak{z}_2ny+\mathfrak{z}_3nz+\frac{\left(25\Pi_2x+6t\Pi_4^2\right)\left(\Pi_4+\sqrt{-100\left(\mathfrak{z}_2^2+\mathfrak{z}_3^2\right)n^2\Pi_2\Pi_3+\Pi_4^2}\right)}{250\Pi_2^2}} nd_0\Bigg)^2 \\
\Pi_4\left(\Pi_4+\sqrt{-100(\mathfrak{z}_2^2+\mathfrak{z}_3^2)n^2\Pi_2\Pi_3+\Pi_4^2}\right)\Bigg].
\end{cases}
\tag{36}
$$

6.2. Graphical Simulation

In this section, we present a detailed discussion of the solitary-wave solutions derived through the Paul–Painlevé approach for the proposed $(3+1)$-dimensional ZK–Burgers model. The solutions are demonstrated in Figures 11–15, where different parameter sets lead to distinct nonlinear wave structures such as periodic waves, bright solitons, combined states, and dark–bright excitations. These results emphasize the physical richness of the model and its relevance to dusty plasmas with quantum corrections.

Figure 11 corresponds to Equation (29) and represents a bright soliton solution derived for the parameter values $\Pi_1 = 0.3$, $\Pi_2 = 0.02$, $\Pi_3 = 0.06$, $\Pi_4 = -0.03$, $d_0 = -0.9$, $n = 0.1$, $k = -0.4$, $a_1 = 0.03$, $\omega = 0.1$, $z = 0.3$, $\mathfrak{Q} = 0.78$, $\mathfrak{z}_2 = -0.02$, $y = 0.2$. The solution explains a localized wave packet of enhanced amplitude that preserves its shape while propagating. Physically, bright solitons arise due to a balance between dispersion and nonlinearity, and they are significant in modeling coherent energy transport in plasma devices as well as in astrophysical-plasma environments.

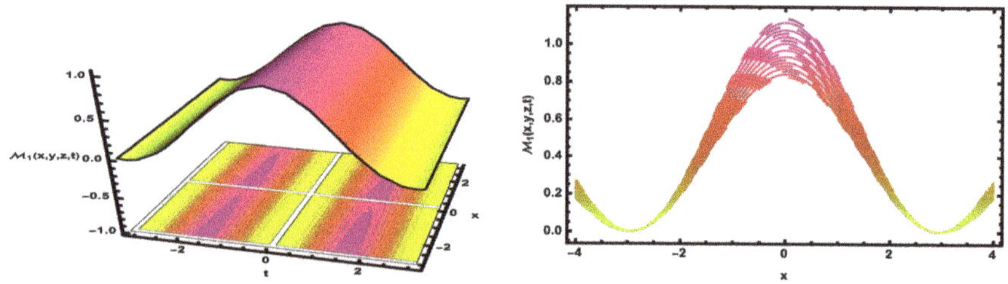

Figure 11. Physical visualization of the solution (29) for $\Pi_1 = 0.3, \Pi_2 = 0.02, \Pi_3 = 0.06, \Pi_4 = -0.03$, $d_0 = -0.9, n = 0.1, k = -0.4, a_1 = 0.03, \omega = 0.1, z = 0.3, \mathfrak{Q} = 0.78, \mathfrak{z}_2 = -0.02, y = 0.2$.

Figure 12, associated with Equation (30), shows a periodic solution for the parameters $\Pi_1 = 0.5$, $\Pi_2 = 0.04$, $\Pi_3 = 0.06$, $\Pi_4 = -0.06$, $d_0 = -0.3$, $n = 0.4$, $k = -0.2$, $\omega = 0.7$, $z = 0.7$, $\mathfrak{Q} = 0.56$, $\mathfrak{z}_2 = 0.2$, $y = 0.8$. The oscillatory pattern represents the presence of nonlinear wave trains that may be generated in plasmas under resonant conditions. Such periodic states are relevant to plasma resonance studies, wave–particle interactions, and nonlinear communication systems.

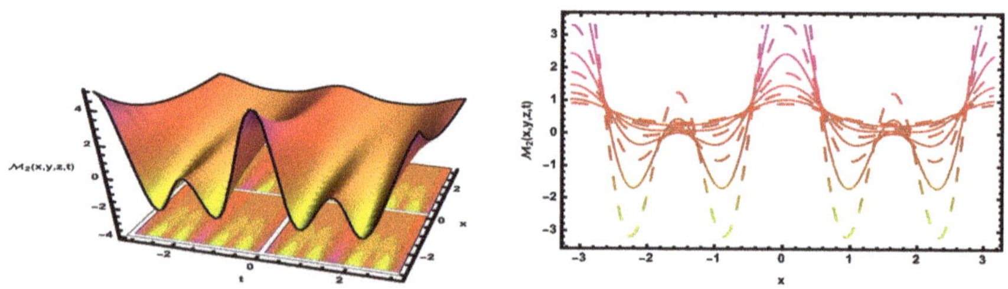

Figure 12. Physical visualization of the solution (30) for $\Pi_1 = 0.5, \Pi_2 = 0.04, \Pi_3 = 0.06, \Pi_4 = -0.06$, $d_0 = -0.3, n = 0.4, k = -0.2, \omega = 0.7, z = 0.7, \mathfrak{Q} = 0.56, \mathfrak{z}_2 = 0.2, y = 0.8$.

Figure 13, determined from Equation (32) with $\Pi_1 = 0.75$, $\Pi_2 = 0.05$, $\Pi_3 = 0.06$, $\Pi_4 = -0.06$, $d_0 = -0.04$, $\mathfrak{z}_3 = 0.6$, $n = 0.4$, $k = -0.4$, $z = 0.3$, $\mathfrak{Q} = 0.6$, $\mathfrak{z}_2 = 0.82$, $y = 0.3$, illustrates a combo solution. This solution contains both solitary and oscillatory characteristics, reflecting the coexistence of localized and periodic modes. Physically, such hybrid behaviors can be used to describe multi-mode interactions in dusty plasmas, where nonlinear excitations coexist due to strong coupling effects or quantum corrections.

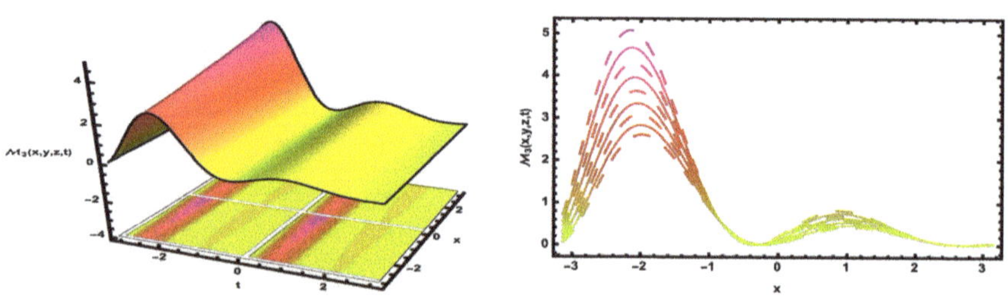

Figure 13. Physical visualization of the solution (32) for $\Pi_1 = 0.75, \Pi_2 = 0.05, \Pi_3 = 0.06, \Pi_4 = -0.06$, $d_0 = -0.04, \mathfrak{z}_3 = 0.6, n = 0.4, k = -0.4, z = 0.3, \mathfrak{Q} = 0.6, \mathfrak{z}_2 = 0.82, y = 0.3$.

Figure 14, corresponding to Equation (34), also represents a combined solution, derived for $\Pi_1 = 0.85, \Pi_2 = 0.04, \Pi_3 = 0.06, \Pi_4 = -0.06, d_0 = -0.02, \mathfrak{z}_3 = 0.6, n = 0.4, k = -0.2$, $z = 0.7, \mathfrak{Q} = 0.56, \mathfrak{z}_2 = 0.92, y = 0.8$. In this case, the coexistence of solitary and periodic waves appears, with different amplitude distributions compared to Figure 13, suggesting parameter-sensitive dynamics. These solutions are valuable for modeling nonlinear wave coupling and modulation processes in strongly magnetized plasmas.

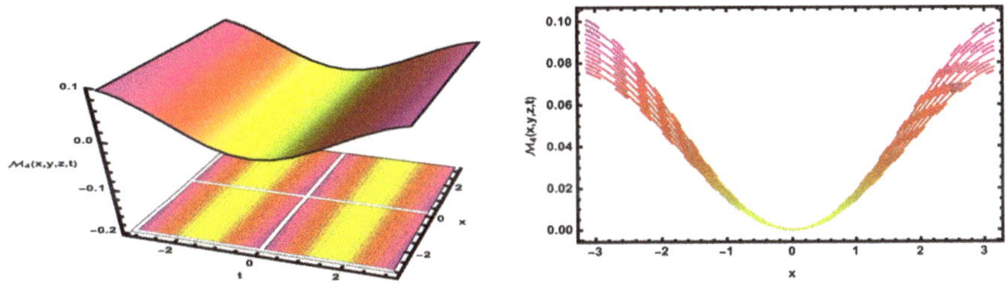

Figure 14. Physical visualization of the solution (34) for $\Pi_1 = 0.85, \Pi_2 = 0.04, \Pi_3 = 0.06, \Pi_4 = -0.06$, $d_0 = -0.02$, $\mathfrak{z}_3 = 0.6$, $n = 0.4$, $k = -0.2$, $z = 0.7$, $\mathfrak{Q} = 0.56$, $\mathfrak{z}_2 = 0.92$, $y = 0.8$.

Finally, Figure 15, related to Equation (36), depicts a dark–bright soliton solution for $\Pi_1 = 0.75$, $\Pi_2 = 0.5$, $\Pi_3 = 0.6$, $\Pi_4 = -0.06$, $d_0 = -0.04$, $\mathfrak{z}_3 = 0.74$, $n = 0.4$, $k = -0.4$, $z = 0.3$, $\mathfrak{Q} = 0.6$, $\mathfrak{z}_2 = 0.02$, $y = 0.3$. This type of solution demonstrates the coexistence of a localized intensity dip (dark soliton) and a localized intensity hump (bright soliton). Such states are highly significant in the context of energy localization, modulational instability, and turbulence in plasma systems. They also present analogies to dark–bright solitons observed in optical fibers, where nonlinear waveguides support coexisting dip–hump structures. Overall, the derived solutions indicate that the $(3+1)$-dimensional ZK–Burgers system supports a wide range of nonlinear excitations depending on parameter choices. These results expand our understanding of plasma nonlinearities, providing practical insights for applications in dusty and quantum plasmas, nonlinear optics, plasma turbulence control, and astrophysical wave modeling.

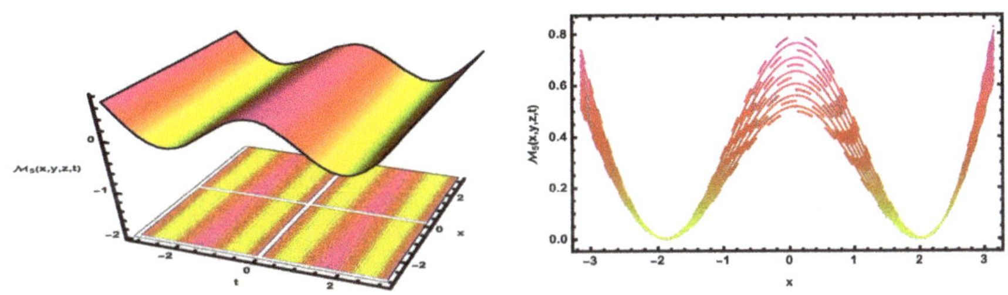

Figure 15. Physical visualization of the solution (36) for $\Pi_1 = 0.75, \Pi_2 = 0.5, \Pi_3 = 0.6, \Pi_4 = -0.06$, $d_0 = -0.04$, $\mathfrak{z}_3 = 0.74$, $n = 0.4$, $k = -0.4$, $z = 0.3$, $\mathfrak{Q} = 0.6$, $\mathfrak{z}_2 = 0.02$, $y = 0.3$.

6.3. Comparison

In contrast to prior quantum ZK–type studies [28–31], which consider dust-free or nondissipative settings and chiefly report solitary/exact solutions, we analyze a (3+1)-D ZK–Burgers model for dusty quantum plasma (including dissipation), derive multiple solution families via the Paul–Painlevé approach, and conduct a comprehensive nonlinear-dynamics/chaos analysis. A concise side-by-side comparison is provided in Table 2.

Table 2. Side-by-side comparison of the present work with additional published studies [28–31].

Aspect	Goswami et al. [28]	Arshed et al. [29]	Zhang et al. [30]	Shah & Mahmood [31]	Present Work
Model/equation	Electron-acoustic waves (inner magnetosphere; relativistic degeneracy)	(3+1)-D extended quantum ZK	(3+1)-D extended quantum ZK	(2+1)-D quantum ZK (no dust)	(3+1)-D ZK–Burgers in dusty quantum plasma
Method	Shock/solitary-structure analysis	Generalized Kudryashov; modified Khater	Exact solution techniques (incl. peakons)	Analytical solitary-wave analysis	Paul–Painlevé + full dynamical diagnostics
Reported solutions	Shocks; solitary structures	Families of exact solutions	Peakons; new solitary waves	Bright solitary waves	Bright, periodic, hybrid (combo), dark–bright
Dynamical analysis	No	No	No	No	**Yes**: LEs, bifurcation, spectra, basins, multistability
Scope	Space-plasma regime, relativistic effects	Parametric exact solutions (no dynamics)	Extended quantum ZK without dissipation	Baseline quantum ZK framework	Dissipation + dusty medium; solution families + comprehensive dynamics
Novelty	Shock/solitary in different regimes	Exact families w/o dynamics	New exact forms w/o dissipation	Baseline for quantum ZK	First integration of Paul–Painlevé exact solutions with full dynamical/chaotic analysis for dusty (3+1)-D ZK–Burgers

7. Conclusions and Future Work

In this study, we studied the $(3+1)$-dimensional Zakharov–Kuznetsov–Burgers equation in the framework of quantum dusty plasma to examine the mechanisms underlying shock-wave phenomena. The nonlinear model was analyzed through a comprehensive dynamical framework that incorporated bifurcation theory, Lyapunov exponents, multistability, return map analysis, chaotic attractors, Poincaré maps, and phase portraits. The analysis revealed a rich variety of dynamical regimes, including chaotic, quasi-periodic, and periodic structures, as well as sensitivity of the system to frequency-response and time-delay effects. These results contribute to a deeper understanding of the nonlinear structures that arise in dispersive–dissipative-plasma environments. After establishing the global dynamics, traveling-wave solutions were constructed via the Paul–Painlevé approach. The obtained analytical solutions present explicit representations of shock- and solitary-wave profiles, thereby linking the dynamical picture with exact solution structures. This dual framework provides valuable insight into the interplay between nonlinear excitations, dissipation, and dispersion in plasmas with charged dust particles under quantum effects. Building on this work, several promising avenues may be pursued. First, the model can be extended to include additional physical effects such as nonthermal particle distributions, external magnetic fields, or higher-order quantum corrections. Second, numerical simulations may be performed to validate the analytical and dynamical results, specifically in regimes where multistability and coexistence of attractors are predicted. Third, connections to experimental plasma systems can be explored, allowing the identification of parameter regimes relevant to laboratory dusty-plasma and astrophysical-plasma conditions. Finally, the methodology employed here may be generalized to other nonlinear dispersive equations, broadening its impact in plasma physics, nonlinear optics, and related engineering applications.

Author Contributions: Conceptualization, L.Z.; Methodology, H.X.; Formal analysis, H.X.; Investigation, L.Z.; Resources, H.X.; Writing—original draft, H.X.; Writing—review & editing, L.Z. All authors have read and agreed to the published version of the manuscript.

Funding: This work was supported in part by the National Natural Science Foundation (NSF) of China under Grant 12372009, in part by the NSF of Hanshan Normal University under Grant PNB221103, and in part by the Education Science Planning Project of Guangdong under Grant 2023GXJK385.

Data Availability Statement: The original contributions presented in this study are included in the article. Further inquiries can be directed to the corresponding author.

Conflicts of Interest: The authors declare that they have no conflicts of interest.

Appendix A. Outline of the Paul–Painlevé Approach

For completeness, we present here a concise description of the Paul–Painlevé approach, which is often employed in the analysis of nonlinear differential equations to distinguish between regular and chaotic solution behaviors.

Step 1: Reduction to an ordinary differential equation

We begin with the general nonlinear partial differential equation

$$\mathfrak{I}(\mathcal{M}, \mathcal{M}_x, \mathcal{M}_y, \mathcal{M}_z, \mathcal{M}_t, \cdots) = 0. \tag{A1}$$

Introducing the traveling-wave transformation

$$\mathcal{M}(x,y,z,t) = \mathcal{Q}(\tau), \qquad \tau = \mathfrak{z}_1 x + \mathfrak{z}_2 y + \mathfrak{z}_3 z - \omega t, \tag{A2}$$

the PDE (A1) is reduced to an ordinary differential equation of the form

$$\mathfrak{U}(\mathcal{Q}, \mathcal{Q}', \mathcal{Q}'', \cdots) = 0. \tag{A3}$$

Step 2: Construction of the Trial Solution

A suitable trial solution for Equation (A3) is established, expressed as

$$\mathcal{Q}(\tau) = \sum_{i=1}^{M} \left[\mathfrak{P}_i \, \mathcal{P}^i(\mathfrak{G}) \, e^{-in\tau} \right], \tag{A4}$$

where $\mathfrak{P}_i$ $(i = 1, 2, \ldots, m)$ are constants to be determined. The auxiliary function $\mathcal{P}(\mathfrak{G})$ satisfies the Riccati-type equation

$$\frac{d\mathcal{P}}{d\mathfrak{G}} - k\mathcal{P}^2 = 0,$$

with $\mathfrak{G} = \mathfrak{E}(\tau) = A_1 - \frac{e^{-n\tau}}{n}$. Its solution can be written as

$$\mathcal{P}(\mathfrak{G}) = \frac{1}{k\mathfrak{G} - d_0}. \tag{A5}$$

Step 3: Determination of the Balance Number

The parameter m in Equation (A4) is obtained using the balancing principle, which requires that the highest-order derivative in Equation (A3) be balanced with the highest-degree nonlinear term.

Step 4: Coefficient Identification

Substituting Equations (A4) and (A5) into Equation (A1) produces a polynomial in powers of $\mathcal{P}^i(\mathfrak{G})$, $(i = 0, 1, 2, \ldots)$. By equating coefficients of identical powers to zero, one obtains an algebraic system of equations. This system is then solved using a computer algebra system (CAS), such as *Mathematica*, yielding explicit forms for the unknown parameters and thereby constructing the final solution set. *Remark:* This appendix has been included to provide readers with a structured overview of the Paul–Painlevé procedure. The approach is especially valuable in classifying solution behaviors of nonlinear models and in generating closed-form structures that highlight integrability properties.

References

1. Zhu, X.; Xia, P.; He, Q.; Ni, Z.; Ni, L. Ensemble Classifier Design Based on Perturbation Binary Salp Swarm Algorithm for Classification. *Comput. Model. Eng. Sci. CMES* **2023**, *135*, 653. [CrossRef]
2. ur Rahman, M.; Akram, S.; Asif, M. Chaotic behavior, sensitive analysis and dynamics of invariant formulation of nonclassical symmetries to the nonlinear Tzitzéica equation arising in mathematical physics. *Bound. Value Probl.* **2025**, *2025*, 123. [CrossRef]
3. Zhang, X.; Yang, X.; He, Q. Multi-scale systemic risk and spillover networks of commodity markets in the bullish and bearish regimes. *N. Am. J. Econ. Financ.* **2022**, *62*, 101766. [CrossRef]
4. Moslem, W.M.; Ali, S.; Shukla, P.K.; Tang, X.Y.; Rowlands, G. Solitary, explosive, and periodic solutions of the quantum Zakharov-Kuznetsov equation and its transverse instability. *Phys. Plasmas* **2007**, *14*, 082308. [CrossRef]
5. El-Shorbagy, M.A.; Akram, S.; ur Rahman, M.; Nabwey, H.A. Analysis of bifurcation, chaotic structures, lump and $M-W$-shape soliton solutions to (2 + 1) complex modified Korteweg-de-Vries system. *AIMS Math.* **2024**, *9*, 16116–16145. [CrossRef]
6. Li, B.; Liang, H.; He, Q. Multiple and generic bifurcation analysis of a discrete Hindmarsh-Rose model. *Chaos Solitons Fractals* **2021**, *146*, 110856. [CrossRef]
7. Akram, S.; ur Rahman, M.; AL-Essa, L.A. A comprehensive dynamical analysis of (2 + 1)-dimensional nonlinear electrical transmission line model with Atangana–Baleanu derivative. *Phys. Lett. A* **2025**, *555*, 130762. [CrossRef]
8. Iqbal, M.; Faridi, W.A.; Alrashdi, H.D.; Aljohani, A.; Murad, M.A.S.; Mohammad, N.; Alsubaie, A.S. Nonlinear behavior of dispersive solitary wave solutions for the propagation of shock waves in the nonlinear coupled system of equations. *Sci. Rep.* **2025**, *15*, 27535. [CrossRef]
9. Mahmood, T.; Alhawael, G.; Akram, S.; ur Rahman, M. Exploring the Lie symmetries, conservation laws, bifurcation analysis and dynamical waveform patterns of diverse exact solution to the Klein–Gordan equation. *Opt. Quantum Electron.* **2024**, *56*, 1978. [CrossRef]
10. Eskandari, Z.; Avazzadeh, Z.; Ghaziani, R.K.; Li, B. Dynamics and bifurcations of a discrete-time Lotka–Volterra model using nonstandard finite difference discretization method. *Math. Methods Appl. Sci.* **2025**, *48*, 7197–7212. [CrossRef]
11. Zubair Raza, M.; Iqbal, M.A.B.; Khan, A.; Almutairi, D.K.; Abdeljawad, T. Soliton solutions of the (2 + 1)-dimensional Jaulent-Miodek evolution equation via effective analytical techniques. *Sci. Rep.* **2025**, *15*, 3495. [CrossRef]
12. Xu, P.; Huang, H.; Wang, K. Dynamics of real and complex multi-soliton solutions, novel soliton molecules, asymmetric solitons and diverse wave solutions to the Kadomtsev-Petviashvili equation. *Alex. Eng. J.* **2025**, *125*, 537–544. [CrossRef]
13. Baber, M.Z.; Ahmed, N.; Xu, C.; Iqbal, M.S.; Sulaiman, T.A. A computational scheme and its comparison with optical soliton solutions for the stochastic Chen–Lee–Liu equation with sensitivity analysis. *Mod. Phys. Lett. B* **2025**, *39*, 2450376. [CrossRef]
14. Mohan, B.; Kumar, S. Painlevé analysis, restricted bright-dark N-solitons, and N-rogue waves of a (4 + 1)-dimensional variable-coefficient generalized KP equation in nonlinear sciences. *Nonlinear Dyn.* **2025**, *113*, 11893–11906. [CrossRef]
15. El-Shorbagy, M.A.; Akram, S.; ur Rahman, M. Investigation of lump, breather and multi solitonic wave solutions to fractional nonlinear dynamical model with stability analysis. *Partial. Differ. Equ. Appl. Math.* **2024**, *12*, 100955. [CrossRef]
16. Hussein, H.H.; Ahmed, H.M.; Alexan, W. Analytical soliton solutions for cubic-quartic perturbations of the Lakshmanan-Porsezian-Daniel equation using the modified extended tanh function method. *Ain Shams Eng. J.* **2024**, *15*, 102513. [CrossRef]
17. Hossain, A.K.M.; Sazzad, K.; Akter, H.; Akbar, M.A. Soliton solutions of DSW and Burgers equations by generalized $(\frac{G'}{G})$-expansion method. *Opt. Quantum Electron.* **2024**, *56*, 653. [CrossRef]
18. Samir, I.; Ahmed, H.M.; Rabie, W.; Abbas, W.; Mostafa, O. Construction optical solitons of generalized nonlinear Schrödinger equation with quintuple power-law nonlinearity using Exp-function, projective Riccati, and new generalized methods. *AIMS Math.* **2025**, *10*, 3392–3407. [CrossRef]
19. Anjum, N.; Rasheed, A.; He, J.I.; Alsolami, A.A. Free vibration of a tapered beam by the Aboodh transform-based variational iteration method. *J. Comput. Appl. Mech.* **2024**, *55*, 440–450.
20. Yasmin, H.; Alshehry, A.S.; Ganie, A.H.; Mahnashi, A.M.; Shah, R. Perturbed Gerdjikov–Ivanov equation: Soliton solutions via Backlund transformation. *Optik* **2024**, *298*, 171576. [CrossRef]
21. Farooq, A.; Khan, M.I.; Ma, W.X. Exact solutions for the improved mKdv equation with conformable derivative by using the Jacobi elliptic function expansion method. *Opt. Quantum Electron.* **2024**, *56*, 542. [CrossRef]

22. El-Shorbagy, M.A.; Akram, S.; ur Rahman, M. Propagation of solitary wave solutions to (4 + 1)-dimensional Davey–Stewartson–Kadomtsev–Petviashvili equation arise in mathematical physics and stability analysis. *Part. Differ. Equ. Appl. Math.* **2024**, *10*, 100669. [CrossRef]
23. Guo, N. On the inverse scattering transform problem for the modified intermediate long wave equation: Deep-and shallow-water limits. *Commun. Nonlinear Sci. Numer. Simul.* **2025**, *152*, 109099. [CrossRef]
24. Faridi, W.A.; Iqbal, M.; Riaz, M.B.; AlQahtani, S.A.; Wazwaz, A. The fractional soliton solutions of dynamical system arising in plasma physics: The comparative analysis. *Alex. Eng. J.* **2024**, *95*, 247–261. [CrossRef]
25. El-Awady, E.I.; Hussain, S.; Akhtar, N. On the analytical soliton approximations to damping forced Zakharov-Kuznetsov equation arising in dissipative nonthermal magnetized plasma. *Phys. Scr.* **2024**, *99*, 115263. [CrossRef]
26. Saini, N.S.; Chahal, B.S.; Bains, A.S.; Bedi, C. Zakharov-Kuznetsov equation in a magnetized plasma with two temperature superthermal electrons. *Phys. Plasmas* **2014**, *21*, 022114. [CrossRef]
27. Sindi, C.T.; Manafian, J. Soliton solutions of the quantum Zakharov-Kuznetsov equation which arises in quantum magneto-plasmas. *Eur. Phys. J. Plus* **2017**, *132*, 67. [CrossRef]
28. Goswami, J.; Chandra, S.; Ghosh, B. Shock waves and the formation of solitary structures in electron acoustic wave in inner magnetosphere plasma with relativistically degenerate particles. *Astrophys. Space Sci.* **2019**, *364*, 65. [CrossRef]
29. Arshed, S.; Akram, G.; Sadaf, M.; Khan, A. Solutions of (3 + 1)-dimensional extended quantum nonlinear Zakharov–Kuznetsov equation using the generalized Kudryashov method and the modified Khater method. *Opt. Quantum Electron.* **2023**, *55*, 922. [CrossRef]
30. Zhang, B.-g.; Li, W.; Li, X. Peakons and new exact solitary wave solutions of extended quantum Zakharov-Kuznetsov equation. *Phys. Plasmas* **2017**, *24*, 062113. [CrossRef]
31. Shah, H.A.; Mahmood, S. Zakharov–Kuznetsov Equation in Quantum Plasmas. *Phys. Plasmas* **2011**, *18*, 022301.
32. Tao, L.-L.; Wei, L.; Liu, B.; Zhang, H.; Duan, W. The effect of dust size distribution on shock wave in quantum dusty plasma. *Pramana* **2021**, *95*, 111. [CrossRef]
33. Manfredi, G. How to model quantum plasmas. *Fields Inst. Commun.* **2005**, *46*, 263–287.
34. Suvorov, A.G.; Mastrano, A.; Melatos, A. Spin paramagnetic deformation of a neutron star. *Mon. Not. R. Astron. Soc.* **2016**, *456*, 731–738. [CrossRef]
35. Shukla, P.K.; Ali, S. Dust acoustic waves in quantum plasmas. *Phys. Plasmas* **2005**, *12*, 114502. [CrossRef]
36. Han, J.-F.; Gao, D.; Zhang, H.; Wang, X.; Duan, W. Effects of the dust size distribution in one-dimensional quantum dusty plasma. *Front. Phys.* **2015**, *10*, 105201. [CrossRef]
37. El-Labany, S.K.; El-Siragy, N.M.; El-Taibany, W.F.; Behery, E.E. The effect of dust size distribution on quantum dust acoustic wave. *Phys. Plasmas* **2009**, *16*, 093701. [CrossRef]
38. El-Tantawy, S.A. Effect of ion viscosity on dust ion-acoustic shock waves in a nonextensive magnetoplasma. *Astrophys. Space Sci.* **2016**, *361*, 249. [CrossRef]
39. Qi, X.; Xu, Y.; Duan, W.; Zhang, L.; Yang, L. Particle-in-cell simulation of the head-on collision between two ion acoustic solitary waves in plasmas. *Phys. Plasmas* **2014**, *21*, 082118. [CrossRef]
40. De Angelis, U.; Formisano, V.; Giordano, M. Ion plasma waves in dusty plasmas: Halley's comet. *J. Plasma Phys.* **1988**, *40*, 399–406. [CrossRef]
41. Magnitskii, N.A. Wave Propagation and Chaotic Behavior in Conservative and Dissipative Sawada–Kotera Models. *Fluid Dyn. Mater. Process.* **2025**, *21*, 1529. [CrossRef]
42. Akram, S.; Ur Rahman, M. Exploring Nonlinear Dynamics and Soliton Structures in the Spin Reduced Hirota-Maxwell-Bloch System via Atangana's Conformable Operator. *Chin. J. Phys.* **2025**, *97*, 1514–1538. [CrossRef]

mathematics

MDPI

Article

Truncated M-Fractional Exact Solutions, Stability Analysis, and Modulation Instability of the Classical Lonngren Wave Model

Haitham Qawaqneh [1], Abdulaziz Khalid Alsharidi [2,*]

[1] Department of Mathematics, Faculty of Science and Information Technology, Al-Zaytoonah University of Jordan, Amman 11733, Jordan; h.alqawaqneh@zuj.edu.jo
[2] Department of Mathematics and Statistics, College of Science, King Faisal University, Al-Hasa 31982, Saudi Arabia
* Correspondence: akalsharidi@kfu.edu.sa

Abstract

Many types of exact solutions to the truncated M-fractional classical Lonngren wave model are explored in this paper. The classical Lonngren wave model is a significant electronics equation. This model is used to explain the electronic signals within semiconductor materials, especially tunnel diodes. Through the application of a modified (G'/G^2)-expansion technique and an extended sinh-Gordon equation expansion (EShGEE) method, we obtained various wave solutions, including periodic, kink, singular, dark, bright, and dark–bright types, among others. To ensure that the solutions in question are stable, linear stability analysis is also carried out. Moreover, the stationary solutions of the concerning equation are studied through modulation instability. The obtained results are useful in various areas, including electronic physics, soliton physics, plasma physics, nonlinear optics, acoustics, etc. Both techniques are useful for solving nonlinear partial fractional differential equations. Both techniques provide exact solutions, which can be important for understanding complex phenomena. Both techniques are reliable and yield distinct types of exact soliton solutions.

Keywords: classical Lonngren wave model; qualitative analysis; analytical methods; fractional form exact solutions; applications in mathematical physics

MSC: 35C07; 35C08; 83C15

1. Introduction

Fractional differential equations are used in many fields of science and engineering. Various fractional differential models have been developed, including the fractional stochastic Biswas–Arshed equation [1], the fractional Van der Waals equation [2], the fractional single-joint robot arm model [3], the fractional generalized Pochhammer–Chree equation [4], the fractional Boussinesq–Burgers system [5], the fractional Pareto probability distribution model [6], the fractional Riemann wave equation [7], the fractional coupled Konno–Onno equation [8], the Sharma–Tasso–Olver equation [9], the fractional advection diffusion equations [10], the fractional Boussinesq–Burgers system [11], the fractional Schrödinger–Hirota equation [12], the fractional Westervelt model [13], etc. There are many methods to obtain the exact wave solitons and other solutions, including the Sardar sub-equation method [14], the Moser iterative method [15], the unified method [16], the new extended direct algebraic method [17], the Crank–Nicolson finite difference method [18], the Fourier-Jacobi Polynomials method [19], the Hirota bilinear method [20], etc.

The model we focus on is the classical Lonngren wave model, which is given as follows [21]:

$$(v_{xx} - \theta v + \kappa v^2)_{tt} + v_{xx} = 0 \tag{1}$$

Here, v is a real-valued function. Symbols θ and κ are the arbitrary constants. Equation (1) has its physical basis in the behavior of electrical signals within Sony's tunnel diode, which falls under the category of semiconductor materials [22]. Moreover, Equation (1) has applications in elucidating the propagation of electrical signals through materials exhibiting semiconductor properties and mechanisms underlying energy storage in circuits featuring electrical charge. Various methods are used to obtain the different types of solutions of Equation (1), including the Sine–Gordon expansion method [23], the auxiliary equation method [24], the $(1/G')$-expansion method [25], Lie group analysis [26], etc.

In this paper, the authors utilized the EShGEE technique and the modified (G'/G^2)-expansion technique. The proposed methods are used for many models. Specifically, the EShGEE method is applied to the Biswas–Arshed equation [27], the hyperbolic and cubic-quintic non-linear Schrödinger models [28], the generalized non-linear Schrödinger model [29], and the Kundu–Eckhaus model [30]. The modified (G'/G^2)-expansion technique is utilized for multiple models, as discussed in [31–33], etc.

The aim of this work was to obtain novel exact wave solitons of the classical Lonngren wave model with a truncated M-fractional derivative. Moreover, we performed qualitative analysis to describe the accuracy and stability of the obtained results.

The motivation for our research is to explore the different types of exact soliton solutions of the classical Lonngren wave model in the truncated M-fractional derivative form. The truncated M-fractional derivative shares properties of both the fractional derivatives and integer-order derivatives. This definition of a fractional derivative provides solutions that are close to the numerical solutions of the model. The techniques employed here provide multiple kinds of exact soliton solutions. These techniques have not yet been applied to the classical Lonngren wave model. The applied techniques are also applicable for other nonlinear partial fractional differential equations. Additionally, the effect of the truncated M-fractional derivative on the obtained solutions is also discussed through two-dimensional graphs. Moreover, stability and modulation instability analyses are utilized for the first time for the classical Lonngren wave model.

This paper comprises multiple sections: a description of the EShGEE scheme and modified (G'/G^2)-expansion method in Section 2; mathematical analysis and exact wave solutions in Section 3; a graphical explanation in Section 4; qualitative analysis in Section 5; and the conclusion in Section 6.

Definition 1. *Suppose $w(y) : [0, \infty) \to \Re$, so TMFD of w of order ϵ [34]*

$$D_{M,t}^{\epsilon,\varrho} w(t) = \lim_{\epsilon \to 0} \frac{w\,(t\,E_\varrho(\epsilon t^{1-\epsilon})) - w(t)}{\epsilon}, \quad \epsilon \in (0,1], \ \ \varrho > 0,$$

here $E_\varrho(.)$ denotes TML profile [35]

$$E_\varrho(z) = \sum_{j=0}^{i} \frac{z^j}{\Gamma(\varrho j + 1)}, \ \ \varrho > 0 \ \ and \ \ z \in C.$$

Theorem 1. *Suppose $a,b \in \Re$ and g, f are $\epsilon-$ differentiable for $t > 0$. The following property is taken from [34]:*

$$(a)\ D_{M,t}^{\epsilon,\varrho}(ag(t) + bf(t)) = aD_{M,t}^{\epsilon,\varrho} g(t) + bD_{M,t}^{\epsilon,\varrho} f(t).$$

To prove the linearity property, we will use the definition of the fractional derivative operator $D_{M,t}^{\epsilon,\varrho}$.

Step 1: Apply the definition to the linear combination. Let us consider $D_{M,t}^{\epsilon,\varrho}(ag(t)+bf(t))$ *using the given definition:*

$D_{M,t}^{\epsilon,\varrho}(ag(t)+bf(t)) = \lim_{\epsilon\to 0} \frac{(ag(t\ E_{\varrho}(\epsilon t^{1-\epsilon}))+bf(t\ E_{\varrho}(\epsilon t^{1-\epsilon})))-(ag(t)+bf(t))}{\epsilon}$

Step 2: Distribute the limit. $D_{M,t}^{\epsilon,\varrho}(ag(t)+bf(t)) = \lim_{\epsilon\to 0} \frac{ag(t\ E_{\varrho}(\epsilon t^{1-\epsilon}))+bf(t\ E_{\varrho}(\epsilon t^{1-\epsilon}))-ag(t)-bf(t)}{\epsilon}$

Step 3: Separate the terms. $D_{M,t}^{\epsilon,\varrho}(ag(t)+bf(t)) = \lim_{\epsilon\to 0} \frac{a(g(t\ E_{\varrho}(\epsilon t^{1-\epsilon}))-g(t))+b(f(t\ E_{\varrho}(\epsilon t^{1-\epsilon}))-f(t))}{\epsilon}$

Step 4: Factor out constants. $D_{M,t}^{\epsilon,\varrho}(ag(t)+bf(t)) = \lim_{\epsilon\to 0} a\frac{g(t\ E_{\varrho}(\epsilon t^{1-\epsilon}))-g(t)}{\epsilon} + \lim_{\epsilon\to 0} b\frac{f(t\ E_{\varrho}(\epsilon t^{1-\epsilon}))-f(t)}{\epsilon}$

Step 5: Apply the definition of the fractional derivative. $D_{M,t}^{\epsilon,\varrho}(ag(t)+bf(t)) = a\,D_{M,t}^{\epsilon,\varrho}g(t)$ $+\, bD_{M,t}^{\epsilon,\varrho}f(t)$

The final answer is $\boxed{aD_{M,t}^{\epsilon,\varrho}g(t)+bD_{M,t}^{\epsilon,\varrho}f(t)}$

Similarly, we can prove the following theorems.

$$(b)\ D_{M,t}^{\epsilon,\varrho}(g(t)\cdot f(t)) = g(t)D_{M,t}^{\epsilon,\varrho}f(t)+f(t)D_{M,t}^{\epsilon,\varrho}g(t).$$

$$(c)\ D_{M,t}^{\epsilon,\varrho}(\frac{g(t)}{f(t)}) = \frac{f(t)D_{M,t}^{\epsilon,\varrho}g(t)-g(t)D_{M,t}^{\epsilon,\varrho}f(t)}{(f(t))^2}$$

$$(d)\ D_{M,t}^{\epsilon,\varrho}(C)=0,\ \text{ where C is a constant.}$$

$$(e)\ D_{M,t}^{\epsilon,\varrho}g(t) = \frac{t^{1-\epsilon}}{\Gamma(\varrho+1)}\frac{dg(t)}{dt}.$$

The truncated M-fractional derivative has several physical justifications and mathematical advantages:

(i) It captures the memory effect of the system, which is essential in modeling complex phenomena. (ii) It accounts for non-local interactions, allowing for a more accurate representation of physical systems. (iii) It provides flexibility in modeling various physical systems, including those with different types of nonlinearities. (iv) It is a generalized form that encompasses various fractional derivatives, including the Riemann–Liouville and Caputo derivatives. (v) It converges to the classical derivative when the fractional order approaches an integer value. (vi) It allows for the derivation of analytical solutions for certain types of differential equations. (vii) It can be implemented numerically, providing an efficient way to solve complex problems.

Remark 1. *For* $\epsilon\to 1$*, the term* $t^{1-\epsilon}$ *approaches* $t^0=1$*. Thus,* $\epsilon t^{1-\epsilon}$ *approaches* ϵ*. The function* $E_{\varrho}(\epsilon t^{1-\epsilon})$ *would approach* $E_{\varrho}(\epsilon)$*.*

Given the specific form of the limit definition and without the exact form of E_{ϱ}*, we can hypothesize that as* $\epsilon\to 1$*, the operator might approach a form consistent with classical differentiation if* $E_{\varrho}(\epsilon t^{1-\epsilon})$ *behaves in a manner that reduces the fractional nature of the derivative to an integer-order derivative.*

2. Description of Techniques

2.1. Description of EShGEE Scheme

Now, we explain the phases of the proposed scheme.

Phase 1:

Consider an FNLPD equation

$$F(g, D^{\varepsilon,\varrho}_{M,t}g^2, g^2 D^{\varepsilon,\varrho}_{M,x}g, D^{\varepsilon,\varrho}_{M,x}g, \ldots) = 0. \tag{2}$$

where g denotes the profile.

Applying the given transformation in [36] within the framework of the truncated M-fractional derivative, we obtain the following:

$$g = G(\Omega),\ \Omega = \Gamma(1+\varrho)(\frac{x^{\varepsilon}}{\varepsilon} - \lambda\frac{t^{\varepsilon}}{\varepsilon}). \tag{3}$$

Inserting Equation (3) in Equation (2) yields

$$H(G, G^2G', G'', \ldots) = 0. \tag{4}$$

Phase 2:

Assume the solution of Equation (4) takes the form

$$G(f) = \alpha_0 + \sum_{j=1}^{m}(\beta_j \sinh(f) + \alpha_j \cosh(f))^j. \tag{5}$$

Here, $\alpha_0, \alpha_j, \beta_j$ $(j = 1, 2, 3, \ldots, m)$ are unknowns. A novel function f of Ω satisfies the following:

$$\frac{df}{d\Omega} = \sinh(f). \tag{6}$$

Positive integer "m" is obtained through utilizing the homogenous balance rule. Equation (6) is obtained by applying the following:

$$q_{xt} = \kappa \sinh(v). \tag{7}$$

By using [37], we obtain a solution of Equation (7) in the form

$$\sinh f(\Omega) = \pm\operatorname{csch}(\Omega) \quad OR \quad \cosh f(\Omega) = \pm\coth(\Omega). \tag{8}$$

and

$$\sinh f(\Omega) = \pm\iota\ \operatorname{sech}(\Omega) \quad OR \quad \cosh f(\Omega) = \pm\tanh(\Omega). \tag{9}$$

$\iota^2 = -1.$

Phase 3:

Using Equation (5) and Equation (6) in Equation (4) yields the following set of equations.

Phase 4:

Simplifying the obtained set yields undetermined values. Using the obtained results, Equations (8) and (9) give the results for Equation (4) in the form

$$G(\Omega) = \alpha_0 + \sum_{j=1}^{m}(\pm\beta_j \operatorname{csch}(\Omega) \pm \alpha_j \coth(\Omega))^j \tag{10}$$

and

$$G(\Omega) = \alpha_0 + \sum_{j=1}^{m}(\pm\iota\beta_j \operatorname{sech}(\Omega) \pm \alpha_j \tanh(\Omega))^j. \tag{11}$$

2.2. *Description of Modified $(G'/G^2)-$ Expansion Scheme*

Here, basic steps of the scheme are presented [38].

Step 1:
Consider Equations (2)–(4).
Step 2:
Consider the solution of Equation (4) in the form

$$Q(\Omega) = \sum_{i=0}^{m} \alpha_i (\frac{G'}{G^2})^i. \tag{12}$$

Here, $\alpha_i (i = 0, 1, 2, 3, \ldots, m)$ are unknowns where $\alpha_i \neq 0$. A new auxiliary function $G = G(\Omega)$ satisfies

$$(\frac{G'}{G^2})' = a + b(\frac{G'}{G^2})^2. \tag{13}$$

Here, a and b represent the parameters. The results obtained by the authors for Equation (13) depend on a, as follows:

Case 1: $ab < 0$ yields

$$(\frac{G'}{G^2}) = -\frac{\sqrt{|ab|}}{b} + \frac{\sqrt{|ab|}}{2} (\frac{C_1 \sinh(\sqrt{ab}\,\Omega) + C_2 \cosh(\sqrt{ab}\,\Omega)}{C_1 \cosh(\sqrt{ab}\,\Omega) + C_2 \sinh(\sqrt{ab}\,\Omega)}), \tag{14}$$

Case 2: if $ab > 0$, then

$$(\frac{G'}{G^2}) = \sqrt{\frac{a}{b}} (\frac{C_1 \cos(\sqrt{ab}\,\Omega) + C_2 \sin(\sqrt{ab}\,\Omega)}{C_1 \sin(\sqrt{ab}\,\Omega) - C_2 \sin(\sqrt{ab}\,\Omega)}), \tag{15}$$

Case 3: if $a = 0$ and $b \neq 0$, then

$$(\frac{G'}{G^2}) = -\frac{C_1}{b(C_1\Omega + C_2)}. \tag{16}$$

Here, C_1 and C_2 are constants.

Step 3:
Put Equation (12) into the Equation (4) with Equation (13) and collect the coefficients of each power of $(\frac{G'}{G^2})^i$ equal to zero, then solve the obtained set having α_i, a, b, ν.
Step 4:
By substituting α_i, ν, and the other parameters obtained in Step 3 from Equation (12) into Equation (4), one can derive the results of Equation (2).

3. Mathematical Analysis

Equation (1) in the form of a fractional derivative is given as follows:

$$D^{\varepsilon,2\varrho}_{M,t}(D^{\varepsilon,2\varrho}_{M,x}v - \theta v + \kappa v^2) + D^{\varepsilon,2\varrho}_{M,x}v = 0. \tag{17}$$

Consider the following wave transformation:

$$v(x,t) = V(\Omega), \qquad \Omega = \frac{\Gamma(1+\varrho)}{\varepsilon}(x^{\varepsilon} - \rho t^{\varepsilon}). \tag{18}$$

Here, ρ represents the soliton velocity.

$$D^{\varepsilon,\varrho}_{M,x}v = V', \quad D^{\varepsilon,2\varrho}_{M,x}v = V''. \tag{19}$$

$$D^{\varepsilon,\varrho}_{M,t}v = -\rho V', \quad D^{\varepsilon,2\varrho}_{M,t}v = \rho^2 V''. \tag{20}$$

$$D^{\varepsilon,\varrho}_{M,t}v^2 = -2\rho V V', \quad D^{\varepsilon,2\varrho}_{M,t}v^2 = 2\rho^2 (V V'' + (V')^2). \tag{21}$$

$$D_{M,t}^{\varepsilon,\varrho}(D_{M,x}^{\varepsilon,2\varrho}v) = -\rho V''', \quad D_{M,t}^{\varepsilon,2\varrho}(D_{M,x}^{\varepsilon,2\varrho}v) = \rho^2 V^{(4)}. \tag{22}$$

By substituting Equations (19)–(22) into Equation (17), we get

$$\rho^2 V^{(4)} + \left(1 - \theta\rho^2\right)V'' + 2\kappa\rho^2 VV'' + 2\kappa\rho^2 (V')^2 = 0. \tag{23}$$

By using the homogenous balance technique and balancing the terms V^4 and VV'', we find that the value of m is two.

3.1. Exact Wave Solutions Through the EShGEE Technique

Equation (5) reduces to the following for $m = 2$:

$$V(\Omega) = \alpha_0 + \alpha_1 \cosh(f(\Omega)) + \beta_1 \sinh(f(\Omega)) + (\alpha_2 \cosh(f(\Omega)) + \beta_2 \sinh(f(\Omega)))^2. \tag{24}$$

Using Equation (24) in Equation (23) along with Equation (6), we obtain a system containing α_0, α_1, β_1, λ, and other parameters. Solving the system with the use of Mathematica software, provides the following sets:

Set 1;

$$\left\{\alpha_0 = \frac{(\theta+8)\rho^2 - 1}{2\kappa\rho^2}, \alpha_1 = 0, \alpha_2 = \pm\frac{\sqrt{6}}{\sqrt{-\kappa}}, \beta_1 = 0, \beta_2 = 0\right\}. \tag{25}$$

$$v(x,t) = \frac{(\theta+8)\rho^2 - 1}{2\kappa\rho^2} - \frac{6}{\kappa}\coth^2\left(\frac{\Gamma(1+\varrho)}{\varepsilon}(x^{\varepsilon} - \rho t^{\varepsilon})\right). \quad \rho,\kappa > 0 \tag{26}$$

$$v(x,t) = \frac{(\theta+8)\rho^2 - 1}{2\kappa\rho^2} - \frac{6}{\kappa}\tanh^2\left(\frac{\Gamma(1+\varrho)}{\varepsilon}(x^{\varepsilon} - \rho t^{\varepsilon})\right). \quad \rho,\kappa > 0 \tag{27}$$

Set 2;

$$\left\{\alpha_0 = \frac{(\theta+2)\rho^2 - 1}{2\kappa\rho^2}, \alpha_1 = 0, \alpha_2 = \pm\frac{\sqrt{3}}{\sqrt{-2\kappa}}, \beta_1 = 0, \beta_2 = \mp\frac{\sqrt{3}}{\sqrt{-2\kappa}}\right\}. \tag{28}$$

$$v(x,t) = \frac{(\theta+2)\rho^2 - 1}{2\kappa\rho^2} - \frac{3}{2\kappa}\left(\coth\left(\frac{\Gamma(1+\varrho)}{\varepsilon}(x^{\varepsilon} - \rho t^{\varepsilon})\right) - \operatorname{csch}\left(\frac{\Gamma(1+\varrho)}{\varepsilon}(x^{\varepsilon} - \rho t^{\varepsilon})\right)\right)^2. \quad \rho,\kappa > 0 \tag{29}$$

$$v(x,t) = \frac{(\theta+2)\rho^2 - 1}{2\kappa\rho^2} - \frac{3}{2\kappa}\left(\tanh\left(\frac{\Gamma(1+\varrho)}{\varepsilon}(x^{\varepsilon} - \rho t^{\varepsilon})\right) - \imath\,\operatorname{sech}\left(\frac{\Gamma(1+\varrho)}{\varepsilon}(x^{\varepsilon} - \rho t^{\varepsilon})\right)\right)^2. \quad \rho,\kappa > 0 \tag{30}$$

Set 3;

$$\left\{\alpha_0 = \frac{(\theta-4)\rho^2 - 1}{2\kappa\rho^2}, \alpha_1 = 0, \alpha_2 = 0, \beta_1 = 0, \beta_2 = \pm\frac{\sqrt{6}}{\sqrt{-\kappa}}\right\}. \tag{31}$$

$$v(x,t) = \frac{(\theta-4)\rho^2 - 1}{2\kappa\rho^2} - \frac{6}{\kappa}\operatorname{csch}^2\left(\frac{\Gamma(1+\varrho)}{\varepsilon}(x^{\varepsilon} - \rho t^{\varepsilon})\right). \quad \rho,\kappa < 0 \tag{32}$$

$$v(x,t) = \frac{(\theta-4)\rho^2 - 1}{2\kappa\rho^2} + \frac{6}{\kappa}\operatorname{sech}^2\left(\frac{\Gamma(1+\varrho)}{\varepsilon}(x^{\varepsilon} - \rho t^{\varepsilon})\right). \quad \rho < 0, \kappa > 0 \tag{33}$$

3.2. Exact Wave Solutions Through Modified $(G'/G^2)-$ Expansion Technique

In our case, Equation (12) transforms to

$$Q(\Omega) = \alpha_0 + \alpha_1\left(\frac{G'(\Omega)}{G^2(\Omega)}\right) + \alpha_2\left(\frac{G'(\Omega)}{G^2(\Omega)}\right)^2. \tag{34}$$

Here, α_0, α_1, and α_2 are unknowns. Substituting Equations (13) and (34) into Equation (23) and solving the equation the help of Mathematica software yields the following set:

Set:

$$\left\{\alpha_0 = \frac{-8ab\rho^2 + \theta\rho^2 - 1}{2\kappa\rho^2}, \alpha_1 = 0, \alpha_2 = -\frac{6b^2}{\kappa}\right\}. \tag{35}$$

Case 1: If $ab < 0$,

$$v(x,t) = \frac{-8ab\rho^2 + \theta\rho^2 - 1}{2\kappa\rho^2} - \frac{6b^2}{\kappa}\Big(-\frac{\sqrt{|ab|}}{b} + \frac{\sqrt{|ab|}}{2}$$
$$\Big(\frac{C_1 \sinh(\sqrt{ab}\,\frac{\Gamma(1+\varrho)}{\varepsilon}(x^\varepsilon - \rho t^\varepsilon)) + C_2 \cosh(\sqrt{ab}\,\frac{\Gamma(1+\varrho)}{\varepsilon}(x^\varepsilon - \rho t^\varepsilon))}{C_1 \cosh(\sqrt{ab}\,\frac{\Gamma(1+\varrho)}{\varepsilon}(x^\varepsilon - \rho t^\varepsilon)) + C_2 \sinh(\sqrt{ab}\,\frac{\Gamma(1+\varrho)}{\varepsilon}(x^\varepsilon - \rho t^\varepsilon))}\Big)\Big)^2. \quad \rho,\kappa < 0 \tag{36}$$

Case 2: If $ab > 0$,

$$v(x,t) = \frac{-8ab\rho^2 + \theta\rho^2 - 1}{2\kappa\rho^2} - \frac{6a}{b\kappa}\Big(\frac{C_1 \cos(\sqrt{ab}\,\frac{\Gamma(1+\varrho)}{\varepsilon}(x^\varepsilon - \rho t^\varepsilon)) + C_2 \sin(\sqrt{ab}\,\frac{\Gamma(1+\varrho)}{\varepsilon}(x^\varepsilon - \rho t^\varepsilon))}{C_1 \sin(\sqrt{ab}\,\frac{\Gamma(1+\varrho)}{\varepsilon}(x^\varepsilon - \rho t^\varepsilon)) - C_2 \sin(\sqrt{ab}\,\frac{\Gamma(1+\varrho)}{\varepsilon}(x^\varepsilon - \rho t^\varepsilon))}\Big)^2. \quad \rho,\kappa < 0 \tag{37}$$

Case 3: If $a = 0$ and $b \neq 0$,

$$v(x,t) = \frac{\theta\rho^2 - 1}{2\kappa\rho^2} - \frac{6}{\kappa}\left(\frac{C_1}{(C_1\frac{\Gamma(1+\varrho)}{\varepsilon}(x^\varepsilon - \rho t^\varepsilon) + C_2)}\right)^2. \quad \rho,\kappa < 0 \tag{38}$$

4. Graphical Representation

Graphical representations of the obtained solutions of the truncated M-fractional classical Lonngren wave model will be explained in this section. The authors use contour, three-dimensional, and two-dimensional plots to illustrate the results in this section. Graphs for $\epsilon = 0.5, 0.7, 1$ are also used to illustrate the effect of the fractional derivative. The following graphs were drawn using Mathematica software 11.0

5. Qualitative Analysis

5.1. Stability Analysis

Stability analysis is employed to describe how the system reacts over time and how it acts in response to outside influences. To describe the stability of the governing equation in applications, stability analysis is carried out by testing some of the obtained solutions, applying the characteristics of the Hamiltonian system. The stability analysis of various models has been covered in the literature, including by [39,40].

By performing stability analysis on the classical Lonngren wave model, we can gain valuable insights into the behavior of waves in various physical systems that can ultimately lead to improved designs and applications. We consider the energy-like functional for stability

$$\mathcal{S} = \frac{1}{2}\int_{-\infty}^{\infty} v^2\,dx. \tag{39}$$

Here, $v(x,t)$ is the field variable and $\mathcal{S}$ denotes the energy-like L^2 functional. We now present a prerequisite for stable soliton solutions.

$$\frac{\partial \mathcal{S}}{\partial \rho} > 0, \tag{40}$$

Here, ρ indicates the wave speed. Substituting Equation (26) into Equation (39) yields

$$\mathcal{S} = \frac{1}{2}\int_{-2}^{2}\Big(\frac{(\theta+8)\rho^2 - 1}{2\kappa\rho^2} - \frac{6}{\kappa}\coth^2\Big(\frac{\Gamma(1+\varrho)}{\varepsilon}(x^\varepsilon - \rho t^\varepsilon)\Big)\Big)^2 dx, \tag{41}$$

and by applying the condition described by Equation (40), one obtains

$$\frac{1}{4\kappa^2\rho^5}(8\theta\rho^2 - 32\rho^2 - 12\theta\rho^5 t\,\mathrm{csch}^2(\rho t+2) + 12\theta\rho^5 t\,\mathrm{csch}^2(2-\rho t) + \theta\rho^2\log(\sinh(\rho t)+\cosh(\rho t))^2 - \theta\rho^2\log(\sinh(2\rho t)-\cosh(2\rho t)) - 24\rho^5 t\,\mathrm{csch}^2(\rho t+2) + 24\rho^5 t\,\mathrm{csch}^2(2-\rho t) + 72\rho^5 t\coth^2(\rho t+2)\,\mathrm{csch}^2(\rho t+2) - 72\rho^5 t\coth^2(2-\rho t)\,\mathrm{csch}^2(2-\rho t) + 12\rho^3 t\,\mathrm{csch}^2(\rho t+2) - 12\rho^3 t\,\mathrm{csch}^2(2-\rho t) + 24\rho^2\coth(\rho t+2) + 24\rho^2\coth(2-\rho t) - 4\rho^2\log(\sinh(\rho t)+\cosh(\rho t))^2 + 4\rho^2\log(\sinh(2\rho t)-\cosh(2\rho t)) - \log(\sinh(\rho t)+\cosh(\rho t))^2 + \log(\sinh(2\rho t)-\cosh(2\rho t)) - 8) > 0. \quad (42)$$

Hence, Equation (26) shows the stable solution. Similarly, the stability of the other solutions can be checked.

5.2. Modulation Instability (MI) Analysis

An equation to examine a steady-state method for solving the classical Lonngren wave model is given below [41,42]:

$$v(x,t) = \left(V(x,t) + \sqrt{\tau}\right)e^{\iota\tau t}. \quad (43)$$

The anstaz given in Equation (43) is used to study the stability of a continuous wave solution.

Here, τ indicates the optical normalizing power.

Substitute Equation (43) into Equation (1). By linearization, one gets

$$\theta\tau^{5/2} + \theta\tau^2 - 2\theta\iota\tau V_t - \theta V_{tt} - \tau^2 V_{xx} + V_{xx} + 2\iota\tau V_{xxt} + V_{xxtt} = 0. \quad (44)$$

Supposing the solution of Equation (44) mentioned as:

$$V(x,t) = A_1 e^{\iota(px-qt)} + A_2 e^{-\iota(px-qt)}. \quad (45)$$

Here, q and p are the parameters that represent the growth rate and wave number, respectively. Equation (45) is substituted into Equation (44). After solving the determinant of the coefficient matrix, the authors obtain the dispersion relation by adding the coefficients of $e^{\iota(px-qt)}$ and $e^{-\iota(px-qt)}$.

$$p^4q^4 - 2p^4q^2\tau^2 - 2p^4q^2 + p^4\tau^4 - 2p^4\tau^2 + p^4 + 2\theta p^2q^4 - 6\theta p^2q^2\tau^2 - 2\theta p^2q^2 + \theta^2q^4 - 4\theta^2q^2\tau^2 = 0. \quad (46)$$

The dispersion relation can be found from Equation (46) for q, with the following results:

$$q = \pm\tau \pm \frac{\sqrt{\theta^2\tau^2 + p^4 + \theta p^2\tau^2 + \theta p^2}}{\theta + p^2}. \quad (47)$$

The solution in the steady state is unstable when

$$\theta^2\tau^2 + p^4 + \theta p^2\tau^2 + \theta p^2 < 0. \quad (48)$$

Instability arises when $Imq > 0$. It is possible to obtain the modulation instability (MI) gain spectrum $G(p)$ as follows:

$$G(p) = 2Im(q) = \pm\tau \pm \frac{\sqrt{\theta^2\tau^2 + p^4 + \theta p^2\tau^2 + \theta p^2}}{\theta + p^2}. \quad (49)$$

6. Conclusions

Several types of exact waves of the non-linear classical Lonngren wave model with the TMFD were presented in this paper. By utilizing the modified (G'/G^2)-expansion technique and the EShGEE method, the authors obtained novel types of exact solitons. The obtained results were also explained through 2D, 3D, and contour graphs, as shown in Figures 1–7. To ensure that the obtained solutions were stable, stability analysis was carried out. Modulation instability was also checked and explained through Figure 8. The obtained results may be useful in various fields, including fluid dynamics, plasma physics, soliton physics, etc. In the future, bifurcation analysis and sensitivity analysis, as well as analysis of quasi-periodic, periodic, and chaotic behavior can be studied for the concerned model. Moreover, the obtained soliton solutions can be compared with the numerical solutions of the governing model in the future.

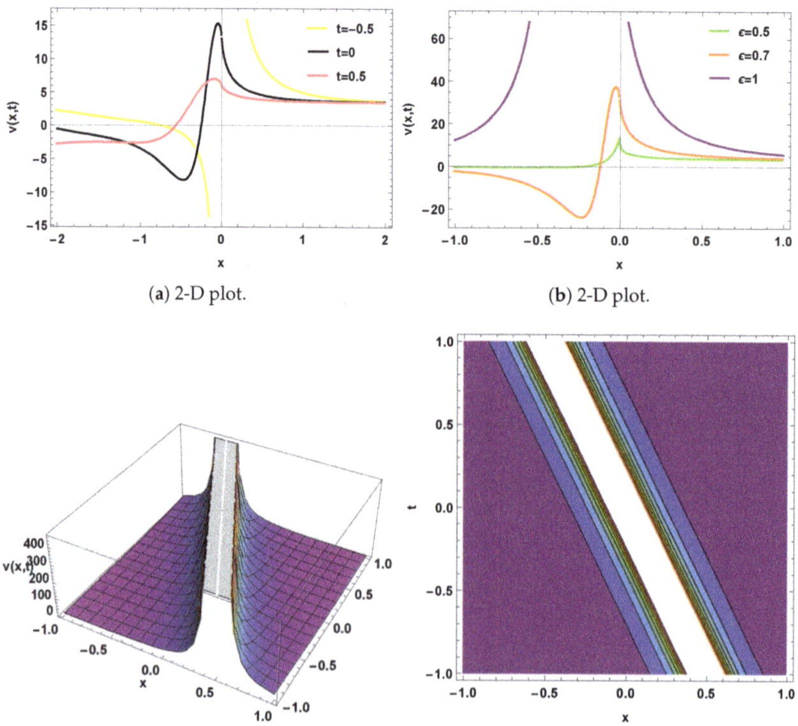

(**a**) 2-D plot. (**b**) 2-D plot.

(**c**) 3-D plot. (**d**) Contour plot.

Figure 1. Graphs of $v(x,t)$ for Equation (26) for $\theta = 1$, $\rho = -0.5$, $\kappa = -1$, and $\varrho = 1$. (**a**) is the two-dimensional plot if $-2 < x < 2$ and $\varepsilon = 0.7$; the yellow shape represents values if $t = -0.5$; the black shape represents values if $t = 0$; the pink shape represents values if $t = 0.5$. (**b**) is the two-dimensional plot if $-1 < x < 1$ and $t = 0.5$; the green shape represents values if $\epsilon = 0.5$; the orange shape represents values if $\epsilon = 0.7$; the purple shape represents values if $\epsilon = 1$. (**c**) is a 3-D graph for $-1 < x < 1$ and $\epsilon = 1$ with $-1 < t < 1$. (**d**) represents the contour graph when $-1 < x < 1$ and $\epsilon = 1$ for $t \in (-1, 1)$.

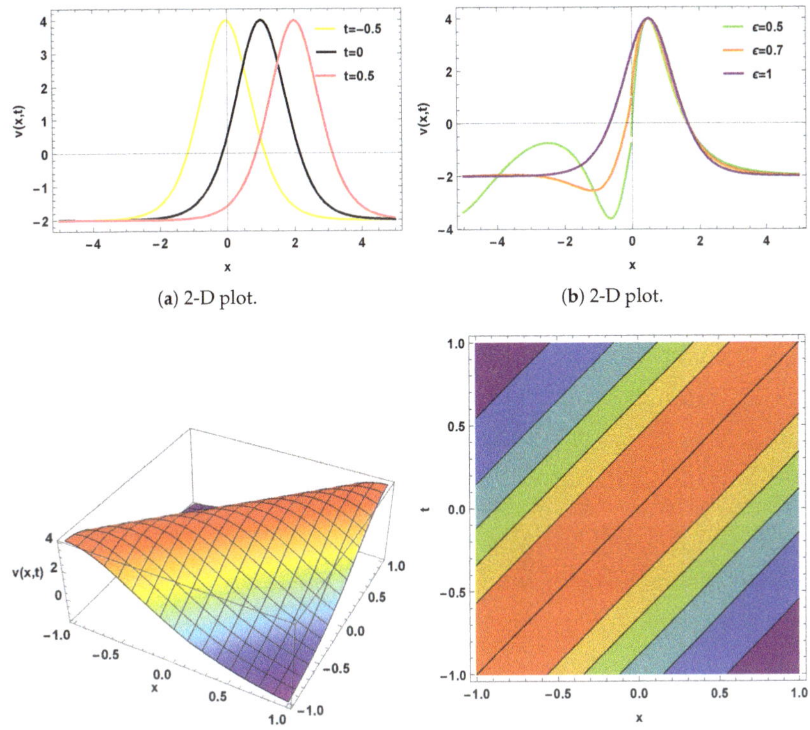

(a) 2-D plot. (b) 2-D plot.

(c) 3-D plot. (d) Contour plot.

Figure 2. Graph of $v(x,t)$ in Equation (27) for $\theta = 1$, $\rho = 1$, $\kappa = 1$, and $\varrho = 1$. (**a**) is the two-dimensional plot if $-5 < x < 5$ and $\varepsilon = 1$; the yellow shape represents values if $t = -0.5$; the black shape represents values if $t = 0$; the pink shape represents values if $t = 0.5$. (**b**) is the two-dimensional plot if $-5 < x < 5$ and $t = 0.5$; the green shape represents values if $\epsilon = 0.5$; the orange shape represents values if $\epsilon = 0.7$; the purple shape represents values if $\epsilon = 1$. (**c**) is a 3-D graph for $-1 < x < 1$ and $\epsilon = 1$ with $-1 < t < 1$. (**d**) represents the contour graph when $-1 < x < 1$ and $\epsilon = 1$ for $t \in (-1, 1)$.

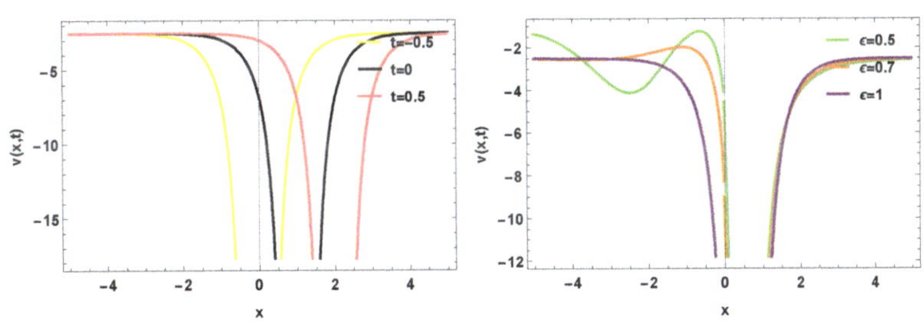

(**a**) 2-D plot. (**b**) 2-D plot.

Figure 3. *Cont.*

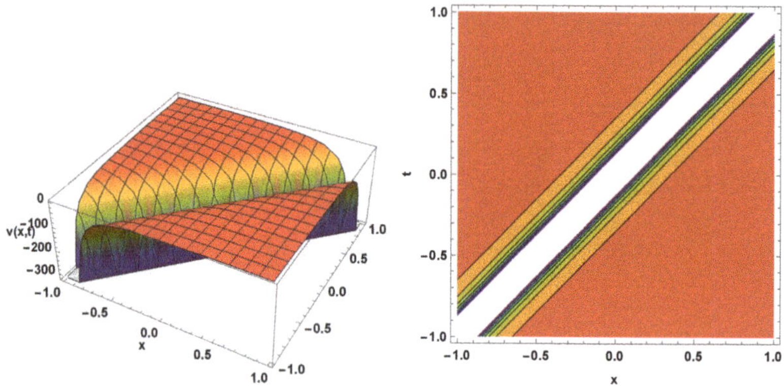

Figure 3. Graph for $v(x,t)$ is denoted through Equation (32) for; $\theta = -0.01$, $\rho = 1$, $\kappa = 1$, and $\varrho = 1$. (**a**) is the two-dimensional plot if $-3 < x < 3$ and $\varepsilon = 1$; the yellow shape represents values if $t = -0.5$; the black shape represents values if $t = 0$; the pink shape represents values if $t = 0.5$. (**b**) is the two-dimensional plot if $-5 < x < 5$ and $t = 0.5$; the green shape represents values if $\epsilon = 0.5$; the orange shape represents values if $\epsilon = 0.7$; the purple shape represents values if $\epsilon = 1$. (**c**) is a 3-D graph for $-5 < x < 5$ and $\epsilon = 1$ with $-1 < t < 1$. (**d**) represents the contour graph when $-1 < x < 1$ and $\epsilon = 1$ for $t \in (-1,1)$.

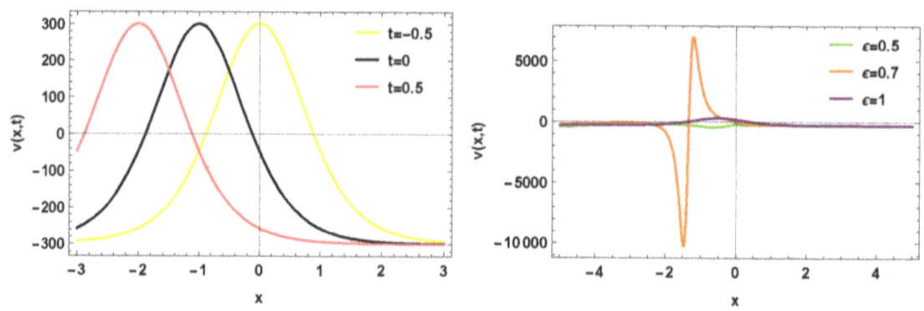

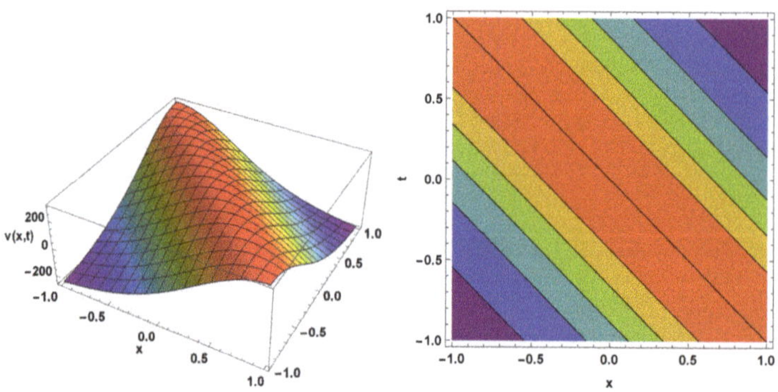

Figure 4. Graph for $v(x,t)$ is denoted through Equation (33) for; $\theta = -1$, $\rho = -1$, $\kappa = 0.01$, and $\varrho = 1$. (**a**) is the two-dimensional plot if $-3 < x < 3$ and $\varepsilon = 1$; the yellow shape represents values if $t = -0.5$; the black shape represents values if $t = 0$; the pink shape represents values if $t = 0.5$. (**b**) is the two-dimensional plot if $-5 < x < 5$ and $t = 0.5$; the green shape represents values if $\epsilon = 0.5$; the orange shape represents values if $\epsilon = 0.7$; the purple shape represents values if $\epsilon = 1$. (**c**) is a 3-D graph for $-1 < x < 1$ and $\epsilon = 1$ with $-1 < t < 1$. (**d**) represents the contour graph when $-1 < x < 1$ and $\epsilon = 1$ for $t \in (-1,1)$.

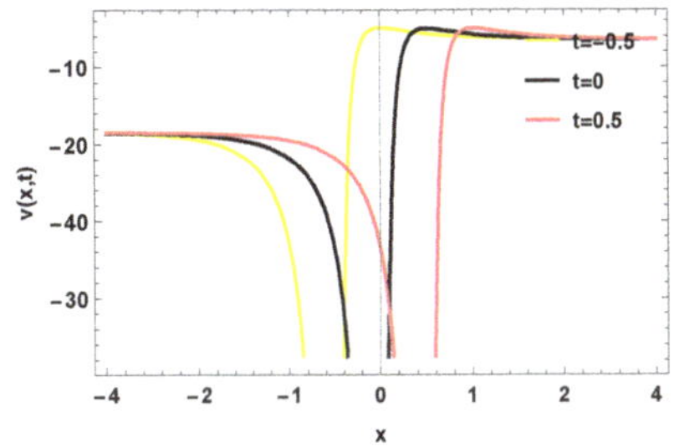

(a) 2-D plot.

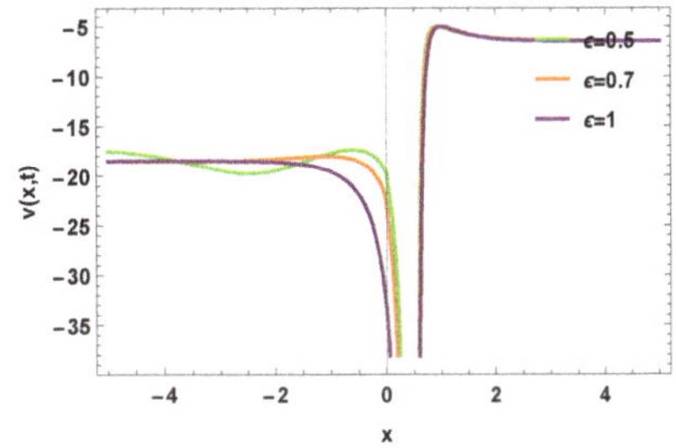

(b) 2-D plot.

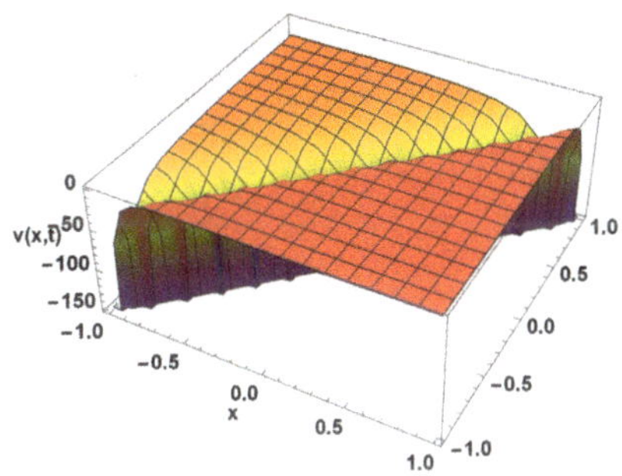

(c) 3-D plot.

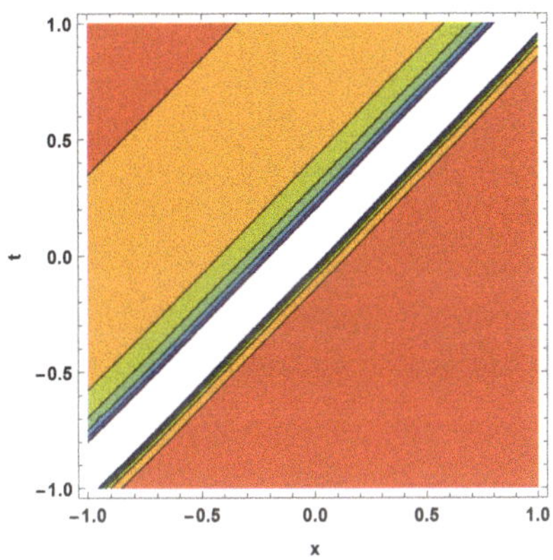

(d) Contour plot.

Figure 5. A graph of $v(x,t)$ in Equation (36) for $\theta = -1$, $\rho = 1$, $\kappa = 1$, $a = 1$, $b = 1$, $C_1 = 0.005$, $C_2 = 0.1$, and $\varrho = 1$. (**a**) is the two-dimensional plot if $-3 < x < 3$ and $\varepsilon = 1$; the yellow shape represents values if $t = -0.5$; the black shape represents values if $t = 0$; the pink shape represents values if $t = 0.5$. (**b**) is the two-dimensional plot if $-5 < x < 5$ and $t = 0.5$; the green shape represents values if $\epsilon = 0.5$; the orange shape represents values if $\epsilon = 0.7$; the purple shape represents values if $\epsilon = 1$. (**c**) is a 3-D graph for $-1 < x < 1$ and $\epsilon = 1$ with $-1 < t < 1$. (**d**) represents the contour graph when $-1 < x < 1$ and $\epsilon = 1$ for $t \in (-1, 1)$.

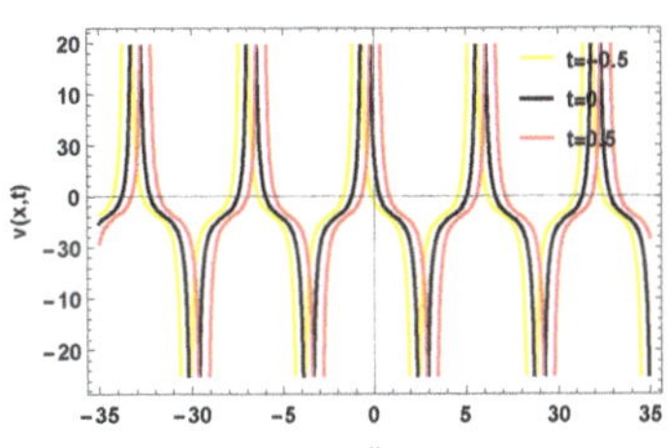

(a) 2-D plot.

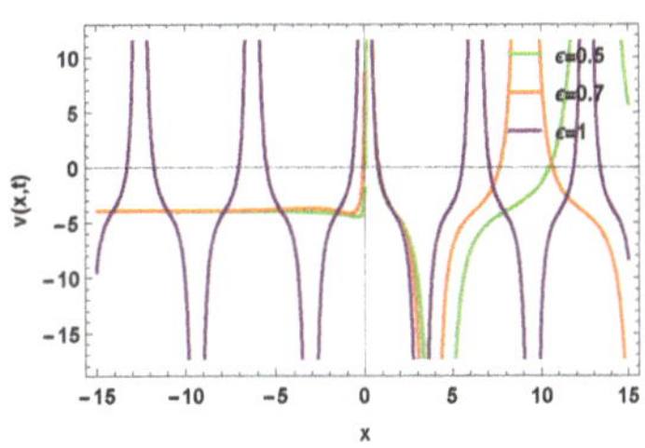

(b) 2-D plot.

Figure 6. *Cont.*

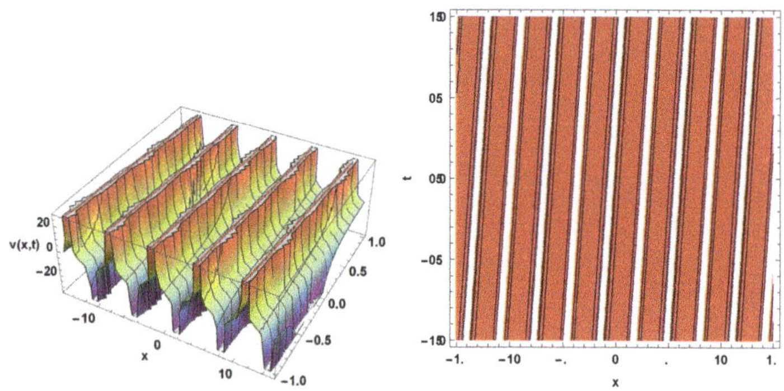

(**c**) 3-D plot. (**d**) Contour plot.

Figure 6. A graph of $v(x,t)$ in Equation (37) for $\theta = 1, \rho = 1, \kappa = 1, a = 1, b = 1, C_1 = -2, C_2 = 1$, and $\varrho = 1$. (**a**) is the two-dimensional plot if $-15 < x < 15$ and $\varepsilon = 1$; the yellow shape represents values if $t = -0.5$; the black shape represents values if $t = 0$; the pink shape represents values if $t = 0.5$. (**b**) is the two-dimensional plot if $-15 < x < 15$ and $t = 0.5$; the green shape represents values if $\epsilon = 0.5$; the orange shape represents values if $\epsilon = 0.7$; the purple shape represents values if $\epsilon = 1$. (**c**) is a 3-D graph for $-15 < x < 15$ and $\epsilon = 1$ with $-1 < t < 1$. (**d**) represents the contour graph when $-15 < x < 15$ and $\epsilon = 1$ for $t \in (-1,1)$.

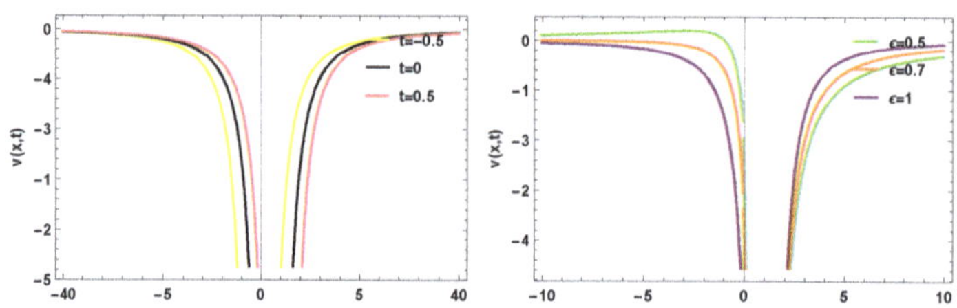

(**a**) 2-D plot. (**b**) 2-D plot.

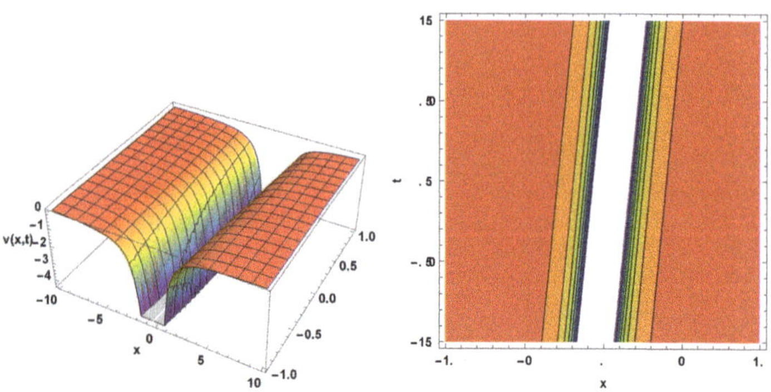

(**c**) 3-D plot. (**d**) Contour plot.

Figure 7. A graph of $v(x,t)$ in Equation (38) for $\theta = 1, \rho = 1, \kappa = 1, a = 1, b = 1, C_1 = -2, C_2 = 1$, and $\varrho = 1$. (**a**) is the two-dimensional plot if $-10 < x < 10$ and $\varepsilon = 1$; the yellow shape represents values if $t = -0.5$; the black shape represents values if $t = 0$; the pink shape represents values if $t = 0.5$. (**b**) is the two-dimensional plot if $-10 < x < 10$ and $t = 0.5$; the green shape represents values if $\epsilon = 0.5$; the orange shape represents values if $\epsilon = 0.7$; the purple shape represents values if $\epsilon = 1$. (**c**) is a 3-D graph for $-10 < x < 10$ and $\epsilon = 1$ with $-1 < t < 1$. (**d**) represents the contour graph when $-10 < x < 10$ and $\epsilon = 1$ for $t \in (-1,1)$.

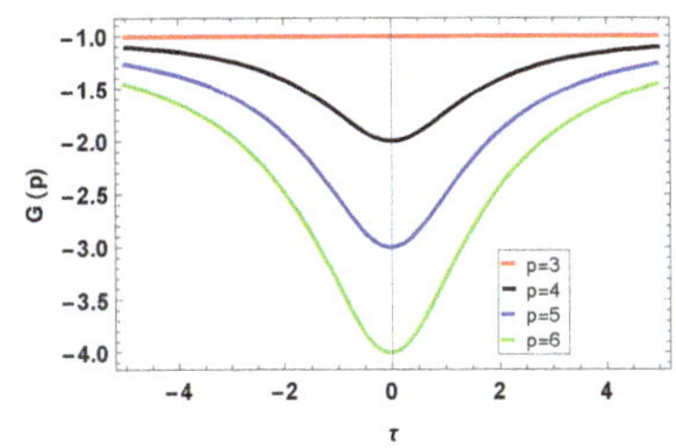

(**a**) Two-dimensional graph at $p = 3, 4, 5, 6$.

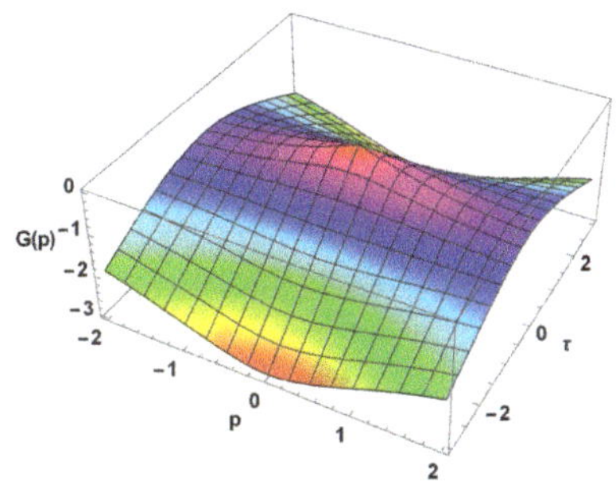

(**b**) 3-D plot.

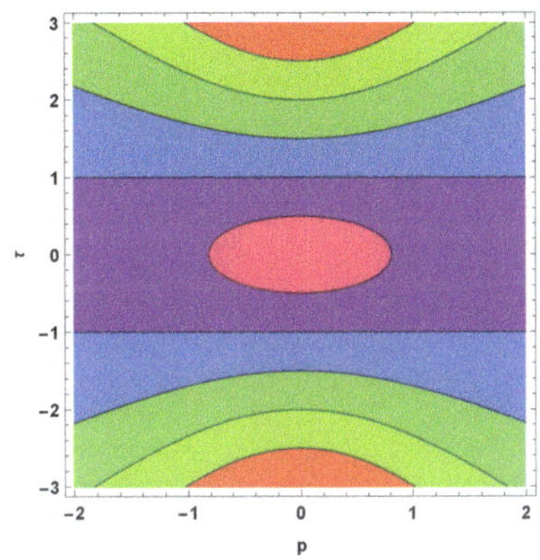

(**c**) Contour plot.

Figure 8. MI gain spectrum for the values $\theta = 2$ and $p = 3, 4, 5, 6$. (**a**) represents the two-dimensional graph when $-5 < \tau < 5$ and $p = 3, 4, 5, 6$. (**b**) shows the three-dimensional graph when $-3 < \tau < 3$ and $-2 < p < 2$. (**c**) represents the contour graph when $-3 < \tau < 3$ and $-2 < p < 2$.

Author Contributions: H.Q.: Writing—review and editing, Conceptualization, Methodology, Project administration; A.K.A.: Funding, Conceptualization, Methodology, Formal Analysis; Supervision. All authors have read and agreed to the published version of the manuscript.

Funding: This work was supported by the Deanship of Scientific Research, Vice Presidency for Graduate Studies and Scientific Research, King Faisal University, Saudi Arabia [Grant No. KFU253149].

Data Availability Statement: The original contributions presented in this study are included in the article. Further inquiries can be directed to the corresponding author.

Conflicts of Interest: The authors declare no conflicts of interest.

References

1. Ahmad, J.; Akram, S.; Rehman, S.U.; Turki, N.B.; Shah, N.A. Description of Soliton and Lump Solutions to M-Truncated Stochastic Biswas–Arshed Model in Optical Communication. *Results Phys.* **2024**, *51*, 106719.
2. Qawaqneh, H.; Manafian, J.; Alharthi, M.; Alrashedi, Y. Stability Analysis, Modulation Instability, and Beta-Time Fractional Exact Soliton Solutions to the Van der Waals Equation. *Mathematics* **2024**, *12*, 2144.
3. Batiha, I.M.; Njadat, S.A.; Batyha, R.M.; Zraiqat, A.; Dababneh, A.; Momani, S. Design Fractional-Order PID Controllers for Single-Joint Robot Arm Model. *Int. J. Adv. Soft Comput. Appl.* **2022**, *14*, 96–114.
4. Liu, C. The Traveling Wave Solution and Dynamics Analysis of the Fractional Order Generalized Pochhammer–Chree Equation. *AIMS Math.* **2024**, *9*, 33956–33972.

5. Qawaqneh, H.; Jari, H.A.; Altalbe, A.; Bekir, A. Stability Analysis, Modulation Instability, and the Analytical Wave Solitons to the Fractional Boussinesq-Burgers System. *Phys. Scr.* **2024**, *99*, 125235.
6. Judeh, D.A.; Hammad, M.A. Applications of Conformable Fractional Pareto Probability Distribution. *Int. J. Adv. Soft Comput. Appl.* **2022**, *14*, 115–124.
7. Mohammed, W.W.; Cesarano, C.; Iqbal, N.; Sidaoui, R.; Ali, E.E. The Exact Solutions for the Fractional Riemann Wave Equation in Quantum Mechanics and Optics. *Phys. Scr.* **2024**, *99*, 085245.
8. Chahlaoui, Y.; Ali, A.; Ahmad, J.; Javed, S. Dynamical Behavior of Chaos, Bifurcation Analysis and Soliton Solutions to a Konno-Onno Model. *PLoS ONE* **2023**, *18*, e0291197.
9. Mehdi, K.B.; Mehdi, Z.; Samreen, S.; Siddique, I.; Elmandouh, A.A.; Elbrolosy, M.E.; Osman, M.S. Novel Exact Traveling Wave Solutions of the Space-Time Fractional Sharma–Tasso–Olver Equation via Three Reliable Methods. *Partial Differ. Equ. Appl. Math.* **2024**, *11*, 100784.
10. Ahmed, S.; Jahan, S.; Nisar, K.S. Haar Wavelet Based Numerical Technique for the Solutions of Fractional Advection Diffusion Equations. *J. Math. Comput. Sci.* **2024**, *34*, 217–233.
11. Altaf, S.; Alderremy, A.A.; Mahmoud, E.E. Exact Wave Solutions of Truncated M-Fractional Boussinesq-Burgers System via an Effective Method. *Phys. Scr.* **2024**, *99*, 095263.
12. Akram, S.; Ahmad, J.; Rehman, S.U.; Younas, T. Stability Analysis and Dispersive Optical Solitons of Fractional Schrödinger–Hirota Equation. *Opt. Quantum Electron.* **2023**, *55*, 664.
13. Qawaqneh, H.; Zafar, A.; Raheel, M.; Zaagan, A.A.; Zahran, E.H.; Cevikel, A.; Bekir, A. New Soliton Solutions of M-Fractional Westervelt Model in Ultrasound Imaging via Two Analytical Techniques. *Opt. Quantum Electron.* **2024**, *56*, 737.
14. Mahmood, T.; Alhawael, G.; Akram, S.; Rahman, M.U. Exploring the Lie Symmetries, Conservation Laws, Bifurcation Analysis and Dynamical Waveform Patterns of Diverse Exact Solution to the Klein–Gordon Equation. *Opt. Quantum Electron.* **2024**, *56*, 1978.
15. Al Oweidi, K.F.; Aal-Rkhais, H.A. Existence Results for a Nonlinear Degenerate Parabolic Equation Involving p-Laplacian Type Diffusion Process. *Iraqi J. Sci.* **2024**, *65* , 5081–5094.
16. Akram, S.; Ahmad, J.; Alkarni, S.; Shah, N.A. Exploration of Solitary Wave Solutions of Highly Nonlinear KDV–KP Equation Arise in Water Wave and Stability Analysis. *Results Phys.* **2023**, *54*, 107054.
17. Alqahtani, A.; Akram, S.; Alosaimi, M. Study of Bifurcations, Chaotic Structures with Sensitivity Analysis and Novel Soliton Solutions of Non-Linear Dynamical Model. *J. Taibah Univ. Sci.* **2024**, *18*, 2399870.
18. Luo, M.; Qiu, W.; Nikan, O.; Avazzadeh, Z. Second-Order Accurate, Robust and Efficient ADI Galerkin Technique for the Three-Dimensional Nonlocal Heat Model Arising in Viscoelasticity. *Appl. Math. Comput.* **2023**, *440*, 127655.
19. Aal-Rkhais, H.A.; Kamil, A.H.; Al Oweidi, K.F. The Approximation of Weighted Hölder Functions by Fourier-Jacobi Polynomials to the Singular Sturm-Liouville Operator. *Baghdad Sci. J.* **2022**, *19*, 2636.
20. El-Shorbagy, M.A.; Akram, S.; Rahman, M.U.; Nabwey, H.A. Analysis of Bifurcation, Chaotic Structures, Lump and M-W-Shape Soliton Solutions to (2+1) Complex Modified Korteweg-de-Vries System. *AIMS Math.* **2024**, *9*, 16116–16145.
21. Lephoko, M.Y.T.; Khalique, C.M. A Study of the Exact Solutions and Conservation Laws of the Classical Lonngren Wave Equation for Communication Signals. *Malays. J. Math. Sci.* **2024**, *18*, 209–226.
22. Lonngren, K.E.; Hsuan, H.C.S.; Ames, W.F. On the Soliton, Invariant, and Shock Solutions of a Fourth-Order Nonlinear Equation. *J. Math. Anal. Appl.* **1975**, *52*, 538–545.
23. Baskonus, H.M.; Bulut, H.; Sulaiman, T.A. New Complex Hyperbolic Structures to the Lonngren-Wave Equation by Using Sine-Gordon Expansion Method. *Appl. Math. Nonlinear Sci.* **2019**, *4*, 129–138.
24. Yokuş, A. Simulation of Bright–Dark Soliton Solutions of the Lonngren Wave Equation Arising the Model of Transmission Lines. *Mod. Phys. Lett. B* **2021**, *35*, 2150484.
25. Duran, S. Travelling Wave Solutions and Simulation of the Lonngren Wave Equation for Tunnel Diode. *Opt. Quantum Electron.* **2021**, *53*, 458.
26. Hussain, A.; Usman, M.; Zaman, F.D.; Almalki, Y. Lie Group Analysis for Obtaining the Abundant Group Invariant Solutions and Dynamics of Solitons for the Lonngren-Wave Equation. *Chin. J. Phys.* **2023**, *86*, 447–457.
27. Zafar, A.; Bekir, A.; Raheel, M.; Razzaq, W. Optical Soliton Solutions to Biswas–Arshed Model with Truncated M-Fractional Derivative. *Optik* **2020**, *222*, 165355.
28. Seadawy, A.R.; Kumar, D.; Chakrabarty, A.K. Dispersive Optical Soliton Solutions for the Hyperbolic and Cubic-Quintic Nonlinear Schrödinger Equations via the Extended Sinh-Gordon Equation Expansion Method. *Eur. Phys. J. Plus* **2018**, *133*, 182.
29. Bezgabadi, A.S.; Bolorizadeh, M.A. Analytic Combined Bright-Dark, Bright and Dark Solitons Solutions of Generalized Nonlinear Schrödinger Equation Using Extended Sinh-Gordon Equation Expansion Method. *Results Phys.* **2021**, *30*, 104852.
30. Kumar, D.; Manafian, J.; Hawlader, F.; Ranjbaran, A. New Closed Form Soliton and Other Solutions of the Kundu–Eckhaus Equation via the Extended Sinh-Gordon Equation Expansion Method. *Optik* **2018**, *160*, 159–167.

31. Behera, S.; Behera, D. Nonlinear Wave Dynamics of (1+1)-Dimensional Conformable Coupled Nonlinear Higgs Equation Using Modified (G'/G^2)-Expansion Method. *Phys. Scr.* 2025, *in press*.
32. Saboor, A.; Shakeel, M.; Liu, X.; Zafar, A.; Ashraf, M. A Comparative Study of Two Fractional Nonlinear Optical Model via Modified (G'/G^2)-Expansion Method. *Opt. Quantum Electron.* **2024**, *56*, 259.
33. Aljahdaly, N.H. Some Applications of the Modified (G'/G^2)-Expansion Method in Mathematical Physics. *Results Phys.* **2019**, *13*, 102272.
34. Sulaiman, T.A.; Yel, G.; Bulut, H. M-Fractional Solitons and Periodic Wave Solutions to the Hirota-Maccari System. *Mod. Phys. Lett. B* **2019**, *33*, 1950052.
35. Sousa, J.V.D.A.C.; Oliveira, E.C.D. A New Truncated M-Fractional Derivative Type Unifying Some Fractional Derivative Types with Classical Properties. *Int. J. Anal. Appl.* **2018**, *16*, 83–96.
36. Lu, J. New Exact Solutions for Kudryashov–Sinelshchikov Equation. *Adv. Differ. Equ.* **2018**, *2018*, 374.
37. X. L. Yang, X.L; J. S. Tang, J.S. Travelling wave solutions for Konopelchenko-Dubrovsky equation using an extended sinh-Gordon equation expansion method. Commun. *Theor. Phys.* **2008**, *50*, 1047.
38. Zhang, Y.; Zhang, L.; Pang, J. Application of (G'/G^2) Expansion Method for Solving Schrödinger's Equation with Three-Order Dispersion. *Adv. Appl. Math.* **2017**, *6*, 212–217.
39. Qawaqneh, H.; Alrashedi, Y. Mathematical and Physical Analysis of Fractional Estevez–Mansfield–Clarkson Equation. *Fractal Fract.* **2024**, *8*, 467.
40. Tariq, K.U.; Wazwaz, A.-M.; Javed, R. Construction of Different Wave Structures, Stability Analysis and Modulation Instability of the Coupled Nonlinear Drinfel'd–Sokolov–Wilson Model. *Chaos Solitons Fractals* **2023**, *166*, 112903.
41. Rehman, S.U.; Ahmad, J. Modulation Instability Analysis and Optical Solitons in Birefringent Fibers to RKL Equation without Four Wave Mixing. *Alex. Eng. J.* **2021**, *60*, 1339–1354.
42. Qawaqneh, H.; Manafian, J.; Alsubaie, A.S.; Ahmad, H. Investigation of Exact Solitons to the Quartic Rosenau-Kawahara-Regularized-Long-Wave Fluid Model with Fractional Derivative and Qualitative Analysis. *Phys. Scr.* **2024**, *100*, 015270.

mathematics

MDPI

Article

Bifurcation Analysis and Solitons Dynamics of the Fractional Biswas–Arshed Equation via Analytical Method

Asim Zafar [1], Waseem Razzaq [1], Abdullah Nazir [1], Mohammed Ahmed Alomair [2], Abdulaziz S. Al Naim [3] and Abdulrahman Alomair [3,*]

[1] Department of Mathematics, COMSATS University Islamabad, Vehari Campus, Vehari 61100, Pakistan; asimzafar@cuivehari.edu.pk (A.Z.); mathcentr@gmail.com (W.R.); abdullahnazir0306@gmail.com (A.N.)
[2] Department of Quantitative Methods, School of Business, King Faisal University, Al-Ahsa 31982, Saudi Arabia; ma.alomair@kfu.edu.sa
[3] Department of Accounting, School of Business, King Faisal University, Al-Ahsa 31982, Saudi Arabia; asaudalnaim@kfu.edu.sa
* Correspondence: aamalomair@kfu.edu.sa

Abstract

This paper investigates soliton solutions of the time-fractional Biswas–Arshed (BA) equation using the Extended Simplest Equation Method (ESEM). The model is analyzed under two distinct fractional derivative operators: the β-derivative and the M-truncated derivative. These approaches yield diverse solution types, including kink, singular, and periodic-singular forms. Also, in this work, a nonlinear second-order differential equation is reconstructed as a planar dynamical system in order to study its bifurcation structure. The stability and nature of equilibrium points are established using a conserved Hamiltonian and phase space analysis. A bifurcation parameter that determines the change from center to saddle-type behaviors is identified in the study. The findings provide insight into the fundamental dynamics of nonlinear wave propagation by showing how changes in model parameters induce qualitative changes in the phase portrait. The derived solutions are depicted via contour plots, along with two-dimensional (2D) and three-dimensional (3D) representations, utilizing Mathematica for computational validation and graphical illustration. This study is motivated by the growing role of fractional calculus in modeling nonlinear wave phenomena where memory and hereditary effects cannot be captured by classical integer-order approaches. The time-fractional Biswas–Arshed (BA) equation is investigated to obtain diverse soliton solutions using the Extended Simplest Equation Method (ESEM) under the β-derivative and M-truncated derivative operators. Beyond solution construction, a nonlinear second-order equation is reformulated as a planar dynamical system to analyze its bifurcation and stability properties. This dual approach highlights how parameter variations affect equilibrium structures and soliton behaviors, offering both theoretical insights and potential applications in physics and engineering.

Keywords: extended simplest equation method (ESEM); bifurication analysis; exact solutions; solitons; time-fractional Biswas–Arshed (BA) model; β and M-truncated fractional derivatives

MSC: 35C07; 35C07; 83C15

1. Introduction

Fractional calculus has fascinated many specialists due to its implications in uncovering deeper aspects of present reality. Although fractional derivatives were introduced nearly three centuries ago, they were not entirely a new concept [1]. Recent research on nonlinear fractional partial differential equations (NLFPDEs) has risen significantly, highlighting their diverse applications across various domains, including engineering, medical fields, controlled thermonuclear fusion, plasma physics, stochastic dynamical processes, acoustics, diffusive transport, chemical physics, solid state physics, electric networks, astrophysics, electromagnetic theory, fluid mechanics, geochemistry, fractional dynamics, manipulation theory, chemical kinematics, system identification, biogenetics, optical fibers, and many others [2–5]. The above-mentioned topics are closely related to engineering concepts such as response, diffusion, convection, and dispersion, and NLFPDEs can be applied to accurately solve them. Fractional calculus is the principal technique for differentiating and integrating averages of any order, enabling the construction and understanding of various physical features associated with continuous transitions from stationary to oscillatory phenomena. Due to the prevalence of fractional nonlinear differential equations (FNLDEs) throughout several engineering and scientific fields, numerous researchers focus their efforts on deriving exact or approximate solutions to these dynamic FNLDEs. Ahmed et al. [6] derive a rational solution, singular-periodic wave, periodic wave solution, dark, and collective dark–bright solutions of space-time NLFE for communication lines via the improved generalized Riccati equation technique.The single-wave solutions of the generalized Rosenau–Korteweg-de Vries (RKDv) regularized long-wave model were examined by Avazzadeh et al. [7]. Asjad et al. [8] examined nonlinear differential time-fractional equation to derive solutions like trigonometric functions, exponential functions, rational functions, and hyperbolic functions utilizing the EDA approach. Zaman et al. [9] investigated nonlinear fractional Allen Cahn (AC) and space-time Phi-4 equations via $(\frac{G'}{G})$-expansion technique to obtain periodic soliton, singular kink, dynamical compaction, and single soliton-type solutions. Sadiya et al. [10] derived single solitons, kink type, bell shape, double solitons and multiple solitons types results by applying tanh-function technique to the Klein–Gordon and nonlinear time-fractional Sine-Gordon (SG) model. To analyze coupled approximate-long-water wave and space-time nonlinear fractional coupled systems, Zaman et al. [11] implemented the tanh-function method. To derive soliton solutions, such as bell-shape and kink-type solutions, use the Whitham–Broer–Kaup equation. Arefin et al. [12] utilized the Riemann–Liouville fractional derivative along with the two-variable $(\frac{G'}{G}, \frac{1}{G})$-expansion technique to obtain exact solutions for the space-time NLF (2 + 1)-dimensional diffusive long-wave equation and the approximated long water-wave equation. During the application of the fractional differential sub-equation technique. RASHED et al. [13] examined the space-time NLF differential modified Benjamin Bona-Mahony model. Furthermore, two-variable $(\frac{G'}{G}, \frac{1}{G})$-expansion technique [14,15], Sine–Gordon expansion method [16], $(\frac{G'}{G^2})$-expansion technique [17], modified extended tanh function approach [18], sine cosine and sinh cosh method [19], a novel modified extended direct algebraic method [20], extended generalized Riccati equation mapping method [21], Paul–Painlevé method [22], Laplace Pade–Caputo-fractional differential transform technique [23], generalized Kudryashov technique [24], explicit finite-difference technique [25], the Yang decomposition technique and homotopy perturbation technique [26], optimized decomposition technique [27], Chelyshkov wavelets method [28], differential inequality technique and integral transformation method [29], hybrid local fractional approach [30], natural decomposition technique [31], Mohand variational iteration transform technique and novel approximate analytical technique [32], iterative method [33], fractional new analytic technique [34], F-expansion approach [35], Elzaki transform technique [36], Adomia -decomposition and Jafari transform technique [37], Laplace residual power series approach [38], Bernstein spectral approach [39] are adopted by different researchers to solve NFFDEs. Here, our concern is to solve the Biswas arshed (BA) equation. Biswas and Arshed [40] introduced an innovative concept aimed at reducing issues by attaining an optimal equilibrium between dispersion and nonlinearity to preserve solitons in metamaterials, crystal fibers, optical fibers, and photonic crystal fibers, possibly leading to reduced group velocity dispersion and an absence of nonlinearity. In this instance, they recovered the combo, bright, and singular solitons to demonstrate that solitons still exist for BA equation. Many researchers have recently provided an explanation of the BA equation. Alhojilan et al. [41] find stochastic bright solutions, stochastic dark solutions, stochastic singular solutions, stochastic rational solution, stochastic singular-bright solutions, stochastic periodic solutions, and stochastic bright-dark solutions by investigating the Biswas–Arshed equation via modified extended mapping technique. Cinar et al. [42] used an extended sine cosine approach and extended sinh-cosh approach and obtain singular solitons solutions, dark solitons solutions, and singular-periodic soliton solutions from Biswas Arshed equation. Zhao Li et al. [43] obtain optical and traveling wave solitons solutions by investigating the BA equation including beta-derivative via Li's three-step technique. Ghazala et al. [44] formed trigonometric function solutions, rational function solutions and hyperbolic function solutions by investigating BA model through the improved auxiliary equation method. Akbulut and Rayhanul [45] applied improved extended auxiliary equation and improved F-expansion technique to BA equation, including the β-derivative to gain rational function solutions, trigonometric function solutions, and hyperbolic function solutions. Sachin and Monika [46] investigated BA equation via a generalized exponential-rational function method and kudryashov's technique to extract solitons solutions.

The governing model has the following form:

$$ij_t + a_1 j_{xx} + a_2 j_{xt} + i(b_1 j_{xxx} + b_2 j_{xxt}) = i[\delta(|j|^2 j)_x + \mu(|j|^2)_x j + \lambda |j|^2 j_x], \tag{1}$$

where $j(x,t)$ rely on x and t characterizes soliton profile, x represents the distance and t represents the time variables. a_1 represents the group velocity dispersion (GVD), while a_2, b_1 are the spatio-temporal dispersion coefficient and b_2 for the third-order dispersion coefficient. The nonlinearity is defined by the third component in the equation on the right-hand side, where δ denotes the influence of self-steepening, while λ and μ indicate the nonlinear dispersion effect. Another powerful technique has been offered by Kudryashov in his research [47,48], the simplest equation technique is the name given to this methodology. Recently, Bilige et al. [49,50] modified this technique which is named the modified simplest equation technique. Subsequently, numerous researchers [51,52] applied this technique to gain novel exact solitons solutions for NLPDEs. This study uses extended-simplest equation technique to find new trigonometric, hyperbolic, and rational solutions for the BA equation and explains the resulting solutions, which include the β-derivative and M-truncated by their graphical representations. In this paper, We conduct a comprehensive comparison of the β and M-truncated fractional derivatives applied to the Biswas–Arshed equation utilizing the Extended Simplest Equation technique. Unlike earlier research, which focused primarily on individual fractional derivatives or conventional analytical approaches, ours uniquely mixes beta and M-truncated derivatives within the same framework. This makes a direct comparative study, which the literature has not yet extensively investigated, feasible. Furthermore, we derive a more general and effective solution method, thereby generating a class of soliton solutions. This study offers innovative analytical perspectives that surpass prior research and elucidates the progression of fractional derivatives in nonlinear equations. This facilitates future progress in fractional calculus and its applications in complex physical systems.

This paper is organized as follows: Preliminaries are outlined in Section 2. The proposed approaches are summarized in Section 3. The governing models are outlined in Section 4. Section 5 discusses the application of the proposed methodologies to the governing system for extracting precise solutions. Section 6 presents graphical representations of several findings. Bifurcation analysis are described in Section 7. Section 8 contains the presentation of the conclusion and future work.

2. Preliminaries

2.1. β-Derivative

Definition 1 (Atangana et al. [53]). *Let $u(z)$ be a function that is defined for any non-negative z. Therefore, the β-derivative of $u(z)$ is as follows:*

$$T^{\beta}(u(z)) = \frac{d^{\beta}u(z)}{dz^{\beta}} = \lim_{\xi \to 0} \frac{u\left(z + \xi\left(z + \frac{1}{\Gamma(\beta)}\right)^{1-\beta}\right) - u(z)}{\xi}, \ 1 < \beta \leq 1. \tag{2}$$

Theorem 1. *Let $u(z)$ and $v(z)$ be β-differentiable functions for all $z > 0$ and $\beta \in (0,1]$ (Martínez et al. [54]). Then,*

$$T^{\beta}(ru(z) + sv(z)) = rT^{\beta}(u(z)) + sT^{\beta}(v(z)), \forall r,s \in \mathbb{R}.$$

$$T^{\beta}(u(z)v(z)) = v(z)T^{\beta}(u(z)) + u(z)T^{\beta}(v(z)).$$

$$T^{\beta}\left(\frac{u(z)}{v(z)}\right) = \frac{v(z)T^{\beta}(u(z)) - u(z)T^{\beta}(v(z))}{v^2(z)}.$$

$$T^{\beta}(u(z)) = \left(z + \frac{1}{\Gamma(\beta)}\right)^{1-\beta}\frac{du(z)}{dz}.$$

2.2. M-Truncated Derivative

Definition 2. *The Truncated-Mittag–Leffler function [55] is defined as follows:*

$$_{i}\mathbb{E}_{\beta}(g(z)) = \sum_{m=0}^{i} \frac{g(z)^m}{\Gamma(\beta m + 1)}, \tag{3}$$

where $g \in \mathbb{C}$ and $\beta > 0$

Definition 3. *Let v: $[0,\infty) \to R$ be a function. The M-truncated derivative of v of order γ, where $\gamma \in (0,1)$ with respect to z, is defined as*

$$\mathbb{D}^{(\gamma,\beta)}_{(M,z)}v(z) = \lim_{h \to 0} \frac{v(z + {}_{i}\mathbb{E}_{\beta}(hz^{-\beta})) - v(z)}{h}, \beta, z > 0, \tag{4}$$

where $_{i}\mathbb{E}_{\beta}(.)$ is the truncated Mittag–Leffler function.

Theorem 2. *Let us assume that $0 < \gamma \leq 1, p, q \in \mathbb{R}, \beta > 0$, ψ and φ be a γ-diferentiable at any $z > 0$. Then,*

$$\mathbb{D}^{(\gamma,\beta)}_{(M,z)}(p\psi + q\varphi)(z) = p\mathbb{D}^{(\gamma,\beta)}_{(M,z)}\psi(z) + q\mathbb{D}^{(\gamma,\beta)}_{(M,z)}\varphi(z), \ p, q \in \mathbb{R}.$$

$$\mathbb{D}^{(\gamma,\beta)}_{(M,z)}(\psi\varphi)(z) = \psi(z)\mathbb{D}^{(\gamma,\beta)}_{(M,z)}\varphi(z) + \varphi(z)\mathbb{D}^{(\gamma,\beta)}_{(M,z)}\psi(z).$$

$$\mathbb{D}_{(M,z)}^{(\gamma,\beta)}\left(\frac{\psi}{\varphi}\right)(z) = \frac{\psi(z)\mathbb{D}_{(M,z)}^{(\gamma,\beta)}\varphi(z) - \varphi(z)\mathbb{D}_{(M,z)}^{(\gamma,\beta)}\psi(z)}{\varphi(z)^2}.$$

If ψ is diferentiable, then

$$\mathbb{D}_{(M,z)}^{(\gamma,\beta)}(\psi)(z) = \frac{z^{1-\gamma}}{\Gamma(\beta+1)}\frac{d\psi(z)}{dz}.$$

3. Description of the Method

To explain this method, initially consider the following projective Riccati equation:

$$f'(\chi) = -f(\chi)g(\chi), \; g'(\chi) = -g^2(\chi) + \sigma f(\chi) - \rho, \; \rho \neq 0 \tag{5}$$

where ρ and σ are constants. Consider

$$f(\chi) = \frac{1}{\phi(\chi)}, \; g(\chi) = \frac{\phi'(\chi)}{\phi(\chi)}, \; \phi(\chi) \neq 0 \tag{6}$$

$\phi(\chi)$ is the result of the following ODE of order two.

$$\sigma = \phi''(\chi) + \rho\phi(\chi). \tag{7}$$

For this ODE, there are three different kinds of solutions.

(1) **For $\rho < 0$,** hyperbolic function solution exist:

$$\phi(\chi) = B_1 cosh(\chi\sqrt{-\rho}) + B_2 sinh(\chi\sqrt{-\rho}) + \frac{\sigma}{\rho}. \tag{8}$$

Due to this,

$$\left(\frac{\phi'(\chi)}{\phi(\chi)}\right)^2 - \Delta_1\left(\frac{1}{\phi(\chi)}\right) - \frac{2\sigma}{\phi(\chi)} + \rho = 0, \tag{9}$$

where, $\Delta_1 = \rho B_1^2 - \rho B_2^2 - \frac{\sigma^2}{\rho}$

(2) **For $\rho > 0$,** trigonometric function solution exist:

$$\phi(\chi) = B_1 cos(\chi\sqrt{\rho}) + B_2 sin(\chi\sqrt{\rho}) + \frac{\sigma}{\rho}. \tag{10}$$

Due to this,

$$\left(\frac{\phi'(\chi)}{\phi(\chi)}\right)^2 - \Delta_2\left(\frac{1}{\phi(\chi)}\right) - \frac{2\sigma}{\phi(\chi)} + \rho = 0, \tag{11}$$

where, $\Delta_2 = \rho B_1^2 - \rho B_2^2 - \frac{\sigma^2}{\rho}$

(3) **For $\rho = 0$,** the solution is as follows:

$$\phi(\chi) = \frac{\sigma\chi^2}{2} + B_1\chi + B_2. \tag{12}$$

Due to this,

$$\left(\frac{\phi'(\chi)}{\phi(\chi)}\right)^2 - \Delta_3\left(\frac{1}{\phi(\chi)}\right) - \frac{2\sigma}{\phi(\chi)} = 0, \tag{13}$$

where, $\Delta_3 = B_1^2 - 2\sigma B_2$.

Here, B_1 and B_2 are arbitrary constants.

Examine the nonlinear $(n+1)$-dimensional partial differential equation (PDE)

$$H(j, j_x, j_t, j_{xx}, j_{xt}, j_{tt}, \ldots) = 0, \tag{14}$$

where F is a polynomial in $j(x,t)$ and its partial derivatives, containing the highest order derivatives and the nonlinear terms.

The key components of this methodology are outlined as follows:
Stage (1): With the aid of a traveling wave theory.

$$j(x,t) = J(\chi)e^{i\chi}, \chi = x - \frac{\tau}{\beta}\left(\frac{1}{\Gamma(\beta)} + t\right)^{\beta}, \eta = -dx + \frac{v}{\beta}\left(\frac{1}{\Gamma(\beta)} + t\right)^{\beta} + \epsilon.$$

$$j(x,t) = J(\chi)e^{i\eta}, \chi = x - \frac{\tau\Gamma(\beta+1)t^{\gamma}}{\gamma}, \eta = -dx + \frac{v\Gamma(\beta+1)t^{\gamma}}{\gamma} + \epsilon. \tag{15}$$

The traveling wave theory transforms (15) the nonlinear PDE (14) into the nonlinear ODE as follows

$$\mathbb{G}(j, j', j'', \ldots) = 0, \tag{16}$$

where $\mathbb{G}$ is a polynomial in $j(\chi)$ and its total derivative with respect to χ.
Stage (2): Assume the following solution to Equation (16).

$$j(\chi) = \sum_{i=0}^{M} \alpha_i \left[\frac{\phi'(\chi)}{\phi(\chi)}\right]^i + \sum_{j=0}^{M-1} \beta_j \left[\frac{\phi'(\chi)}{\phi(\chi)}\right]^i \frac{1}{\phi(\chi)}, \tag{17}$$

where $\phi(\chi)$ is the solution of second order ODE (7) and α_i and β_j are arbitrary constants.
Stage (3): By substitution (7), (9), (11), (13), and (17) to Equation (16), collect all terms with the same order of $\left(\frac{1}{\phi^i(\chi)}\right)$ and $\left(\frac{1}{\phi^j(\chi)}\right)\left(\frac{\phi'(\chi)}{\phi(\chi)}\right)$ together and a set of algebraic equations results from setting them to zero. Find $\rho, \sigma, \alpha_i, \beta_i\, a_1, a_2, b_1, b_2$ by solving this system with the aid of Mathematica.

4. Governing Models

In this part, define the governing model equations including both β derivatives and M-truncated derivatives.

4.1. Biswas Arshed Equation Including β-Derivative

Han T. et al. [56] defined BA equation including β-derivative as

$$i\frac{\partial^{\beta} j}{\partial t^{\beta}} + a_1\frac{\partial^2 j}{\partial x^2} + a_2\frac{\partial^{\beta}}{\partial t^{\beta}}\left(\frac{\partial j}{\partial x}\right) - i\left(\delta\frac{\partial |j|^2 j}{\partial x} + \mu j\frac{\partial |j|^2}{\partial x} + \lambda |j|^2\frac{\partial j}{\partial x}\right)$$

$$+ i\left(b_1\frac{\partial^3 j}{\partial x^3} + b_2\frac{\partial^{\beta}}{\partial t^{\beta}}\left(\frac{\partial^2 j}{\partial x^2}\right)\right) = 0,\ 0 < \beta \leq 1, \tag{18}$$

where i represent the imaginary part, j is the function of x and t, $\frac{\partial^{\beta}}{\partial t^{\beta}}$ is the operator for β-derivative, β represents fractional order, a_1, a_2, b_1, and b_2 are arbitrary constants, δ, μ, and λ are nonzero parameters, the wave transformations listed below will be used:

$$j(x,t) = J(\chi)e^{i\eta},\ \chi = x - \frac{\tau}{\beta}\left(\frac{1}{\Gamma(\beta)} + t\right)^{\beta},\ \eta = -dx + \frac{v}{\beta}\left(\frac{1}{\Gamma(\beta)} + t\right)^{\beta} + \epsilon, \tag{19}$$

where η , v, τ, and ϵ are non-zero parameters.

4.2. Biswas Arshed Equation Including M-Truncated Derivative

$$i\mathbb{D}^{(\gamma,\beta)}_{(M,z)}(j) + a_1\frac{\partial^2 j}{\partial x^2} + a_2\mathbb{D}^{(\gamma,\beta)}_{(M,z)}\left(\frac{\partial j}{\partial x}\right) - i\left(\delta\frac{\partial|j|^2 j}{\partial x} + \mu j\frac{\partial|j|^2}{\partial x} + \lambda|j|^2\frac{\partial j}{\partial x}\right)$$
$$+i\left(b_1\frac{\partial^3 j}{\partial x^3} + b_2\mathbb{D}^{(\gamma,\beta)}_{(M,z)}\left(\frac{\partial^2 j}{\partial x^2}\right)\right) = 0,\ 0 < \gamma \leq 1,\ \beta > 0, \tag{20}$$

where i represent the imaginary part, J is the function of x and t, $\mathbb{D}^{(\gamma,\beta)}_{(M,z)}$ is operator for the γ-derivative, γ represents fractional order, a_1, a_2, b_1, and b_2 are arbitrary constants, δ, μ, and λ are nonzero parameters, the wave transformations listed below will be used:

$$j(x,t) = J(\chi)e^{i\eta}, \chi = x - \frac{\tau\Gamma(\beta+1)t^\gamma}{\gamma}, \eta = -dx + \frac{v\Gamma(\beta+1)t^\gamma}{\gamma} + \epsilon, \tag{21}$$

where η, v, τ, and ϵ are non-zero parameters. In this study, we considered fractional operators defined on the whole memory interval [0, T]. However, in many real-world systems, distant past effects gradually diminish, and it is more realistic to restrict the fractional operator to a finite memory horizon, often referred to as the "short-memory principle." In such cases, the fractional kernel is truncated so that only the most recent history contributes to the system's dynamics. This concept has been shown to provide accurate models for viscoelastic and structural materials with fading memory effects [57,58]. Extending the Biswas–Arshed model to incorporate short-memory operators would therefore be an interesting future direction, offering a balance between computational efficiency and physical realism. The parameters β and γ represent the fractional orders in the β-derivative and the M-truncated derivative, respectively. Physically, these parameters quantify the extent of memory and hereditary effects in the system. When $\beta = 1$ (or $\gamma = 1$), the model reduces to the classical integer-order form without memory. For $0 < \beta, \gamma < 1$, the model incorporates anomalous diffusion and long-range temporal correlations. Smaller values correspond to stronger memory effects, where past states significantly influence present dynamics, while larger values closer to unity indicate weaker memory and near-classical behavior. In the case of the M-truncated operator, γ also introduces a tempered Mittag–Leffler kernel that effectively restricts the memory influence, making it particularly suitable for systems with fading memory such as viscoelastic materials oranomalous transport with cutoff effects.

5. Applications

This section employs the extended simplest equation method to resolve the Biswas–Arshed equation, including both β and M-truncated derivatives. By substituting the wave transformations specified in (19) and (21) into (18) and (20), the resulting nonlinear ordinary differential equations are derived by separating the imaginary and real components, respectively.

$$(b_1 - b_2\tau)J^{(3)}(\chi) + J'(\chi)(d(a_2\tau - 2a_1 + 2b_2v) + a_2v + d^2(b_2\tau - 3b_1) - \tau)$$
$$-(J(\chi))^2(\eta + 3\delta + 2\mu)J'(\chi) = 0. \tag{22}$$

$$J''(\chi)(a_1 - a_2\tau - 2b_2d\tau + 3b_1d - b_2v) - (J(\chi))^3d(\eta + \delta)$$
$$+J(\chi)(v(a_2d + b_2d^2 - 1) - a_1d^2 - b_1d^3) = 0. \tag{23}$$

The following are the constraint conditions that can be found from Equation (22)

$$\tau = \frac{b_1}{b_2}, \delta = -\frac{1}{3}(\eta + 2\mu), v = -\frac{a_2b_1d - 2a_1b_2d - 2b_1b_2d^2 - b_1}{b_2(a_2 + 2b_2d)}. \tag{24}$$

Inserting Equation (24) into Equation (23)

$$d_1 J''(\chi) + d_2 J(\chi) + d_3 (J(\chi))^3 = 0, \tag{25}$$

where

$$\begin{aligned} d_1 &= -\frac{a_2 b_1}{b_2} + a_1 + b_1 d + d_4, \\ d_2 &= -\frac{a_2 d_4 d}{b_2} - a_1 d^2 + \frac{d_4}{b^2} - b_1 d^3 - d_4 d^2, \\ d_3 &= -\lambda d + \frac{1}{3} d(\lambda + 2\mu), \\ d_4 &= \frac{a_2 b_1 d - 2a_1 b_2 d - 2b_1 b_2 d^2 - b_1}{a_2 + 2b_2 d}. \end{aligned}$$

Equation (25) is used to determine the homogeneous balance number through the terms $J''(\chi)$ and $(J(\chi))^3$, we got M = 1 and the following formal solution from Equation (25).

$$J(\chi) = \frac{\alpha_1 \phi'(\chi)}{\phi(\chi)} + \alpha_0 + \frac{\beta_0}{\phi(\chi)}. \tag{26}$$

Type 1. **For** $\rho < 0$.

Substitute Equation (26) with the linear OD Equation (7) and relation (9) into Equation (25), accumulate all the expression with the identical power of $\left(\frac{1}{\phi^i(\chi)}\right)$ and $\left(\frac{1}{\phi^j(\chi)}\right)\left(\frac{\phi'(\chi)}{\phi(\chi)}\right)$ and put them equal to zero, the system of algebraic equations below is obtained.

Utilizing MATHEMATICA to resolve these nonlinear algebraic equations obtains the results given below:

Result:

$$\Bigg\{ \alpha_0 = 0, \alpha_1 = \pm \frac{\sqrt{\frac{3}{2}}\sqrt{b_1}}{\sqrt{2a_2 b_2 \lambda d^3 - 2a_2 b_2 d^3 \mu + a_2 b_2 \rho \lambda d - a_2 b_2 \rho d \mu - 4b_2 \lambda d^2 + 4b_2 d^2 \mu}},$$

$$\beta_0 = \pm \frac{\sqrt{\frac{3}{2}}\sqrt{b_1}\sqrt{\Delta_1}}{\sqrt{2a_2 b_2 \lambda d^3 - 2a_2 b_2 d^3 \mu + a_2 b_2 \rho \lambda d - a_2 b_2 \rho d \mu - 4b_2 \lambda d^2 + 4b_2 d^2 \mu}},$$

$$a_1 = \frac{b_1 (a_2^2 \rho + 2a_2^2 d^2 - 4a_2 d + b_2 \rho + 2b_2 d^2 + 2)}{b_2 (a_2 \rho + 2a_2 d^2 - 4d)} \Bigg\} \tag{27}$$

From Equations (8), (15), (26) and (27), obtain the hyperbolic solution of Equation (1) as follows:

For β-derivative:

$$J(x,t) = \left(\frac{\pm\sqrt{b_1}\sqrt{\frac{3}{2}}}{\sqrt{2a_2 b_2 \lambda d^3 - 2a_2 b_2 d^3 \mu + a_2 b_2 \rho \lambda d - a_2 b_2 \rho d \mu - 4b_2 \lambda d^2 + 4b_2 d^2 \mu}} \right)$$

$$\left(\sqrt{-\rho}\vartheta_1(\chi) + \sqrt{\Delta_1}\vartheta_1(\chi)\right) e^{-dx + \frac{v}{\beta}\left(\frac{1}{\Gamma(\beta)} + t\right)^\beta + \epsilon}, \tag{28}$$

where

$$\vartheta_1(\chi) = \frac{B_1 \sinh(\chi\sqrt{-\rho}) + B_2 \cosh(\chi\sqrt{-\rho})}{B_1 \cosh(\chi\sqrt{-\rho}) + B_2 \sinh(\chi\sqrt{-\rho}) + \frac{\sigma}{\rho}},$$

$$\vartheta_2(\chi) = \frac{1}{B_1 \cosh(\chi\sqrt{-\rho}) + B_2 \sinh(\chi\sqrt{-\rho}) + \frac{\sigma}{\rho}}.$$

In particular, if set $B_1 = 0, B_2 \neq 0, \sigma = 0$ in Equation (28), obtain singular wave solution

$$J(x,t) = \left(\frac{\pm\sqrt{b_1}\sqrt{\frac{3}{2}}}{\sqrt{2a_2b_2\lambda d^3 - 2a_2b_2d^3\mu + a_2b_2\rho\lambda d - a_2b_2\rho d\mu - 4b_2\lambda d^2 + 4b_2d^2\mu}} \right)$$

$$\left(\coth\left(\sqrt{-\rho}\chi\right) + \operatorname{csch}\left(\sqrt{-\rho}\chi\right)\right)e^{-dx+\frac{v}{\beta}\left(\frac{1}{\Gamma(\beta)}+t\right)^{\beta}+\epsilon}, \tag{29}$$

For M-truncated derivative:

$$J(x,t) = \left(\frac{\pm\sqrt{b_1}\sqrt{\frac{3}{2}}}{\sqrt{2a_2b_2\lambda d^3 - 2a_2b_2d^3\mu + a_2b_2\rho\lambda d - a_2b_2\rho d\mu - 4b_2\lambda d^2 + 4b_2d^2\mu}} \right)$$

$$\left(\sqrt{-\rho}\vartheta_1(\chi) + \sqrt{\Delta_1}\vartheta_2(\chi)\right)e^{-dx+\frac{v\Gamma(\beta+1)t^{\gamma}}{\gamma}+\epsilon}, \tag{30}$$

where

$$\vartheta_1(\chi) = \frac{B_1\sinh(\chi\sqrt{-\rho}) + B_2\cosh(\chi\sqrt{-\rho})}{B_1\cosh(\chi\sqrt{-\rho}) + B_2\sinh(\chi\sqrt{-\rho}) + \frac{\sigma}{\rho}},$$

$$\vartheta_2(\chi) = \frac{1}{B_1\cosh(\chi\sqrt{-\rho}) + B_2\sinh(\chi\sqrt{-\rho}) + \frac{\sigma}{\rho}}.$$

In particular, if set $B_1 = 0, B_2 \neq 0, \sigma = 0$ in Equation (30), obtain singular wave solution

$$J(x,t) = \left(\frac{\pm\sqrt{\frac{3}{2}}\left(\sqrt{b_1}\sqrt{-\rho}\right)}{\sqrt{2a_2b_2\lambda d^3 - 2a_2b_2d^3\mu + a_2b_2\rho\lambda d - a_2b_2\rho d\mu - 4b_2\lambda d^2 + 4b_2d^2\mu}} \right)$$

$$\left(\coth\left(\sqrt{-\rho}\chi\right) + \operatorname{csch}\left(\sqrt{-\rho}\chi\right)\right)e^{-dx+\frac{v\Gamma(\beta+1)t^{\gamma}}{\gamma}+\epsilon}. \tag{31}$$

Type 2. **For $\rho > 0$.**

Substitute Equation (26) with the linear OD Equation (7), and relation (11) into Equation (25), accumulate all the expression with the identical power of $\left(\frac{1}{\phi^i(\chi)}\right)$ and $\left(\frac{1}{\phi^i(\chi)}\right)\left(\frac{\phi'(\chi)}{\phi(\chi)}\right)$ and put them equal to zero, the system of algebraic equations below is obtained.

By using Mathematica to solve these nonlinear algebraic equations and obtain results are shown below.

Result:

$$\begin{cases} \alpha_0 = 0, \alpha_1 = \pm\frac{\sqrt{\frac{3}{2}}\sqrt{b_1}}{\sqrt{2a_2b_2\lambda d^3 - 2a_2b_2d^3\mu + a_2b_2\rho\lambda d - a_2b_2\rho d\mu - 4b_2\lambda d^2 + 4b_2d^2\mu}}, \\ \beta_0 = \pm\frac{\sqrt{\frac{3}{2}}\sqrt{b_1}\sqrt{\Delta_2}}{\sqrt{2a_2b_2\lambda d^3 - 2a_2b_2d^3\mu + a_2b_2\rho\lambda d - a_2b_2\rho d\mu - 4b_2\lambda d^2 + 4b_2d^2\mu}}, \\ a_1 = \frac{b_1\left(a_2^2\rho + 2a_2^2d^2 - 4a_2d + b_2\rho + 2b_2d^2 + 2\right)}{b_2(a_2\rho + 2a_2d^2 - 4d)} \end{cases} \tag{32}$$

From Equations (10), (15), (26) and (32), obtain the trigonometric solution of Equation (1) as follows:

For β-derivative:

$$J(x,t) = \left(\frac{\pm\sqrt{b_1}\sqrt{\frac{3}{2}}}{\sqrt{2a_2b_2\lambda d^3 - 2a_2b_2d^3\mu + a_2b_2\rho\lambda d - a_2b_2\rho d\mu - 4b_2\lambda d^2 + 4b_2d^2\mu}} \right)$$

$$\left(\sqrt{\rho}\vartheta_1(\chi)+\sqrt{\Delta_2}\vartheta_2(\chi)\right)e^{-dx+\frac{v}{\beta}\left(\frac{1}{\Gamma(\beta)}+t\right)^{\beta}+\epsilon}, \tag{33}$$

where

$$\vartheta_1(\chi)=\frac{-B_1\sin(\chi\sqrt{\rho})+B_2\cos(\chi\sqrt{\rho})}{B_1\cos(\chi\sqrt{\rho})+B_2\sin(\chi\sqrt{\rho})+\frac{\sigma}{\rho}},$$

$$\vartheta_2(\chi)=\frac{1}{B_1\cos(\chi\sqrt{\rho})+B_2\sin(\chi\sqrt{\rho})+\frac{\sigma}{\rho}}.$$

In particular, if set $B_1=0, B_2\neq 0, \sigma=0$, Equation (33) and obtain periodic wave solution

$$J(x,t)=\left(\frac{\pm\sqrt{b_1}\sqrt{\frac{3}{2}}}{\sqrt{2a_2b_2\lambda d^3-2a_2b_2d^3\mu+a_2b_2\rho\lambda d-a_2b_2\rho d\mu-4b_2\lambda d^2+4b_2d^2\mu}}\right)$$

$$(\cot(\sqrt{\rho}\chi)+\csc(\sqrt{\rho}\chi))e^{-dx+\frac{v}{\beta}\left(\frac{1}{\Gamma(\beta)}+t\right)^{\beta}+\epsilon}. \tag{34}$$

In particular, if set $B_1\neq 0, B_2=0, \sigma=0$, Equation (33) and obtain periodic wave solution

$$J(x,t)=\left(\frac{\pm\sqrt{b_1}\sqrt{\frac{3}{2}}}{\sqrt{2a_2b_2\lambda d^3-2a_2b_2d^3\mu+a_2b_2\rho\lambda d-a_2b_2\rho d\mu-4b_2\lambda d^2+4b_2d^2\mu}}\right)$$

$$(\tan(\sqrt{\rho}\chi)-\sec(\sqrt{\rho}\chi))e^{-dx+\frac{v}{\beta}\left(\frac{1}{\Gamma(\beta)}+t\right)^{\beta}+\epsilon}, \tag{35}$$

For M-truncated derivative:

$$J(x,t)=\left(\frac{\pm\sqrt{b_1}\sqrt{\frac{3}{2}}}{\sqrt{2a_2b_2\lambda d^3-2a_2b_2d^3\mu+a_2b_2\rho\lambda d-a_2b_2\rho d\mu-4b_2\lambda d^2+4b_2d^2\mu}}\right)$$

$$\left(\sqrt{\rho}\vartheta_1(\chi)+\sqrt{\Delta_2}\vartheta_2(\chi)\right)e^{-dx+\frac{v\Gamma(\beta+1)t^{\gamma}}{\gamma}+\epsilon}, \tag{36}$$

where

$$\vartheta_1(\chi)=\frac{-B_1\sin(\chi\sqrt{\rho})+B_2\cos(\chi\sqrt{\rho})}{B_1\cosh(\chi\sqrt{\rho})+B_2\sinh(\chi\sqrt{-\rho})+\frac{\sigma}{\rho}},$$

$$\vartheta_2(\chi)=\frac{1}{B_1\cos(\chi\sqrt{\rho})+B_2\sin(\chi\sqrt{\rho})+\frac{\sigma}{\rho}}.$$

In particular, if set $B_1=0, B_2\neq 0, \sigma=0$, Equation (36), obtain periodic wave solution

$$J(x,t)=\left(\frac{\pm\sqrt{\frac{3}{2}}(\sqrt{b_1}\sqrt{\rho})}{\sqrt{2a_2b_2\lambda d^3-2a_2b_2d^3\mu+a_2b_2\rho\lambda d-a_2b_2\rho d\mu-4b_2\lambda d^2+4b_2d^2\mu}}\right)$$

$$(\cot(\sqrt{\rho}\chi)+\csc(\sqrt{\rho}\chi))e^{-dx+\frac{v\Gamma(\beta+1)t^{\gamma}}{\gamma}+\epsilon}. \tag{37}$$

In particular, if set $B_1\neq 0, B_2=0, \sigma=0$, Equation (36) and obtain periodic wave solution

$$J(x,t)=\left(\frac{\pm\sqrt{\frac{3}{2}}(\sqrt{b_1}\sqrt{\rho})}{\sqrt{2a_2b_2\lambda d^3-2a_2b_2d^3\mu+a_2b_2\rho\lambda d-a_2b_2\rho d\mu-4b_2\lambda d^2+4b_2d^2\mu}}\right)$$

$$(\tan(\sqrt{\rho}\chi)-\sec(\sqrt{\rho}\chi))e^{-dx+\frac{v\Gamma(\beta+1)t^{\gamma}}{\gamma}+\epsilon}. \tag{38}$$

Type 3. **For** $\rho = 0$.

Substitute Equation (26) with the linear OD Equation (7), and relation (13) into Equation (25), accumulate all the expression with the identical power of $\left(\frac{1}{\phi^i(\chi)}\right)$ and $\left(\frac{1}{\phi^j(\chi)}\right)\left(\frac{\phi'(\chi)}{\phi(\chi)}\right)$ and put them equal to zero, the system of algebraic equations below is obtained.

$$\left(\frac{1}{\phi(\chi)}\right)^0 : -\frac{1}{3}\alpha_0 d\left(2\alpha_0^2(\lambda-\mu)+3a_1 d+3b_1 d^2\right) + \frac{\alpha_0\left(a_2 d+b_2 d^2-1\right)\left(b_1\left(-a_2 d+2b_2 d^2+1\right)+2a_1 b_2 d\right)}{b_2(a_2+2b_2 d)} = 0,$$

$$\left(\frac{1}{\phi(\chi)}\right) : -d\left(\beta_0 d(a_1+b_1 d)+2\alpha_0^2\beta_0(\lambda-\mu)+4\alpha_1^2\alpha_0\sigma(\lambda-\mu)\right) + \frac{\beta_0\left(a_2 d+b_2 d^2-1\right)\left(b_1\left(-a_2 d+2b_2 d^2+1\right)+2a_1 b_2 d\right)}{b_2(a_2+2b_2 d)} = 0,$$

$$\left(\frac{1}{\phi(\chi)}\right)^2 : 3a_1\beta_0\sigma+d\left(3b_1\beta_0\sigma-2(\lambda-\mu)\left(\alpha_1^2(\alpha_0\Delta_3+2\beta_0\sigma)+\alpha_0\beta_0^2\right)\right) - \frac{3\beta_0\sigma\left(b_2\left(2a_1 b_2 d+b_1\left(2b_2 d^2+1\right)\right)+a_2 b_1 b_2 d+a_2^2 b_1\right)}{b_2(a_2+2b_2 d)} = 0,$$

$$\left(\frac{1}{\phi(\chi)}\right)^3 : \frac{1}{3}(-2)\beta_0\left(\beta_0^2 d(\lambda-\mu)-3\Delta_3\left(a_1+d\left(\alpha_1^2(\mu-\lambda)+b_1\right)\right)\right) - \frac{2\beta_0\Delta_3\left(b_2\left(2a_1 b_2 d+b_1\left(2b_2 d^2+1\right)\right)+a_2 b_1 b_2 d+a_2^2 b_1\right)}{b_2(a_2+2b_2 d)} = 0,$$

$$\left(\frac{\phi'(\chi)}{\phi(\chi)}\right) : \alpha_1(-d)\left(2\alpha_0^2(\lambda-\mu)+a_1 d+b_1 d^2\right) + \frac{\alpha_1\left(a_2 d+b_2 d^2-1\right)\left(b_1\left(-a_2 d+2b_2 d^2+1\right)+2a_1 b_2 d\right)}{b_2(a_2+2b_2 d)} = 0,$$

$$\left(\frac{1}{\phi(\chi)}\right)^2\left(\frac{\phi'(\chi)}{\phi(\chi)}\right) : -\frac{1}{3}\alpha_1\left(d\left(4(\lambda-\mu)\left(3\alpha_0\beta_0+\alpha_1^2\sigma\right)-3b_1\sigma\right)-3a_1\sigma\right) - \frac{\alpha_1\sigma\left(b_2\left(2a_1 b_2 d+b_1\left(2b_2 d^2+1\right)\right)+a_2 b_1 b_2 d+a_2^2 b_1\right)}{b_2(a_2+2b_2 d)} = 0,$$

$$\left(\frac{1}{\phi(\chi)}\right)^3\left(\frac{\phi'(\chi)}{\phi(\chi)}\right) : \frac{1}{3}(-2)\alpha_1\left(3\beta_0^2 d(\lambda-\mu)-\Delta_3\left(3a_1+d\left(\alpha_1^2(\mu-\lambda)+3b_1\right)\right)\right) - \frac{2\alpha_1\Delta_3\left(b_2\left(2a_1 b_2 d+b_1\left(2b_2 d^2+1\right)\right)+a_2 b_1 b_2 d+a_2^2 b_1\right)}{b_2(a_2+2b_2 d)} = 0.$$

Utilizing Mathematica to resolve these nonlinear algebraic equations obtains the results given below.

Result:

$$\left\{\alpha_0 = 0, \alpha_1 = \frac{\pm\sqrt{b_1}\sqrt{3}}{2\sqrt{a_2 b_2\lambda d^3-a_2 b_2 d^3\mu-2b_2\lambda d^2+2b_2 d^2\mu}}, \beta_0 = \frac{\pm\sqrt{3}\sqrt{b_1}\sqrt{\Delta_3}}{2\sqrt{a_2 b_2\lambda d^3-a_2 b_2 d^3\mu-2b_2\lambda d^2+2b_2 d^2\mu}}, a_1 = \frac{b_1\left(a_2^2 d^2-2a_2 d+b_2 d^2+1\right)}{b_2 d(a_2 d-2)}\right\} \quad (39)$$

From Equations (12), (15), (26) and (39), obtain the rational solution of Equation (1) as follows:

For β-derivative:

$$J(x,t) = \frac{\left(\pm\sqrt{b_1}\sqrt{3}\right)\left(\sqrt{\Delta_3}\vartheta_2(\chi) + \vartheta_1(\chi)\right)e^{-dx+\frac{v}{\beta}\left(\frac{1}{\Gamma(\beta)}+t\right)^{\beta}+\epsilon}}{2\sqrt{a_2b_2\lambda d^3 - a_2b_2d^3\mu - 2b_2\lambda d^2 + 2b_2d^2\mu}}, \tag{40}$$

For M-truncated derivative:

$$J(x,t) = \frac{\pm\left(\sqrt{b_1}\sqrt{3}\right)\left(\sqrt{\Delta_3}\vartheta_2(\chi) + \vartheta_1(\chi)\right)e^{-dx+\frac{v\Gamma(\beta+1)t^{\gamma}}{\gamma}+\epsilon}}{2\sqrt{a_2b_2\lambda d^3 - a_2b_2d^3\mu - 2b_2\lambda d^2 + 2b_2d^2\mu}}, \tag{41}$$

where

$$\vartheta_1(\chi) = \frac{B_1 + \chi\sigma}{B_1\chi + B_2 + \frac{\chi^2\sigma}{2}},$$

$$\vartheta_2(\chi) = \frac{1}{B_1\chi + B_2 + \frac{\chi^2\sigma}{2}}.$$

Since the Biswas–Arshed equation is a time-space fractional model, appropriate initial and boundary conditions are necessary to ensure well-posedness. In the context of optical solitons, the initial condition at $t = 0$ typically corresponds to a localized input pulse with finite amplitude. Moreover, the boundary condition is taken as follows:

$$\lim_{|x|\to\infty} J(x,t) = 0,$$

meaning that the soliton amplitude vanishes at spatial infinity. These conditions reflect the physical reality of solitary waves that are localized in space and evolve from prescribed input profiles in time.

6. Physical Behavior of Solitons

This section contained the physical characteristics of the gained solitons with M-truncated and β fractional derivative like kink, singular and periodic- singular types.

In Figure 1, the physical behavior of solution $J(x,t)$ with the M-truncated fractional derivative shown in Equation (29), in Figure 1a 3-dim, with $d = 0.1, \nu = -0.5, \delta = -1$, $\lambda = -0.2, \mu = -1.2, a_2 = 0.2, b_1 = 2, b_2 = -0.5; \xi = 0; \beta = 0.5; \tau = 0.5$, Figure 1b 2-dim with $t = 0,1,2,3$ and Figure 1c contour.

In Figure 2, the physical behavior of solution $J(x,t)$ with the β fractional derivative shown in Equation (31), in Figure 2a 3-dim, with $d = 0.1, \nu = -0.5, \delta = -1, \lambda = -0.2$, $\mu = -1.2, a_2 = 0.2, b_1 = 2, b_2 = -0.5; \xi = 0; \beta = 0.5; \tau = 0.5; \alpha = 1$, Figure 2b 2-dim with $t = 0,1,2,3$ and Figure 2c contour.

In Figure 3, the physical behavior of solution $J(x,t)$ with the M-truncated fractional derivative shown in Equation (34), in Figure 3a 3-dim, with $d = 0.1, \nu = -0.5, \delta = -1$, $\lambda = -0.2, \mu = -1.2, a_2 = 0.2, b_1 = 2, b_2 = -0.5; \xi = 0; \beta = 0.5; \tau = 0.5$, Figure 3b 2-dim with $t = 0,1,2,3$ and Figure 3c contour.

In Figure 4, the physical behavior of solution $J(x,t)$ with the β fractional derivative shown in Equation (37), in Figure 4a 3-dim, with $d = 0.1, \nu = -0.5, \delta = -1, \lambda = -0.2$, $\mu = -1.2, a_2 = 0.2, b_1 = 2, b_2 = -0.5; \xi = 0; \beta = 0.5; \tau = 0.5; \alpha = 1$, Figure 4b 2-dim with $t = 0,1,2,3$ and Figure 4c contour.

In Figure 5, the physical behavior of solution $J(x,t)$ with the M-truncated fractional derivative shown in Equation (35), in Figure 5a 3-dim, with $d = 0.1, \nu = -0.5, \delta = -1$, $\lambda = -0.2, \mu = -1.2, a_2 = 0.2, b_1 = 2, b_2 = -0.5; \xi = 0; \beta = 0.5; \tau = 0.5$, Figure 5b 2-dim with $t = 0,1,2,3$ and Figure 5c contour.

In Figure 6, the physical behavior of solution $J(x,t)$ with the β fractional derivative shown in Equation (38), in Figure 6a 3-dim, with $d = 0.1, \nu = -0.5, \delta = -1, \lambda = -0.2$,

$\mu = -1.2, a_2 = 0.2, b_1 = 2, b_2 = -0.5; \xi = 0; \beta = 0.8; \tau = 0.5$, Figure 6b 2-dim with $t = 0, 1, 2, 3$ and Figure 6c contour.

In Figures 1–6 same behavior of the soliton with M-truncated and β fractional derivative.

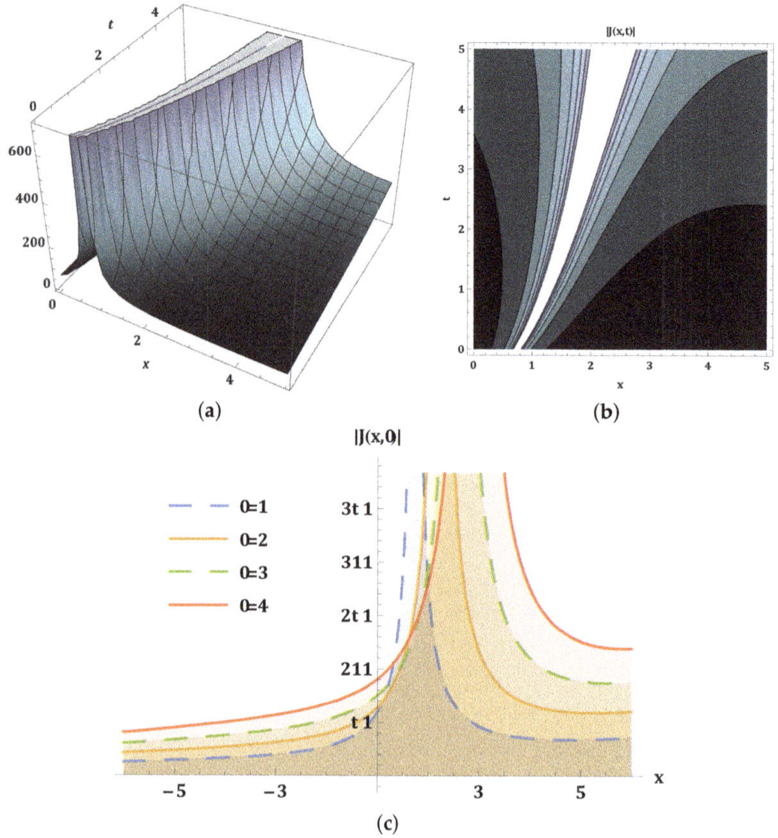

Figure 1. Physical behavior of $J(x,t)$ shown in Equation (29) in (**a**) 3-dim, (**b**) 2-dim and (**c**) contour graphs.

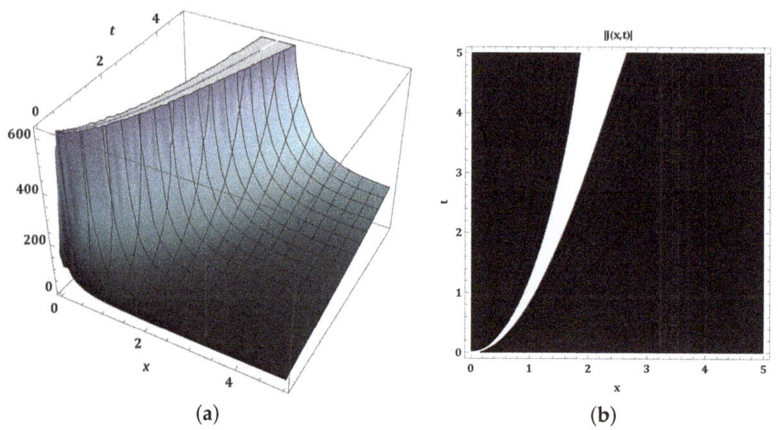

Figure 2. *Cont.*

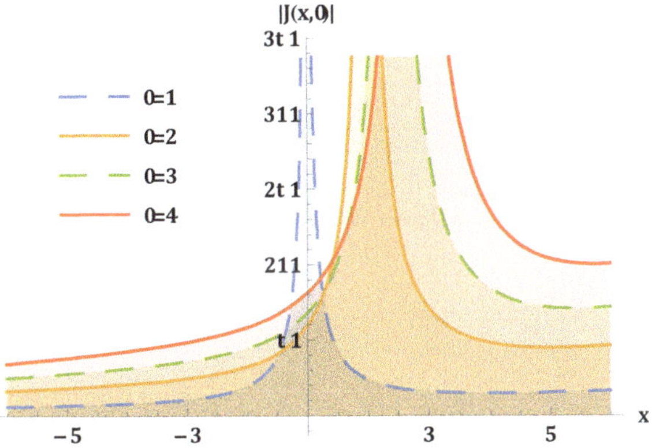

(c)

Figure 2. Physical behavior of $J(x,t)$ shown in Equation (31) in (**a**) 3-dim, (**b**) 2-dim and (**c**) contour graphs.

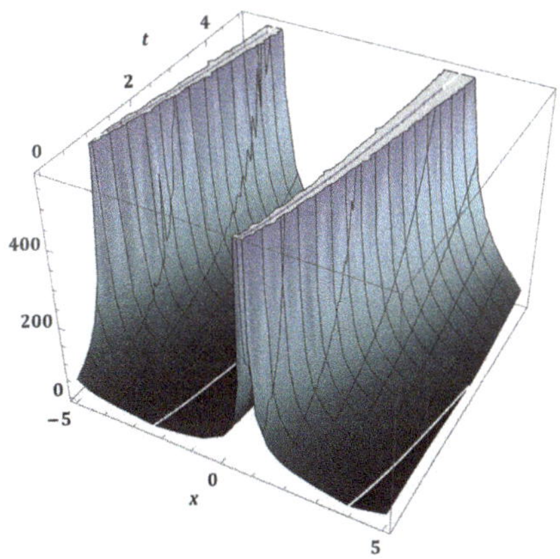

(a)

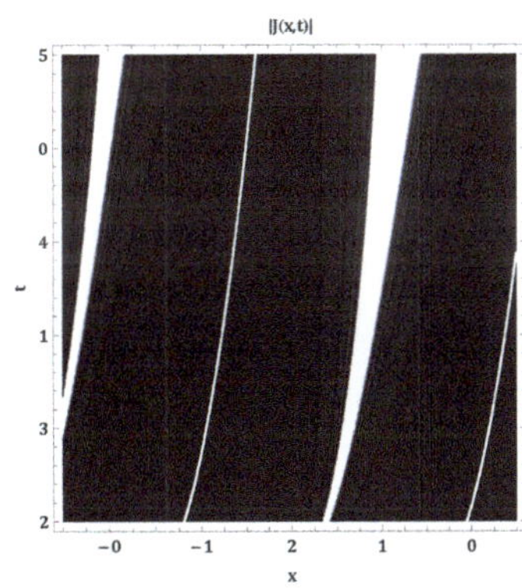

(b)

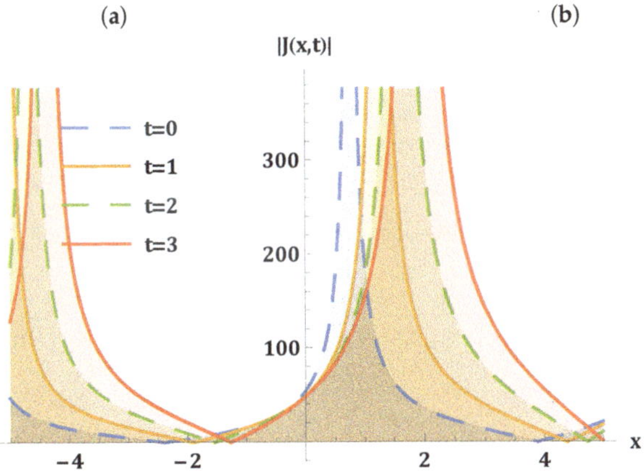

(c)

Figure 3. Physical behavior of $J(x,t)$ shown in Equation (34) in (**a**) 3-dim, (**b**) 2-dim and (**c**) contour graphs.

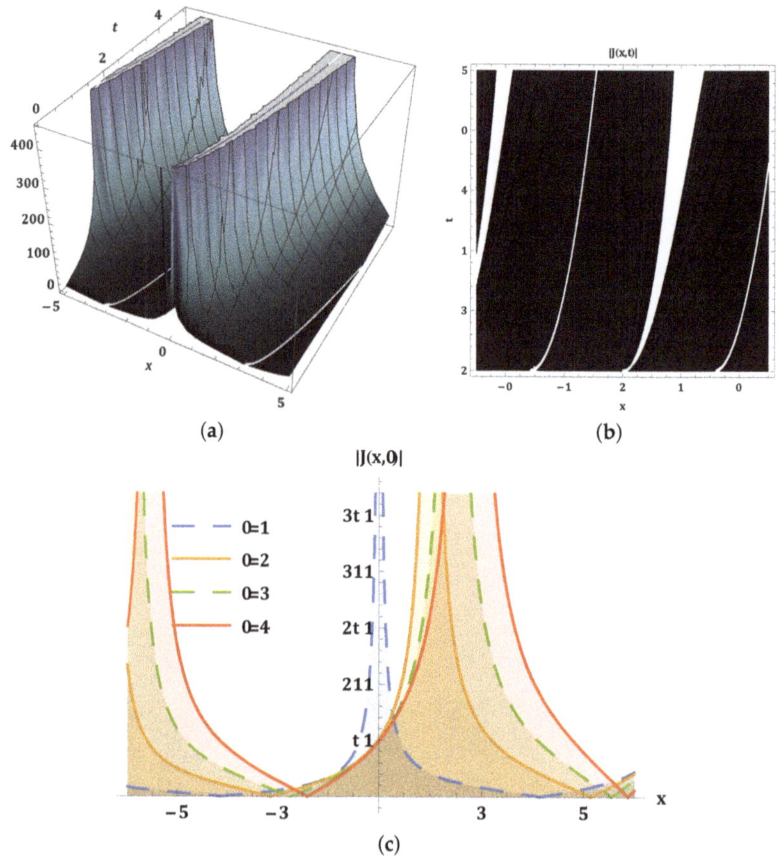

Figure 4. Physical behavior of $J(x,t)$ shown in Equation (37) in (**a**) 3-dim, (**b**) 2-dim and (**c**) contour graphs.

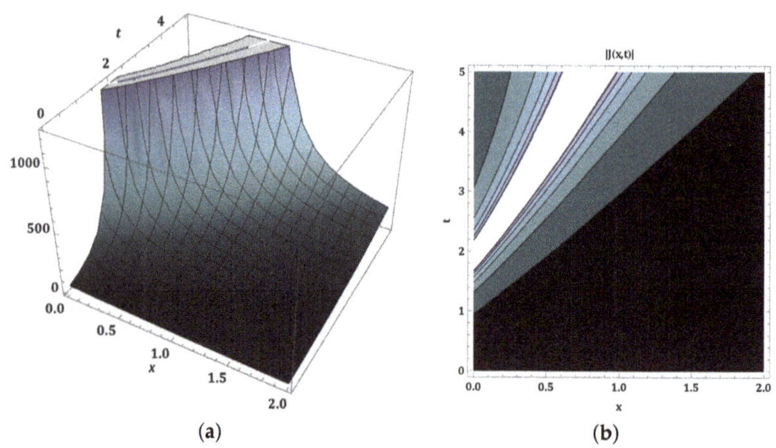

Figure 5. *Cont.*

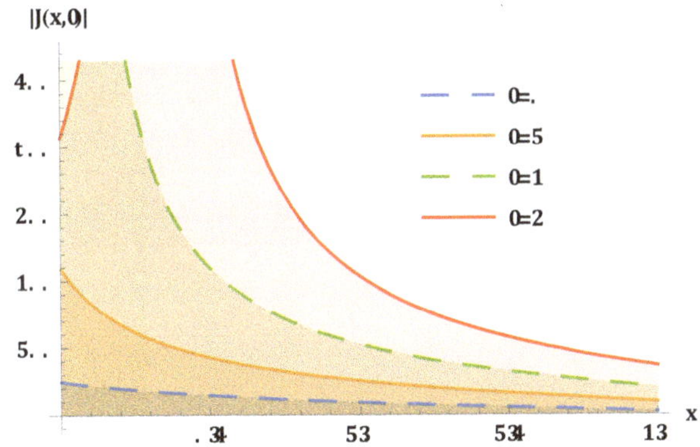

(c)

Figure 5. Physical behavior of $J(x,t)$ shown in Equation (35) in (**a**) 3-dim, (**b**) 2-dim and (**c**) contour graphs.

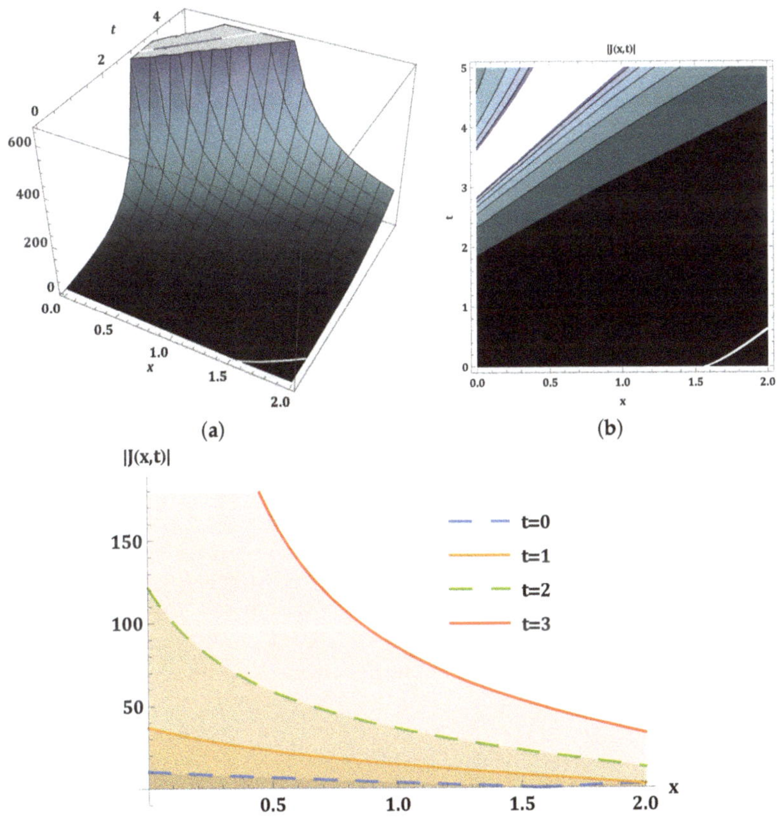

(c)

Figure 6. Physical behavior of $J(x,t)$ shown in Equation (38) in (**a**) 3-dim, (**b**) 2-dim and (**c**) contour graphs.

To highlight the influence of fractional dynamics, we performed a parametric analysis of the obtained soliton solutions with respect to the fractional orders β and γ. The results show that varying β or γ strongly affects the amplitude, width, and stability of the soliton profiles. For example, decreasing β from 0.9 to 0.5 leads to broader and slower-decaying waveforms, reflecting enhanced memory effects. Conversely, values closer to unity recover sharper, more localized solitons resembling the classical case. A similar trend is observed for γ, where smaller values correspond to stronger fading memory and slower propagation dynamics. These findings confirm that fractional orders act as tunable parameters controlling the balance between dispersion and nonlinearity, thereby offering a richer description of wave evolution in complex media.

7. Bifurication Analysis

The bifurcation analysis of the time-fractional BA model is investigated in this section using a planar dynamical system. In order to simplify this analysis, the dynamical system in Equation (25) is assumed to be represented as follows:

$$\begin{cases} \dfrac{dP}{d\chi} = Q, \\ \dfrac{dQ}{d\chi} = -\dfrac{d_2}{d_1}P - \dfrac{d_3}{d_1}P^3, \end{cases} \tag{42}$$

where $P(\chi) = J(\chi)$ and $Q(\chi) = J'(\chi)$. This system displays wave solutions of the time-fractional BA model alongside the established phase portraits in the (P, Q)-plane. The Hamiltonian canonical equations $P'(\chi) = \frac{\partial H}{\partial Q}$ and $Q'(\chi) = -\frac{\partial H}{\partial P}$ are applied to the equivalent Hamiltonian function, as illustrated in Equation (25) or Equation (42), to derive the correlated Hamiltonian function.

$$H(P, Q) = \frac{d_1}{2}Q^2 + \frac{d_2}{2}P^2 + \frac{d_3}{4}P^4. \tag{43}$$

To assess the stability of the solution, H must remain constant along trajectories $(dH/d\chi = 0)$. The system (42) contains two equilibrium points (EPs): $EP_1 = (0,0)$ and $EP_2 = (\pm\sqrt{-\frac{d_2}{d_3}}, 0)$, dependent upon the condition $\frac{d_2}{d_3} < 0$. Here, EP_2 functions as both a saddle point and a center, whereas EP_1 serves as a center point, exhibiting a trajectory as illustrated in the Figure 7. We can write the characteristic equation of the Jacobian matrix as follows:

$$\eta^2 = -(\frac{d_2}{d_1} + 3\frac{d_3}{d_1}P^2). \tag{44}$$

The characteristic roots of the EP_1 are $\pm\sqrt{E}$, where $E = -\frac{d_2}{d_1}$ and $d_1 \neq 0$, in order to assure its stability. If $E > 0$, the eigenvalues are real and of the opposite sign, implying that the specified EP_1 is a saddle point. The EP_1 is a stable center or of elliptic type if $E < 0$ and the eigenvalues are imaginary. Alternatively, the characteristic roots are $\pm i\sqrt{2E}$ for the stability of the point $(\pm\sqrt{-\frac{d_2}{d_3}}, 0)$, where $\frac{d_2}{d_3} < 0$. If $E > 0$, the eigenvalues are imaginary, signifying that the given EP_2 is a stable center. If $E < 0$, the eigenvalues are real and of opposite signs, signifying that EP_2 represents a saddle point. The phase portraits in Figure 7 illustrate how the bifurcation parameter $E = \frac{d_2}{d_1}$ governs the stability of equilibrium points in the BA model. For $E > 0$, Figure 7 demonstrate that EP_1 acts as an unstable saddle point with divergent trajectories, while EP_2 functions as a stable center enclosed by periodic orbits. On the contrary, when $E < 0$, Figure 7, the stability is reversed: EP_1 converts into a stable center defined by closed orbits, while EP_2 becomes an unstable saddle. The contour plots provide additional validation for these systems, illustrating energy level curves that correspond with saddle (hyperbolic) and center (elliptic) dynamics. For the Hamiltonian system Equation (43), we produce three-dimensional representations of the total surface energy, as illustrated in Figure 8. This research highlights the model's complex dynamical structure, with implications for solitary and periodic wave phenomena.

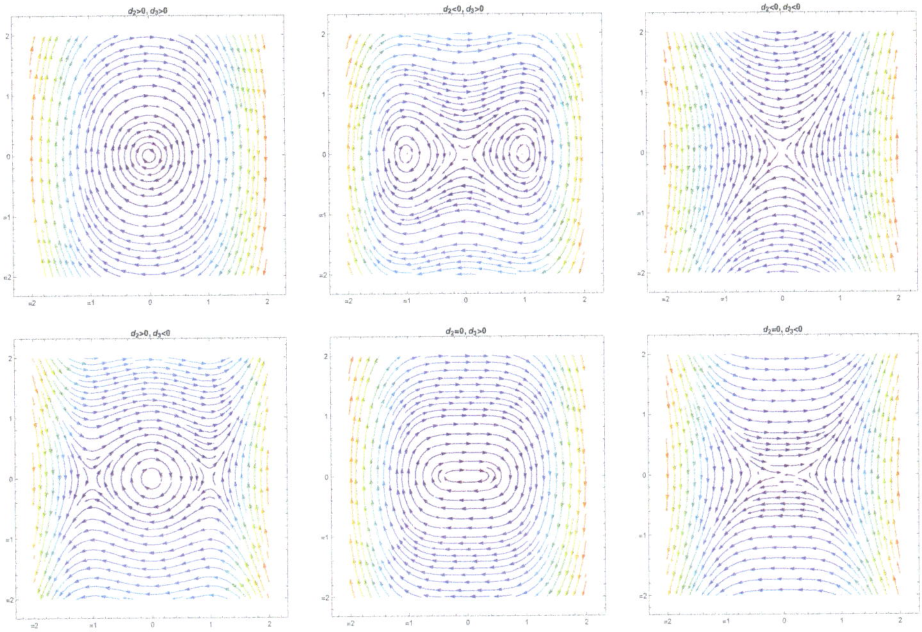

Figure 7. Phase Portrait.

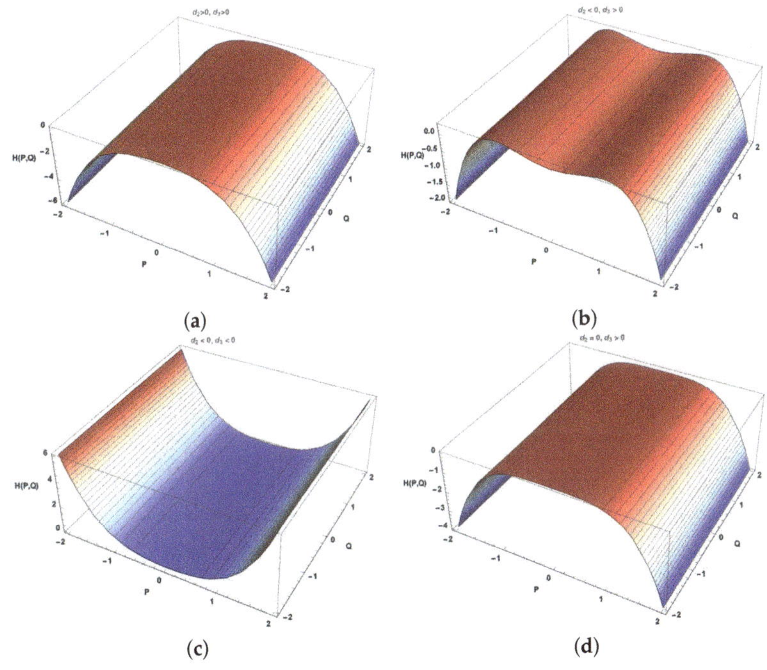

Figure 8. *Cont.*

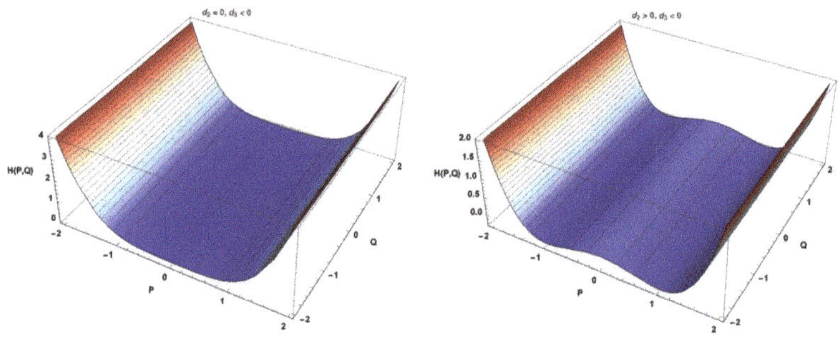

(e) (f)

Figure 8. Three-dimensional representations of the total surface energy.

8. Conclusions

This study presents new optical soliton solutions to the time-fractional Biswas–Arshed (BA) equation by employing the extended simplest equation approach in conjunction with both β-fractional and M-truncated derivatives. The effectively established a range of solution types, including kink, singular, and periodic-singular forms, by choosing random values for the free parameters by using the computational program called Mathematica. These solutions are important because they provide new ideas and instruments to address the complex problems posed by higher-order and dispersive nonlinear partial differential equations. The findings not only improve the theoretical knowledge of the investigated models, but they also have potential uses in clarifying the physical events driven by these equations. The computational method shown here is a strong and efficient mathematical instrument that provides a solid basis for investigating wave solutions in a broad spectrum of complicated nonlinear models across several spheres of nonlinear research. This paper also presents a bifurcation analysis of a nonlinear second-order differential equation by transforming it to a planar dynamical system and determining its Hamiltonian structure. The critical points were obtained analytically, and their stability was assessed using linearization and eigenvalue analysis. It was demonstrated that the nature of the equilibrium points, whether saddle or center, relies on the sign of a bifurcation parameter derived from the system's coefficients. This parameter defines the boundary between qualitatively distinct solution behaviors in the phase space. These results demonstrate the importance of bifurcation theory in anticipating structural changes in nonlinear systems. Although the present study establishes exact soliton solutions and bifurcation analysis for the fractional Biswas–Arshed equation, several limitations should be acknowledged. First, the analysis is restricted to two specific fractional operators: namely the β-derivative and the M-truncated derivative, whereas other modern definitions such as the Caputo–Fabrizio or Atangana–Baleanu operators may yield different behaviors. Second, the approach is primarily analytical and does not include full-scale numerical simulations of the governing PDE, which would be necessary to validate the robustness of the solutions under perturbations. Third, the obtained soliton solutions are derived under certain parametric constraints, which may limit their direct applicability to arbitrary parameter regimes. Finally, only whole-memory operators were considered, while short-memory formulations—known to be important in fading-memory materials—remain an open direction for future research.

Author Contributions: A.Z., W.R. and A.N.—idea, methodology, investigation, writing—review and editing. M.A.A., A.S.A.N. and A.A.—formal analysis, resources, visualization, writing—review and editing. All authors have read and agreed to the published version of the manuscript.

Funding: This work was supported by the Deanship of Scientific Research, Vice Presidency for Graduate Studies and Scientific Research, King Faisal University, Saudi Arabia [KFU253379].

Data Availability Statement: All the data generated during analyzed is available in the manuscript.

Conflicts of Interest: All authors agreed there is no conflicts of interest.

References

1. Laplace, P.S. Mémoire sur les suites. *Mém. Acad. R. Sci. Paris* **1779**, *1782*, 207–309.
2. Zaman, U.H.M.; Arefin, M.A.; Akbar, M.A.; Uddin, M.H. Comprehensive dynamic-type multi-soliton solutions to the fractional order nonlinear evolution equation in ocean engineering. *AIN Shams Eng. J.* **2024**, *15*, 102935. [CrossRef]
3. Khatun, M.A.; Arefin, M.A.; Islam, M.Z.; Akbar, M.A.; Uddin, M.H. New dynamical soliton propagation of fractional type couple modified equal-width and Boussinesq equations. *Alex. Eng. J.* **2022**, *61*, 9949–9963. [CrossRef]
4. Miller, K.S. *An Introduction to the Fractional Calculus and Fractional Differential Equations*; Academic Press: Cambridge, MA, USA, 1993.
5. Iqbal, M.A.; Miah, M.M.; Ali, H.S.; Shahen, N.H.M.; Deifalla, A. New applications of the fractional derivative to extract abundant soliton solutions of the fractional order PDEs in mathematics physics. *Partial. Differ. Equ. Appl. Math.* **2024**, *9*, 100597. [CrossRef]
6. Ahmed, N.; Rani, M.; Dragomir, S.S.; Akgul, A. New exact solutions to space-time fractional telegraph equation with conformable derivative. *Int. J. Mod. Phys. B* **2023**, *37*, 2350275. [CrossRef]
7. Avazzadeh, Z.; Nikan, O.; Machado, J.A.T. Solitary wave solutions of the generalized Rosenau-KdV-RLW equation. *Mathematics* **2020**, *8*, 1601. [CrossRef]
8. Asjad, M.I.; Inç, M.; Faridi, W.A.; Bakar, M.A.; Muhammad, T.; Rezazadeh, H. Optical solitonic structures with singular and non-singular kernel for nonlinear fractional model in quantum mechanics. *Opt. Quantum Electron.* **2023**, *55*, 1–20. [CrossRef]
9. Zaman, U.H.M.; Arefin, M.A.; Akbar, M.A.; Uddin, M.H. Analyzing numerous travelling wave behavior to the fractional-order nonlinear Phi-4 and Allen-Cahn equations throughout a novel technique. *Results Phys.* **2022**, *37*, 105486. [CrossRef]
10. Sadiya, U.; Inç, M.; Arefin, M.A.; Uddin, M.H. Consistent travelling waves solutions to the non-linear time fractional Klein-Gordon and Sine-Gordon equations through extended tanh-function approach. *J. Taibah Univ. Sci.* **2022**, *16*, 594–607. [CrossRef]
11. Zaman, U.H.M.; Arefin, M.A.; Akbar, M.A.; Uddin, M.H. Analytical behavior of soliton solutions to the couple type fractional-order nonlinear evolution equations utilizing a novel technique. *Alex. Eng. J.* **2022**, *61*, 11947–11958. [CrossRef]
12. Arefin, M.A.; Khatun, M.A.; Uddin, M.H.; Inç, M. Investigation of adequate closed form travelling wave solution to the space-time fractional non-linear evolution equations. *J. Ocean Eng. Sci.* **2022**, *7*, 292–303. [CrossRef]
13. Rashed, A.S.; Mostafa, A.N.M.; Wazwaz, A.M.; Mabrouk, S.M. Dynamical behavior and soliton solutions of the Jumarie's space-time fractional modified Benjamin-Bona-Mahony equation in plasma physics. *Rom. Rep. Phys.* **2023**, *75*, 104.
14. Gasimov, Y.; Manafian, J.; Aliyeva, A. New approach of (G'/G)-expansion method to solve the fractional differential equations arising in fluid mechanics. *J. Contemp. Appl. Math.* **2025**, *15*, 124–141.
15. Mohammed, W.W.; Khatun, M.M.; Algolam, M.S.; Sidaoui, R.; Akbar, M.A. Analytical Solitary Wave Solutions of Fractional Tzitzéica Equation Using Expansion Approach: Theoretical Insights and Applications. *Fractal Fract.* **2025**, *9*, 438. [CrossRef]
16. Akbar, M.A.; Akinyemi, L.; Yao, S.W.; Jhangeer, A.; Rezazadeh, H.; Khater, M.M.; Inc, M. Soliton solutions to the Boussinesq equation through sine-Gordon method and Kudryashov method. *Results Phys.* **2021**, *25*, 104228. [CrossRef]
17. Mumtaz, A.; Shakeel, M.; Manan, A.; Shah, N.A.; Ahmed, S.F. A comparative study of new traveling wave solutions for the (2+1)-dimensional fractional Wazwaz–Kaur Boussinesq equation using novel modified (G'/G^2)-expansion method. *AIP Adv.* **2025**, *15*, 035204. [CrossRef]
18. Samir, I.; Ahmed, H.M. Retrieval of solitons and other wave solutions for stochastic nonlinear Schrödinger equation with non-local nonlinearity using the improved modified extended tanh-function method. *J. Opt.* **2024**, 1–10. [CrossRef]
19. Muniyappan, A.; Manik, K.; Saparbekova, A.; Serikbayev, N. Exploring the dynamics of dark and singular solitons in optical fibers using extended rational sinh–cosh and sine–cosine methods. *Symmetry* **2024**, *16*, 561. [CrossRef]
20. Bilal, M.; Khan, A.; Ullah, I.; Khan, H.; Alzabut, J.; Alkhawar, H.M. Application of modified extended direct algebraic method to nonlinear fractional diffusion reaction equation with cubic nonlinearity. *Boundary Value Probl.* **2025**, *2025*, 16. [CrossRef]
21. Hassaballa, A.A.; Satty, A.; Salih, M.; Adam, A.M.; MA, O.; Hamed, Z.; Mohammed, M.S.; Mahmoud, A.F.; Gumma, E.A. Analytical solutions for the nonlinear fractional stochastic KdV equation: Application of the generalized Riccati equation mapping method. *J. Appl. Sci. Eng.* **2025**, *29*, 511–519.
22. Shagolshem, S.; Bira, B.; Nagaraja, K.V. Analysis of soliton wave structure for coupled Higgs equation via Lie symmetry, Paul Painlevé approach and the Unified method. *Nonlinear Dyn.* **2025**, *113*, 11999–12020. [CrossRef]
23. Deresse, A.T.; Mussa, Y.O.; Gizaw, A.K. Approximate analytical solution of two-dimensional nonlinear time-fractional damped wave equation in the Caputo fractional derivative operator. *Math. Probl. Eng.* **2022**, *2022*, 7004412. [CrossRef]

24. Alam, M.N.; Ilhan, O.A.; Manafian, J.; Asjad, M.I.; Rezazadeh, H.; Baskonus, H.M.; Macias-Diaz, J.E. New results of some of the conformable models arising in dynamical systems. *Adv. Math. Phys.* **2022**, *2022*, 7753879. [CrossRef]
25. Abdulla, S.O.; Abdulazeez, S.T.; Modanli, M. Comparison of third-order fractional partial differential equation based on the fractional operators using the explicit finite difference method. *Alex. Eng. J.* **2023**, *70*, 37–44. [CrossRef]
26. Naeem, M.; Yasmin, H.; Shah, R.; Shah, N.A.; Chung, J.D. A comparative study of fractional partial differential equations with the help of Yang transform. *Symmetry* **2023**, *15*, 146. [CrossRef]
27. Laoubi, M.; Odibat, Z.; Maayah, B. Effective optimized decomposition algorithms for solving nonlinear fractional differential equations. *J. Comput. Nonlinear Dyn.* **2023**, *18*, 021001. [CrossRef]
28. Erman, S.; Demir, A.; Ozbilge, E. Solving inverse non-linear fractional differential equations by generalized Chelyshkov wavelets. *Alex. Eng. J.* **2023**, *66*, 947–956. [CrossRef]
29. Chatzarakis, G.E.; Logaarasi, K. Forced oscillation of impulsive fractional partial differential equations. *Partial Differ. Equ. Appl. Math.* **2023**, *7*, 100478. [CrossRef]
30. Kumar, D.; Dubey, V.P.; Dubey, S.; Singh, J.; Alshehri, A.M. Computational analysis of local fractional partial differential equations in realm of fractal calculus. *Chaos Solitons Fractals* **2023**, *167*, 113009. [CrossRef]
31. Alesemi, M.; Shahrani, J.S.A.; Iqbal, N.; Shah, R.; Nonlaopon, K. Analysis and numerical simulation of system of fractional partial differential equations with non-singular kernel operators. *Symmetry* **2023**, *15*, 233. [CrossRef]
32. Alderremy, A.A.; Shah, R.; Shah, N.A.; Aly, S.; Nonlaopon, K. Comparison of two modified analytical approaches for the systems of time fractional partial differential equations. *AIMS Math.* **2023**, *8*, 7142–7162. [CrossRef]
33. Mallick, B.; Sahu, P.K.; Routaray, M. An iterative method for solving time-fractional partial differential equations with proportional delays. *Mathematics* **2023**, *11*, 74.
34. Sultana, M.; Arshad, U.; Abdel-Aty, A.H.; Akgül, A.; Mahmoud, M.; Eleuch, H. New numerical approach of solving highly nonlinear fractional partial differential equations via fractional novel analytical method. *Fractal Fract.* **2022**, *6*, 512. [CrossRef]
35. Razzaq, W.; Zafar, A.; Nazir, A.; Ahmad, H.; Zaagan, A.A. Dark, bright and singular optical solitons for Biswas–Milovic equation with Kerr and dual power law nonlinearities. *Mod. Phys. Lett. B* **2024**, *39*, 2450443. [CrossRef]
36. Mohamed, M.; Yousif, M.; Hamza, A.E. Solving nonlinear fractional partial differential equations using the Elzaki transform method and the homotopy perturbation method. *Abstr. Appl. Anal.* **2022**, *2022*, 743234. [CrossRef]
37. Rashid, S.; Ashraf, R.; Jarad, F. Strong interaction of Jafari decomposition method with nonlinear fractional-order partial differential equations arising in plasma via the singular and nonsingular kernels. *AIMS Math.* **2022**, *7*, 7936–7963. [CrossRef]
38. Alderremy, A.A.; Shah, R.; Iqbal, N.; Aly, S.; Nonlaopon, K. Fractional series solution construction for nonlinear fractional reaction-diffusion Brusselator model utilizing Laplace residual power series. *Symmetry* **2022**, *14*, 1944. [CrossRef]
39. Pandey, P.; Singh, J. An efficient computational approach for nonlinear variable order fuzzy fractional partial differential equations. *Comput. Appl. Math.* **2022**, *41*, 38. [CrossRef]
40. Biswas, A.; Arshed, S. Optical solitons in presence of higher order dispersions and absence of self-phase modulation. *Optik* **2018**, *174*, 452–459. [CrossRef]
41. Alhojilan, Y.; Ahmed, H.M.; Rabie, W.B. Stochastic solitons in birefringent fibers for Biswas–Arshed equation with multiplicative white noise via Itô calculus by modified extended mapping method. *Symmetry* **2023**, *15*, 207. [CrossRef]
42. Cinar, M.; Secer, A.; Bayram, M. On the optical soliton solutions of time-fractional Biswas–Arshed equation including the beta or M-truncated derivatives. *Opt. Quantum Electron.* **2023**, *55*, 186. [CrossRef]
43. Li, Z. Bifurcation and traveling wave solution to fractional Biswas–Arshed equation with the beta time derivative. *Chaos Solitons Fractals* **2022**, *160*, 112249. [CrossRef]
44. Akram, G.; Sadaf, M.; Zainab, I. The dynamical study of Biswas–Arshed equation via modified auxiliary equation method. *Optik* **2022**, *255*, 168614. [CrossRef]
45. Akbulut, A.; Islam, S.R. Study on the Biswas–Arshed equation with the beta time derivative. *Int. J. Appl. Comput. Math.* **2022**, *8*, 167. [CrossRef]
46. Kumar, S.; Niwas, M. New optical soliton solutions of Biswas–Arshed equation using the generalised exponential rational function approach and Kudryashov's simplest equation approach. *Pramana* **2022**, *96*, 204. [CrossRef]
47. Kudryashov, N.A. Simplest equation method to look for exact solutions of nonlinear differential equations. *Chaos Solitons Fractals* **2005**, *24*, 1217–1231. [CrossRef]
48. Kudryashov, N.A. Exact solitary waves of the Fisher equation. *Phys. Lett. A* **2005**, *342*, 99–106. [CrossRef]
49. Bilige, S.; Chaolu, T.; Wang, X. Application of the extended simplest equation method to the coupled Schrödinger–Boussinesq equation. *Appl. Math. Comput.* **2013**, *224*, 517–523. [CrossRef]
50. Bilige, S.; Chaolu, T. An extended simplest equation method and its application to several forms of the fifth-order KdV equation. *Appl. Math. Comput.* **2010**, *216*, 3146–3153. [CrossRef]
51. Shehata, M.S.; Bekir, A. New perceptions for the bright and dark soliton solutions to the modified nonlinear Schrödinger equation. *Int. J. Mod. Phys. B* **2023**, *37*, 2350204. [CrossRef]

52. Wang, K.J.; Wang, G.D. Exact traveling wave solutions for the system of the ion sound and Langmuir waves by using three effective methods. *Results Phys.* **2022**, *35*, 105390. [CrossRef]
53. Atangana, A.; Baleanu, D. New fractional derivatives with nonlocal and non-singular kernel: Theory and application to heat transfer model. *arXiv* **2016**, arXiv:1602.03408. [CrossRef]
54. Yépez-Martínez, H.; Gómez-Aguilar, J.F.; Baleanu, D. Beta-derivative and sub-equation method applied to the optical solitons in medium with parabolic law nonlinearity and higher order dispersion. *Optik* **2018**, *155*, 357–365. [CrossRef]
55. Sousa, J.V.D.C.; de Oliveira, E.C. A new truncated *M*-fractional derivative type unifying some fractional derivative types with classical properties. *arXiv* **2017**, arXiv:1704.08187.
56. Han, T.; Li, Z.; Yuan, J. Optical solitons and single traveling wave solutions of Biswas–Arshed equation in birefringent fibers with the beta-time derivative. *AIMS Math.* **2022**, *7*, 15282–15297. [CrossRef]
57. Sumelka, W.; Łuczak, B.; Gajewski, T.; Voyiadjis, G.Z. Modelling of AAA in the framework of time-fractional damage hyperelasticity. *Int. J. Solids Struct.* **2020**, *206*, 30–42. [CrossRef]
58. Zhou, Y.; Zhang, Y. Noether symmetries for fractional generalized Birkhoffian systems in terms of classical and combined Caputo derivatives. *Acta Mech.* **2020**, *231*, 3017–3029. [CrossRef]

mathematics

Article

Nonlinear Dynamica Analysis of a Diffusion-Driven Bacterial Density Model: Integrability and Bifurcation Analysis

Adel Elmandouh

Department of Mathematics and Statistics, College of Science, King Faisal University, P.O. Box 400, Al-Ahsa 31982, Saudi Arabia; aelmandouh@kfu.edu.sa

Abstract

This work investigates the dynamical properties of the Kolmogorov–Petrovskii–Piskunov (KPP) equation. We begin by establishing its non-integrability through the Painlevé test. Using a traveling wave transformation, we reduce the equation to a planar dynamical system, which we identify as non-conservative. A subsequent bifurcation analysis, supported by Bendixson's criterion, rules out the existence of periodic orbits and, thus, periodic solutions—a finding further validated by phase portraits. Furthermore, we classify the types and co-dimensions of the bifurcations present in the system. We demonstrate that under certain conditions, the system can exhibit saddle-node, transcritical, and pitchfork bifurcations, while Hopf and Bogdanov–Takens bifurcations cannot occur. This study concludes by systematically deriving a power series solution for the reduced equation.

Keywords: Kolmogorov–Petrovskii–Piskunov; bifurcation; Painlevé analysis

MSC: 35C07; 35C08; 37K40; 83C15

1. Introduction

The combination of mathematical modeling with experimental biology has profoundly advanced our understanding of complex biological phenomena in recent decades. These models, grounded in empirical data, formally describe the components, architecture, and interactive processes of a system. They are not merely descriptive but predictive tools that allow for the simulation of scenarios, the extension of biological theory, and the formulation of novel hypotheses. The quantitative power of this approach is evidenced by its applications in solving real-world problems, such as predicting outcomes precisely prior to action being taken, and so on [1,2]. In recent years, researchers in mathematics and physics have shown growing interest in exploring the fundamental characteristics of bacterial cells, which are essential to sustaining all animal life on Earth. Their investigations often rely on theoretical frameworks, mathematical modeling, and abstract representations of biological systems to understand bacterial morphology, growth dynamics, and behavioral patterns. Bacteria constitute a vast group of proteolytic microorganisms, typically measuring only a few micrometers and exhibiting diverse shapes, such as spherical, rod-like, and spiral forms. Recognized as among the earliest life forms to emerge on the planet, bacteria thrive in extreme environments—including radioactive waste, subterranean layers of the Earth's crust, soil, aquatic habitats, and acidic thermal springs. Despite their ubiquity, only about 27% of bacterial species are cultivable under laboratory conditions, a small fraction compared to the estimated global population of approximately 5×10^{30} cells. The scientific discipline dedicated to understanding bacterial biology and its implications for human life is known as bacteriology [3–5].

The growing capacity to model complex natural systems represents a significant advance in nonlinear science. This progress is largely driven by the application of nonlinear differential equations, which provide the essential mathematical framework for phenomena across disciplines such as biology, fluid dynamics, and the physical sciences. As a result, these equations are a central focus of contemporary theoretical and applied research [6–9]. This study is devoted to the analysis of nonlinear partial differential equations (NLPDEs), which are pivotal in modeling a broad spectrum of complex phenomena. Consequently, the pursuit of exact solutions for these equations has emerged as a central and dynamic area of research. A principal objective in this field is the derivation of such solutions, particularly solitary wave and traveling wave solutions, to gain deeper insight into the underlying systems. To this end, a diverse suite of analytical techniques have been developed and applied to various NLPDE models. Notable methods cited in the literature include the generalized exponential rational function method [10] and the generalized Kudryashov method [11,12]. The analytical toolkit is further enriched by techniques such as the improved simple equation method, the modified F-expansion method [13], the exp-function method [14], the modified Jacobi elliptic function expansion method [15], Painlevé analysis [16–18], Hirota's method [19,20], auto-Bäcklund transformations [21–23], and bifurcation methods [24–26].

We consider the nonlinear KPP equation:

$$\mathcal{N}_t - \mathcal{N}_{xx} + \rho\mathcal{N} + \delta\mathcal{N}^2 + \sigma\mathcal{N}^3 = 0, \tag{1}$$

where ρ, δ, and σ are real-valued parameters, the subscripts represent the partial derivatives, and $\mathcal{N}(x,t)$ represents the state variable in a spatiotemporal domain. Originally introduced by the Russian mathematicians Kolmogorov, Petrovsky, and Piskunov in 1937 [27,28], the KPP equation provides a foundational framework for modeling a wide array of phenomena in population dynamics, chemical kinetics, and physics. The KPP equation has been the subject of extensive research, with numerous studies addressing it from various perspectives. The existing literature reveals a rich tapestry of analytical and numerical techniques applied to this model. For instance, several studies have focused on deriving exact solutions. The generalized Kudryashov method was employed in [29] to obtain general solutions, all of which were expressed in exponential form. Similarly, Ref. [30] constructed exact solutions by combining the Riccati equation method with a generalized extended (G'/G)-expansion, while [31] utilized a modified sub-equation method for the same purpose. Other analytical approaches include the G'/G-expansion method applied in [32] for traveling wave solutions and the simple equation technique used in [33] to obtain time-dependent variable solitons. On the numerical front, diverse schemes have been developed. The work in [34] introduced a novel algorithm based on Adams–Bashforth extrapolation, reporting superior efficiency over traditional methods. Furthermore, Ref. [35] applied a hybrid approach, using the generalized Sinh–Gordon equation method alongside B-spline schemes to acquire numerical solutions. Approximate analytical oscillatory solutions for a generalized KPP equation were also discussed in [36] using dynamical systems theory and a hypothesis undetermined method. The framework of the KPP equation has also been extended in several directions. A prominent area of research involves its generalization through fractional derivatives, applied to either spatial or temporal coordinates, or both. Within this context, the homotopy perturbation method was used in [37] to find approximate solutions for the fractional KPP equation, and the modified extended direct algebraic method was applied in [38] to construct propagating soliton solutions for this fractional variant. Another significant extension incorporates random effects by adding stochastic perturbation terms.

The significance of the KPP Equation (1) is further underscored by its role as a unifying framework for several seminal models. Specific parameter choices recover well-known equations: for instance, the Fitzhugh–Nagumo equation for nerve impulse transmission is obtained with $\sigma = 1$ and $\delta = -(\rho + 1)$ $(0 < \rho < 1)$, where $\mathcal{N}(x,t)$ represents the electric potential [39,40]. Similarly, the Fisher equation, describing the spread of an advantageous gene ($\mathcal{N}(x,t)$ being its density), results from the parameters $\rho = -1$, $\delta = 1$, and $\sigma = 0$ [41,42]. Furthermore, the Huxley equation, which models cross-bridge dynamics in muscle physiology, corresponds to the case where $\sigma = 1$ and $\delta = -(\rho + 1)$ with $\rho \neq 0$ [43].

Despite the KPP equation's significance in modeling numerous phenomena, a comprehensive analysis of its integrability and bifurcation behavior remains absent from the literature, a gap that this work aims to address.

The remainder of this work is structured as follows: The integrability of the KPP equation is analyzed in Section 2 using Painlevé analysis. Bifurcation analysis and phase portraits are conducted in Section 3. Section 4 involves a proof of the non-existence of periodic solutions for the KPP equation and derives a series solution. Finally, Section 5 summarizes the results of the study.

2. Integrability Analysis

The integrability of the governing equation (Equation (1)) is investigated here by assessing its Painlevé property. This is accomplished through a singularity analysis based on the ARS algorithm, which is summarized in Appendix A to ensure a self-contained presentation. The fundamental question addressed is whether all possible solutions exhibit single-valued expansion about any movable singularity manifold.

We consider a solution expansion in the neighborhood of a non-characteristic singular manifold $\phi(x,t) = 0$ $(\phi_x \phi_t \neq 0)$:

$$\mathcal{N}(x,t) = \phi^{\nu}(x,t) \sum_{s=0}^{\infty} f_s(x,t)\phi^{s}(x,t), \tag{2}$$

where ν is a negative integer and the coefficients $f_s(x,t)$ are analytic near $\phi = 0$, with $f_0 \neq 0$.

Leading-Order Analysis: The dominant behavior emerges from the leading term:

$$\mathcal{N}(x,t) \approx f_0(x,t)\phi^{\nu}(x,t). \tag{3}$$

Substituting Expression (3) into Equation (1) reveals that the most singular terms balance when $\nu = -1$. The leading coefficient follows from the ϕ^{-3} terms:

$$f_0(x,t) = \sqrt{\frac{2}{\sigma}}\phi_x. \tag{4}$$

Resonance Analysis: The positions where arbitrary functions may enter Series (2) are identified by substituting

$$\mathcal{N}(x,t) = f_0\phi^{-1} + f_p\phi^{p-1}, \tag{5}$$

and collecting ϕ^{p-3} terms yields the resonance condition:

$$f_p\phi_x^2(p+1)(p-4) = 0. \tag{6}$$

The functions $f_p(x,t)$ are arbitrary if $p = -1, 4$ which are named the resonances. The value $p = -1$ is the only acceptable resonance corresponding to the free location of the singularity manifold itself, while $p = 4$ suggests possible arbitrariness at the fifth term in Series (2).

Verification of Compatibility Conditions: To validate the Painlevé property, we examine whether sufficient arbitrariness exists at the resonance positions. Substituting the finite expansion

$$\mathcal{N}(x,t) = \sum_{s=0}^{4} f_s(x,t)\phi^{s-1} \tag{7}$$

into Equation (1) generates determining equations for the coefficients by examining different powers of ϕ:

Power ϕ^{-3}: Confirms the leading coefficient (Equation (4)).

Power ϕ^{-2}: Determines the coefficient $f_1(x,t)$ as follows:

$$f_1(x,t) = -\frac{2\delta\phi_x + \sqrt{2\sigma}(3\phi_{xx} - \phi_t)}{6\sigma\phi_x}. \tag{8}$$

Power ϕ^{-1}: Yields the second coefficient:

$$f_2(x,t) = \frac{\sqrt{2}\left[6\sigma\phi_x(\phi_{xxx} - 6\phi_{xt}) + 2(\delta^2 - 3\rho\sigma)\phi_x^2 - \sigma\phi_t(\phi_t - 6\phi_{xx}) - 9\sigma\phi_{xx}^2\right]}{36\sigma^{3/2}\phi_x^3}. \tag{9}$$

Power ϕ^0: Provides the third coefficient:

$$\begin{aligned} f_3(x,t) = \frac{1}{216\sqrt{\sigma^7}\phi_x^5}\Big\{&\sigma^3\sqrt{2}[-9\phi_{xxxx}\phi_x^2 - 18\phi_x\phi_{xxx}(\phi_t - 3\phi_{xx}) + 18\phi_{txx}\phi_x^2 - 54\phi_{xx}^2(1+\phi_t)] \\ &-6\sigma^2\sqrt{2}\phi_{xx}[9\sigma\phi_x\phi_{xt} + (3\sigma\rho - \delta^2)\phi_x^2 + 4\sigma\phi_t^2] + 3\sigma^3\sqrt{2}(10\phi_t\phi_x\phi_{xt} - 3\phi_{tt}\phi_x^2) \\ &+2\delta\sqrt{\sigma^3}(9\rho\sigma - 2\delta^2)\phi_x^3 + 6\sigma^2\sqrt{2}(3\rho\sigma - \delta^2)\phi_t\phi_x^2 + 4\sigma^3\sqrt{2}\phi_t^3\Big\}. \end{aligned} \tag{10}$$

Power ϕ^1 (Resonance $p = 4$): The condition at the resonance produces

$$\begin{aligned} 3(\sigma f_0^2 - 2\phi_x^2)f_4 = {} & 2f_3\phi_{xx} + f_{2,xx} + 4f_{3,x}\phi_x - 2f_3\phi_t - f_{2,t} \\ & - [3\sigma f_2^2 + (6\sigma f_1 + 2\delta)f_3]f_0 - (3\sigma f_1^2 + 2\delta f_1 + \rho)f_2. \end{aligned} \tag{11}$$

Substitution of the known coefficients f_0–f_3 into Equation (11) demonstrates that f_4 cannot be chosen arbitrarily—the compatibility condition fails at the resonance $p = 4$.

The failure to satisfy the necessary condition at resonance $p = 4$ establishes that Equation (1) lacks the Painlevé property, leading to the following theorem:

Theorem 1. *Equation* (1) *does not possess the Painlevé property and is therefore non-integrable in the Painlevé sense.*

3. Bifurcation Analysis

The non-integrability of Equation (1) immediately implies that it cannot be solved using standard integrability-based techniques, such as the inverse scattering transform or soliton theory, which are characteristic of integrable PDEs. Non-integrable PDEs are typically nonlinear and present a greater challenge for analytical solution. They generally do not possess explicit analytic solutions or an infinite set of conserved quantities [44]. Consequently, researchers typically rely on approximate, numerical, or perturbative methods for their study. Furthermore, a dynamical systems approach can be effectively employed to gain qualitative insights into the nature of their solutions.

This section aims to employ the dynamical systems framework to conduct a qualitative examination of the solutions to Equation (1). We consider solutions of the KPP Equation (1) in the form of

$$\mathcal{N} = \psi(\theta), \quad \theta = ax - t, \tag{12}$$

where ψ is a real-valued function, a is a non-zero constant representing the wave number, and θ is the wave variable. Substituting this form of Equation (12) into Equation (1), it simplifies to an ODE. Consequently, the resulting equation is

$$a^2\psi'' + \psi' - \rho\psi - \delta\psi^2 - \sigma\psi^3 = 0, \tag{13}$$

where $'$ indicates the derivative with respect to θ. This section endeavors to explore some dynamical aspects to Equation (1). The qualitative theory for planar integrable systems [45] is applied to analyze Equation (13), which is equivalent to the dynamical system

$$\begin{aligned} \psi' &= y, \\ y' &= \frac{1}{a^2}[-y + \rho\psi + \delta\psi^2 + \sigma\psi^3]. \end{aligned} \tag{14}$$

The dynamical system (14) is non-conservative, since $\mathrm{div}(\psi', y') = -\frac{1}{a^2} \neq 0$. To be more precise, it is chaotic because $\mathrm{div}(\psi', y')$ is always negative. The equilibrium states of (14) are given by the points $Q = (\psi_0, 0)$, where ψ_0 represents the real solutions of the cubic equation

$$\psi_0[\sigma\psi_0^2 + \delta\psi_0 + \rho] = 0. \tag{15}$$

On the other hand, to determine the nature of the equilibrium points, we consider that the linearized system of (14) with respect to the equilibrium point $(\psi_0, 0)$ is

$$\begin{aligned} \begin{pmatrix} \xi_1 \\ \xi_2 \end{pmatrix}' &= \begin{pmatrix} 0 & 1 \\ \frac{1}{a^2}[3\sigma\psi_0^2 + 2\delta\psi_0 + \rho] & \frac{-1}{a^2} \end{pmatrix} \begin{pmatrix} \xi_1 \\ \xi_2 \end{pmatrix}, \\ &= J_0(\psi_0, 0) \begin{pmatrix} \xi_1 \\ \xi_2 \end{pmatrix}. \end{aligned} \tag{16}$$

Here, ξ_1 and ξ_2 denote the perturbed variables, and $J_0(\psi_0, 0)$ represents the coefficient matrix of the linearized system (16). More precisely, it corresponds to the Jacobian matrix of the nonlinear system (14) evaluated at the equilibrium point $(\psi_0, 0)$. The associated eigenvalues are given by

$$\lambda_{1,2} = \frac{1}{2}\left[\tau \pm \sqrt{\tau^2 - 4\det(J_0(\psi_0, 0))}\right], \tag{17}$$

where

$$\tau = -\frac{1}{a^2}, \qquad \det(J_0) = -\frac{1}{a^2}(\rho + 2\delta\psi_0 + 3\sigma\psi_0^2). \tag{18}$$

The stability of the equilibrium point $(\psi_0, 0)$ is detected by evaluating the magnitude and sign of the eigenvalues derived from Equation (17). In particular, the point is deemed stable if both eigenvalues have negative real parts, unstable when at least one exhibits a positive real part, and neutrally stable if the real parts of both eigenvalues vanish. Moreover, a broader classification of the equilibrium behavior can be established based on the qualitative nature of the eigenvalues; for further discussion, refer to [45].

The bifurcation structure and phase portrait of the planar dynamical system (14) are analyzed with respect to the parameters σ, ρ, and δ. To begin, we identify the system's equilibrium points by introducing the discriminant $\Delta = \delta^2 - 4\sigma\rho$. The number of these equilibrium points is governed by the sign of Δ: whether it is negative, zero, or positive. Accordingly, each case is examined separately to capture the distinct dynamical behaviors that emerge.

Case A: If $\Delta < 0$, which is equivalent to $|\delta| < 2\sqrt{\sigma\rho}$ with $\sigma\rho > 0$, then Equation (15) admits a unique real solution, namely, $\psi_0 = 0$. Consequently, the point $Q_0 = (0,0)$ serves as the sole equilibrium of the system described by Equation (14). To detect the nature of the equilibrium point Q_0, we compute the eigenvalues (17) at Q_0 and obtain

$$\lambda_{1,2}(Q_0) = \frac{1}{2a^2}\left[-1 \pm \sqrt{1+4a^2\rho}\right]. \tag{19}$$

Since $\sigma\rho > 0$, the parameters σ and ρ own the same sign. This leads to the following possible scenarios:

(a) If $(\sigma,\rho) \in \mathbb{R}^+ \times \mathbb{R}^+$, then the eigenvalues $\lambda_{1,2}(Q_0)$ are real and satisfy the inequality $\lambda_2(Q_0) < 0 < \lambda_1(Q_0)$. This configuration indicates that the equilibrium point Q_0 is a saddle point, exhibiting hyperbolic behavior. Since one of the eigenvalues is positive, the equilibrium is inherently unstable. The corresponding phase portrait is illustrated in Figure 1a.

(b) For parameter values $(\sigma,\rho) \in \mathbb{R}^- \times (-\infty, -\frac{1}{4a^2})$, the eigenvalues given in Equation (19) are complex with negative real parts. This indicates that the equilibrium point Q_0 behaves as a stable focus or stable spiral point. The corresponding phase portrait is illustrated in Figure 1b.

(c) For $(\sigma,\rho) \in \mathbb{R}^- \times (-\frac{1}{4a^2}, 0)$, the eigenvalues are real and strictly negative, satisfying $\lambda_2(Q_0) < \lambda_1(Q_0) < 0$. This configuration implies that the equilibrium point Q_0 is a stable node. The associated phase portrait is presented in Figure 1c.

(d) Finally, when $(\sigma,\rho) \in \mathbb{R}^- \times \left\{\frac{-1}{4a^2}\right\}$, the eigenvalues coincide and are strictly negative, given by $\lambda_1(Q_0) = \lambda_2(Q_0) = -\frac{1}{2a^2}$. This configuration characterizes the equilibrium point Q_0 as a stable star. The corresponding phase portrait is illustrated in Figure 1d.

We summarize the nature of the equilibrium point Q_0 in Table 1.

Table 1. The nature of the equilibrium point Q_0 if $|\delta| < 2\sqrt{\sigma\rho}$ and $\sigma\rho > 0$.

No.	Sign of σ	Sign of ρ	Classification of Q_0	Figure
1.	$+$	$+$	Saddle point	Figure1a
2.	$-$	$(-\infty, \frac{-1}{4a^2})$	Stable focus or Stable spiral point	Figure 1b
3.	$-$	$(-\frac{1}{4a^2}, 0)$	Stable node	Figure 1c
4.	$-$	$\frac{-1}{4a^2}$	Stable star	Figure 1d

Case B: If $\Delta = 0$, which implies $|\delta| = 2\sqrt{\sigma\rho}$ provided that $\sigma\rho > 0$, then Equation (15) admits two real-valued solutions: $\psi_0 = 0$ and $\psi_0 = -\frac{\delta}{2\sigma}$. As a result, the planar dynamical system (14) possess two equilibrium points: $Q_0 = (0,0)$ and $Q_1 = (-\frac{\delta}{2\sigma}, 0)$. To assort the nature of these points, we compute the eigenvalues (19) at them. We find

$$\lambda_{1,2}(Q_0) = \frac{1}{2a^2}\left[-1 \pm \sqrt{1+4a^2\rho}\right], \qquad \lambda_{1,2}(Q_1) = 0, -\frac{1}{a^2}. \tag{20}$$

The equilibrium Q_1 is non-hyperbolic, possessing one zero and one negative eigenvalue, which commonly indicates a saddle-node type. The behavior of Q_0, on the other hand, depends on the parameter ρ, and its type is exactly as described in Table 1. Table 2 summarizes the nature of these equilibrium points and the corresponding phase portraits.

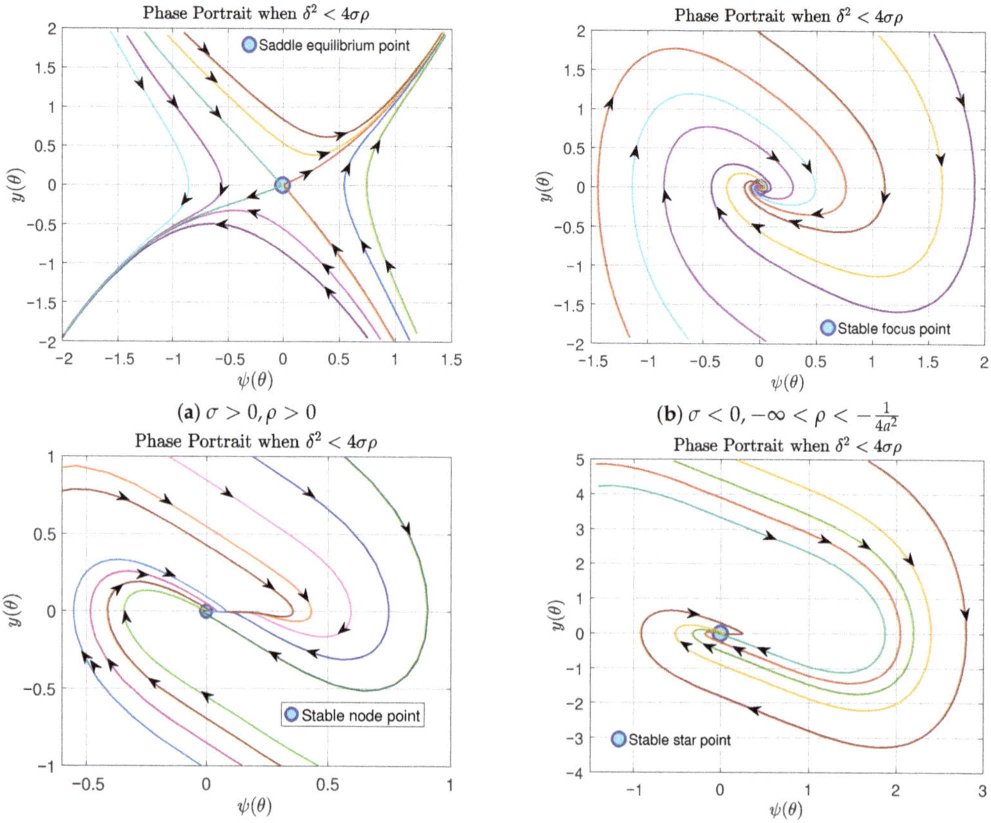

(**a**) $\sigma > 0, \rho > 0$ (**b**) $\sigma < 0, -\infty < \rho < -\frac{1}{4a^2}$

(**c**) $\sigma < 0, -\frac{1}{4a^2} < \rho < 0$ (**d**) $\sigma < 0, \rho = -\frac{1}{4a^2}$

Figure 1. Phase portrait of system (14) corresponding to the case $\delta^2 < 4\sigma\rho$.

Table 2. Classifications of the equilibrium points $Q_{0,1}$ if $\delta = 2\sqrt{\sigma\rho}$ and $\sigma\rho > 0$.

No.	Sign of		Classification of		Figure
	σ	ρ	Q_0	Q_2	
1.	+	+	Saddle point	Saddle node	Figure 2a
2.	−	$(-\infty, \frac{-1}{4a^2})$	Stable focus		Figure 2b
3.	−	$(-\frac{1}{4a^2}, 0)$	Stable node		Figure 2c
4.	−	$\frac{-1}{4a^2}$	Stable star		Figure 2d

Case C: When $\Delta > 0$, corresponding to the condition $\delta^2 > 4\sigma\rho$, Equation (15) yields two distinct real solutions: $\psi_0 = 0$ and $\psi_0 = \frac{1}{2\sigma}[-\delta \pm \sqrt{\delta^2 - 4\sigma\rho}]$. Accordingly, the planar dynamical system Equation (14) possesses two equilibrium points: $Q_0 = (0,0)$ and $Q_{2,3} = (\frac{1}{2\sigma}[-\delta \pm \sqrt{\delta^2 - 4\sigma\rho}], 0)$. To explore the nature of these equilibrium points, we compute the eigenvalues (19) at them. We find

$$\lambda_{1,2}(Q_0) = \frac{1}{2a^2}\left[-1 \pm \sqrt{1 + 4a^2\rho}\right],$$
$$\lambda_{1,2}(Q_{2,3}) = \frac{1}{2a^2}\left[-1 \pm \frac{\sqrt{2a^2\sigma(\Delta - \delta\sqrt{\Delta}) + \sigma^2}}{\sigma}\right]. \quad (21)$$

Consequently, two distinct regimes arise when $\sigma\rho > 0$, corresponding to either $\delta > 2\sqrt{\sigma\rho}$ or $\delta < -2\sqrt{\sigma\rho}$. Additionally, in the case where $\sigma\rho < 0$, the inequality $\delta^2 > 4\sigma\rho$ holds automatically. Let us consider these scenarios, separately:

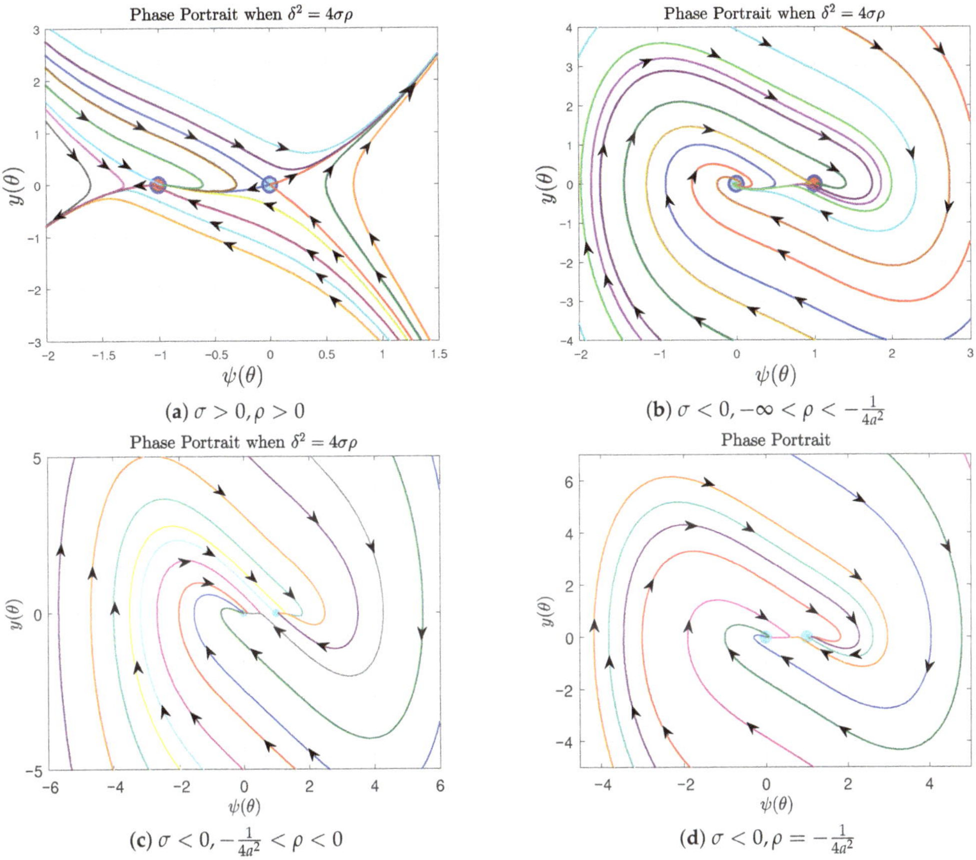

(**a**) $\sigma > 0, \rho > 0$ (**b**) $\sigma < 0, -\infty < \rho < -\frac{1}{4a^2}$

(**c**) $\sigma < 0, -\frac{1}{4a^2} < \rho < 0$ (**d**) $\sigma < 0, \rho = -\frac{1}{4a^2}$

Figure 2. Phase portrait of system (14) corresponding to the case $\delta^2 = 4\sigma\rho$.

I. We analyze the case in which $\delta > 2\sqrt{\sigma\rho}$ provided that $\sigma\rho > 0$.

(a) When $(\sigma, \rho) \in \mathbb{R}^+ \times \mathbb{R}^+$, the eigenvalues $\lambda_{1,2}(Q_{0,2})$ are real and satisfy $\lambda_2(Q_{0,2}) < 0 < \lambda_1(Q_{0,2})$, indicating that the equilibrium points Q_0 and Q_2 are saddle points with hyperbolic character. In contrast, the eigenvalues $\lambda_{1,2}(Q_3)$ are complex with negative real parts, signifying that Q_3 is a stable focus or stable spiral point. The corresponding phase portrait is depicted in Figure 3a.

(b) When $(\sigma, \rho) \in \mathbb{R}^- \times \left(-\frac{1}{4a^2}, 0\right)$, the eigenvalues $\lambda_{1,2}(Q_{0,2,3})$ are real and satisfy the inequality $\lambda_2(Q_{0,2,3}) < \lambda_1(Q_{0,2,3}) < 0$. This indicates that the equilibrium points Q_0, Q_2, and Q_3 are stable nodes. The phase portrait corresponding to System (15) is shown in Figure 3b.

(c) When $(\sigma, \rho) \in \mathbb{R}^- \times \left(-\infty, \frac{-1}{4a^2}\right)$, the eigenvalues $\lambda_{1,2}(Q_0)$ and $\lambda_{1,2}(Q_2)$ are complex with negative real parts, indicating that the equilibrium points Q_0 and Q_2 are stable foci (stable spiral points). In contrast, the eigenvalues $\lambda_{1,2}(Q_3)$ are real and satisfy $\lambda_2(Q_3) < 0 < \lambda_1(Q_3)$, which implies that Q_3 is a saddle point with hyperbolic character. The corresponding phase portrait for this configuration is illustrated in Figure 3c.

(d) When $(\sigma, \rho) \in \mathbb{R}^- \times \{\frac{-1}{4a^2}\}$, the equilibrium points exhibit distinct stability properties. Q_0, with a repeated negative eigenvalue $\lambda_{1,2} = -\frac{1}{2a^2}$, is a stable star. Q_2 is a stable spiral, as its eigenvalues are complex with a negative real part. In contrast, Q_3 is a saddle point (hyperbolic equilibrium point) because its real eigenvalues satisfy $\lambda_2(Q_3) < 0 < \lambda_1(Q_3)$. This configuration is illustrated in the phase portrait of Figure 4d.

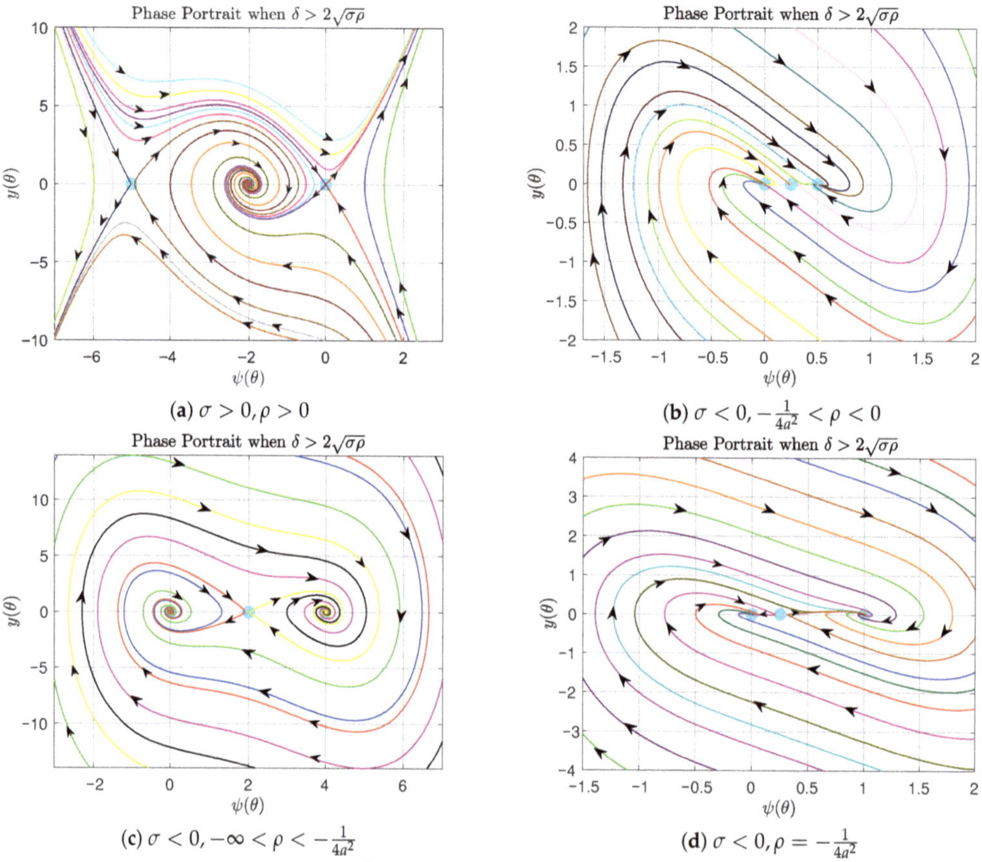

(**a**) $\sigma > 0, \rho > 0$ (**b**) $\sigma < 0, -\frac{1}{4a^2} < \rho < 0$

(**c**) $\sigma < 0, -\infty < \rho < -\frac{1}{4a^2}$ (**d**) $\sigma < 0, \rho = -\frac{1}{4a^2}$

Figure 3. Phase portrait of system (14) corresponding to the case $\delta^2 > 4\sigma\rho$.

The dynamical system (14) exhibits a qualitatively similar phase portrait under the condition $\delta < -2\sqrt{\sigma\rho}$ with $\sigma\rho > 0$. Thus, we introduce a summary of these results without details in Table 3.

Table 3. Classifications of the equilibrium points $Q_{0,2,3}$ if $\delta < -2\sqrt{\sigma\rho}$ and $\sigma\rho > 0$.

No.	Sign of		Classification of			Figure
	σ	ρ	Q_0	Q_2	Q_3	
1.	+	+	Saddle point	Stable focus	Saddle point	Figure 4a
2.	−	$(\frac{-1}{4a^2}, 0)$	Stable node	Saddle point	Stable node	Figure 4b
3.	−	$(-\infty, -\frac{1}{4a^2})$	Stable focus	Saddle point	Stable focus	Figure 4c
4.	−	$\frac{-1}{4a^2}$	Stable star	Saddle point	Stable focus	Figure 4d

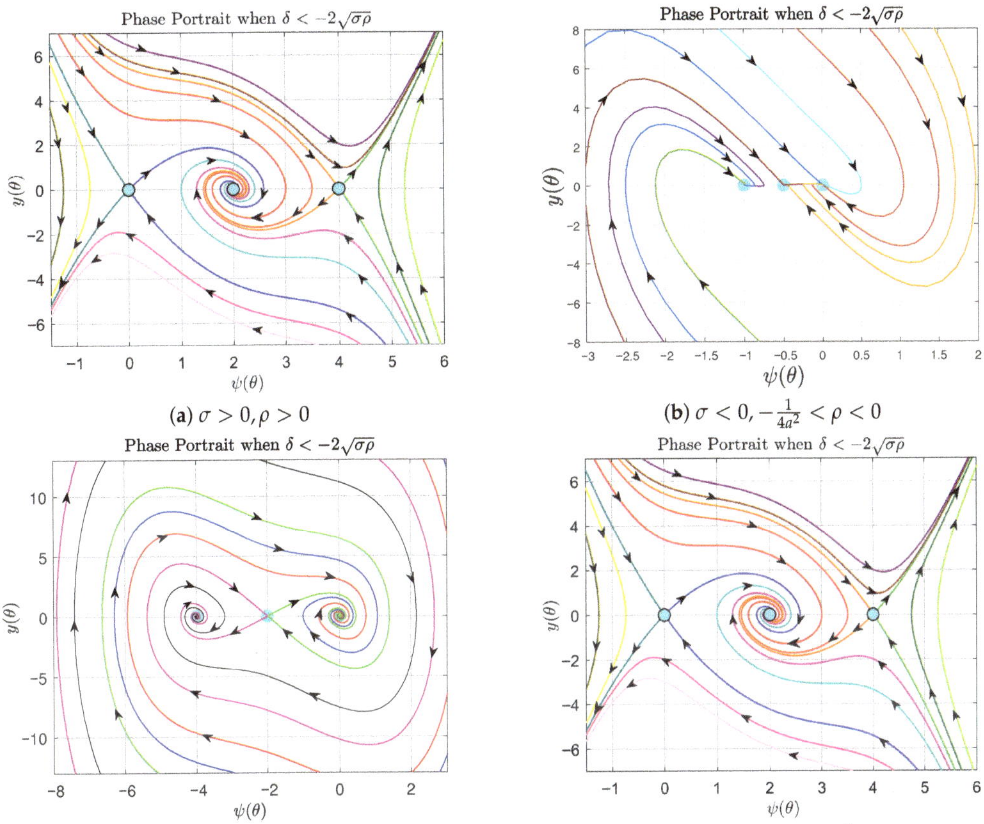

(**a**) $\sigma > 0, \rho > 0$

(**b**) $\sigma < 0, -\frac{1}{4a^2} < \rho < 0$

(**c**) $\sigma < 0, -\infty < \rho < -\frac{1}{4a^2}$

(**d**) $\sigma < 0, \rho = -\frac{1}{4a^2}$

Figure 4. Phase portrait of system (14) corresponding to the case $\delta^2 > 4\sigma\rho$ with $\sigma\rho > 0$.

II. Our analysis now turns to the regime where $\sigma\rho < 0$. In this regime, the condition $\delta^2 > 4\sigma\rho$ is automatically satisfied, leading to two distinct possibilities:

(a) For the parameter region $(\sigma, \rho) \in \mathbb{R}^+ \times \mathbb{R}^-$, the eigenvalues at Q_0 form a complex conjugate pair with a negative real part, while the eigenvalues at Q_2 and Q_3 are real and satisfy $\lambda_2(Q_{2,3}) < 0 < \lambda_1(Q_{2,3})$. Consequently, Q_0 is a stable focus, and Q_2 and Q_3 are both saddle points (hyperbolic equilibria). The corresponding phase portrait is shown in Figure 5a.

(b) When $(\sigma, \rho) \in \mathbb{R}^- \times \mathbb{R}^+$, the equilibrium point Q_0 is a saddle, as indicated by its real eigenvalues $\lambda_2(Q_0) < 0 < \lambda_1(Q_0)$. In contrast, Q_2 and Q_3 are stable foci, characterized by complex eigenvalues with negative real parts. This behavior is illustrated in the phase portrait of Figure 5b.

We now summarize the types and co-dimensions of the bifurcations occurring in system (14). For a more detailed explanation, please refer to Appendix B.

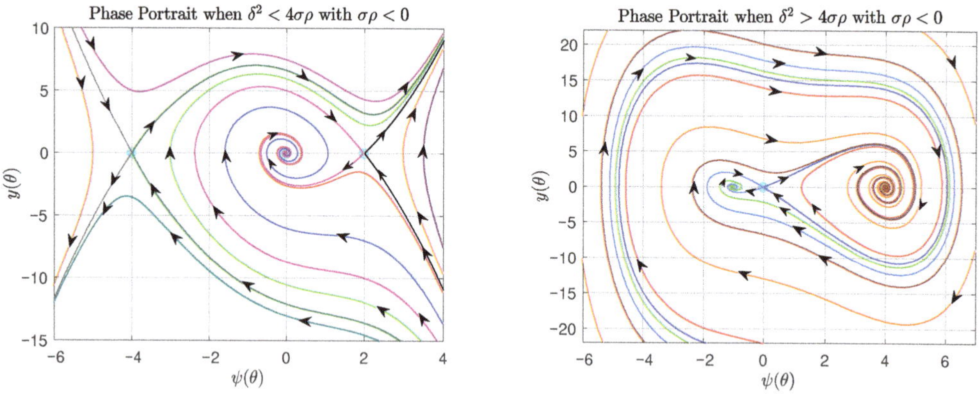

(**a**) $\sigma > 0, \rho < 0$ (**b**) $\sigma < 0, \rho > 0$

Figure 5. Phase portrait of system (14) corresponding to the case $\delta^2 > 4\sigma\rho$ with $\sigma\rho < 0$.

4. Solutions

While numerous studies have focused on constructing specific solutions to Equation (1)—particularly traveling wave solutions—these have predominantly yielded non-periodic forms. This observation prompts a fundamental question: does Equation (1) admit any periodic solutions? To address this, we employ Bendixson's criterion [23]. This theorem states that the dynamical system does not have any closed orbit if its divergence does not vanish in a simply connected zone D.

We proceed by computing the divergence of the dynamical system (14):

$$\nabla \cdot (y', \psi') = \frac{-1}{a^2} \neq 0. \tag{22}$$

This divergence is a negative constant, and consequently, it is neither zero nor changes sign anywhere in the plane. Since $\mathbb{R}^2$ is simply connected, Bendixson's criterion directly precludes the existence of periodic orbits in the entire phase plane. This conclusion is further corroborated by phase portrait analysis, as illustrated in Figures 1–5. We thus establish the following theorem:

Theorem 2. *The dynamical system* (14), *and consequently Equation* (1), *possesses no periodic solutions.*

Given the absence of periodic solutions, we turn to numerical and approximate analytical techniques. In the subsequent subsection, we develop a series solution for Equation (1) using a power series expansion approach, drawing inspiration from the methodology presented in [46].

Series Solution

We begin by postulating a power series solution for Equation (13) of the form

$$\psi(\theta) = \sum_{m=0}^{\infty} d_m \theta^m, \tag{23}$$

where the coefficients d_m are to be determined. The necessary derivatives and nonlinear terms are given by

$$\begin{aligned}\psi'(\theta) &= \sum_{m=0}^{\infty}(m+1)d_{m+1}\theta^m,\\ \psi''(\theta) &= \sum_{m=0}^{\infty}(m+1)(m+2)d_{m+2}\theta^m,\\ \psi^2(\theta) &= \sum_{m=0}^{\infty}\left(\sum_{s=0}^{m}d_s d_{m-s}\right)\theta^m,\\ \psi^3(\theta) &= \sum_{m=0}^{\infty}\left(\sum_{s=0}^{m}\sum_{l=0}^{s}d_l d_{s-l} d_{m-s}\right)\theta^m.\end{aligned} \tag{24}$$

Substituting the expressions from (23) and (24) into Equation (13) yields

$$\begin{aligned}a^2\sum_{m=0}^{\infty}(m+1)(m+2)d_{m+2}\theta^m + \sum_{m=0}^{\infty}(m+1)d_{m+1}\theta^m - \rho\sum_{m=0}^{\infty}d_m\theta^m&\\ -\delta\sum_{m=0}^{\infty}\left(\sum_{s=0}^{m}d_s d_{m-s}\right)\theta^m - \sigma\sum_{m=0}^{\infty}\left(\sum_{s=0}^{m}\sum_{l=0}^{s}d_l d_{s-l}d_{m-s}\right)\theta^m &= 0.\end{aligned} \tag{25}$$

To satisfy this identity for all θ, we equate the coefficients for each power of θ, leading to the following recurrence relations: For $m = 0$,

$$d_2 = \frac{1}{2a^2}\left[-d_1 + \rho d_0 + \delta d_0^2 + \sigma d_0^3\right]. \tag{26}$$

For $m \geq 1$, the general recurrence relation is

$$d_{m+2} = \frac{-1}{a^2(m+1)(m+2)}\left[-(m+1)d_{m+1} + \rho d_m + \delta\sum_{s=0}^{m}d_s d_{m-s} + \sigma\sum_{s=0}^{m}\sum_{l=0}^{s}d_l d_{s-l}d_{m-s}\right]. \tag{27}$$

Consequently, the power series solution to Equation (13)—and, hence, to Equation (1)—is given by

$$\begin{aligned}\mathcal{N}(x,t) = \psi(\theta) = d_0 + d_1(ax-t) + \frac{1}{2a^2}\left[-d_1 + \rho d_0 + \delta d_0^2 + \sigma d_0^3\right](ax-t)^2&\\ + \sum_{m=1}^{\infty}\left\{\frac{-1}{a^2(m+1)(m+2)}\left[-(m+1)d_{m+1} + \rho d_m\right.\right.&\\ \left.\left. + \delta\sum_{s=0}^{m}d_s d_{m-s} + \sigma\sum_{s=0}^{m}\sum_{l=0}^{s}d_l d_{s-l}d_{m-s}\right]\right\}(ax-t)^{m+2},&\end{aligned} \tag{28}$$

where d_0 and d_1 are arbitrary constants, and the subsequent coefficients $\{d_m\}_{m=2}^{\infty}$ are generated recursively from Equation (27).

5. Conclusions

This study presents a detailed investigation of the KPP equation, which serves as a mathematical model for various phenomena observed in biological and chemical systems. The research addresses several aspects that have not been thoroughly examined in the existing literature. Specifically, the integrability characteristics of the KPP equation were investigated through Painlevé analysis, employing the well-established ARS algorithm. The results demonstrate that the KPP equation does not possess the Painlevé property, thereby establishing its non-integrability within the Painlevé framework. This finding further suggests that the equation may exhibit intricate and chaotic dynamical behavior. The non-integrability of Equation (1) immediately implies that it cannot be solved using standard integrability-based techniques, such as the inverse scattering transform or soliton theory, which are characteristic of integrable PDEs. It generally does not possess explicit analytic solutions or an infinite set of conserved quantities. Consequently, a dynamical systems approach can be effectively employed to gain qualitative insights into the nature of their solutions. We assume that the KPP Equation (1) has a solution in the form (12), which is utilized to transform the original $(1+1)$-dimensional partial differential equation into a second-order ordinary differential equation, which can be interpreted as a two-dimensional non-conservative autonomous dynamical system in the phase plane. We conducted a comprehensive bifurcation analysis of the reduced system, revealing diverse dynamical structures. The existence and stability characteristics of equilibrium points depend fundamentally on the parameters ρ, δ, and σ through the discriminant $\Delta = \delta^2 - 4\sigma\rho$. By examining phase portraits corresponding to three distinct cases—$\Delta < 0$, $\Delta = 0$, and $\Delta > 0$—we identified various equilibrium configurations, including saddle points, stable nodes, stable foci, and stable star nodes. This systematic classification enables a complete qualitative characterization of all admissible traveling wave solutions to the KPP equation. Furthermore, we classified the types and co-dimensions of the bifurcations present in the system. We demonstrated that under certain conditions, the system can exhibit saddle-node, transcritical, and pitchfork bifurcations, while Hopf and Bogdanov–Takens bifurcations cannot occur. This is completely proven in Appendix B and tabulated in Table 4.

Table 4. Complete bifurcation classification with co-dimensions.

Bifurcation Type	Condition	Co-dimension	Non-Degeneracy	Exist	Theorem
Saddle-Node	$\delta^2 - 4\sigma\rho = 0$	1	$\delta \neq 0$	Yes	Theorem A1
Transcritical	$\rho = 0$	1	$\delta \neq 0$	Yes	Theorem A2
Pitchfork	$\rho = 0, \delta = 0$	2	$\sigma \neq 0$	Yes	Theorem A3
Cusp	$\rho = 0, \delta = 0$	2	$\sigma \neq 0$	Yes	Theorem A4
Hopf	$\tau = 0$	1	—	No	Theorem A5
Bogdanov–Takens	$\tau = 0$, det $= 0$	2	—	No	Theorem A6

An important theoretical result established in this study is the absence of periodic orbits in the reduced dynamical system, which we proved rigorously using the Bendixson criterion (Theorem 2). Since the divergence of the vector field remains uniformly negative throughout the simply connected domain $\mathbb{R}^2$, no closed trajectories can exist. This analytical finding is further supported by our detailed examination of the phase portraits, which consistently exhibit no periodic behavior across all parameter regimes. Given the established non-integrability and the proven absence of periodic orbits, we pursued an alternative approach by developing approximate analytical solutions through power series expansion. We derived a recurrence relation that determines the series coefficients systematically, offering a computationally tractable framework for constructing solutions parameterized by two arbitrary constants, d_0 and d_1.

In summary, we conducted a detailed multi-perspective study of the KPP equation. The demonstrated non-integrability, characterized bifurcation dynamics, and proven absence of periodic solutions collectively deepen our theoretical insight into this well-known model. The power series technique developed herein also offers a practical means for approximating solutions. These contributions bridge existing gaps in the literature and provide a platform for future work, potentially including numerical bifurcation studies, extensions to fractional-order or stochastic frameworks, and investigations of chaotic dynamics in higher dimensions.

Funding: This work was supported by the Deanship of Scientific Research, Vice Presidency for Graduate Studies and Scientific Research, King Faisal University, Saudi Arabia [Grant No. KFU253612].

Data Availability Statement: The original contributions presented in this study are included in the article. Further inquiries can be directed to the corresponding author.

Conflicts of Interest: The author declares no conflicts of interest.

Appendix A. Painlevé Analysis

This appendix outlines the Painlevé test for integrability analysis. It is applied to a general NLPDE of the form

$$\mathcal{F}(u, u_t, u_x, u_{xx}, u_{xt}, u_{tt}, \dots) = 0, \tag{A1}$$

where $\mathcal{F}$ is a polynomial function in u and its partial derivatives, and u is a complex-valued function of the real variables x and t. The Painlevé analysis provides a systematic criterion for identifying integrable nonlinear systems by examining the singularity structure of their solutions. The central concept is the Painlevé property, which requires that all solutions of a PDE be single-valued around any movable singularity—a singularity whose position depends on initial or boundary conditions. This approach, with roots in the work of Kowalevskaya on rigid-body dynamics [47], and later extended by Painlevé and others, was formalized for PDEs through the algorithmic procedure developed by Ablowitz, Ramani, and Segur [44,48]. The following steps summarize the application of the ARS algorithm to Equation (A1):

The analysis begins with a Laurent-series ansatz for the solution in the neighborhood of a movable singular manifold $\phi(x,t) = 0$:

$$u(x,t) = \phi^{\nu}(x,t) \sum_{i=0}^{\infty} u_i(x,t)\phi^{i}(x,t), \quad u_0(x,t) \neq 0, \tag{A2}$$

where ν is a negative integer and $\phi_x \phi_t \neq 0$.

Step 1: Leading-Order Analysis

To determine the leading-order exponent ν and coefficient u_0, we substitute the dominant form

$$u(x,t) \sim u_0(x,t)\phi^{\nu}(x,t), \tag{A3}$$

into the governing PDE (A1). Balancing the most singular terms yields the value of ν and, subsequently, an algebraic equation for u_0.

Step 2: Determination of Resonances

Resonances (p) are the powers in the Laurent series at which arbitrary functions may appear. They are found by substituting the perturbation

$$u(x,t) = u_0(x,t)\phi^{\nu}(x,t) + u_p(x,t)\phi^{p+\nu}(x,t), \tag{A4}$$

into (A1) and keeping the terms linear in u_p. The condition for a non-trivial u_p produces an eigenvalue problem whose solutions are the resonances. The resonance $p = -1$, corresponding to the arbitrary location of the singular manifold, is always present. A necessary condition for the Painlevé property is that all other resonances are non-negative integers.

Step 3: Verification of Compatibility Conditions

The final step involves verifying the consistency of the Laurent series at each resonance. The truncated expansion

$$u(x,t) = \phi^{\nu}(x,t) \sum_{i=0}^{p_{\max}} u_i(x,t)\phi^{i}(x,t), \tag{A5}$$

where $p_{\max}$ is the largest resonance, is substituted into (A1). At each resonance p, the corresponding coefficient u_p must be an arbitrary function, or the equation for u_p must be identically satisfied. If this holds for all resonances, the PDE passes the Painlevé test and is deemed integrable in the Painlevé sense.

Appendix B. Complete Bifurcation Classification and Co-Dimension

This appendix presents a comprehensive bifurcation classification and co-dimension analysis for the dynamical system (14). For an in-depth discussion of these concepts, the reader is referred to [49]. In the following, we prove the main theorems related to this analysis.

Appendix B.1. Saddle-Node Bifurcation (Co-Dimension 1)

Theorem A1. *A saddle-node bifurcation occurs in the system* (14) *under the condition* $\delta^2 - 4\sigma\rho = 0$*, provided that* $\delta\sigma \neq 0$.

Proof. The necessary condition for a saddle-node bifurcation is the presence of a non-hyperbolic equilibrium with a zero eigenvalue, which is equivalent to the vanishing of the Jacobian determinant. Thus, Equation (18) gives

$$\det(J_0)(\psi_0, 0) = \rho + 2\delta\psi_0 + 3\sigma\psi_0^2 = 0. \tag{A6}$$

Simultaneously, the non-zero equilibrium point ψ_0 must satisfy Equation (15):

$$\rho + \delta\psi_0 + \sigma\psi_0^2 = 0. \tag{A7}$$

To find the parameter relationship that enables this bifurcation, we subtract (A7) from (A6), yielding

$$\psi_0(\delta + 2\sigma\psi_0) = 0. \tag{A8}$$

Excluding the trivial solution $\psi_0 = 0$, we obtain the relevant equilibrium point at $\psi_0 = -\delta/(2\sigma)$. Substituting this value into Equation (A7) gives

$$\delta^2 - 4\sigma\rho = 0, \tag{A9}$$

and, hence,

$$\rho_c = \frac{\delta^2}{4\sigma}, \tag{A10}$$

where ρ_c refers to the critical bifurcation value. We now verify the non-degeneracy conditions. First, we analyze the local behavior near the bifurcation point, and then we translate the equilibrium to the origin by setting

$$\psi = \psi_0 + \eta, \qquad y = y, \qquad \rho = \rho_c + \varepsilon, \tag{A11}$$

where ε is very small. Inserting the expressions (A11) into the system (14) results in

$$\begin{aligned} x' &= y, \\ y' &= \frac{1}{a^2}[-y + g(\psi_0 + \eta, \rho_c + \varepsilon)], \end{aligned} \tag{A12}$$

where $g(\psi,\rho) = \rho\psi + \delta\psi^2 + \sigma\psi^3$. By expanding g about the point (ψ_0, ρ_c) and taking into account $g(\psi_0, \rho_c) = 0$ and $g_\psi(\psi_0, \rho_c) = 0$, we obtain

$$g(\psi_0 + \eta, \rho_c + \varepsilon) = \tfrac{1}{2} g_{\psi\psi}(\psi_0, \rho_c)\,\eta^2 + g_\rho(\psi_0, \rho_c)\,\varepsilon + \mathcal{O}(|\eta|^3, |\eta|\varepsilon, \varepsilon^2). \tag{A13}$$

Hence, the coefficient of the quadratic term in the normal form is

$$\frac{1}{2} g_{\psi\psi}(\psi_0, \rho_c) = -\delta \neq 0. \tag{A14}$$

Second, we check the transversality condition

$$w^T \frac{\partial \mathbf{f}}{\partial \rho}(\psi_0, 0, \rho_c) \neq 0, \tag{A15}$$

where w is left null eigenvectors of the Jacobian $J_0(\psi_0, \rho_c)$ and

$$\mathbf{f}(\psi, y, \rho) = \left(y, \frac{1}{a^2}(-y + \rho\psi + \sigma\psi^3) \right)^T, \tag{A16}$$

is a vector field corresponding to the system (14). After some calculations, we have

$$w^T \frac{\partial \mathbf{f}}{\partial \rho}(\psi_0, 0, \rho_c) = \frac{\psi_0}{a^2} = \frac{-\delta}{2a^2\sigma}. \tag{A17}$$

Both conditions (A14) and (A17) are met provided $\delta \neq 0$, which, along with $\sigma \neq 0$ to ensure that the equilibrium point is finite, completes the proof. □

Appendix B.2. Transcritical Bifurcation (Co-Dimension 1)

Theorem A2. *The system* (14) *undergoes a transcritical bifurcation when* $\rho = 0$.

Proof. A transcritical bifurcation occurs when two distinct equilibrium branches intersect and exchange stability [49]. To establish the occurrence of a transcritical bifurcation, we must verify the standard necessary and sufficient conditions at the bifurcation point.

When $\rho = 0$, Equation (15) simplifies to

$$\psi_0^2(\delta + \sigma\psi_0) = 0,$$

yielding two distinct equilibrium points:

$$E_0 : \psi_0 = 0 \quad \text{and} \quad E_1 : \psi_0 = -\frac{\delta}{\sigma} \quad (\sigma \neq 0).$$

Thus, the equilibria E_0 and E_1 intersect and exchange stability as the parameter ρ passes through zero.The Jacobian matrix evaluated at the origin $(0,0)$ when $\rho = 0$ is given by

$$J_0(0,0) = \begin{pmatrix} 0 & 1 \\ 0 & -\frac{1}{a^2} \end{pmatrix}.$$

This matrix has a zero determinant, $\det(J) = 0$, confirming that the origin is a non-hyperbolic equilibrium with a zero eigenvalue, as required.

Similar to Theorem A1, direct calculations show that the bifurcation is non-degenerate, since both the transversality condition and the non-vanishing quadratic term are satisfied. □

Appendix B.3. Pitchfork Bifurcation (Co-Dimension 2)

Theorem A3. *The system undergoes a pitchfork bifurcation at the equilibrium $\psi = 0$ when the parameters satisfy $\rho = 0$ and $\delta = 0$, provided the cubic coefficient is non-zero ($\sigma \neq 0$). The bifurcation is supercritical if $\sigma < 0$ and subcritical if $\sigma > 0$.*

Proof. To establish the occurrence of a pitchfork bifurcation, we must verify the necessary conditions: the existence of a symmetry, a non-hyperbolic equilibrium, and specific non-degeneracies.

First, setting $\delta = 0$ simplifies the system (14) to

$$\psi' = y, \tag{A18}$$

$$y' = \frac{1}{a^2}\left[-y + \rho\psi + \sigma\psi^3\right]. \tag{A19}$$

Let $\mathbf{f}(\psi, y) = \left(y, \frac{1}{a^2}(-y + \rho\psi + \sigma\psi^3)\right)^T$ be the vector field. We observe that

$$\begin{aligned} \mathbf{f}(-\psi, -y) &= \left(-y, \frac{1}{a^2}(-(-y) + \rho(-\psi) + \sigma(-\psi)^3)\right)^T = \left(-y, \frac{1}{a^2}(y - \rho\psi - \sigma\psi^3)\right)^T, \\ &= -\mathbf{f}(\psi, y). \end{aligned} \tag{A20}$$

This confirms that the system has the odd symmetry $\mathbf{f}(-\mathbf{x}) = -\mathbf{f}(\mathbf{x})$, a prerequisite for a pitchfork bifurcation.

Following Equation (15), the equilibrium points are the roots of the equation

$$\rho\psi_0 + \sigma\psi_0^3 = \psi_0(\rho + \sigma\psi_0^2) = 0. \tag{A21}$$

This equation has the following solutions:

$$\psi_0 = 0 \quad \text{and} \quad \psi_0 = \pm\sqrt{-\rho/\sigma} \quad \text{(which exist when } \rho\sigma < 0). \tag{A22}$$

Thus, for $\rho \neq 0$, the system has either one or three fixed points due to the symmetry.

The bifurcation occurs when $\rho = 0$. At this point, the three fixed points merge into one at the origin: $\psi_0 = 0$. The Jacobian matrix at the origin $(\psi_0, 0) = (0, 0)$ when $\rho = 0$ is

$$J_0(0,0) = \begin{pmatrix} 0 & 1 \\ 0 & -\frac{1}{a^2} \end{pmatrix}.$$

This matrix has eigenvalues 0 and $-1/a^2$, confirming that the origin is a non-hyperbolic equilibrium.

We now verify the non-degeneracy conditions. The first non-degeneracy condition requires a non-zero cubic coefficient in the dynamics restricted to the center manifold. For our system, this coefficient is σ. The condition $\sigma \neq 0$ ensures that the bifurcation is non-degenerate.

The second non-degeneracy condition is the transversality of the bifurcation parameter. We must check that the growth rate of the critical eigenvalue with respect to ρ is non-zero. A calculation shows that $\partial(\lambda(\rho))/\partial\rho \neq 0$ at $\rho = 0$, confirming that the bifurcation unfolds generically.

The sign of the cubic coefficient σ determines the type of pitchfork bifurcation:

- If $\sigma < 0$, the cubic term is stabilizing, and the two new symmetric branches that emerge for $\rho > 0$ (or $\rho < 0$, depending on the sign of the transversality condition) are stable. This is a supercritical pitchfork bifurcation.

- If $\sigma > 0$, the cubic term is destabilizing, and the two new symmetric branches are unstable. This is a subcritical pitchfork bifurcation.

The satisfaction of the symmetry, the merging of three equilibria, the zero eigenvalue, and the non-degeneracy conditions confirms that the system undergoes a pitchfork bifurcation at $\rho = 0, \delta = 0$. □

Appendix B.4. Cusp Singularity (Co-Dimension 2)

Theorem A4. *The system has a cusp singularity at the origin in the parameter space, defined by* $\rho = 0$ *and* $\delta = 0$*, provided the cubic coefficient is non-zero,* $\sigma \neq 0$.

Proof. A cusp singularity is the organizing center for bifurcations of co-dimension 2, where both the first and second derivatives of the vector field (restricted to the center manifold) vanish. Our goal is to show that this happens at the point where the transcritical and pitchfork bifurcation conditions coincide.

Recall that the dynamics on the center manifold can be expressed in a reduced form as $\psi' = g(\psi, \rho, \delta)$. The conditions for an equilibrium point to be non-hyperbolic are $g(0,0,0) = 0, \quad g_\psi(0,0,0) = 0$. These conditions are satisfied at $\psi_0 = 0$ with parameters $\rho = 0, \delta = 0$, as verified in the proofs for the transcritical and pitchfork bifurcations.

For a higher-order degeneracy, we must check the second derivative:

$$g_{\psi\psi}(0,0,0) = 2\delta + 6\sigma\psi\big|_{\psi=0,\delta=0} = 0. \tag{A23}$$

This confirms that the quadratic term also vanishes at the singularity. A point where $g = g_\psi = g_{\psi\psi} = 0$ is a candidate for a cusp.

The universal unfolding of this singularity, which captures all possible perturbed behaviors in a two-parameter neighborhood, is given by the normal form

$$\psi' = \mu_1 + \mu_2\psi + \sigma\psi^3 + \mathcal{O}(\psi^4), \tag{A24}$$

where $\mu_1 = \rho$ and $\mu_2 = \delta$ serve as the unfolding parameters that perturb the system away from the singular point. The critical non-degeneracy condition is that the cubic coefficient is non-zero:

$$g_{\psi\psi\psi}(0,0,0) = 6\sigma \neq 0, \tag{A25}$$

which holds if only and only if $\sigma \neq 0$. This condition ensures that the singularity is of co-dimension 2 and is not more degenerate (e.g., of co-dimension 3). When $\sigma \neq 0$, the two-parameter bifurcation diagram in the (ρ, δ)-plane features a curve of saddle-node bifurcations that meet at the cusp point ($\rho = 0, \delta = 0$) with a tangency. Within the cusp-shaped region, the system has three equilibrium points, and outside of it, only one.

Since all conditions for a cusp singularity are met—specifically, $g = g_\psi = g_{\psi\psi} = 0$ and $g_{\psi\psi\psi} \neq 0$ at the origin—we can conclude that the system has a cusp singularity at $\rho = 0$, $\delta = 0$. □

Appendix B.5. Hopf Bifurcation

Theorem A5. *The system* (14) *cannot undergo a Hopf bifurcation for any values of its parameters.*

Proof. Recall that a Hopf bifurcation, which gives rise to limit cycles from an equilibrium point, requires two necessary conditions at the bifurcation point [49]:

1. The trace of the Jacobian matrix must be zero ($\tau = 0$).
2. The determinant of the Jacobian matrix must be positive ($\det(J_0) > 0$).

The first condition ensures a pair of purely imaginary eigenvalues, while the second ensures that the equilibrium is of a focus or center type (non-saddle) before the bifurcation.

Now, consider the general form of the system. The Jacobian matrix J_0 at any equilibrium point $(\psi_0, 0)$ has a trace given by

$$\tau = \mathrm{Tr}(J_0) = \frac{\partial \psi'}{\partial \psi} + \frac{\partial y'}{\partial y} = -\frac{1}{a^2}.$$

Since the parameter a^2 is a positive constant related to the system's inertia or damping, the trace is strictly negative for all parameter values and at all equilibria:

$$\tau = -\frac{1}{a^2} < 0 \quad \text{for all } \rho, \delta, \sigma.$$

The failure of the first necessary condition ($\tau = 0$) is sufficient to conclude that a Hopf bifurcation is impossible in this system. The constant, non-zero trace indicates that the real part of the eigenvalues can never cross the imaginary axis, which is the essential mechanism for a Hopf bifurcation. □

Theorem A6. *The system* (14) *cannot undergo a Bogdanov–Takens bifurcation for any values of its parameters.*

Proof. A Bogdanov–Takens bifurcation is a co-dimension 2 bifurcation that occurs when an equilibrium point has a Jacobian matrix with a double-zero eigenvalue (a nilpotent Jordan block of size 2) [49]. The necessary and sufficient linear algebra conditions for this are as follows:

1. The trace of the Jacobian is zero: $\tau = 0$.
2. The determinant of the Jacobian is zero: $\det(J_0) = 0$.

The first condition ($\tau = 0$) ensures that the sum of the eigenvalues is zero, and the second ($\det(J_0) = 0$) ensures that their product is zero, together implying that both eigenvalues are exactly zero.

Now, consider the Jacobian matrix J of the system. Its trace is given by

$$\tau = \frac{\partial \psi'}{\partial \psi} + \frac{\partial y'}{\partial y} = -\frac{1}{a^2}.$$

The parameter a^2 is a positive constant representing a time-scale or damping factor. Therefore, the trace is a strictly negative constant for all states and parameter values:

$$\tau = -\frac{1}{a^2} < 0 \quad \text{for all } \rho, \delta, \sigma.$$

Since the first necessary condition for a Bogdanov–Takens bifurcation ($\tau = 0$) is violated universally, it is impossible for the system to exhibit this bifurcation. The constant negative trace prevents the eigenvalues from ever both being zero. □

References

1. Figueiredo, I.N.; Leal, C.; Romanazzi, G.; Engquist, B. Biomathematical model for simulating abnormal orifice patterns in colonic crypts. *Math. Biosci.* **2019**, *315*, 108221. [CrossRef]
2. Hawkins-Daarud, A.; Johnston, S.K.; Swanson, K.R. Quantifying uncertainty and robustness in a biomathematical model–based patient-specific response metric for glioblastoma. *JCO Clin. Cancer Inform.* **2019**, *3*, 1–8. [CrossRef] [PubMed]
3. Ibargüen-Mondragón, E.; Romero-Leiton, J.P.; Esteva, L.; Burbano-Rosero, E.M. Mathematical modeling of bacterial resistance to antibiotics by mutations and plasmids. *J. Biol. Syst.* **2016**, *24*, 129–146. [CrossRef]

4. Leclerc, Q.J.; Lindsay, J.A.; Knight, G.M. Mathematical modelling to study the horizontal transfer of antimicrobial resistance genes in bacteria: Current state of the field and recommendations. *J. R. Soc. Interface* **2019**, *16*, 20190260. [CrossRef] [PubMed]
5. Dudhagara, P.R.; Patel, A. Enhance the bacterial nitrate reductase production using mathematical and statistical model to formulate the affordable silver nanoparticle for the production of nanofinished fabric. *Biomath Commun. Suppl.* **2018**, *5*, 1–10.
6. Khattak, S.; Khan, M.N.; Riaz, M.B.; Lu, D.; Hussien, M.; Albalwi, M.D.; Jhangeer, A. Insights of temperature-dependent fluid characteristics on micropolar material in a rotating frame with cubic autocatalysis chemical reaction. *J. Comput. Des. Eng.* **2024**, *11*, 29–39. [CrossRef]
7. Elmandouh, A. Dynamical Analysis of a Soliton Neuron Model: Bifurcations, Quasi-Periodic Behaviour, Chaotic Patterns, and Wave Solutions. *Mathematics* **2025**, *13*, 1912. [CrossRef]
8. Hassan, T.S.; Elmandouh, A.; Attiya, A.A.; Khedr, A.Y. Bifurcation Analysis and Exact Wave Solutions for the Double-Chain Model of DNA. *J. Math.* **2022**, *2022*, 7188118. [CrossRef]
9. Hussain, A.; Riaz, M.B.; Dar, M.N.R.; Kanwal, R.; Sarwar, L.; Jhangeer, A. Computational study of effect of hybrid nanoparticles on hemodynamics and thermal transfer in ruptured arteries with pathological dilation. *Sci. Rep.* **2024**, *14*, 13400. [CrossRef]
10. Kumar, S.; Kumar, A.; Mohan, B. Evolutionary dynamics of solitary wave profiles and abundant analytical solutions to a (3+1)-dimensional burgers system in ocean physics and hydrodynamics. *J. Ocean. Eng. Sci.* **2023**, *8*, 1–14. [CrossRef]
11. Hosseini, K.; Mayeli, P.; Kumar, D. New exact solutions of the coupled sine-Gordon equations in nonlinear optics using the modified Kudryashov method. *J. Mod. Opt.* **2018**, *65*, 361–364. [CrossRef]
12. Gaber, A. Solitary and periodic wave solutions of (2+1)-dimensions of dispersive long wave equations on shallow waters. *J. Ocean. Eng. Sci.* **2021**, *6*, 292–298. [CrossRef]
13. Ali, A.; Seadawy, A.R. Dispersive soliton solutions for shallow water wave system and modified Benjamin-Bona-Mahony equations via applications of mathematical methods. *J. Ocean. Eng. Sci.* **2021**, *6*, 85–98. [CrossRef]
14. Ravi, L.; Saha Ray, S.; Sahoo, S. New exact solutions of coupled Boussinesq–Burgers equations by Exp-function method. *J. Ocean. Eng. Sci.* **2017**, *2*, 34–46. [CrossRef]
15. Shen, S.; Zhang, J.; Ye, C.; Pan, Z. New exact solutions of the (2+1)-dimensional KdV equation with variable coefficients. *Phys. Lett. A* **2005**, *337*, 101–106. [CrossRef]
16. Elmandouh, A.; Aljuaidan, A.; Elbrolosy, M. The integrability and modification to an auxiliary function method for solving the strain wave equation of a flexible rod with a finite deformation. *Mathematics* **2024**, *12*, 383. [CrossRef]
17. Albalawi, S.M.; Elmandouh, A.A.; Sobhy, M. Integrability and dynamic behavior of a piezoelectro-magnetic circular rod. *Mathematics* **2024**, *12*, 236. [CrossRef]
18. Elbrolosy, M.; Elmandouh, A. Painlevé analysis, Lie symmetry and bifurcation for the dynamical model of radial dislocations in microtubules. *Nonlinear Dyn.* **2025**, *113*, 13699–13714. [CrossRef]
19. Li, L.; Duan, C.; Yu, F. An improved Hirota bilinear method and new application for a nonlocal integrable complex modified Korteweg-de Vries (MKdV) equation. *Phys. Lett. A* **2019**, *383*, 1578–1582. [CrossRef]
20. Yomba, E.; TC, K.; FB, P. On exact solutions of the generalized modified Ginzburg-Landau equation using Hirota S method. *J. Phys. Soc. Jpn.* **1996**, *65*, 2337–2338. [CrossRef]
21. Gao, X.Y. Auto-Bäcklund transformation with the solitons and similarity reductions for a generalized nonlinear shallow water wave equation. *Qual. Theory Dyn. Syst.* **2024**, *23*, 181. [CrossRef]
22. Guo, X.; Li, L. Auto-Bäcklund transformation and exact solutions for a new integrable (2+1)-dimensional shallow water wave equation. *Phys. Scr.* **2024**, *99*, 115233. [CrossRef]
23. Zhang, J.; Feng, B. *Geometric Theory of Ordinary Differential Equations and Bifurcation Problems*; Peking University Press: Beijing, China, 2000.
24. Alharbi, M.; Elmandouh, A.; Elbrolosy, M. Study of Soliton Solutions, Bifurcation, Quasi-Periodic, and Chaotic Behaviour in the Fractional Coupled Schrödinger Equation. *Mathematics* **2025**, *13*, 3174. [CrossRef]
25. Roshid, M.M.; Rahman, M.; Roshid, H.-O. Bifurcation, modulation instability analysis, observation of closed solutions and effect of dispersion coefficient on soliton in relativity and quantum mechanics. *Alex. Eng. J.* **2025**, *130*, 662–671. [CrossRef]
26. Gu, Q.; Wang, L. Bifurcation Analysis and Exact Solutions of the (2+1)-Dimensional Mixed Fractional Broer-Kaup-Kupershmidt System Involving the Riemann-Liouville Fractional Derivative. *Phys. Lett. A* **2025**, *560*, 130947. [CrossRef]
27. Kolmogorov, A.N.; Petrovsky, I.G.; Piskunov, N.S. Investigation of the Equation of Diffusion Combined with Increasing of the Substance and Its Application to a Biology Problem. *Vestn. Mosk. Univ. Seriya I Mat. I Mekhanika* **1937**, *1*, 1–25.
28. Fisher, R.A. The wave of advance of advantageous genes. *Ann. Eugen.* **1937**, *7*, 355–369. [CrossRef]
29. Aydın, Z.; Taşcan, F. Application of the generalized Kudryashov method to the Kolmogorov-Petrovskii-Piskunov equation. *Eskişeh. Tech. Univ. J. Sci. Technol. A Appl. Sci. Eng.* **2024**, *25*, 320–330. [CrossRef]
30. Zayed, E.; Al-Nowehy, A.G. The Riccati equation method combined with the generalized extended (G'/G)-expansion method for solving the nonlinear KPP equation. *J. Math. Res. Appl.* **2017**, *37*, 577–590.

31. Durur, H. The modified sub equation method to Kolmogorov-Petrovskii-Piskunov equation. *Celal Bayar Univ. J. Sci.* **2025**, *21*, 137–144. [CrossRef]
32. Feng, J.; Li, W.; Wan, Q. Using G'/G-expansion method to seek the traveling wave solution of Kolmogorov–Petrovskii–Piskunov equation. *Appl. Math. Comput.* **2011**, *217*, 5860–5865.
33. Roshid, M.M.; Rahman, M.; Or-Roshid, H. Effect of the nonlinear dispersive coefficient on time-dependent variable coefficient soliton solutions of the Kolmogorov-Petrovsky-Piskunov model arising in biological and chemical science. *Heliyon* **2024**, *10*, e31294. [CrossRef]
34. Bezrodnykh, S.; Pikulin, S. Numerical-Analytical Method for Nonlinear Equations of Kolmogorov–Petrovskii–Piskunov Type. *Comput. Math. Math. Phys.* **2024**, *64*, 2484–2509. [CrossRef]
35. Khater, M.M.A.; Mohamed, M.S.; Attia, R.A.M. On semi analytical and numerical simulations for a mathematical biological model; the time-fractional nonlinear Kolmogorov–Petrovskii–Piskunov (KPP) equation. *Chaos Solitons Fractals* **2021**, *144*, 110676. [CrossRef]
36. Zhang, W.G.; Hu, X.K.; Ling, X.Q.; Li, W.X. Approximate analytical solution of the generalized Kolmogorov-Petrovsky-Piskunov equation with cubic nonlinearity. *Acta Math. Appl. Sin. Engl. Ser.* **2023**, *39*, 424–449. [CrossRef]
37. Gepreel, K.A. The homotopy perturbation method applied to the nonlinear fractional Kolmogorov–Petrovskii–Piskunov equations. *Appl. Math. Lett.* **2011**, *24*, 1428–1434. [CrossRef]
38. Ullah, I.; Shah, K.; Abdeljawad, T. Study of traveling soliton and fronts phenomena in fractional Kolmogorov-Petrovskii-Piskunov equation. *Phys. Scr.* **2024**, *99*, 055259. [CrossRef]
39. Li, H.; Guo, Y. New exact solutions to the Fitzhugh–Nagumo equation. *Appl. Math. Comput.* **2006**, *180*, 524–528. [CrossRef]
40. Shih, M.; Momoniat, E.; Mahomed, F. Approximate conditional symmetries and approximate solutions of the perturbed Fitzhugh–Nagumo equation. *J. Math. Phys.* **2005**, *46*, 1839276. [CrossRef]
41. Wazwaz, A.M. Analytic study on Burgers, Fisher, Huxley equations and combined forms of these equations. *Appl. Math. Comput.* **2008**, *195*, 754–761. [CrossRef]
42. Ross, J.; Villaverde, A.F.; Banga, J.R.; Vázquez, S.; Morán, F. A generalized Fisher equation and its utility in chemical kinetics. *Proc. Natl. Acad. Sci. USA* **2010**, *107*, 12777–12781. [CrossRef] [PubMed]
43. Lecarpentier, Y.; Blanc, F.X.; Quillard, J.; Hébert, J.L.; Krokidis, X.; Coirault, C. Statistical mechanics of myosin molecular motors in skeletal muscles. *J. Theor. Biol.* **2005**, *235*, 381–392. [CrossRef]
44. Tabor, M. *Chaos and Integrability in Nonlinear Dynamics: An Introduction*; Wiley-Interscience: Hoboken, NJ, USA, 1989.
45. Nemytskii, V.V. *Qualitative Theory of Differential Equations*; Princeton University Press: Princeton, NJ, USA, 2015.
46. Arora, R.; Chauhan, A. Lie Symmetry Analysis and Some Exact Solutions of (2+1)-Dimensional KdV-Burgers Equation. *Int. J. Appl. Comput. Math.* **2019**, *15*, 603–605. [CrossRef]
47. Yehia, H. *Rigid Body Dynamics*; Springer: Berlin/Heidelberg, Germany; Birkhäuser: Basel, Switzerland, 2022.
48. Ablowitz, M.J.; Ramani, A.; Segur, H. A connection between nonlinear evolution equations and ordinary differential equations of P-type. II. *J. Math. Phys.* **1980**, *21*, 1006–1015. [CrossRef]
49. Kuznetsov, Y.A. *Elements of Applied Bifurcation Theory*; Springer: New York, NY, USA, 1998.

mathematics

MDPI

Article

Qualitative Analysis for Modifying an Unstable Time-Fractional Nonlinear Schrödinger Equation: Bifurcation, Quasi-Periodic, Chaotic Behavior, and Exact Solutions

M. M. El-Dessoky [1,*], A. A. Elmandouh [2,3] and A. A. Alghamdi [1]

1 Mathematics Department, Faculty of Science, King Abdulaziz University, P.O. Box 80203, Jeddah 21589, Saudi Arabia; aaalghamdi6@kau.edu.sa
2 Department of Mathematics and Statistics, College of Science, King Faisal University, P.O. Box 400, Al-Ahsa 31982, Saudi Arabia; aelmandouh@kfu.edu.sa
3 Department of Mathematics, Faculty of Science, Mansoura University, Mansoura 35516, Egypt
* Correspondence: mahmed4@kau.edu.sa

Abstract

This work explores the qualitative dynamics of the modified unstable time-fractional nonlinear Schrödinger equation (mUNLSE), a model applicable to nonlinear wave propagation in plasma and optical fiber media. By transforming the governing equation into a planar conservative Hamiltonian system, a detailed bifurcation study is carried out, and the associated equilibrium points are classified using Lagrange's theorem and phase-plane analysis. A family of exact wave solutions is then constructed in terms of both trigonometric and Jacobi elliptic functions, with solitary, kink/anti-kink, periodic, and super-periodic profiles emerging under suitable parameter regimes and linked directly to the type of the phase plane orbits. The validity of the solutions is discussed through the degeneracy property which is equivalent to the transmission between the phase orbits. The influence of the fractional derivative order on amplitude, localization, and dispersion is illustrated through graphical simulations, exploring the memory impacts in the wave evolution. In addition, an externally periodic force is allowed to act on the mUNLSE model, which is reduced to a perturbed non-autonomous dynamical system. The response to periodic driving is examined, showing transitions from periodic motion to quasi-periodic and chaotic regimes, which are further confirmed by Lyapunov exponent calculations. These findings deepen the theoretical understanding of fractional Schrödinger-type models and offer new insight into complex nonlinear wave phenomena in plasma physics and optical fiber systems.

Keywords: Schrödinger equations; bifurcation theory; phase portrait; quasi behaviour; chaotic pattern; wave solutions

MSC: 35C07; 35C08; 37K40; 83C15

1. Introduction

Nonlinear phenomena appear in a wide range of scientific and engineering disciplines, including physics [1], engineering [2], applied mathematics [3], chemistry [4], and biology [5]. These phenomena are often modeled through nonlinear evolution equations (NLEEs). The significance of nonlinearity in wave dynamics has become increasingly evident in recent years, leading to substantial efforts aimed at developing analytical solutions for NLEE models [6,7]. Among the various nonlinear models, the nonlinear Schrödinger equation (NLSE) stands out due to its broad applicability across numerous scientific domains. These include mathematical finance [8], optical fiber communications [9], fluid dynamics [10], quantum mechanics [11], plasma physics [12], quantum field theory [13], and wave propagation in piezoelectric materials [14]. Explicit solutions to NLEEs often exhibit soliton-like behavior, which plays a crucial role in modern technologies. In particular, solitons are fundamental in optical fiber systems for digital information transmission [15].

A key aspect of mathematical analysis in understanding the dynamics of nonlinear evolution equations (NLEEs) lies in constructing explicit solutions that accurately describe these processes. Over the past decades, significant efforts have been devoted to developing comprehensive analytical approaches for such models. Numerous mathematical techniques have been proposed and refined, including the generalized auxiliary equation technique [16,17], Kudryashov technique [18], classical Lie symmetry analysis [19,20], Hirota and modified Hirota bilinear method [21,22], sub-equation technique [23], extended direct algebraic technique [24], and bifurcation approach [25–29].

Within plasma physics and optical fiber research, nonlinear Schrödinger-type equations (NLSEs) provide a foundational modeling framework. A specific variant, known as the modified unstable nonlinear Schrödinger equation (mUNLSE), is particularly relevant for modeling phenomena such as two-layer baroclinic instability and symmetric two-stream plasma dynamics in lossless media. In this work, we investigate exact analytical solutions of the mUNLSE, formulated as follows [30]:

$$i\,{}_{n}\mathbb{D}_{t}^{\gamma,\nu} R + R_{xx} + 2\mu R|R|^{2} + m\,{}_{n}\mathbb{D}_{t}^{\gamma,\nu}(R_{x}) = 0, \tag{1}$$

where $R(x,t)$ represents the complex-valued field envelope, x corresponds to the normalized longitudinal coordinate along the fiber, and t denotes the retarded time coordinate. Partial derivatives are expressed using subscript notation, and the parameter λ quantifies the strength of the self-phase modulation (SPM) effect. While ${}_{n}\mathbb{D}_{t}^{\gamma,\nu}(\cdot)$ for $\nu > 0$ and $\gamma \in (0,1]$, is the M-fractional derivative of order γ. The truncated M-fractional derivative used in Equation (1) belongs to a class of fractional operators that generalize classical definitions while preserving key properties of ordinary calculus, such as the product, quotient, and chain rules. The definition, main properties, and a detailed comparison with classical fractional operators are provided in Appendix A, in order to keep the article self-contained.

Fractional derivatives are widely used as modeling tools to achieve more accurate results in real-world applications. In the present problem, the nonlocal nature of the M-fractional derivative captures memory effects in wave propagation—the evolution at time t depends on previous states, a characteristic feature of fractional dynamics in plasmas and in optical fibers with hereditary behavior.

Equation (1) has been examined in a number of recent studies. For instance, the extended Jacobi elliptic function expansion and certain unified schemes have been employed to explore wave propagation and optical soliton dynamics in this setting [31]. In addition, an amended extended hyperbolic tangent approach was applied in [32] to analyze the solution structure of Equation (1). Furthermore, the MEM technique was utilized in [33] to construct optical soliton solutions of Equation (1). In [34,35], bright and dark soliton solutions, together with elliptic-function-type waves for the mUNLSE, were obtained via the modified extended direct algebraic method (MEDAM) and the simple equation method (SEM). A direct algebraic strategy was adopted in [36] to investigate the mUNLSE and its associated optical solitons, while a modified extended auxiliary equation mapping technique was proposed in [37] to derive soliton solutions for the mNLSE in fiber optics.

To the best of our knowledge, we note the following:

https://doi.org/10.3390/math14020354

1. The lack of bifurcation studies, as well as analyses of quasi-periodic and chaotic behavior, for the time-fractional mUNLSE;
2. The importance of constructing exact solutions that are directly linked to phase-portrait structures through degeneracy analysis;
3. The insufficient exploration of the physical significance of memory effects and external perturbations in plasma and optical-fiber applications compared with purely soliton-based studies.

These gaps motivate us to further develop and complete the existing literature.

The paper is organized as follows: Section 2 presents the reduction of Equation (1) to a planar conservative dynamical system. Section 3 provides the bifurcation analysis and corresponding phase portraits. Section 4 introduces exact solutions to Equation (1). Section 5 illustrates graphical representations of the solutions and highlights the effect of the fractional derivative order. Section 6 investigates quasi-periodic behavior and chaotic patterns. Section 7 summarizes the key findings of the study.

2. Mathematical Analysis

We assume Equation (1) has a solution in the form

$$R(x,t) = e^{\mathrm{i}z}\Omega(\rho), \qquad z = p_1 x - \frac{q_1\Gamma(\nu+1)}{\gamma}t^{\gamma}, \qquad \rho = p_2 x - \frac{q_2\Gamma(\nu+1)}{\gamma}t^{\gamma}, \tag{2}$$

where p_i and q_i with $i = 1,2$ are arbitrary constants while $\Omega(\rho)$ is a real valued function. Based on the properties of the truncated M-fractional derivative in Appendix A, we obtain

$$\begin{aligned} R_x &= e^{\mathrm{i}z}[\mathrm{i}p_1\Omega(\rho) + p_2\Omega'(\rho)], \\ R_{xx} &= e^{\mathrm{i}z}[p_2^2\Omega''(\rho) + 2\mathrm{i}p_1p_2\Omega'(\rho) - p_1^2\Omega(\rho)], \\ {}_n\mathbb{D}_t^{\gamma,\nu} R &= -e^{\mathrm{i}z}[q_2\Omega'(\rho) + \mathrm{i}q_1\Omega(\rho)], \\ {}_n\mathbb{D}_t^{\gamma,\nu} R_x &= -e^{\mathrm{i}z}[-p_2q_2\Omega''(\rho) - \mathrm{i}(p_1q_2 + p_2q_1)\Omega'(\rho) + q_1p_1\Omega]. \end{aligned} \tag{3}$$

Inserting the expression (3) into Equation (1) and separating the real and imaginary parts gives the following:

Real part:

$$p_2(p_2 - mq_2)\Omega''(\rho) + 2\mu\Omega^3(\rho) + (mp_1q_1 - p_1^2 + q_1)\Omega(\rho) = 0. \tag{4}$$

Imaginary part:

$$[m(p_1q_2 + p_2q_1) - 2p_1p_2 + q_2]\Omega'(\rho) = 0. \tag{5}$$

Equation (5) is identically verified if

$$m = \frac{2p_1p_2 - q_2}{p_1q_2 + p_2q_1}. \tag{6}$$

Inserting the expression (6) into Equation (4) implies

$$\Omega'' - \ell_1\Omega^3(\rho) + \ell_2\Omega(\rho) = 0, \tag{7}$$

where ℓ_1 and ℓ_2 are new constants introduced for simplicity and they are given by

$$\ell_1 = \frac{2\mu(p_1q_2 + p_2q_1)}{p_2(p_1p_2q_2 - p_2^2q_1 - q_2^2)}, \qquad \ell_2 = \frac{p_1^3q_2 - p_1^2p_2q_1 - p_2q_1^2}{p_2(p_1p_2q_2 - p_2^2q_1 - q_2^2)}. \tag{8}$$

https://doi.org/10.3390/math14020354

Defining $\Omega' = \Upsilon(\rho)$, Equation (7) reduces to a two-dimensional dynamical system in the form

$$\begin{aligned} \Omega' &= \Upsilon \\ \Upsilon' &= \ell_1\Omega^3 - \ell_2\Omega. \end{aligned} \tag{9}$$

The dynamical system (9) is conservative because $\mathrm{div}(\Omega', \Upsilon') = 0$. Moreover, it is Hamiltonian because it can be obtained from the Hamilton function

$$H = \frac{1}{2}\Upsilon^2 - \frac{\ell_1}{4}\Omega^4 + \frac{\ell_2}{2}\Omega^2, \tag{10}$$

by using Hamilton canonical equations [38]. Due to $\partial_\rho H = 0$, the Hamilton function (10) itself is a conserved quantity, i.e., it has a constant value along any trajectories. Thus, we have

$$H = \frac{1}{2}\Upsilon^2 - \frac{\ell_1}{4}\Omega^4 + \frac{\ell_2}{2}\Omega^2 = a, \tag{11}$$

where a is free parameter. The Hamiltonian (11) is elucidated physically via the 1D motion of a unit mass particle under the impact of two parameters' potential functions in the form

$$V(\Omega) = -\frac{\ell_1}{4}\Omega^4 + \frac{\ell_2}{2}\Omega^2. \tag{12}$$

Hence, the solution of the Hamiltonian system (9) is obtained by quadrature, and consequently, we obtain the solution to Equation (1). Inserting the first equation in Equation (9) into Equation (11) and separating the variables gives

$$\pm\sqrt{2}\mathrm{d}\rho = \frac{\mathrm{d}\Omega}{\sqrt{G_4(\Omega)}}, \tag{13}$$

where the quartic polynomial $G_4(\Omega)$ is given by

$$G_4(\Omega) = a - \frac{\ell_2}{2}\Omega^2 + \frac{\ell_1}{4}\Omega^4. \tag{14}$$

To integrate both sides of Equation (13), we must find the range of the parameters a, ℓ_1, ℓ_2 and the intervals of the real solution because $\Omega(\rho)$ is real valued function. The phase portrait analysis for the system (9) is investigated not only to determine this range of the parameters but also because it provides the types of the solution before constructing them.

3. Qualitative Analysis

In this section, we examine the qualitative dynamics of the Hamiltonian system (9) by means of its phase portrait and investigate the nature of the corresponding trajectories using the Hamiltonian concepts. The equilibrium points of system (9) arise as the critical points to the potential function (12), i.e., they are $\Omega_0, 0$, where Ω_0 is a solution to $\partial_\Omega V(\Omega_0) = \Omega_0(\ell_2 - \ell_1\Omega_0^2) = 0$. When $\ell_1\ell_2 < 0$, the system possesses a single equilibrium point, namely the trivial solution at the origin, $O = (0,0)$. Conversely, if $\ell_1\ell_2 > 0$ with $\ell_1 \neq 0$, three distinct equilibrium points emerge: the origin together with two symmetric nontrivial equilibria, $O = (0,0)$, $C_{1,2} = \left(\pm\sqrt{\frac{\ell_2}{\ell_1}}, 0\right)$. To specify the nature these equilibria, we proceed by applying Lagrange's theorem [39], which states that the isolated equilibrium point is either stable or unstable if it is either the minimum or maximum point of the potential function. Therefore, we compute $\partial_{\Omega\Omega}V$ at the equilibrium points. Hence, we have

$$\partial_{\Omega\Omega}V|_{\Omega=0} = \ell_2, \qquad \partial_{\Omega\Omega}V\Big|_{\Omega=\pm\sqrt{\frac{\ell_2}{\ell_1}}} = -2\ell_2. \tag{15}$$

https://doi.org/10.3390/math14020354

Following Lagrange's theorem [39], the equilibrium point O is classified as a center when $\ell_2 > 0$ and $\ell_1 < 0$, whereas it becomes a saddle point when $\ell_2 < 0$ and $\ell_1 > 0$. In the case $\ell_2 < 0$ and $\ell_1 < 0$, the origin O is a saddle, while the two nontrivial equilibria $C_{1,2}$ are centers. Conversely, if $\ell_2 > 0$ and $\ell_1 > 0$, the origin O is a center and the equilibria $C_{1,2}$ are saddles. Figure 1 describes the phase portrait for the system (9).

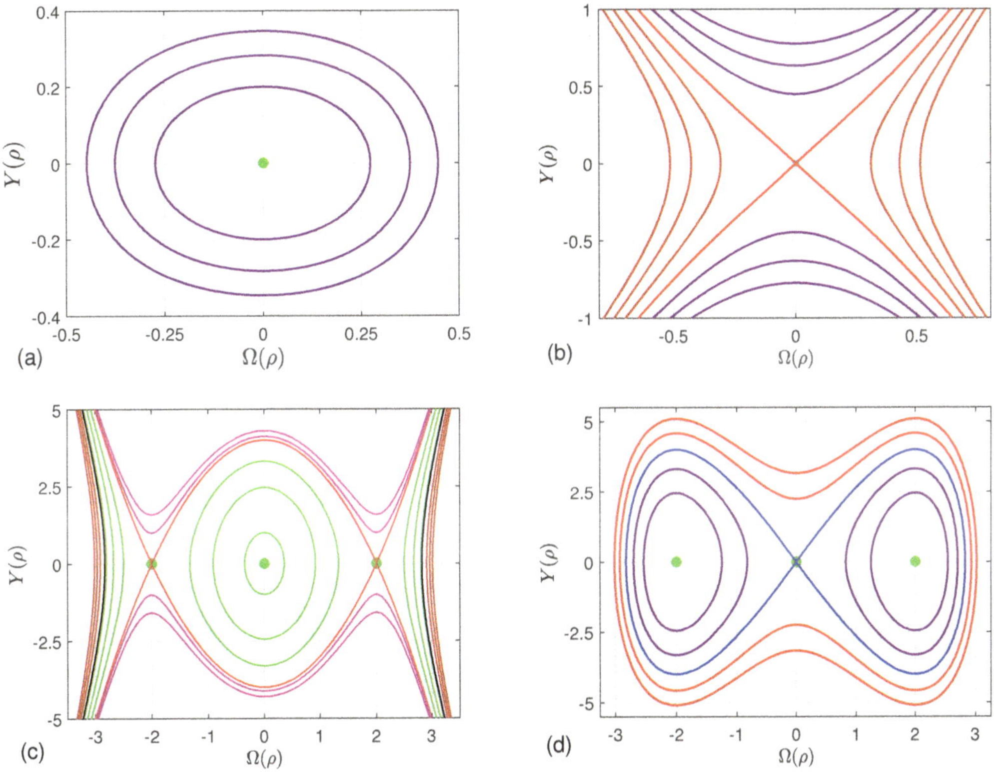

Figure 1. Phase portraits for system (9): (**a**) $\ell_1 < 0, \ell_2 > 0$; (**b**) $\ell_1 > 0, \ell_2 < 0$; (**c**) $\ell_1 > 0, \ell_2 > 0$; (**d**) $\ell_1 < 0, \ell_2 < 0$.

To describe the phase portrait more concretely, we compute the energy levels at the equilibrium points:

$$a_1 = H(O) = 0, \qquad a_2 = H(C_{1,2}) = \frac{{\ell_2}^2}{4\ell_1}. \tag{16}$$

To provide a more concrete description of the phase portrait, we first evaluate the energy levels at the equilibrium points:

$$\mathcal{N}_a = \left\{(\Omega, \mathrm{Y}) \in \mathbb{R} \times \mathbb{R} : \tfrac{1}{2}\mathrm{Y}^2 = F_4(\Omega)\right\}. \tag{17}$$

In the phase portrait of system (9), every trajectory is associated with an energy level curve defined by its corresponding energy value.

We now provide a qualitative description of the phase portraits associated with system (9).

(A) For $\ell_1 < 0$ and $\ell_2 > 0$, the system admits a single equilibrium point at the origin O, which behaves as a center. When the energy level satisfies $a > 0$, the trajectories form

https://doi.org/10.3390/math14020354

a continuous family of closed periodic curves, denoted by $\{\mathcal{N}_a : a > 0\}$, encircling the center O. This configuration is illustrated in Figure 1a.

(B) For $\ell_1 > 0$ and $\ell_2 < 0$, the origin O becomes a saddle equilibrium. At the critical energy level $a = 0$, the system supports a distinguished unbounded trajectory (highlighted in red), denoted by $\mathcal{N}_{a=0}$, as shown in Figure 1b. For $a > 0$, the dynamics give rise to a family of unbounded trajectories (depicted in purple), $\{\mathcal{N}_a : a > 0\}$. Conversely, for $a < 0$, another family of unbounded trajectories (depicted in gold) emerges. As the energy approaches zero, both families (purple and gold) converge to the unique orbit $\mathcal{N}_{a=0}$.

(C) For $\ell_1 > 0$ and $\ell_2 > 0$, the dynamical system (9) admits three equilibrium points: two saddles and one center, as depicted in Figure 1c. At $a = 0$, the system generates a black unbounded trajectory with a hyperbolic profile in addition to the equilibrium point O. When $a < 0$, it produces a gold family of unbounded orbits, all sharing the same hyperbolic geometry. Within the interval $0 < a < a_2$, a green family of solutions emerges, consisting of two distinct parts: one bounded by the heteroclinic curve $\mathcal{N}_{a=a_2}$ (shown in red), and another with hyperbolic form. For $a > a_2$, the system displays a pink family of unbounded trajectories. As $a \to 0$, the gold family collapses into the black unbounded orbit, while the hyperbolic branch of the green family also converges to the same black orbit. Meanwhile, the periodic green family enclosed by the heteroclinic orbit contracts to the equilibrium point O. As $a \to a_2$, the pink unbounded family is absorbed into the red heteroclinic orbit, and the green family likewise transitions into the red heteroclinic structure.

(D) For $\ell_1 < 0$ and $\ell_2 < 0$, system (9) admits three equilibrium points: one saddle and two centers, as illustrated in Figure 1d. At the energy level $a = 0$, the system exhibits a homoclinic trajectory (shown in blue) that departs from the saddle point O and returns to it. For intermediate values $a_2 < a < 0$, two distinct families of closed periodic trajectories (depicted in purple) appear inside the homoclinic loop. When $a > 0$, the dynamics reduce to a single family of bounded periodic trajectories.

4. Solution Construction

The purpose of this section is to obtain bounded wave solutions of Equation (1). These solutions can be classified into three main types: solitary waves, kink (or anti-kink) waves, and periodic waves. Although the adopted method is sufficiently general to construct unbounded solutions, such cases are excluded here because they are not physically relevant. For clarity in the forthcoming analysis, the conditions that lead to periodic, super-periodic, solitary, and homoclinic solutions are summarized in Table 1. This organization highlights the correspondence between the wave forms of system (9) and the nature of their phase trajectories: periodic and super-periodic waves arise from periodic and super-periodic phase orbits, solitary waves are associated with homoclinic orbits, and kink (or anti-kink) waves originate from heteroclinic orbits.

Table 1. Existence and classification of the solutions.

Case	ℓ_1	ℓ_2	a	Figure/Orbit Color	Solution's Type
1.	$-$	$-$	0	Figure 1d/blue	Solitary
2.	$+$	$+$	a_2	Figure 1c/red	Kink(anti-kink)
3.	$-$	$+$	$+$	Figure 1a/purple	periodic
4.	$+$	$+$	$(0, a_2)$	Figure 1c/green	periodic
5.	$-$	$-$	$(a_2, 0)$	Figure 1d/purple	periodic
6.	$-$	$-$	$+$	Figure 1d/red	Super-periodic

https://doi.org/10.3390/math14020354

Proceeding to integrate the differential form given in (13), we apply the parameter conditions summarized in Table 1 to identify admissible solutions.

4.1. Solitary Solution

The condition listed in the first row of Table 1 corresponds to the existence of a solitary-wave solution. We now construct this solution explicitly. When the parameters ℓ_1, ℓ_2, and a satisfy the third condition of first row of Table 1, system (9) possesses two blue homoclinic orbits that cross the Ω-axis at three distinct points, as shown in Figure 1d. Consequently, the polynomial $F_4(\Omega)$ admits four real roots: a double root at the origin and two simple roots at $\Omega = \pm\sqrt{2\ell_2/\ell_1}$. Hence, $F_4(\Omega)$ can be written as $F_4(\Omega) = -\frac{\ell_1}{4}\Omega^2\left(\frac{2\ell_2}{\ell_1} - \Omega^2\right)$. For a real-valued solution we require $\Omega \in \left(-\sqrt{\frac{2\ell_2}{\ell_1}}, 0\right) \cup \left(0, \sqrt{\frac{2\ell_2}{\ell_1}}\right)$. Setting the initial condition $\Omega(\rho_0) = \pm\sqrt{2\ell_2/\ell_1}$ and integrating (13) gives the solitary-wave profile

$$\Omega(\rho) = \pm\sqrt{\frac{2\ell_2}{\ell_1}}\operatorname{sech}\left(\sqrt{-\ell_2}\,(\rho - \rho_0)\right). \tag{18}$$

Using both Equations (2) and (18) produces a new solution to Equation (1) in the form

$$R(x,t) = \pm\sqrt{\frac{2\ell_2}{\ell_1}}e^{\mathrm{i}(p_1 x - \frac{q_1\Gamma(\nu+1)}{\gamma}t^{\gamma})}\operatorname{sech}\left(\sqrt{-\ell_2}\,(p_2 x - \frac{q_2\Gamma(\nu+1)}{\gamma}t^{\gamma} - \rho_0)\right). \tag{19}$$

4.2. Kink (Anti-Kink) Solution

The second row outlined in Table 1 guarantees that a heteroclinic orbit links the saddle equilibria C_1 and C_2, indicating the possibility of kink/anti-kink wave solutions. We now derive this solution explicitly. When the parameters ℓ_1, ℓ_2, and a meet the criterion of the second row, system (9) supports a red heteroclinic trajectory (see Figure 1c), which intersects the Ω-axis at two locations. Accordingly, the polynomial $F_4(\Omega)$ possesses a pair of double roots at $\Omega = \pm\sqrt{\ell_2/\ell_1}$, allowing it to be factored as $F_4(\Omega) = \frac{\ell_1}{4}\left(u^2 - \frac{\ell_2}{\ell_1}\right)^2$. Real solutions are restricted to the intervals $\Omega \in \left(-\sqrt{\frac{\ell_2}{\ell_1}}, 0\right) \cup \left(0, \sqrt{\frac{b}{a}}\right)$. Choosing the initial condition $\Omega(\rho_0) = 0$ and integrating (13) yields the kink profile

$$\Omega(\rho) = \pm\sqrt{\frac{\ell_2}{\ell_1}}\tanh\left(\sqrt{\frac{\ell_2}{2}}\,(\rho - \rho_0)\right). \tag{20}$$

Substituting this result into Equation (2) givesa new solution to Equation (1) in the form

$$R(x,t) = \pm\sqrt{\frac{\ell_2}{\ell_1}}e^{\mathrm{i}(p_1 x - \frac{q_1\Gamma(\nu+1)}{\gamma}t^{\gamma})}\tanh\left(\sqrt{\frac{\ell_2}{2}}\,(p_2 x - \frac{q_2\Gamma(\nu+1)}{\gamma}t^{\gamma} - \rho_0)\right). \tag{21}$$

4.3. Periodic Solution

We consider the third, fourth, and fifth rows of Table 1 individually.

(i) If the parameters satisfy $\ell_1 < 0$, $\ell_2 > 0$, and $a > 0$, the phase portrait of system (9) contains a periodic orbit encircling the equilibrium O. This closed trajectory meets the Ω-axis at two distinct points, implying that the associated polynomial $F_4(\Omega)$ has two real roots and a pair of complex-conjugate roots. It can therefore be written in the factorized form $F_4(\Omega) = -\frac{\ell_1}{4}(\vartheta_1^2 - \Omega^2)(\vartheta_2^2 + \Omega^2)$. A real-valued solution is admissible only for Ω lying in the open interval $(-\vartheta_1, \vartheta_2)$. Setting the initial condition $\Omega(\rho_0) = \vartheta_1$ and integrating Equation (9) leads to the periodic solution expressed via the Jacobi elliptic cosine:

$$\Omega(\rho) = \vartheta_1 \mathrm{cn}\left(\sqrt{\frac{-\ell_1(\vartheta_1^2+\vartheta_2^2)}{2}}\,(\rho-\rho_0),\ \frac{\vartheta_1}{\sqrt{\vartheta_1^2+\vartheta_2^2}}\right). \tag{22}$$

Substituting this result into Equation (2) results in a new solution to Equation (1) in the form

$$R(x,t) = \vartheta_1 e^{\mathrm{i}(p_1 x - \frac{q_1\Gamma(\nu+1)}{\gamma}t^{\gamma})} \mathrm{cn}\left(\sqrt{\frac{-\ell_1(\vartheta_1^2+\vartheta_2^2)}{2}}\,(p_2 x - \frac{q_2\Gamma(\nu+1)}{\gamma}t^{\gamma}-\rho_0),\ \frac{\vartheta_1}{\sqrt{\vartheta_1^2+\vartheta_2^2}}\right). \tag{23}$$

(ii) When the parameters are chosen such that $\ell_1 < 0$, $\ell_2 < 0$, and $a_2 < a < 0$, system (9) admits a pair of green periodic orbits (see Figure 1d), each crossing the Ω-axis at four distinct locations. Consequently, the polynomial $F_4(\Omega)$ possesses four real roots, which we denote by $\pm\vartheta_3$ and $\pm\vartheta_4$ with $0 < \vartheta_3 < \vartheta_4$. It can therefore be factored as $F_4(\Omega) = -\frac{\ell_1}{4}(\Omega^2 - \vartheta_3^2)(\vartheta_4^2 - \Omega^2)$. Real, bounded solutions are confined to the intervals $\Omega \in (-\vartheta_4, -\vartheta_3) \cup (\vartheta_3, \vartheta_4)$. Taking the initial condition $\Omega(\rho_0) = \pm\vartheta_4$ and integrating (13) produces the solution in terms of the Jacobi elliptic dn function:

$$\Omega(\rho) = \pm\vartheta_4 \mathrm{dn}\left(\vartheta_4\sqrt{\frac{-\ell_1}{2}}(\rho-\rho_0),\ \frac{\sqrt{\vartheta_4^2-\vartheta_3^2}}{\vartheta_4}\right). \tag{24}$$

Using both Equations (2) and (24) produces a new solution to Equation (1) in the form

$$R(x,t) = \pm\vartheta_4 e^{\mathrm{i}(p_1 x - \frac{q_1\Gamma(\nu+1)}{\gamma}t^{\gamma})} \mathrm{dn}\left(\vartheta_4\sqrt{\frac{-\ell_1}{2}}(p_2 x - \frac{q_2\Gamma(\nu+1)}{\gamma}t^{\gamma}-\rho_0),\ \frac{\sqrt{\vartheta_4^2-\vartheta_3^2}}{\vartheta_4}\right). \tag{25}$$

(iii) When the parameters are fixed with $\ell_1 > 0$, $\ell_2 > 0$, and $a_2 < a < 0$, system (9) displays three distinct trajectories: a single periodic orbit together with two families of unbounded orbits. Correspondingly, the polynomial $F_4(\Omega)$ admits four simple real roots, which we label as $\pm\vartheta_5$ and $\pm\vartheta 6$, ordered such that $0 < \vartheta_5 < \vartheta_6$. It therefore factors as $F_4(\Omega) = \frac{\ell_1}{4}(\Omega^2 - \vartheta_5^2)(\Omega^2 - \vartheta_6^2)$. Bounded, real-valued solutions are only possible for Ω in the disjoint intervals $\Omega \in (-\vartheta_5, 0) \cup (0, \vartheta_5)$. Imposing the initial condition $\Omega(\rho_0) = 0$ and integrating (13) leads to a solution expressed by the Jacobi elliptic sine function:

$$\Omega(\rho) = \pm\vartheta_5 \mathrm{sn}\left(\vartheta_6\sqrt{\frac{\ell_1}{2}}\,(\rho-\rho_0),\ \frac{\vartheta_5}{\vartheta_6}\right). \tag{26}$$

Using both Equations (2) and (26) provides a new solution to Equation (1) in the form

$$R(x,t) = \pm\vartheta_5 e^{\mathrm{i}(p_1 x - \frac{q_1\Gamma(\nu+1)}{\gamma}t^{\gamma})} \mathrm{sn}\left(\vartheta_6\sqrt{\frac{\ell_1}{2}}\,(p_2 x - \frac{q_2\Gamma(\nu+1)}{\gamma}t^{\gamma}-\rho_0),\ \frac{\vartheta_5}{\vartheta_6}\right). \tag{27}$$

4.4. Super-Periodic Solution

The last row in Table 1 refers to the existence of a super-periodic wave solution to Equation (1). Under parameter values ℓ_1, ℓ_2, and a that fulfill this condition, the phase portrait of system (9) contains a red super-periodic orbit (Figure 1d), which meets the Ω-axis at two locations. This geometric feature implies that the associated polynomial $F_4(\Omega)$ possesses a pair of real roots, $\pm\vartheta_7$, together with a pair of purely imaginary conjugate roots, $\pm\mathrm{i}\vartheta_8$. Consequently, the polynomial factors as $F_4(\Omega) = -\frac{\ell_1}{4}(\vartheta_7^2 - \Omega^2)(\Omega^2 + \vartheta_8^2)$.

https://doi.org/10.3390/math14020354

A physically relevant (real) solution is obtained only when Ω lies in the open interval $(-\vartheta_7, \vartheta_7)$. Choosing the initial value $\Omega(\rho_0) = \vartheta_7$ and integrating (13) gives the super-periodic profile, in terms of the Jacobi elliptic cosine,

$$\Omega(\rho) = \pm\vartheta_7 \mathrm{cn}\left(\sqrt{\frac{-\ell_1(\vartheta_7^2+\vartheta_8^2)}{2}}\,(\rho-\rho_0),\ \frac{\vartheta_7}{\sqrt{\vartheta_7^2+\vartheta_8^2}}\right). \tag{28}$$

Substituting this expression into Equation (2) yields

$$R(x,t) = \pm\vartheta_7 e^{\mathrm{i}(p_1 x - \frac{q_1\Gamma(\nu+1)}{\gamma}t^\gamma)} \mathrm{cn}\left(\sqrt{\frac{-\ell_1(\vartheta_7^2+\vartheta_8^2)}{2}}\,(p_2 x - \frac{q_2\Gamma(\nu+1)}{\gamma}t^\gamma - \rho_0),\ \frac{\vartheta_7}{\sqrt{\vartheta_7^2+\vartheta_8^2}}\right). \tag{29}$$

The solution (29) is a new solution to Equation (1).

4.5. Solution Validity

This subsection verifies the consistency and validity of the derived solutions using the degeneracy property. This property is defined by the study of solution degeneracy through the phase orbit transition for limiting values of the bifurcation parameter a.

I. As the parameter a tends to zero, the family of blue periodic orbits shown in Figure 1a contracts toward the equilibrium point at the origin, O. In this limit, the root ϑ_1 approaches zero, causing solution (22) to vanish. The zero value corresponds to the Ω-coordinate of the equilibrium O. Furthermore, solution (23) reduces to $R(x,t) = 0$, which is the trivial solution of Equation (1).

II. In the limit $a \to 0^-$, the family of purple periodic orbits deforms continuously into the blue homoclinic orbits, as illustrated in Figure 1d. Hence, we have $\vartheta_3 = 0$ and $\vartheta_4 = \sqrt{2\ell_2/\ell_1}$. As a result, the periodic solution given in (25) reduces to the solitary-wave profile described by Equation (19).

III. In the limit $a \to 0^+$, the red super-periodic orbits merge into the blue homoclinic orbit depicted in Figure 1d. In this limit, the parameters become $\vartheta_7 = \sqrt{2\ell_2/\ell_1}$ and $\vartheta_8 = 0$. As a result, solution (29) simplifies to the form:

$$\begin{aligned} R(x,t) &= \pm\vartheta_7 e^{\mathrm{i}(p_1 x - \frac{q_1\Gamma(\nu+1)}{\gamma}t^\gamma)} \mathrm{cn}\left(\sqrt{\frac{-\ell_1(\vartheta_7^2+\vartheta_8^2)}{2}}\,(p_2 x - \frac{q_2\Gamma(\nu+1)}{\gamma}t^\gamma - \rho_0),\ 1\right), \\ &= \pm\sqrt{\frac{2\ell_2}{e^{\mathrm{i}(p_1 x - \frac{q_1\Gamma(\nu+1)}{\gamma}t^\gamma)}\ell_1}}\mathrm{sech}\left(\sqrt{-\ell_2}\,(p_2 x - \frac{q_2\Gamma(\nu+1)}{\gamma}t^\gamma - \rho_0)\right), \end{aligned} \tag{30}$$

which is in agreement with the solution in Equation (19).

IV. As the parameter limit is approached to a_2, the green periodic orbits continuously deform into the red heteroclinic orbit shown in Figure 1c. In this degenerate case, the two roots coincide, giving $\vartheta_5 = \vartheta_6 = \sqrt{\ell_2/\ell_1}$. Consequently, the periodic solution (27) collapses to

$$\begin{aligned} R(x,t) &= \pm\sqrt{\ell_2/\ell_1}\, e^{\mathrm{i}(p_1 x - \frac{q_1\Gamma(\nu+1)}{\gamma}t^\gamma)} \mathrm{sn}\left(\sqrt{\frac{\ell_2}{2}}\,(p_2 x - \frac{q_2\Gamma(\nu+1)}{\gamma}t^\gamma - \rho_0),\ 1\right), \\ &= \pm\sqrt{\frac{\ell_2}{\ell_1}}e^{\mathrm{i}(p_1 x - \frac{q_1\Gamma(\nu+1)}{\gamma}t^\gamma)} \tanh\left(\sqrt{\frac{\ell_2}{2}}\,(p_2 x - \frac{q_2\Gamma(\nu+1)}{\gamma}t^\gamma - \rho_0)\right), \end{aligned} \tag{31}$$

which is in agreement with the solution (21).

https://doi.org/10.3390/math14020354

Hence, the degeneracy property confirms the consistency and validity of the obtained analytical result.

5. Graphical Representation

The purpose of this section is to present graphical interpretations of the derived solutions and to highlight how fractional derivatives influence their behavior.

We arbitrarily assume $\mu = 0.2,\ p_1 = -0.3,\ p_2 = -0.5,\ q_1 = -0.08,\ q_2 = -0.07$. Substituting these values into Equations (6) and (8) yields

$$m = 6.06557377, \qquad \ell_1 = -10.60869565, \qquad \ell_2 = -0.6478260870.$$

Since $(\ell_1, \ell_2) \in \mathbb{R}^- \times \mathbb{R}^-$, the corresponding phase portrait of system (9) is shown in Figure 1d. The solution of Equation (1) is then determined by the value of parameter a. Accordingly, we consider the following three cases:

A. If $a = 0$, Equation (1) has a solution in the form

$$R(x,t) = 0.3494726707\, e^{\left(-0.3x + \frac{0.08\Gamma(\nu+1)t^{\gamma}}{\gamma}\right)i} \operatorname{sech}\left(0.402438221x - \frac{0.056341350951\Gamma(\nu+1)t^{\gamma}}{\gamma} + \rho_0\right). \qquad (32)$$

Figure 2 displays the behavior of the real component of the solution $R(x,t)$ associated with Equation (19). In panel (a), a three-dimensional surface representation of Re.$R(x,t)$ is shown over the (x,t)-plane. The profile forms a sharply localized solitary wave centered near $x = 0$, with its amplitude decreasing rapidly as one moves away from the center, illustrating strong spatial confinement and stable propagation characteristics. Figure 2b depicts the temporal evolution of Re.$R(2,t)$ at the fixed spatial location $x = 2$ for several choices of the fractional derivative order γ. The red curve corresponds to the classical limit $\gamma = 1$, while the green and blue curves illustrate the fractional cases $\gamma = 0.7$ and $\gamma = 0.4$, respectively. A reduction in the fractional order leads to a broader temporal profile and a noticeably slower decay rate, a behavior consistent with the increased memory effects inherent to fractional operators. These observations emphasize how sensitively the wave amplitude, temporal dispersion, and long-time persistence depend on the value of γ.

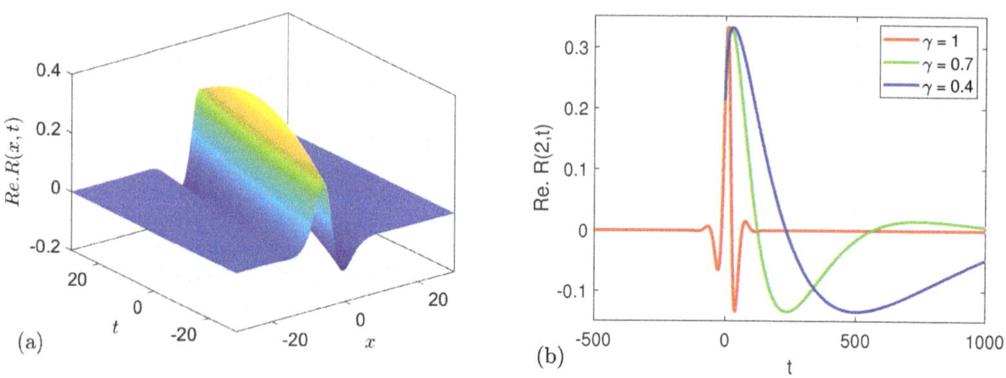

Figure 2. Graphic representation to the real part of the solution (19). (**a**) 3D-representation (**b**) 2D representation for different values of the fractional order derivative.

B. If $a = -0.004944983965 \in ({\ell_2}^2/(4\ell_1), 0) = (-0.009889967930, 0)$, Equation (1) has a solution:

https://doi.org/10.3390/math14020354

$$R(x,t) = 0.3228706477e^{\mathrm{i}\left(0.3x - \frac{0.08\Gamma(\nu+1)t^{\gamma}}{\gamma}\right)}\mathrm{dn}\left(0.3718044356x - \frac{0.05205262098\Gamma(\nu+1)t^{\gamma}}{\gamma}\right.$$
$$\left., 0.9101797209\right). \tag{33}$$

Figure 3 illustrates the real part of solution (33). Figure 3a presents a 3D surface of Re.$R(x,t)$, showing a localized wave profile with a pronounced peak and rapid spatial decay. Figure 3b displays the time evolution of Re.$R(2,t)$ for different fractional orders γ. As γ decreases from 1 to 0.4, the waveform broadens and decays more slowly, reflecting the effects in the fractional model.

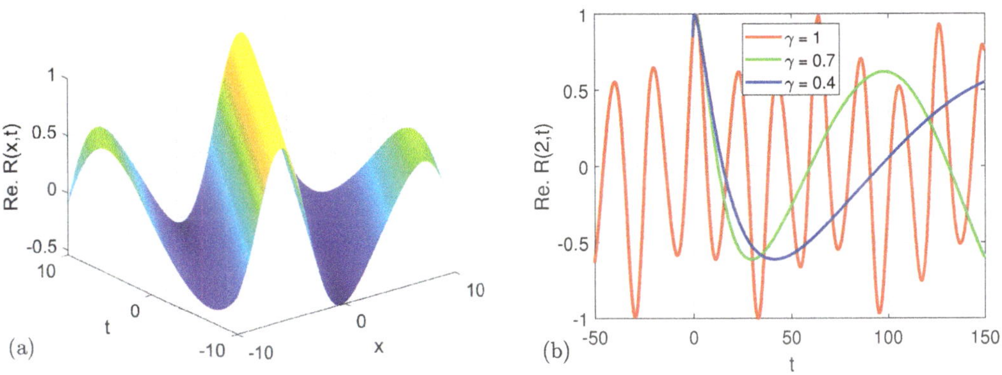

Figure 3. Graphic representation of the real part of the solution (25). (**a**) The 3D representation and (**b**) 2D representation for different values of the fractional order derivative.

C. If $a = 0.9901100321 > 0$, Equation (1) has a solution in the form

$$R(x,t) = 0.8225723213e^{\mathrm{i}\left(0.3x - \frac{0.08\Gamma(\nu+1)t^{\gamma}}{\gamma}\right)}\mathrm{cn}\left(1.277721114x - \frac{0.1788809559\Gamma(\gamma+1)t^{\nu}}{\gamma}\right.$$
$$\left., 0.7413512465\right). \tag{34}$$

Figure 4 illustrates the real part of solution (34). Figure 4a shows a three-dimensional surface plot of Re.$R(x,t)$, revealing a localized wave structure whose amplitude varies in both space and time. Figure 4b presents the temporal evolution of Re.$R(2,t)$ at the fixed point $x = 2$ for several fractional orders γ. The curves corresponding to $\gamma = 1$, $\gamma = 0.7$, and $\gamma = 0.4$ demonstrate that decreasing the fractional order leads to slower decay and broader temporal spreading, reflecting the enhanced memory effects inherent to fractional derivatives.

Hence, physically, γ characterizes memory and nonlocal temporal effects. In plasma media, it accounts for anomalous transport and long-range particle interactions, whereas in optical fibers it reflects delayed nonlinear responses and dispersive memory effects. As illustrated in Figures 2–4, decreasing γ leads to slower decay, broader temporal spreading, and enhanced wave persistence, thereby demonstrating the direct physical influence of fractional dynamics on wave localization and stability.

https://doi.org/10.3390/math14020354

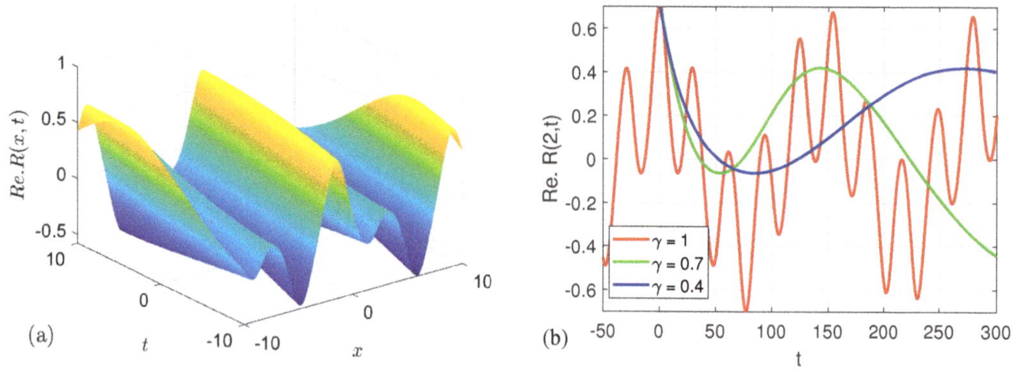

Figure 4. Graphic representation of the real part of the solution (29). (**a**) The 3D representation and (**b**) 2D representation for different values of the fractional order derivative.

6. Perturbed System

We now turn to the autoresonance behavior of the non-autonomous oscillator, wherein the system can self-synchronize with a slowly varying periodic excitation. To incorporate external driving, we augment the original model (1) with a specific time-periodic forcing function $\alpha_0 e^{iz}\mathrm{cn}(\beta\rho,\nu)$. The driven system then takes the form

$$i\,{}_{n}\mathbb{D}_t^{\gamma,\nu} R + R_{xx} + 2\mu R|R|^2 + m\,{}_{n}\mathbb{D}_t^{\gamma,\nu}(R_x) - \alpha_0 e^{iz}\mathrm{cn}(\beta\rho,\nu) = 0. \tag{35}$$

Physically, the added perturbation term represents an external time-periodic excitation acting on the wave envelope, such as a driven electromagnetic field in plasma media or an imposed modulation in optical fiber systems. Its amplitude and frequency quantify the strength and temporal rate of this external driving, which can be tuned experimentally. Including this term converts the autonomous Hamiltonian model into a non-autonomous driven system, enabling the description of resonance, quasi-periodic responses, and the onset of chaotic dynamics arising from the interaction between the medium's intrinsic oscillations and the external forcing.

Applying the transformation (2) and performingthe same procedures as in Section 2, we obtain

$$\begin{aligned} \Omega' &= \Upsilon, \\ \Upsilon' &= \ell_1\Omega^3 - \ell_2\Omega + \alpha\mathrm{cn}(\beta\rho,\nu), \\ \kappa' &= \beta, \end{aligned} \tag{36}$$

where ℓ_1 and ℓ_2 are given by (8) and α is introduced instead of α_0 for simplicity as $\alpha = \frac{\alpha_0(p_1q_2+p_2q_1)}{p_2(p_1p_2q_2-p_2^2q_1-q_2^2)}$. The parameters α and β denote, respectively, the forcing amplitude and frequency of the external periodic drive. In what follows, we shall call (36) the perturbed system.

The analysis of periodic and chaotic dynamics of the wave behavior to the model (1) is complicated by a four-parameter space: the model parameters ℓ_1 and ℓ_2, together with the forcing parameters α and β that define the external perturbation.

We examine the unperturbed system (9) or the perturbed system (36) in the limit where the amplitude of external periodic forcing vanishes. Choosing the parameter set

$$p_1 = 0.3,\ p_2 = 0.03,\ q_1 = 1.859556098,\ q_2 = 0.7,\ \mu = 0.2390496318,\ m = -2.565967537, \tag{37}$$

https://doi.org/10.3390/math14020354

we obtain $\ell_1 = -5.2$ and $\ell_2 = 19.05$. For the initial condition $(\Upsilon(0), \Omega(0)) = (0.1, 0.137066112)$, the constant a is evaluated from Equation (11) as $a = 0.09558$. Hence, $(\ell_1, \ell_2, a) \in \mathbb{R}^- \times \mathbb{R}^+ \times \mathbb{R}^+$. Following the bifurcation analysis, the perturbed system exhibits periodic dynamics, as confirmed by the two-dimensional and three-dimensional phase portraits and by the time series of Ω versus ρ shown in Figure 5a–c.

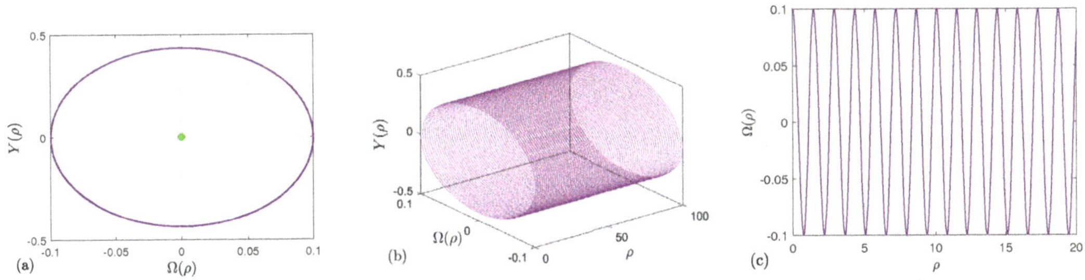

Figure 5. The behavior of the unperturbed system Equation (9) with initial conditions $(\Upsilon(0), \Omega(0)) = (0.1, 0.1370661118)$ and parameter values of $p_1 = 0.3, p_2 = 0.03, q_1 = 1.859556098, q_2 = 0.7, \mu = 0.2390496318, m = -2.565967537$. (**a**) 2D phase orbit; (**b**) 3D phase orbit; (**c**) Time series of $Omega(ho)$ against ho.

We now investigate the impact of an external periodic forcing on the dynamics of the unperturbed system (9). The analysis is carried out in two stages: first, by varying the forcing amplitude while keeping the frequency constant; and second, by altering the frequency while maintaining a fixed amplitude.

For this study, we adopt the parameter values given in Equation (37) and assume the forcing frequency is fixed at $\beta = 3$, while the amplitude α is allowed to vary. When the amplitude is set to $\alpha = 100$, the perturbed system (36) exhibits quasi-periodic behavior, as illustrated by the 2D and 3D phase portraits and the time series of Ω versus ρ in Figure 6a–c. This phenomenon occurs because the ratio of the interacting frequencies is incommensurable. Conversely, when the amplitude of the external forcing is increased to $\alpha = 200$ while the frequency remains fixed at $\beta = 3$, the system transitions to chaotic dynamics, as shown in Figure 7a–c.

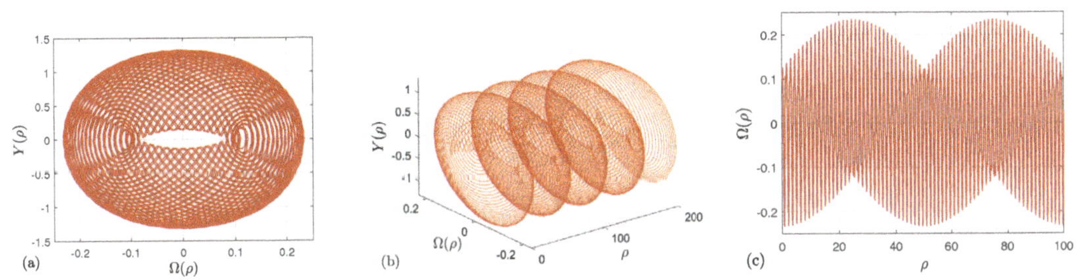

Figure 6. The behavior of the perturbed system Equation (36) with initial conditions $(\Upsilon(0), \Omega(0)) = (0.1, 0.1370661118)$ and frequency $\beta = 3$, amplitude $\alpha = 100$. Parameter values of $p_1 = 0.3$, $p_2 = 0.03$, $q_1 = 1.859556098, q_2 = 0.7, \mu = 0.2390496318, m = -2.565967537$. (**a**) 2D phase orbit; (**b**) 3D phase orbit; (**c**) Time series of $Omega(ho)$ against ho.

We proceed to evaluate the Lyapunov exponents for the perturbed system described in Equation (36), using the same parameter set as in Figure 7. Numerical evaluation of these exponents provides a powerful tool for detecting both the onset of chaos and the stability properties of nonlinear dynamics. However, proper interpretation of the results requires a solid understanding of the system's fundamental behavior, since the exponents

https://doi.org/10.3390/math14020354

depend strongly on specific features of the model under study [40]. In practical terms, Lyapunov exponents serve as indicators of dynamical regimes: a positive value denotes chaotic motion, while a negative value reflects convergence toward stable trajectories.

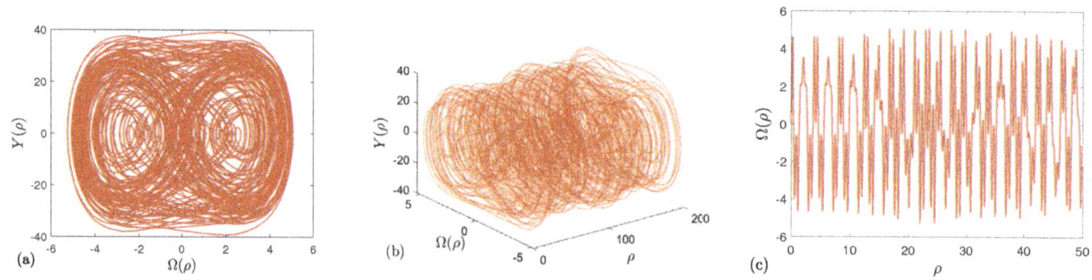

Figure 7. The behavior of the perturbed system Equation (36) with initial conditions $(Y(0), \Omega(0)) = (0.1, 0.1370661118)$ and frequency $\beta = 3$, amplitude $\alpha = 200$. Parameter values of $p_1 = 0.3$, $p_2 = 0.03$, $q_1 = 1.859556098, q_2 = 0.7, \mu = 0.2390496318, m = -2.565967537$. (**a**) 2D phase orbit; (**b**) 3D phase orbit; (**c**) Time series of $Omega(ho)$ against ho.

For the system (36) with the parameter set (37), the Lyapunov exponents are

$$\lambda_1 = 0.07550652, \qquad \lambda_2 = -0.07550652, \qquad \lambda_3 = 0.00.$$

Figure 8 illustrates the convergence of the Lyapunov exponents. The presence of the positive Lyapunov exponent λ_1 confirms the chaotic behavior of the perturbed system (36).

Consequently, the transition to chaos under increased forcing amplitude α mirrors physical scenarios where strong external modulation—such as intense RF heating in plasmas or high-power periodic pumping in fibers—leads to wave turbulence, mode competition, or signal breakdown.

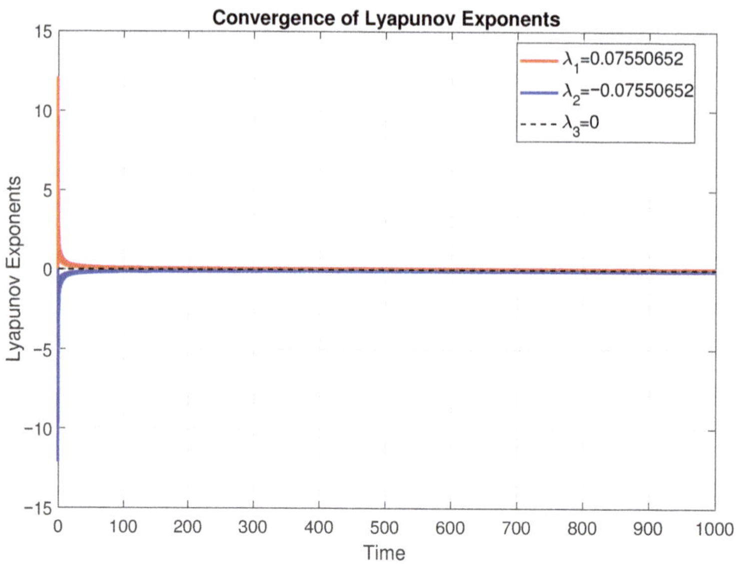

Figure 8. Lyapunov exponents for the perturbed system (36).

https://doi.org/10.3390/math14020354

7. Conclusions

This study focuses on the qualitative dynamics of the modified unstable time-fractional nonlinear Schrödinger equation (mUNLSE), a model relevant to nonlinear wave propagation in plasma and optical fiber media. Through an appropriate transformation, the mUNLSE is reformulated as a conservative autonomous dynamical system. The resulting system is identified as a one-dimensional Hamiltonian framework. The equilibrium points are determined, and their stability is analyzed using the Lagrange theorem for Hamiltonian systems. A phase portrait is constructed and briefly discussed to illustrate the system's behavior.

By integrating the conserved quantity along intervals of real propagation, several exact solutions of the mUNLSE are obtained. The validity and consistency of these solutions are examined through the degeneracy property, which corresponds to studying the transition of solution types across phase-plane trajectories. Selected solutions are presented graphically to highlight their structural features.

Furthermore, the role of the fractional derivative order in shaping amplitude, localization, and dispersion is investigated through numerical simulations, emphasizing the memory effects inherent in fractional dynamics. An external periodic forcing is also introduced, transforming the mUNLSE into a perturbed non-autonomous dynamical system. The system's response to periodic driving is explored, revealing transitions from regular periodic motion to quasi-periodic and chaotic regimes. These behaviors are illustrated using two- and three-dimensional phase portraits as well as time-series analysis, with Lyapunov exponent calculations providing further confirmation.

We compare our results with those presented in two earlier studies, namely [41,42]. Arshad et al. [41] used a modified extended mapping method to analyze the fractional mUNLSE, constructing bright/dark solitons, combined dark–bright solitons, elliptic-function solutions, and periodic solitary waves under particular parameter conditions. Similarly, Zulfiqar and Ahmad [42] utilized the Exp-function approach to derive trigonometric, hyperbolic, and hybrid solutions for the mUNLSE, yielding bright/dark solitons, solitary waves, and periodic structures. In contrast, bifurcation analysis appears in other recent studies such as [43], though these typically overlook the critical intervals of real wave propagation essential for solution construction. Moreover, such works often assume trigonometric cosine perturbations, whereas our study employs Jacobi-elliptic forcing functions that more naturally emerge from the underlying dynamical system.

Overall, the findings enrich the theoretical understanding of fractional Schrödinger-type equations and shed new light on complex nonlinear wave phenomena in plasma physics and optical fiber systems.

Author Contributions: Conceptualization, M.M.E.-D. and A.A.E.; methodology, A.A.A., M.M.E.-D. and A.A.E.; software, A.A.E. and A.A.A.; validation, M.M.E.-D., A.A.E. and A.A.A.; formal analysis, M.M.E.-D. and A.A.E.; investigation, A.A.E. and A.A.A.; resources, A.A.E.; writing—original draft preparation, A.A.A., M.M.E.-D. and A.A.E.; writing—review and editing, M.M.E.-D.; project administration, M.M.E.-D.; funding acquisition, M.M.E.-D. All authors have read and agreed to the published version of the manuscript.

Funding: This Project was funded by the Deanship of Scientific Research (DSR) at King Abdulaziz University, Jeddah, Saudi Arabia under grant no. (IPP: 969–130-2025). The authors, therefore, acknowledge with thanks the DSR for technical and financial support.

Data Availability Statement: The original contributions presented in this study are included in the article. Further inquiries can be directed to the corresponding author.

Acknowledgments: The authors acknowledge the Deanship of Scientific Research (DSR) at King Abdulaziz University, Jeddah, Saudi Arabia, for the financial support.

https://doi.org/10.3390/math14020354

Conflicts of Interest: The authors have no conflicts of interest.

Appendix A. Truncated M-Fractional Differentiation

To ensure this article is self-contained, we begin by presenting the essential definitions and fundamental ideas related to truncated M-fractional differentiation.

The truncated M-fractional derivative operator was introduced to overcome certain drawbacks of classical fractional operators, particularly regarding the validity of rules such as the chain, product, and quotient rules, as well as the mean value theorem. This operator is constructed based on the Mittag-Leffler function.

Definition A1 ([44]). *The truncated Mittag-Leffler function with one parameter, denoted by $M_\delta^n(r)$, is given by*

$$M_\delta^n(r) = \sum_{s=0}^{n} \frac{r^s}{\Gamma(\delta s + 1)}, \tag{A1}$$

where $\delta > 0$ and $r \in \mathbb{C}$.

Next, we introduce a specific form of the truncated M-fractional derivative of order p.

Definition A2 ([44]). *Let $M_\delta^n(r)$ be the truncated Mittag-Leffler function with $\delta > 0$, and let $h : \mathbb{R}^+ \to \mathbb{R}$ be a real-valued function with $0 < \gamma < 1$. The truncated M-fractional derivative of order γ for h is defined as*

$${}_nD^{\gamma,\nu}(h(t)) = \lim_{\eta \to 0} \frac{h\big(t\, M_\delta^n(\eta t^{-\gamma})\big) - h(t)}{\eta}, \tag{A2}$$

for all $t > 0$.

The main properties of the truncated M-fractional derivative are summarized below.

Theorem A1 ([44]). *Let f_1 and f_2 be functions that are truncated M-fractional differentiable of order p for $t > 0$, and let $a_1, a_2 \in \mathbb{R}$. Then the following rules hold:*

1. ${}_nD^{\gamma,\nu}(a_1h_1 + a_2h_2)(t) = a_1\, {}_nD^{\gamma,\nu}h_1(t) + a_2\, {}_nD^{\gamma,\nu}h_2(t)$,
2. ${}_nD^{\gamma,\nu}(t^q) = \dfrac{q}{\Gamma(\nu+1)} t^{q-\gamma}$, *for all* $q \in \mathbb{R}$,
3. ${}_nD^{\gamma,\nu}(h_1h_2)(t) = h_1(t)\, {}_nD^{\gamma,\nu}h_2(t) + h_2(t)\, {}_nD^{\gamma,\nu}h_1(t)$,
4. ${}_nD^{\gamma,\nu}\left(\dfrac{h_1}{h_2}\right)(t) = \dfrac{1}{h_2^2(t)}\Big(h_2(t)\, {}_nD^{\gamma,\nu}h_1(t) - h_1(t)\, {}_nD^{\gamma,\nu}h_2(t)\Big)$,
5. ${}_nD^{\gamma,\nu}(b) = 0$, *where b is a constant,*
6. ${}_nD^{\gamma,\nu}(h)(t) = \dfrac{t^{1-\gamma}}{\Gamma(\gamma+1)} \dfrac{dh(t)}{dt}$, *for differentiable h,*
7. ${}_nD^{\gamma,\nu}(h_1 \circ h_2)(t) = h_1'(h_2(t))\, {}_nD^{\gamma,\nu}h_2(t)$, *provided h_1 is differentiable at $h_2(t)$.*

The truncated M-fractional derivative adopted here differs from classical fractional operators in several ways. The Caputo derivative is defined via a power-law kernel, which is singular at the origin and is particularly suited for problems with physically interpretable initial conditions. The Caputo–Fabrizio derivative uses an exponential kernel, which is non-singular and often preferred for modeling processes with fading memory, such as viscoelasticity [45,46]. In contrast, the truncated M-fractional derivative is based on a truncated Mittag-Leffler kernel, allowing it to interpolate between classical fractional operators and integer-order calculus while preserving standard differentiation rules. This makes it especially convenient for constructing exact solutions and performing bifurcation analysis in nonlinear wave equations, as demonstrated in this work. However, like all fractional

https://doi.org/10.3390/math14020354

operators, its physical interpretation depends on the context: in plasma and optical fiber models, it captures memory and hereditary effects that power-law or exponential kernels may describe differently. The choice of operator thus reflects a trade-off between analytical convenience, physical fidelity, and the specific memory structure of the system under study.

References

1. Gepreel, K.A. Exact soliton solutions for nonlinear perturbed Schrödinger equations with nonlinear optical media. *Appl. Sci.* **2020**, *10*, 8929. [CrossRef]
2. Zobeiry, N.; Humfeld, K.D. A physics-informed machine learning approach for solving heat transfer equation in advanced manufacturing and engineering applications. *Eng. Appl. Artif. Intell.* **2021**, *101*, 104232. [CrossRef]
3. Raza, N.; Ullah, M.A. A comparative study of heat transfer analysis of fractional Maxwell fluid by using Caputo and Caputo–Fabrizio derivatives. *Can. J. Phys.* **2020**, *98*, 89–101. [CrossRef]
4. Sgura, I.; Lawless, A.S.; Bozzini, B. Parameter estimation for a morphochemical reaction-diffusion model of electrochemical pattern formation. *Inverse Probl. Sci. Eng.* **2019**, *27*, 618–647. [CrossRef]
5. Jornet, M. Modeling of Allee effect in biofilm formation via the stochastic bistable Allen–Cahn partial differential equation. *Stoch. Anal. Appl.* **2021**, *39*, 22–32. [CrossRef]
6. Kaplan, M.; Ozer, M.N. Multiple-soliton solutions and analytical solutions to a nonlinear evolution equation. *Opt. Quantum Electron.* **2018**, *50*, 2. [CrossRef]
7. Malik, S.; Kumar, S.; Das, A. A (2+1)-dimensional combined KdV–mKdV equation: Integrability, stability analysis and soliton solutions. *Nonlinear Dyn.* **2022**, *107*, 2689–2701. [CrossRef]
8. Wróblewski, M. Nonlinear Schrödinger approach to European option pricing, author=Wróblewski, Marcin. *Open Phys.* **2017**, *15*, 280–291. [CrossRef]
9. Arora, G.; Rani, R.; Emadifar, H. Numerical solutions of nonlinear Schrodinger equation with applications in optical fiber communication. *Optik* **2022**, *266*, 169661. [CrossRef]
10. Liu, X.z.; Yu, J. A nonlocal nonlinear Schrödinger equation derived from a two-layer fluid model. *Nonlinear Dyn.* **2019**, *96*, 2103–2114. [CrossRef]
11. Shi, L.; Zhou, X. Exact solutions of a coupled space-time fractional nonlinear Schrödinger type equation in quantum mechanics. *Results Phys.* **2022**, *42*, 105967. [CrossRef]
12. Salas, A.H.; El-Tantawy, S.A.; Castillo H., J.E. The hybrid finite difference and moving boundary methods for solving a linear damped nonlinear Schrödinger equation to model rogue waves and breathers in plasma physics. *Math. Probl. Eng.* **2020**, *2020*, 6874870. [CrossRef]
13. Omote, M.; Sakagami, M.; Sasaki, R.; Yamanaka, I. Solvable quantum field theories and polynomial conserved quantities for the quantum nonlinear Schrödinger equation. *Phys. Rev. D* **1987**, *35*, 2423. [CrossRef]
14. Rizvi, S.T.; Seadawy, A.R.; Mustafa, B.; Ali, K.; Ashraf, R. Propagation of chirped periodic and solitary waves for the coupled nonlinear Schrödinger equation in two core optical fibers with parabolic law with weak non-local nonlinearity. *Opt. Quantum Electron.* **2022**, *54*, 545. [CrossRef]
15. Manukure, S.; Booker, T. A short overview of solitons and applications. *Partial Differ. Equ. Appl. Math.* **2021**, *4*, 100140.
16. Zhang, S. A generalized auxiliary equation method and its application to the (2+1)-dimensional Korteweg–de Vries equations. *Comput. Math. Appl.* **2007**, *54*, 1028–1038. [CrossRef]
17. Elmandouh, A.; Aljuaidan, A.; Elbrolosy, M. The integrability and modification to an auxiliary function method for solving the strain wave equation of a flexible rod with a finite deformation. *Mathematics* **2024**, *12*, 383. [CrossRef]
18. Malik, S.; Hashemi, M.S.; Kumar, S.; Rezazadeh, H.; Mahmoud, W.; Osman, M. Application of new Kudryashov method to various nonlinear partial differential equations. *Opt. Quantum Electron.* **2023**, *55*, 8. [CrossRef]
19. Elbrolosy, M.; Elmandouh, A. Painlevé analysis, Lie symmetry and bifurcation for the dynamical model of radial dislocations in microtubules. *Nonlinear Dyn.* **2025**, *113*, 13699–13714. [CrossRef]
20. Kumar, S.; Malik, S.; Rezazadeh, H.; Akinyemi, L. The integrable Boussinesq equation and it's breather, lump and soliton solutions. *Nonlinear Dyn.* **2022**, *107*, 2703–2716. [CrossRef]
21. Li, L.; Duan, C.; Yu, F. An improved Hirota bilinear method and new application for a nonlocal integrable complex modified Korteweg-de Vries (MKdV) equation. *Phys. Lett. A* **2019**, *383*, 1578–1582. [CrossRef]
22. Alhami, R.; Alquran, M. Extracted different types of optical lumps and breathers to the new generalized stochastic potential-KdV equation via using the Cole-Hopf transformation and Hirota bilinear method. *Opt. Quantum Electron.* **2022**, *54*, 553. [CrossRef]
23. Rezazadeh, H.; Neirameh, A.; Eslami, M.; Bekir, A.; Korkmaz, A. A sub-equation method for solving the cubic–quartic NLSE with the Kerr law nonlinearity. *Mod. Phys. Lett. B* **2019**, *33*, 1950197. [CrossRef]

https://doi.org/10.3390/math14020354

24. Rehman, H.U.; Ullah, N.; Imran, M. Optical solitons of Biswas-Arshed equation in birefringent fibers using extended direct algebraic method. *Optik* **2021**, *226*, 165378. [CrossRef]
25. El-Dessoky, M.; Elmandouh, A. Qualitative analysis and wave propagation for Konopelchenko- Dubrovsky equation. *Alex. Eng. J.* **2023**, *67*, 525–535. [CrossRef]
26. Elmandouh, A. Nonlinear Dynamical Analysis of a Diffusion-Driven Bacterial Density Model: Integrability and Bifurcation Analysis. *Mathematics* **2025**, *13*, 3623. [CrossRef]
27. Elmandouh, A. Bifurcation, Quasi-Periodic, Chaotic Pattern, and Soliton Solutions to Dual-Mode Gardner Equation. *Mathematics* **2025**, *13*, 841. [CrossRef]
28. Rafiq, M.H.; Jhangeer, A.; Raza, N. The analysis of solitonic, supernonlinear, periodic, quasiperiodic, bifurcation and chaotic patterns of perturbed Gerdjikov–Ivanov model with full nonlinearity. *Commun. Nonlinear Sci. Numer. Simul.* **2023**, *116*, 106818. [CrossRef]
29. Ahmidi, M.; Mokni, K.; Ch-Chaoui, M. Influence of Prey Harvesting on the Dynamics of a Prey–Predator System: Multi-Parameter Bifurcation Analysis. *Nonlinear Dyn.* **2025**, *113*, 31841–31870. [CrossRef]
30. Lamb, G.L. *Elements of Soliton Theory*; Wiely: New York, NY, USA, 1980.
31. Roshid, M.M.; Uddin, M.; Boulaaras, S.; Osman, M. Dynamic optical soliton solutions of M-fractional modify unstable nonlinear Schrödinger equation via two analytic methods. *Results Eng.* **2025**, *25*, 103757. [CrossRef]
32. Ahmad, J.; Anwar, M.; Mustafa, Z. Nonlinear wave dynamics of fractional unstable and modified unstable nonlinear Schrödinger equations through analytical solutions. *J. Opt.* **2025**, *54*, 2112–2130. [CrossRef]
33. Arshad, M.; Seadawy, A.R.; Lu, D. Optical soliton solutions of the generalized higher-order nonlinear Schrödinger equations and their applications. *Opt. Quantum Electron.* **2018**, *50*, 421. [CrossRef]
34. Seadawy, A.R. Modulation instability analysis for the generalized derivative higher order nonlinear Schrödinger equation and its the bright and dark soliton solutions. *J. Electromagn. Waves Appl.* **2017**, *31*, 1353–1362. [CrossRef]
35. Arshad, M.; Seadawy, A.R.; Lu, D. Exact bright–dark solitary wave solutions of the higher-order cubic–quintic nonlinear Schrödinger equation and its stability. *Optik* **2017**, *138*, 40–49. [CrossRef]
36. Tala-Tebue, E.; Seadawy, A.R.; Djoufack, Z. The modify unstable nonlinear Schrödinger dynamical equation and its optical soliton solutions. *Opt. Quantum Electron.* **2018**, *50*, 380. [CrossRef]
37. Seadawy, A.R.; Iqbal, M.; Lu, D. Construction of soliton solutions of the modify unstable nonlinear Schrödinger dynamical equation in fiber optics. *Indian J. Phys.* **2020**, *94*, 823–832. [CrossRef]
38. Goldstein, H. *Classical Mechanics*; Addison-Wesley Series in Physics; Addison-Wesley: Boston, MA, USA, 1980.
39. Gantmacher, F. *Lectures in Analytical Mechanics*; Mir Publishers: Moscow, Russia, 1975.
40. Layek, G. *An Introduction to Dynamical Systems and Chaos*; Springer: New Delhi, India, 2015; Volume 1.
41. Arshad, M.; Seadawy, A.R.; Lu, D.; Jun, W. Modulation instability analysis of modify unstable nonlinear schrodinger dynamical equation and its optical soliton solutions. *Results Phys.* **2017**, *7*, 4153–4161. [CrossRef]
42. Zulfiqar, A.; Ahmad, J. Soliton solutions of fractional modified unstable Schrödinger equation using Exp-function method. *Results Phys.* **2020**, *19*, 103476. [CrossRef]
43. Harun-Or-Roshid; Abdeljabbar, A.; Uddin, M.S.; Khatun, M.S. Phase portraits and orbit wise dynamics solutions, quasi-periodic and chaotic behavior of heisenberg ferromagnetic spin chains mode. *Partial Differ. Equ. Appl. Math.* **2025**, *13*, 101044. [CrossRef]
44. Sousa, J.V.D.C.; de Oliveira, E.C. A new truncated M-fractional derivative type unifying some fractional derivative types with classical properties. *Inter. J. Anal. Appl.* **2017**, *16*, 83–96.
45. Podlubny, I. *Fractional Differential Equations: An Introduction to Fractional Derivatives, Fractional Differential Equations, to Methods of Their Solution and Some of Their Applications*; Elsevier: Amsterdam, The Netherlands, 1998; Volume 198.
46. Caputo, M.; Fabrizio, M. A new definition of fractional derivative without singular kernel. *Prog. Fract. Differ. Appl.* **2015**, *1*, 73–85.

https://doi.org/10.3390/math14020354

MDPI AG
Grosspeteranlage 5
4052 Basel
Switzerland
Tel.: +41 61 683 77 34

Mathematics Editorial Office
E-mail: mathematics@mdpi.com
www.mdpi.com/journal/mathematics

www.ingramcontent.com/pod-product-compliance
Lightning Source LLC
Chambersburg PA
CBHW061447210926
51850CB00008B/1637